Johanne

Doubleday

New York   London   Toronto   Sydney   Auckland

Joan of Arc

A LIFE
TRANSFIGURED

Kathryn Harrison

All rights reserved. Published in the United States by Doubleday,
a division of Random House LLC, New York, and in Canada by Random House of
Canada Limited, Toronto, Penguin Random House companies.

www.doubleday.com

DOUBLEDAY and the portrayal of an anchor with a dolphin are
registered trademarks of Random House LLC.

Book design by Maria Carella
Maps designed by Jeffrey L. Ward
Jacket design by John Fontana
Jacket image of Joan of Arc: engraving from *Figaro Illustre* magazine, 1903
© DEA/M. SEEMULLER/Getty Images

Library of Congress Cataloging-in-Publication Data
Harrison, Kathryn.
Joan of Arc : a life transfigured / Kathryn Harrison.—First edition.
pages cm
Includes bibliographical references and index.
ISBN 978-0-385-53120-7 (hardcover)—ISBN 978-0-385-53122-1 (eBook)
1. Joan, of Arc, Saint, 1412–1431. 2. France—History—Charles VII,
1422–1461. 3. Christian saints—France—Biography. I. Title.
DC103.H25 2014
944'.026092—dc23
[B]   2014005921

MANUFACTURED IN THE UNITED STATES OF AMERICA

1 3 5 7 9 10 8 6 4 2

First Edition

For Gerry Howard

I used to be a hen,
but I loved an angel and became a peacock.

NIKOS KAZANTZAKIS

Contents

Joan of Arc

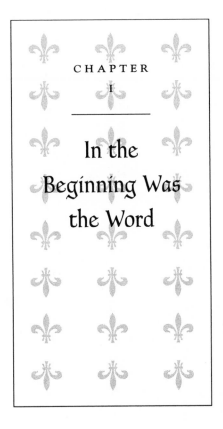

CHAPTER

I

In the
Beginning Was
the Word

*"Have you not heard the prophecy that France
was to be ruined by a woman and restored by a virgin
from the marshes of Lorraine?"*

By the time Joan of Arc proclaimed herself La Pucelle, the virgin sent by God to deliver France from its enemies, the English, she had been obeying the counsel of angels for five years. The voices Joan heard, speaking from over her right shoulder and accompanied by a great light, had been hers alone, a rapturous secret. But when, in 1429, they announced that the time had come for Joan to undertake the quest for which they had been preparing her, they transformed a seemingly undistinguished peasant girl into a visionary heroine who defied every limitation placed on a woman of the late Middle Ages.

Expected by those who raised her to assume nothing more than the workaday cloak of a provincial female, Joan told her family nothing of what her voices asked, lest her parents try to prevent her from fulfilling what she embraced as her destiny: foretold, ordained, inescapable. Seventeen years old, Joan dressed herself in male attire at the command of her heavenly father. She sheared off her hair, put on armor, and took up the sword her angels provided. She was frightened of the enormity of what God had asked of her, and she was feverish in her determination to succeed at what was by anyone's measure a preposterous mission.

As Joan protested to her voices, she "knew not how to ride or lead in war," and yet she roused an exhausted, under-equipped, and impotent army into a fervor that carried it from one unlikely victory to the next. In fact, outside her unshakable faith—or because of that

faith—Joan of Arc was characterized above all by paradox. An illiterate peasant's daughter from the hinterlands, Joan moved purposefully
among nobles, bishops, and royalty, unimpressed by mortal measures
of authority. She had a battle cry that drove her legions forward into
the fray; her voice was described as gentle, womanly. So intent on
vanquishing the enemy that she threatened her own men with violence, promising to cut off the head of any who should fail to heed
her command, she recoiled at the idea of taking a life, and to avoid
having to use her sword, she led her army carrying a twelve-foot banner that depicted Christ sitting in judgment, holding the world in his
right hand, and flanked by angels. In the aftermath of combat, Joan
didn't celebrate victory but mourned the casualties; her men remembered her on her knees weeping as she held the head of a dying enemy
soldier, urging him to confess his sins.

A mortal whose blood flowed red and real from battle wounds,
she had eyes that beheld angels, winged and crowned. When she fell
to her knees to embrace their legs, she felt their flesh solid in her
arms. Her courage outstripped that of seasoned men-at-arms; her
tears flowed as readily as did any other teenage girl's. Not only a virgin, but also an ascetic who held herself beyond the reach of sensual
pleasure, she wept in shock and rage when an English captain called
her a whore. Yet, living as a warrior among warriors, she betrayed no
prudery when time came to bivouac, undressing and sleeping among
lustful young knights who remembered the beauty of a body none
dared approach—not even after Joan chased off any prostitute foolish
enough to tramp after an army whose leader's claim to power was indivisible from her chastity. Under the exigencies of warfare, she didn't
allow her men the small sin of blasphemy; coveting victory above all
else, she righteously seized an advantage falling on a holy day. She
knew God's wishes; she followed his direction; she questioned nothing. Her quest, revealed to her alone, allowed her privileges no pope
would claim. On trial for her life and unfamiliar with the fine points
of Catholic doctrine, she nimbly sidestepped the rhetorical traps of
Sorbonne-trained doctors of the Church bent on proving her a witch
and a heretic. The least likely of commanding officers, she changed
the course of the Hundred Years War, and that of history.

The life of Joan of Arc is as impossible as that of only one other, who also heard God speak: Jesus of Nazareth, prince of paradox as much as peace, a god who suffered and died a mortal, a prophet whose parables were intended to confound, that those who "seeing may not see, and hearing may not understand," a messenger of forgiveness and love who came bearing a sword, inspiring millennia of judgment and violence—the blood of his "new and everlasting covenant" extracted from those who refused his heavenly rule. More than that of any other Catholic martyr, Joan of Arc's career aligns with Christ's, hers "the most noble life that was ever born into this world save only One," Mark Twain wrote. Her birth was prophesied: a virgin warrior would arise to save her people. She had power over the natural world, not walking on water, but commanding the direction of the wind. She foretold the future. If she wasn't transfigured while preaching on a mount, she was, eyewitnesses said, luminous in battle, light not flaring off her armor so much as radiating from the girl within. The English spoke of a cloud of white butterflies unfurling from her banner—proof of sorcery, they called it. Her touch raised the dead. Her feats, which continue six centuries after her birth to frustrate ever more modern and enlightened efforts to rationalize and reduce to human proportions, won the allegiance of tens of wonder-struck thousands and made her as many ardent enemies. The single thing she feared, she said, was treachery.

Captured, Joan was sold to the English and abandoned to her fate by the king to whom she had delivered the French crown. Her passion unfolded in a prison cell rather than a garden, but like Jesus she suffered lonely agonies. Tried by dozens of mostly corrupt clerics, Joan refused to satisfy the ultimatums of Church doctors who demanded she abjure the God she knew and renounce the voices that guided her as the devil's deceit. When she would not, she was condemned to death and burned as a heretic, the stake to which she was bound raised above throngs of jeering onlookers curious to see what fire might do to a witch. She was only nineteen, and her charred body was displayed for anyone who cared to examine it. Had she been a man after all, and if she were, did it explain any of what she'd accomplished?

A sophisticated few of Joan of Arc's contemporaries might have understood the idea of salvation at the hands of a virgin from the marshes of Lorraine as a communal prayer—more a wish for rescue than a prophecy. Probably, most took the idea at face value, some giving it credence, others dismissing it. But only one, a girl who claimed she knew little beyond what she'd learned spinning and sewing and taking her turn to watch over the villagers' livestock, heard it as a vocation. The self-proclaimed agent of God's will, Joan of Arc wasn't immortalized so much as she entered the collective imagination as a living myth, exalted by the angelic company she kept and the powers with which it endowed her.

The woman who "ruined" France was Isabeau of Bavaria, a ruination accomplished by disinheriting her son the dauphin Charles, to whom Joan would restore France's throne, and allowing his paternity to be called into question. It was a credible doubt that might have been cast on any of Isabeau's eight children, as she was notoriously unfaithful to her husband, the mad (we would call him schizophrenic) Charles VI. Bastardy, though it invited dynastic squabbles among opposing crowns with shared ancestry, wasn't a cause for shame among the nobility but was announced if not advertised, a *brisure*, or "bar sinister," added to the coat of arms worn by sons conceived outside a family patriarch's official marriage.[*] In fact, it was an illustrious bastard's invasion of England in 1066 that precipitated the centuries of turf wars between the French and the English. As Duke of Normandy, William the Conqueror claimed England's throne for his own but remained a vassal of the French king, as did those who ruled after him. The arrangement guaranteed centuries of dynastic turmoil, and the house of Valois[†] had the misfortune of presiding over the Hundred Years War, at the beginning of which France had everything to lose. Centuries of crusades following the Norman conquests had established the livre as the currency of international trade, and

---

[*] "Sinister," from the Latin for "left," indicates a stripe moving from the lower left to the upper right quadrant of the coat of arms. À la main gauche, or "by the left hand" (of the father), is a French expression for illegitimate birth.

[†] The cadet line of the Capetian dynasty, whose kings ruled France from 1328 to 1589.

France's wealth purchased its preeminence among nations. French was not used for purposes of haggling alone but was the lingua franca of Europe, the language in which Marco Polo's *Travels* was published.

Punctuated by periods of exhausted stalemates, occasional famine, and the arrival, in 1348, of the bubonic plague, the Hundred Years War ground on until the population of France was halved. When Joan set out on her divine mission, England had taken control of almost all of France north of the Loire River. By the time Isabeau revealed the dauphin's questionable ancestry, effectively barring him from the French throne, portents of salvation by a virgin from the marshes of Lorraine had been circulating for decades, multiplying with the woes that inspired them, the putative historic reach of prophecies concerning Joan's advent reaching ever further back in time as her fame spread. Joan's contemporary the poet and historian Christine de Pizan reported that on the occasion of Joan's first formal ecclesiastical examination—a cautionary investigation the French ministers considered necessary before the dauphin placed his trust in an otherwise untested visionary—she was embraced as a messiah whose coming had been predicted by Merlin, the Sibyl, and the Venerable Bede.* The widowed Christine supported herself and her children by composing love poems for wealthy patrons, but the work for which she would be remembered is *The Book of the City of Ladies*, an allegorical gathering of history's most illustrious and influential women. As the daughter of the court astrologer and physician to Charles V, whose vast royal archives had provided her the education universities denied her sex, Christine made it her purpose to challenge the misogyny that characterized late medieval thought and literature, and she welcomed Joan as a citizen of her utopian vision. "In preference to all the brave men of times past, this woman must wear the crown!" the poet exclaimed. Her *Ditié de Jehanne* (Song of Joan) was the first popular work about the girl who would be remembered as France's savior, an epic ballad she composed at the height of Joan's glory, about a "young maiden, to whom God gives the strength and power to be the champion."

---

* The wizard from the Arthurian legend, a mythical seer, and an English monk of the late seventh and early eighth centuries, respectively.

If a prediction made by a magician who was himself a myth strikes the present-day reader as suspect if not worthless, the medieval mind, preoccupied with sorcery and tales of chivalry and untroubled by the future scholarly detective work that would exhume the sources of the Arthurian legend, gave Merlin's presumed words credence, the Sibyl and the Bede joining him as remote mystical buttresses to the more precise predictions made around the time of Joan's birth. Once Joan had announced herself as the vehicle of God's salvation, her initial examiners turned to prophecy as a means of retroactively validating a declaration they desperately wanted to be true, and during the late Middle Ages, Merlin, the Sibyl, and the Bede were typically summoned as a trio, each associated with pronouncements at once mysterious and archetypal. "A virgin ascends the backs of the archers / and hides the flower of her virginity," was Merlin's contribution. Copied from Geoffrey of Monmouth's twelfth-century *History of the Kings of Britain*, which introduced the Arthurian legend to continental Europe, it invited a broad spectrum of interpretations, as must any lasting prediction. Applied to Joan, it sanctioned her authority to lead men in war and underscored her celibacy, protected by male attire and armor. The Church, whose reflexive revisionism cannibalized any myth that might distract from its doctrine, had long ago consumed and rehabilitated the Sibyl, a legendary seer traced as far back as the fifth century BC and often referred to in the plural. Whether one or many, having left no recorded oracle, the Sibyl could be summoned to reinforce any appeal. The Venerable Bede's presentiment of Joan's saving France was harvested from an Anglo-Saxon poem written six centuries after Bede's death and rested on a single sentence: "Behold, battles resound, the maid carries banners."

Jesus's advent was similarly legitimized. The evangelists applied messianic prophecies as generic as "For unto us a child is born, unto us a son is given, and the government shall be upon his shoulder" to the coming of Christ and revised what they knew of Jesus's life to fit specific predictions made by the prophets Isaiah, Daniel, and Hosea. More significant, Jesus consistently presented himself as the fulfillment of Old Testament prophecy, for example, deliberately staging his Palm Sunday entrance to Jerusalem according to the six-hundred-year-old direction of Zechariah. "Lo your king comes to you," the prophet wrote of the Messiah, "triumphant and victorious is he, humble and riding on an ass." This wasn't prophecy fulfilled so much as a public announcement resting on biblical scholarship, for Jesus was, if nothing else, a Jew who knew his Scripture, knew it as well as did the high priests who called for his death in response to the presumption of his claim of divinity. "All this has taken place," he said to his disciples, "that the Scriptures of the prophets might be fulfilled." He was, Jesus told the temple elders, the Messiah whom Isaiah promised would come to "set at liberty those who are oppressed."

Like Jesus, Joan recognized herself in Scripture, but from the New rather than the Old Testament. "I was sent for the consolation of the poor and destitute," she proclaimed, borrowing her lines from Gospel accounts of a career that, like hers, convinced by means of miracle, spectacle, and prophecy fulfilled.

Of the handful Joan would have heard growing up, the only prophecy she is known to have identified with her mission was particular to her place of birth: France was to be ruined by a woman and restored by a virgin from the marshes of Lorraine. As Old and New Testaments illustrate, prophecy has always been a political medium, broadcasts from a jealous god who distributes land grants to nations worthy of reward. In 1398, when France's national oracle, Marie Robine, foresaw the desolation of her homeland, she came directly to the court in Paris to describe it in full. A recluse of humble origins embraced by the poor and the exalted alike, Marie derived her authority from the attention popes paid her apocalyptic *Book of Revelations*. Refused an audience with Charles VI, who was likely in a state of mental confusion, the seer warned that "great sufferings" would arrive. One vision presented Marie with armor, which frightened her. "But she was told to fear nothing, and that it was not she who would have to wear this armor, but that a Maid who would come after her would wear it and deliver the kingdom of France from its enemies." While witnesses remembered Joan speaking only of the prophecy specific to Lorraine, she undoubtedly knew the content of Marie's visions. Not only were they common lore, but they illustrated her vocation and validated her wearing armor.

At the time of Joan of Arc's birth, in January 1412, France had not only endured seventy-five years of enemy occupation but also devolved into civil war, as the pragmatic Burgundians, assuming the inevitability of English rule, had allied themselves with their presumptive conquerors. The blight of foreign occupation descended on a populace already halved by the previous century's periodic crop failures and famines, as well as the bubonic plague that still smoldered wherever cramped living conditions encouraged the spread of disease. After decades of pillaging the land they coveted, the English found themselves rulers of ghost towns, vineyards and fields of grain reduced to ash, homes and churches to rubble, livestock slaughtered and carcasses left to rot. The French despaired of ever recapturing the land they had lost, served by forces that were unpaid and ill-equipped by their bankrupt government, and the more dire their predicament, the more desperately they redirected hope onto a higher power—the very one from which they believed they needed rescuing. Punishments endured for as long as anyone could remember suggested that God, were God even listening to their petitions, found the French unworthy of salvation. For what, other than the kind of widespread iniquity that had required his smiting a Sodom or a Gomorrah, could explain such unrelieved misery?

When few among the living hadn't seen a putrefying corpse, both high art and popular culture trained a lush and lingering focus on the most gruesome aspects of disease and decay. As the great medievalist Johan Huizinga wrote of the late Middle Ages, it was considered "bad form to praise the world and life openly." The fashion was "to see only its suffering and misery, to discover everywhere signs of decadence and of the near end—in short to condemn the times or to despise them . . . For the true future is the Last Judgment, and that is near at hand." From the masterworks of Brueghel, Bosch, and Holbein to the crude woodcuts illustrating popular chapbooks, the *danse macabre* set the tempo for an accelerated arrival at Judgment Day. Plague made manifest what aristocrats' sumptuary laws tried to obscure. Death was democratic; the great equalizer visited princes and paupers alike and, for those who took comfort in Church doctrine, rewarded the righteous and punished the wicked.

Fifteenth-century Europe was wholly in thrall to the Judeo-Christian reflex that insists on humankind's base nature and God's impulse to destroy transgressors, just as were the Israelites, or eighteenth-century Americans during the Great Awakening, or any contemporary iteration of fundamentalism that explains mortal suffering as the result of sin, especially that of a sexual nature. Without science to provide the countervailing wisdom that weather patterns explain drought and famine, for example, or identify *Xenopsylla cheopis*, the Oriental rat flea, as the disease vector of bubonic plague, the Church commanded an unquestioned—and, during the Inquisition, unquestionable—authority for a people whose religious education stressed "Death by Eve, life by Mary"* as the formula for understanding affliction. To equate female sexuality with disobedience and pollution and judge women exclusively on the basis of their sexual conduct is a cornerstone of Judeo-Christian tradition, a structural and thus indelible doctrine; it is an apologia for misogyny. Saint Bridget of Sweden's *Celestial Revelations*, which she began to record in 1346 and which was subsequently published and given credence across Europe, identified sin as the source of France's devastation. Joan, who showcased her virginity as both proof and symbol of her virtue, believed God had punished the French because "it was his will to suffer them to be beaten for their sins."

A solitary Job might bow his head under the caprices of a deity with a penchant for testing the faith of his followers, but an entire society steeped in the shame and fear of having fallen not only from grace but so far beyond the care of God as to have become a target of his indefinite wrath could imagine only one means of salvation: the emergence of an unpolluted intercessor. If sexual transgression brought death, its inverse, the purity of abstinence, would restore life to a dying nation.

Isabeau, the unchaste queen, had fulfilled the first half of a prophecy that underscored the stain of her promiscuity; the other half would require a virgin immune to temptation.

---

* A popular medieval proverb attributed to Saint Jerome.

The phrase *l'âge de raison*, or "the age of understanding," appears several times in Joan's testimony about a girlhood that ended at twelve, when the guidance she received from her angels delivered her to "understanding" and removed her from the company of her peers, whose carefree games she joined "as little as possible," dismissing them as irrelevant to what she considered the real story of her life, a narrative she was as careful to preserve from the enthusiastic embellishment of her supporters as she was from the slander of her enemies. When Joan's advocates exaggerated and amplified her minimal contribution to the care of her father's sheep to secure her place among Jesus and the shepherds who paid homage to his nativity, as well as the Old Testament prophets Isaiah, Ezekiel, and Zechariah, she was quick to correct any misapprehension, purposeful or not, that she had ever been a shepherdess. But Joan could only protect her story for so long, and the motif of the shepherdess proved impossible to dismiss in a narrative tradition that had chosen the shepherd as an avatar of God a thousand years before the birth of Christ. "The Lord is my shepherd," King David sang, "I shall not want." Five centuries after Joan's birth and two millennia after King David's, Cecil B. DeMille's first epic, *Joan the Woman*, released in 1916, immediately establishes the director's intensely symbolic vision. Joan emerges onto the screen, Christlike in the company of her sheep, walking toward the audience through a landscape of preternatural light that ultimately gathers around her into a radiant nimbus, a halo enveloping her whole body (Fig. 5). Even Georges Duby, the preeminent twentieth-century historian of the French Middle Ages, with limitless access to documented fact, lumped Joan in among the herd of simple shepherdesses.

Of course, there are many stories of Joan's life. She left her own insofar as an autobiography can be assembled from the answers to a set of hostile questions, many repeated over and over in the attempt to wear down her resistance and trick her into perjuring herself. Truth was never what her judges sought, but in this case it couldn't be hidden. Joan's poise under fire demonstrated what she couldn't by herself, even had she been erudite as well as literate. It's one thing to assemble and polish a portrait of oneself, as did Saint Augustine, a professor of philosophy and rhetoric, and another to demonstrate at nineteen an integrity that a chorus of scheming pedants couldn't dismantle, their sophistry displaying Joan's virtues as she could not have done for herself. Few trial transcripts make good reading; only one preserves the voice of Joan of Arc. While the words of the judges are forgettable—all despots sound alike—Joan's transcend the constraints of interrogation. Even threatened with torture and assaulted by prison guards attempting her rape, she could not be forced to assume the outline her judges drew for her. That was their script, their story of Joan's life, and, unlike other such medieval documents, it was reproduced, bound, and distributed by her persecutors with the ironic purpose of establishing their punctiliousness in serving the laws of canon.

The nullification process, undertaken twenty-five years after Joan's death with the purpose of vindicating her, provides a second official narrative, told by 115 witnesses who testified on her behalf: the defense she was denied while living. Beyond these two transcripts, there are contemporaneous chronicles such as the king's counselor Guillaume Cousinot's *Chronique de la Pucelle*, the French poet Alain Chartier's *Epistola de Puella*, and the anonymously authored *Journal du siège d'Orléans* and *Journal d'un bourgeois de Paris*; letters, both those dictated by Joan herself and those written about her by kings, clerics, friends, and foes; poems; theological analyses; and eulogies, biographies, and passion plays undertaken immediately upon her death. Joan was the reluctant object of veneration even before she died, her execution the final and necessary act of a drama that had unfolded before a rapt audience across all of Europe, an audience that consumed every rumor and report of her remarkable life and wove it into narrative.

Like all sacred figures whose extraordinary earthly existence separates them from the broad mass of humanity—including the lives of gods themselves, Allah, Christ—a saint is a story, and Joan of Arc's is like no other. At the time of her birth, the Catholic Church was both center and substance of European culture. Medieval music and art were almost exclusively devotional and found their highest expression within the walls of a cathedral, whose Gothic architecture emphasized light's origin from above, the clerestory showering the faithful gathered under its roof with a spray of heavenly beams, its spires directing the eye upward to the source of that grace, even as they reminded humankind of God's omniscient scrutiny. Each of the hundreds of cathedrals built during the Middle Ages was a great act of propitiation, one city competing with another for the favor of God's grace. So completely did the Church pervade and control the attention of the people that "even cooking instructions called for boiling an egg 'during the length of time wherein you can say a Miserere.'" Far from being separated from government, the Church *was* the state. Rule was by divine right; only an archbishop representing Christ on earth could anoint a king. All across Europe—in Cambridge, Oxford, Bologna, Padua, Naples, Salamanca, Valladolid, Paris, Montpellier, Toulouse, and Orléans—the great centers of thought originated in religious communities.

For the wealthy, patronage of education and art was a means of buying the favor of a deity who, at the approach of a rich man, narrowed the gates of heaven to the size of a needle's eye. For the illiterate poor, the Church offered religious education in the form of allegory and illustration of the Gospels: altarpieces, stained-glass windows, stations of the cross, chapbooks. When academics were paid by the Church, education necessarily reflected its biases and interests, and all medieval culture, from highest to lowest, was permeated by the same anxieties. The underclass in particular focused on the afterlife as a corrective to the endless tribulations of their mortal existence, and stories told around the hearth offered as much religious indoctrination as they did entertainment. Though folktales that would have been familiar to Joan predated—some by millennia—the birth of Christ, they shared themes and symbols with Christianity, the workings of magic taking on the role of divine intervention. The equivalent of the beatitudes' promise that virtue is rewarded by heavenly blessings drove plots forward to judgment and just deserts. The moral of "Cinderella," for example, might well be "Blessed are the meek, for they shall inherit the earth," the heroine's innate goodness and obedience rewarded by a supernatural adjustment that doesn't so much create as unveil her true radiance, freeing her from servitude and delivering her to happily-ever-after in the arms of the king's son. Sleeping Beauty, too, arrives at union with an exalted beloved, woken from sleep at the touch of a prince who cuts through a thicket of thorns to apply a redemptive kiss. Guileless Snow White bites into an apple, a fruit laden with the knowledge of good and evil, proffered by a wicked queen who steps in for the serpent. The incorruptible girl falls dead, beyond the reach of human influence, and waits for the arrival of a prince who, Christlike, resurrects her and bears her off to his kingdom. The fairy-tale forest is Eden's dark inverse, a sunlit garden overgrown by shadow, concealing sin. When Little Red Cap forgets her mother's warning and strays from the path of obedience, she meets the animal that has come to symbolize sexual predation, a wolf. As a narrative genre, hagiography is suspended between biography and fiction, borrowing freely from the second to enhance a truth that may or may not be historical. Some tales of the saints poach not only motifs but also plots directly from folklore, the story of Donkeyskin, for example, revised as that of Saint Dymphna, each pursued by a father who, grieving the death of his wife, tries to take his daughter as his bride. Donkeyskin ends up in the arms of an earthly prince; Dymphna, decapitated when she refuses her father's incestuous advances, gets the heavenly version. Chivalry, too, was permeated by Christianity; the ideal knight served God above any other lord. Galahad never made it back to the Round Table with the Holy Grail before he ascended to heaven in a state of rapture so intense he chose to die in its embrace. Two centuries later, Cervantes's spoof of the chivalric quest cannot escape the Messiah's trajectory. Don Quixote descends into the Cave of Montesinos, which "went down into the abyss"—the underworld—where he remained among the dead for three days before rising.

For centuries, no matter who told the story of Joan of Arc, he or she knew each recorded moment of Jesus's life, knew it so well and from such an early age that it was natural to organize the trajectory of her short life to align with his—just as natural as it was for Joan, a girl Galahad, as she saw herself, to tread his messianic path toward her martyrdom. If her career wasn't predicted in the Scriptures, its outline is there to be found, prefigured by the Gospel narratives that inspired it.

Prophecy, annunciation, virginity. A hidden sword, an angel bearing a crown of jewels. An army of knights, a cloud of butterflies, a phallic arrow that missed its mark. A tower cell, an evil bishop, a king's betrayal. A heart that would not burn, a dove that flew from the flames that failed to dispatch that immortal heart. In Joan, fate, or God, or the gods, or random meaningless chance provided a real-life heroine whose short time on earth struck richly symbolic notes during a period whose limited media relied heavily on symbol. The story of Joan of Arc not only fulfilled a collective dream but also transfigured it, elevating it from the hearth to the heavens. Confounding in its facts, a biography like Joan's invites invention; its provenance is the unconscious; its logic apart from reason. Too, like all good yarns, Joan's spread by mouth, subject to additions and subtractions at the whim of the teller. But while many versions of her life bear a patina of loving details added by the faithful—not so much lying as regarding her through a worshipful lens—it unfolded in public. Witnessed by thousands, its lineaments weren't imagined but known and safeguarded by hard documentation. Her earliest biographers told a story swept into the realm of myth even as it unfolded, one that would demonstrate immunity to mythologizing by virtue of a historical record remarkable in its detail.

The tension between truth and fiction continues to quicken Joan's biography, for a story, like a language, is alive only for as long as it changes. Latin is dead. Joan lives. She has been imagined and reimagined by Shakespeare, Voltaire, Schiller, Twain, Shaw, Brecht, Anouilh, and thousands of writers of less renown. Centuries after her death, she has been embraced by Christians, feminists, French nationalists, Mexican revolutionaries, and hairdressers, her crude cut inspiring the bob worn by flappers as a symbol of independence from patriarchal strictures. Her voices have held the attention of psychiatrists and neurologists as well as theologians. It seems Joan of Arc will never be laid to rest. Is this because stories we understand are stories we forget?

CHAPTER 11

By Angels' Speech and Tongue

Joan's birthplace, Domrémy, lies on the west bank of the upper Meuse River, in northeastern France's region of Lorraine,[*] about 150 miles east of Paris. A census taken in the fourteenth century—it counted hearths rather than individuals—estimated the village's population at a little fewer than 200 inhabitants. Today the head count hovers around 150. With the exception of the Joan of Arc Center and the basilica erected in her honor, Domrémy remains much as it was in her lifetime, the small seat of an agricultural community in a high valley of the Meuse. The climate is more temperate than severe, summer's heat peaking in July at about eighty degrees, winter's grip tightest in January, when the river, shallow and trending into marsh where it winds past town, slows and finally freezes. The soil, dense, clayey, and rich in limestone, is ideal for pasturing livestock and for the cultivation of oats, wheat, rye, and hemp—as well as grapes. Lorraine's vineyards, known today for Beaujolais Nouveau, were first planted during the Roman occupation of Gaul.

Then, as now, a perfectly pastoral landscape spread around Domrémy's tight little clutch of mostly one-story homes: a patchwork of greens, a white spatter of sheep, a river's serpentine course coiling through hills that gradually rose into the Bois Chenu, the looming dark Oak Wood in whose dusky shadows wolves lurked, hoping for a wayward lamb. And there were more fearful predators, for, as everyone knew, it was behind the dark curtain of trees that the devil changed costume, lying in wait for two-legged prey.

---

* Derived from *Lotharingia*, Lorraine was one of the three territorial divisions of the Carolingian Empire, formed in AD 800, when Charlemagne was crowned by Pope Leo III.

Like Vaucouleurs to the north and Neufchâteau to the south, Domrémy was a less provincial village than it might have been were it not located on the Via Agrippa, the network of old Roman roads crisscrossing France and connecting, in the case of Domrémy, Verdun and Dijon by way of Langres. As it was, the town received timely news of the outcome of every skirmish, as well as the dauphin's subsequent response, disseminated by his pages. A less fortunate aspect of Domrémy's position was its vulnerability to passing raids, as a road was as good as an invitation to enjoy the spoils of one town after another. While urbanites in nearby Reims or Metz had the protection of forti-fied walls, the farmers and vintners who lived in the countryside and whose labor provided cities with all they consumed found themselves running every which way from marauding bands of soldiers, as well as deserters, mercenaries, and looters drawn to insufficiently protected property. *Écorcheurs*, they were called, or flayers, and if they didn't skin the land while engaged in what was almost exclusively siege war-fare, when unemployed they plundered whatever they chose. Captain John Fastolf, a respected military tactician whom Joan would face in battle, summarized the modus operandi that accompanied siege war-fare, whose ultimate objective was to capture dynastic rule by kid-napping and ransoming royalty. Occupying armies were directed to systematically ravage the land, burning whatever they didn't steal—homes, grain, fruit trees, crops—and killing livestock they didn't take for their own. The strategy was intended to demoralize as well as ener-vate the citizenry. Once the seemingly interminable war had drained the coffers of France and England both, some soldiers were forced to steal that they might feed and clothe themselves; others succumbed to the temptation of vandalism, rape, and murder that would go unpun-ished. It was an age of unchecked violence, the plague's devastation inuring the populace to grotesque physical torment, which became an object of fascination and even entertainment. The upper class lived for the sanctioned slaughter of warfare punctuated by tournament melees, mock battles that produced unfortunately real effects, differ-ent from Roman gladiatorial contests only in their assuming a veneer of high-minded chivalry. Peasants gaped at heads on pikes and bodies left hanging from gibbets until the flesh dropped off their bones.

By the fifteenth century, famine, plague, and warfare had so drained the land of able bodies that the economic and social fabric no longer supported serfdom, and the system of government that had characterized western Europe for nearly a thousand years had all but collapsed. Those whom the Black Death didn't kill, it freed from bondage. Peasants, serfs, laborers—tens of thousands of commoners— seized the chance to turn on the aristocracy they'd served for as long as anyone could remember, taking over the châteaus of those who had died intestate to feel the warmth of a feather bed and taste the spell a silver goblet imparted to a mouthful of wine. Of course, not everyone turned to murder and thievery. Once out from under vassalage, a skilled worker could demand payment for his labor and make his way up in the world. Born in 1375, when civil unrest was at its most widespread, Joan's father, Jacques d'Arc, lived in a time of unprecedented mobility, when an enterprising man might take advantage of depressed land values to increase his real estate and when the loosening of the social order inspired a similar instability in the fixed systems of thought that had accompanied it. By attacking his creation so indiscriminately and catastrophically, God had lost a little of his power of persuasion, and inasmuch as a man freed himself from the proscribed thoughts of the Church fathers, he had the capacity to think independently. It would be centuries before Western society valued the freethinking individual over the conformist, but a shift had occurred.

A *villein*, or free peasant, from Ceffonds, in Champagne, fifty miles west of Domrémy, Joan's father owned forty acres over which he rotated his crops and pastured his sheep and another ten acres in the Bois Chenu, into which townsfolk ventured only as far as they needed to drive their pigs to forage acorns and grow fat. Jacques d'Arc had his own home, and he owned the furnishings within it. Joan's mother, Isabelle Romée, was born in 1377 and raised in Vouthon, just five miles northwest of Domrémy. It's likely that Isabelle's brother (sometimes identified as her uncle) Henri de Vouthon, the prior of a Benedictine monastery in Sermaize, arranged her betrothal to Jacques d'Arc. Just as the child Joan has been cast in the role of humble shepherdess, her family has often been represented as diminished in circumstances, socially isolated, naive, and untouched by the corruption inherent to worldliness. But few among the peasantry could claim a Church superior in his or her immediate family; few were landed. Isabelle owned property in Vouthon as well as what she would inherit when Jacques died in 1431, of grief, some said, as Joan was executed that year. Romée was not a conventional surname—nor did a fifteenth-century peasant necessarily have a surname—but a distinction conferred on Isabelle (or possibly her mother) for having made a pilgrimage to Rome, a significant expense that bore witness to an unusual commitment to one's faith. To undertake such a journey required not only money but also the willingness to expose oneself to brigands who lay in wait along all pilgrim roads, as well as to plague and leprosy. A medieval pilgrim often sold all he owned to finance a journey from which he didn't necessarily expect to return. As friends and neighbors universally attested, both Jacques d'Arc and Isabelle Romée were "true and good Catholics, upright and brave."

"Honest farmers," they grew rye and oats, but the local diet, and their livelihood, was based on livestock—milk, cheese, eggs, fowl, and pork. The wool Jacques sheared from his sheep each spring bought what the family didn't grow or make for itself. Prosperous among the peasantry, they had a few hundred francs* in savings, as well as food and room enough to offer the occasional traveler dinner and a night's rest, either on the floor before the hearth downstairs or in one of the two lofts that formed the second story of "the only house in the village that was built of stone, not wood and thatch," in an age when almost all dwellings, urban as well as rural, were made of wood.

The fourth of her parents' five children, Joan was born in 1412, after her brothers Jacquemin and Jean and her only sister, Catherine, and before Pierre. Sources are inconsistent as well as incomplete, however, with respect to the birth order of Joan's siblings and their respective ages. According to some, Jacquemin, the eldest, was born

---

* The name given a one-livre coin, minted between 1360 and 1641. Livre, from Latin *libra*, was a measure of weight, like the English pound.

in 1406, when Isabelle was thirty, which would have made him a very young groom in 1419, the year he is said to have married and settled on his mother's land in Vouthon, where he remained until the spring of 1429. By then, Joan's fame had drawn all her siblings into its glare and on into history books, a rare destination for a peasant. After Jean and Pierre followed their little sister into battle, Jacquemin returned to Domrémy to help his parents, who were then in their mid-fifties, run the family's farm. By then, Catherine had married, moved to the neighboring town of Greux, and died, most likely in childbirth.

The accuracy of the day traditionally celebrated as that of Joan's birth, January 6, or Twelfth Night, is called into question by the date's sole extant source, an excitedly florid letter from a courtier within the dauphin's inner circle—a man who was almost certainly not present at a remote village's celebration of a Church feast day. "It was during the night of the Epiphany that she first saw the light in this mortal life," Perceval de Boulainvilliers wrote to the Duke of Milan in June 1429. "Wonderful to relate, the poor inhabitants [of Domrémy] were seized with an inconceivable joy . . . [and] ran one to the other, enquiring what new thing had happened. The cocks, as heralds of this happy news, crowed in a way that had never been heard before, beating their bodies with their wings; continuing for two hours to prophesy this new event." The only of Lord Perceval's letters known to have survived, it was written on June 21, 1429, a month after Joan had raised the siege of Orléans, eclipsing the festering shame of Agincourt and demonstrating God's long-awaited mercy. As king's councillor and a recruiting officer for the French army, Boulainvilliers had reason to celebrate a triumph that made his job not only possible but also effortless. Men who had previously fled from the front made an about-face to chase after Joan for a chance to fight under her command. The court was jubilant, even giddy, but the dauphin Charles of Valois wasn't the center of its attention. That was occupied by Joan, the international sensation to whom France owed its victory. Letters like Boulainvilliers's flew from Chinon to castles and manors across Europe. That every literate European spoke and read French accelerated the trajectory of Joan's fame, the impulse to embroider what was already fantastic as irresistible to a lord as to a gossiping housewife at market. Human prophets had predicted Joan's advent; now nature, one species anyway, had confirmed her arrival. As it was not the habit of medieval people to take note of birth dates, it was that much easier for the unreliable apparatus of human memory to nudge Joan's winter arrival to align with a date befitting her glory. It mattered little whether an Epiphany birthday resulted from heavenly manipulation, happy coincidence, Lord Perceval's imagination, or was the gift of a fabulist somewhere in the chain of rumor that delivered news to the French aristocracy; more important was that Joan's birth be met with fanfare and its date carry meaning. Epiphany marks the Magi's paying homage to Jesus, the infant Messiah who represents the "new heaven and new earth" of Revelation, a book dear to the medieval mind for its wealth of symbol and allegory. For a girl who understood herself as God's agent—"the reason I was born" to save the people of France and deliver its crown to God's chosen king—there was no more fitting birthday. Jesus borrowed December 25 from Sol, who, like most solar deities, had timed his arrival to follow on the heels of the winter solstice, and Jesus took Sol's halo as well—as did the Roman emperors.

Where no tangible historical records or artifacts provide a counterweight to the pull of a narrative tradition shaped by faith, the historical truth of a life like Joan's or Jesus's gives way to religious truth. Deities in mortal form must have parents, places of birth, and childhoods, and Boulainvilliers unwittingly aligned Joan's birthday with an event that might never have taken place. No evidence supports any wise men's pilgrimage to the newborn Son of God; no astronomer recorded any celestial phenomenon that might have been interpreted as a guiding star. The idea of Jesus's being laid in a manger derives from a mistranslation of the Aramaic to the Greek; he was probably born in an underground room used for pressing olives, far from a manger, with no space for receiving shepherds and magi. The Nativity might not have occurred in Bethlehem. Among the five cities archaeologists have identified as possible birthplaces for Jesus, Nazareth is the most likely, as his name suggests. The Evangelist Matthew chose Bethlehem to fulfill a messianic prophecy made eight hundred years earlier by Micah: "You, oh Bethlehem, in the land of Judah, are by no means least among the rulers of Judah; for from you shall come a ruler who will govern my people Israel." John's Gospel chose a different validation: "We have found him of whom Moses in the law and also the prophets wrote, Jesus of Nazareth, the son of Joseph," summoning in the case of Moses a tradition dating as far back as the Bronze Age. As it had been for Jesus, so it would be for Joan; an origin myth was added as a prefix to what was known of her extraordinary life, an auspicious beginning that predicted the subsequent miracles—prophecy applied retroactively to provide context for phenomena witnessed by hundreds of people and, as nothing else explained them, experienced as divine.

Witnesses to Joan's early childhood include friends, neighbors, local clergy, a man who identified himself as Joan's uncle but who was in fact her cousin's husband, and four of her dozen or more godparents. When parishes had yet to keep written records and the majority of the populace was illiterate, twelve wasn't an unusual number of godparents, especially not for the daughter of a prominent villager. The more people who could bear witness to a person's identity, age, and, most important, baptism, the better. Named Jehanne, or Jehannette, after one of her godmothers, Joan never used the name "Arc." As she explained to the notary who each day read her recorded testimony back to her to confirm its accuracy—lest "the said Jehanne should deny having made certain of the replies collected"—in Joan's part of the world, children bore their mother's surname (suggesting to some biographers that her father's mother might have come from Arc, ten miles north of Ceffonds). She supposed she might be Jehanne Romée, but she had always chosen to identify herself as Jehanne la Pucelle, Joan the Virgin, child of her heavenly rather than earthly father.

We have no verifiable likeness of Joan and little physical description. Portraits made during her lifetime, including her profile pressed into, as stated in the trial record, "medals of lead or other metal in her likeness, like those made for the anniversaries of saints canonized by the Church," would have been destroyed in the wake of her execution, no longer devotional objects but devil's play. The single surviving contemporaneous image of Joan is the work of a man who never saw her, more doodle than drawing. Clément de Fauquembergue, the greffier, or "clerk," who recorded the raising of the siege of Orléans in

Paris's parliamentary record, sketched a long-haired girl in the register's margin. Her body is covered by a dress; her face, drawn in profile,
wears a severe expression; and she carries a sword in one hand, her
standard in the other (Fig. 1). If the clerk got one thing right, it was by
accident. Her hair, a strand of which was found caught in the wax seal
of one of her dictated letters, discovered in the mid-nineteenth century, was the color of his ink, black, as corroborated by an eyewitness
at court. It was at court that Boulainvilliers first met the girl whose
exploits would fill his correspondence, and he found her an "elegant"
figure. She "bears herself vigorously," he wrote, "speaks little, shows an
admirable prudence in her words. She has a light feminine voice, eats
little, drinks little wine," and "wears a cheerful countenance." The
Duke of Alençon, who, like others of Joan's comrades-in-arms, "slept
on the straw" with her and had occasion to see her disrobe, praised
her young body as beautiful, quickly adding that he "never had any
carnal desire for her" and attributing the failure to Joan's ability to
banish the lust of any who might admire her, a power to which other
men in her company bore witness. "Although she was a young girl,
beautiful and shapely," her squire, Jean d'Aulon, said, and he "strong,
young, and vigorous," and though in the course of dressing her and
caring for her wounds he had "often seen her breasts, and . . . her legs
quite bare," never was his "body moved to any carnal desire for her."

That so many of Joan's comrades described their inability to summon lust for her as a genuine miracle suggests that she was certainly
not unattractive. Probably she was slender, given how universally
those who had eaten with her commented on her abstemious habits.
As she easily found men's clothing to fit her while waiting for her own
to be made, she might have been taller than most women of her time,
perhaps as tall as five feet eight, the average height of a European
man of the fifteenth century, although the more romantic accounts
of her life tend to present her as petite. A physician who had occasion
to examine Joan when she was a prisoner "found that she was *stricta*,
that is, narrow in the hips." If she and her sister shared that boyish sil-
houette, it might have ended Catherine's life, lost as it probably was in
childbirth. Without doubt, Joan was an athletic girl, and a strong one.
The plate armor she wore immediately upon receiving it, for whole

days at a time, weighed between forty and fifty pounds, enough that knights in training typically took weeks to accustom themselves to carrying the added weight.

As not even a written description of Joan's face survives, imagination has had centuries of unobstructed influence. Shakespeare's portrait of Joan in Henry VI, first produced in 1597, adroitly skirts the question of her physical appearance. "That beauty am I bless'd with which you see," Joan tells the dauphin, is the gift of the Virgin, who "with those clear rays which she infused on me" transformed Joan's appearance, gathering her into the radiance of her purity. "Black and swart before" as the result of "sun's parching heat" to which she "display'd [her] cheeks," now she is fair-skinned, possessing the pallor then held to be beautiful, as only an aristocrat could afford to spend her life in the shade.

Given a blank canvas, many of the painters who have taken Joan as a subject summoned a comely blonde, more Valkyrie than French paysanne, just as they fabricated features for the equally unknown face of Jesus, every portrait not only homage but also projection. The hero must always be handsome and the heroine beautiful, attended by light, not dark, to reveal the perfection virtue demands. The black robe in which a witch could expect to be burned is almost without exception whitewashed for Joan,* more often depicted in her glory, a majestic figure clad in shining armor and mounted on a white horse. To avoid revealing the immodest outline of a woman's legs, the painted Joan's armor tends, like a bodice, to terminate at her waist; from it flows a skirt usually originating under an incongruous peplum fashioned of plate mail (Fig. 2). Held to a lower standard of modesty, Saint Michael, the leader of God's armies, typically wears an abbreviated skirt to absent the problematic groin, a locus of pollution angels don't carry.

---

* That exception is a fifteenth-century mural within the chapel of Notre-Dame de Bermont, a mile north of Domrémy. In it, a black-robed—and blond-haired—Joan awaits execution.

To the years preceding the arrival of her voices, Joan's testimony gives glancing attention. It was a period to which she attached little interest or sentiment, eclipsed as it was by the luster and excitement of what followed. Almost as featureless as her face, Joan's childhood invites invention, and the fabled Joan tells us less about the real woman than she does the standard tropes of Christian narrative. In 1429, the anonymous cleric known as the Bourgeois of Paris recorded in his journal that when Joan "was very small and looked after the sheep, birds would come from the woods and fields when she called them and eat bread in her lap as if they were tame." Birds provide an enduring motif in apocryphal stories of Joan. From the chickens that crowed at her birth to the white dove seen flying from her heart as she died, their presence indicates that of the Holy Spirit, represented in all four Gospels as a dove descending from on high, a dove as old as Noah's olive branch. Friedrich Schiller imagined Joan prophesying her own advent: "A white dove will fly up, brave as an eagle, to attack these vultures that tear our land apart." Anouilh, whose 1955 play about Joan is called *The Lark*, describes her as a bird "in the skies of France, high over the heads of her soldiers, singing a joyous crazy song of courage. There she was, outlined against the sun . . . Every once in a while a lark does appear in [the] sky and then everything stupid and evil is wiped out."

As a child, Jesus, too, had his apocryphal birds, stories of an early life spun between heaven and earth. The *Infancy Gospel of Thomas* describes Jesus "making sparrows, then slapping his hands so that they may fly away." John the Baptist recognized Jesus as the Messiah when he "saw the Spirit of God descending like a dove and alighting on him" and heard "a voice from heaven saying 'this is my beloved Son, with whom I am well pleased.'"

Like virtually all mothers of the time, Isabelle taught her daughters the domestic skills expected of a woman, an apprenticeship that began as soon as a girl was able to fetch and carry. When asked if she had learned any craft in her youth, Joan said that she had indeed, boasting that "in sewing and spinning I fear no woman." As to the importance of those and all other "womanly duties," there were, she added, "enough other women to do them."

Enough wives and daughters to milk the cows, skim the cream, churn the butter, make the cheese, to carry grain to the mill, come home with flour, and bake bread. To feed the fowl, collect their eggs, and to slaughter, pluck, and butcher those destined for the pot. To sow, tend, and reap a kitchen garden, and fetch the water for it as well. To make and mend the family's clothes, render soap from sheep tallow and with it do the washing, then sweep the floor, scrub the pots, collect wood, and lay a fire over which to cook. Enough to suckle and dandle babies, chase toddlers, and nurse whoever fell ill. To follow men into the fields when needed to plow, glean, or thresh. To swing a scythe through the hay, and toss and dry it too. To pick the hops, bring them home to dry, and with them make the beer. And next harvest the flax, winnow out its seeds, soak the stalks, dry and pound them with a mallet, and, at last, spin its fibers into thread. To shear sheep, wash and card their wool, and spin it into yarn.

There was no end to the duties that kept a woman cloistered in her home and under the dominion of her nearest male relation, whether father, grandfather, uncle, brother, or cousin. When something so little as an unwed girl's poking her head out of a window might be interpreted as evidence of promiscuity, it was a man's duty to protect a woman from her own nature, inherited from disobedient Eve, lest she fall prey to idleness, gossip, immodesty, or, worst of all, lust. But long before Joan could be married off or secured in a convent, she was shown a different life, whose singular course would not only free her from domestic servitude but also remove her from the company of her own sex and deliver her into an army of randy, blasphemous men whose age and rank—if not physical strength—far surpassed her own and who followed her with the same unquestioning faith she herself placed in God.

Asked why she rather than another had been chosen to accomplish divine will, Joan said, "It pleased God so to do by a simple maid, to drive back the king's enemies." It's a misleading if not exactly disingenuous statement. True, she was not literate, but Joan was no simple

maid. Though she was uneducated, her mental acuity gave her the
advantage over Sorbonne-trained theologians three times her age.
When she was eleven, her father was appointed the local "dean," testifying to both his character and his affluence, as villagers tended to
select the most prosperous among them to represent their interests.
As a dean, Jacques d'Arc received a stipend to perform administrative chores for Domrémy. He checked weights and measures to ensure
equitable transactions on market day; he collected taxes, organized
the watch, and served as a delegate in local disputes. That same year,
1423, he "accompanied the mayors of Domrémy, Greux, and seven
other 'notable' inhabitants of the two villages to pay protection money
to the Lord of Commercy," twenty-five miles to the north. Jacques's
responsibilities often delivered him into the company of other local
functionaries, all of them gathered together as they wouldn't be under
any other circumstances, eagerly trading news from different parts
of the realm. Travel, and travel alone, carried tidings from town to
town along rutted roads that were muddy when they weren't choked
by dust stirred up by countless feet and hooves. Merchants with wagons and barrows, itinerant weavers carrying looms, clerics peddling
indulgences, pack trains headed to market or castle, tinkers, tax col-
lectors, self-scourging penitent pilgrims covered in ashes and lament:
their voices all flowed together in an endless torrent of rumor and fact.
At home, eating at table, sitting before the fire, talking with friends,
Joan's father would have mentioned the names of the men to whom
her voices would direct her and from whom she would seek help in
making her way to the French court.

Joan was far from the popular conception of her as "the daughter
of a shepherd, who herself followed a flock of sheep," as the prominent
theologian Heinrich von Gorkum described her, echoing his equally
respected colleague Jean Dupuy's description of Joan as a "young girl
who had only watched over animals." Heinrich and Jean were contemporaries of Joan's and wrote about her exploits as they unfolded.
Like the Bourgeois of Paris, they were educated, worldly, and no more
immune to the urge to shape Joan according to the conventions of
hagiography than was the chatty courtier Boulainvilliers. As was true
in most small towns, herding was a communal responsibility in Domrémy, and Joan's legendary career as shepherdess was limited to taking

her turn, along with all the other children, keeping an eye on the villagers' sheep while doing other chores. Usually, Joan brought her spindle with her. The townsfolk had an established routine to secure their livestock when under threat of looters whose imminence made driving their herds to another town impossible. Jacques d'Arc and another townsman, Jean Biget, had led a delegation to lease a small island (long since washed away) in the nearby Meuse from its absentee owner, the Lord of Bourlémont. In so shallow a river, it wasn't the island itself that the citizens of Domrémy wanted but the abandoned fortress on land not even a quarter mile away from the village. The stronghold provided a ready corral, and when the alarm was raised, all the animals were driven across the shallows and onto the island, their owners running behind them. By the time it was safe for them to return to their homes, the villagers would find them plundered, if not burned entirely, a catastrophe that Joan's family was spared, living as they did in a stone house.

⊕

Like most villages throughout Europe, Domrémy retained folk customs to which the Church had applied an inadequate gloss of Christian piety. Each spring, along the short road from Domrémy to Greux, an ancient beech known as the Fairies' Tree gathered the village young people under its wide canopy and provided a good example of the kind of "evidence" spies dispatched to Joan's hometown brought back to her inquisitors, who shaped it into what the Joan of Arc specialist Régine Pernoud calls "mendacious propositions that misrepresented Joan's thoughts," in this case implicating her in pagan rites that suggested sorcery. "Ladies who cast spells—*fairies* they used to call them—*used* to come in the old days and dance under that tree," Joan's godfather Jean Moreau remembered, and one of her godmothers, Jeanne, the wife of Mayor Aubery, claimed she had seen the fairies. Whether or not this was true, Joan didn't know. She herself "never saw the fairies at the tree" and knew nothing about such creatures. In her lifetime, all that remained of such revels had been recast as a celebration of Laetare (from the Latin for "joyful") Sunday, on which it was permitted to break the Lenten fast and heap the altar with flowers. Girls played with boys under "leaves and branches come down to the ground," as a local farmer, Gérardin of Épinal, described it. "Their mothers bake them loaves, and the young people . . . sing and dance there, and then they go to the Fontaine aux Raines"—a reputedly medicinal aquifer that welled up but a stone's throw away—"and eat their bread and drink its waters."

Everyone who spoke of the tree remembered its beauty. Far enough from the village that only its outline could be discerned, the tree's green envelope held one of youth's enchanted realms, sunlight blowing through the leaves.

"Were you not also inclined to go to the Fairies' Tree?" the examiner asked Joan.

"Sometimes I would make garlands for Our Lady of Domrémy."

"What did you do with the garlands?"

"We put them on the branches of the tree. I sometimes hung them there with the other girls. Sometimes we took them away, and sometimes we left them there."

Though Joan had "heard that people sick of the fever drink of this fountain and seek its water to restore their health," she did "not know whether they are cured or not." Nor did she "know whether she had danced near the tree since she had grown to understanding." The Fairies' Tree represented but one of the carefree pleasures Joan gave up once she perceived the gravity of her mission.

The same year that Jacques d'Arc was made dean, the Burgundian governor-general of Barrois attacked and laid siege to Sermaize, where Joan's mother's uncle, the prior, lived. A skirmish of little political consequence, it is remembered for the death of a single soldier, Collot Turlot, whose young widow, Mengette, was Joan's first cousin. Of dire consequence was the Battle of Verneuil, fought on August 17, 1424, a second Agincourt, it was called. Again, French losses were insupportable. Normandy had fallen, as had five French troops to every one enemy soldier, 7,262 in all, more than half of them from Scotland, with which the French were allied. The outcome of Verneuil has been cited as the moment when the dauphin lost hope in God's favor and resigned himself to unrelieved punishment.

Closer to home, in 1425, a local outlaw, notorious in his alliance with the Burgundians, was scapegoated for the theft of livestock from Domrémy and Greux, its sister town immediately to the north. Residents of both villages—if not Joan's father or brothers, then her neighbors—took their vengeance outside the law and murdered the Burgundian sympathizer, who was posthumously acquitted of the crime. The lynching demonstrated how entrenched and reflexive was the enmity of civil war, penetrating the whole of the country even as it reached backward and forward in time, the lives of generations entirely circumscribed by betrayal, destruction, and injustice—"a whole century," history has judged, saturated with "a sombre tone of hatred." Even for those who didn't do battle, war brought hardship and injury, and division colored every aspect of life. The games of children imitated battle, segregating them into factions and providing the younger inhabitants of Domrémy with an excuse to engage in skirmishes with those of Maxey, less than a mile northeast and under Burgundian control. Asked under oath if she had joined in what sounds like the medieval antecedent of cowboys and Indians—with sticks and stones in lieu of cap guns and blunt arrows—Joan said she never did, "as far as I remember." The reply might sound evasive, especially coming from a girl as preoccupied with warmongering as Joan, who did recall other children returning home to Domrémy "much wounded and bleeding," had Joan not consistently distinguished herself from other children.

Soon after the lynching, Joan's village came under attack yet again, by Burgundians, and was raided and burned, this time forcing its inhabitants to flee south to Neufchâteau. Towns like Domrémy that lay on the border between Burgundian- and Armagnac-held territories "belonged to no one, were supported by no one, were spared by no one," as the nineteenth-century French medievalist Jules Michelet characterized them. "Their only liege, their only protector, was God." When she came home, Joan discovered her parish church, Saint-Rémy, had been badly damaged, an affront she would have had to face every time she looked out her window or walked out her own front door, as the church was the family's immediate neighbor. When would she come, the prophesied virgin? When would God forgive France and send a savior?

In the summer of her thirteenth year, Joan received what she described as "a voice from God to help and guide me." The voice came at midday, when Joan was in her father's garden, adjacent to the parish cemetery. If it was a kitchen garden typical of its time and place, it included a row or two of cabbage, as well as onions, garlic, leeks, pole beans, parsnips, beetroots, and medicinal herbs. Every medieval housewife with a patch of dirt to hoe cultivated lovage and rue for everything from catarrh and pinworms to plague. Perhaps Joan was on her knees, the sun on her back, the earth warm to her touch. She might have been weeding or digging up an onion her mother sent her to fetch. At noon the church bell began to ring overhead, and Joan stopped what she was doing and, if she were not already on the ground, fell to her knees. Apart from the sun's transit across the sky, church bells, whether calling farmers home from the fields or summoning Joan to prayer, provided residents of villages like Domrémy their only means of marking time. The sound soared above the clamor of daily life, directing the ear, as a steeple did the eye, toward a realm of beauty and order. When they rang unexpectedly, it was in alarm, warning of fire, wolves, or the approach of human enemies. As it was Joan's father who oversaw the town watch, she lived at the focal point of what little defensive apparatus Domrémy maintained. Literally, there was no one for whom church bells rang more loudly, and the "near continuous incursions and pillaging by outsiders of all sorts" made Joan into a child unusually fixed on the sound of bells, which spoke of God and time and danger.

The local sacristan, Perrin Drappier, remembered that Joan scolded him when he failed to ring the bell for Mass or evening prayers, and when that didn't work, she bribed him, promising him the reward of "galettes," or cakes—the kind Little Red Cap carried in her basket—if he would only fulfill his duties dependably. Jean Waterin, a childhood friend with whom Joan drove her father's plow,

remarked that she "used to go down on her knees every time she heard
the bell tolled" and often slipped away to "speak with God." A different Jean, the Count of Dunois, who would become one of Joan's closest comrades-in-arms, remarked that even at the frantic height of her
military career "it was her habit every day, at Vesper time or at dusk, to
retire into a church and have the bells rung for almost half an hour."
Watching her pray, Dunois saw a woman "seized with a marvelous
rapture," a description far more revealing than any Joan would give.

On this first visitation, noon on a summer day, she had barely
crossed herself at the bell's call before the garden vanished, and the
sky and the earth as well. No church, no river, no patchwork of green.
There was nothing but light, "a great deal of light on all sides, as was
most fitting," Joan told the examiner, reminding him tartly, "Not all
the light comes to you alone!"

The voice's arrival was of consuming interest to Joan's examiners.
How could it not have been? Over and over they questioned her in
the attempt to access, or construct, evidence that might be used to
prove its source demonic. But all the voice had given Joan on that first
afternoon was the kind of mild and perfunctory direction a clergyman
might extend to any child. "Be good," it had said, and "go to church
often." After it had fallen silent and the garden emerged from the
flood of light, Joan found herself "much afraid." Even so, the departure
of the voice left her bereft. "I wept," she said. "I fain would have had
them take me with them too."

"There was more than a single voice?" the examiner asked.

"It was St. Michael," Joan said, "and he was not alone, but accompanied by many angels from heaven, a great host of angels. St. Gabriel
was among them."

Michael: archangel and patron saint of the crusaders, whose slaying the dragon, as Satan is called in the book of Revelation, was considered "the primordial feat of arms" from which knighthood sprang.

Gabriel: the bearer of annunciation to the Virgin Mary.

✦

The judges to whom we commend Joan today are doctors of medicine rather than of the Church. Her voices have inspired retroac-

tive diagnoses of hysteria, schizophrenia, epilepsy, even tuberculosis. Academics don't judge; they interpret. Feminist scholars posit a Joan calculating enough to costume herself as a visionary, like Catherine of Siena or Bridget of Sweden; this was an era when mystical revelation was one of the few routes a woman might take to political power. Cultural anthropology reminds us that it is at times of overwhelming social crises—like those of fifteenth-century France, staggering in the wake of war and plague and famine, and first-century Israel, caught under Rome's heavy heel, its people starving—that visionaries arise. When Jesus delivered the apocalyptic word of God to the Israelites, he spoke to a nation whose land was occupied, its people decimated by famine and disease, its surviving citizens subject to punitive taxation and violent injustice. It was the only mortal world he knew. The Lord's Prayer—"Give us this day our daily bread"—was conceived by a messiah whose parables focused on germination and failed crops and whose impossible multiplication of loaves and fishes to feed hungry masses is held among his greatest miracles.

Joan said of herself, "I am sent to comfort the poor and needy."

Ethnographers identify shamanic figures as a feature of successful societies. Granted passage to states of consciousness that elude the vast majority of us, they are the repository of our fears and hopes as well as our means of petitioning the divine. Neurotheology has discovered "God spots" in the human brain. Four out of five people experience feelings they identify as rapture when specific areas of their temporal lobes are stimulated by a magnetic field. If the brain is wired for faith in a higher being, it must be that faith conveys an evolutionary advantage.

"The first maker of the gods," William James wrote, "was fear."

✦

Among Catholic mystics, Joan is unusual for having left no written account of what Saint Teresa of Avila called the "orison of union" with the divine, a "sublime summit" from whose vantage she perceived truths otherwise withheld and from which she descended convinced that she had "been in God and God in her." If, like Saint Teresa, Joan saw in her angel's hand "a long spear of gold, and at the iron's point . . . a little fire, and if he thrust it into her heart and her very entrails," leaving her "all on fire with a great love of God," she never said. If she saw anything like Saint Bridget of Sweden's vision of the Christ child radiating such an "ineffable light and splendor, that the sun was not comparable to it," she said nothing about that either.

Drawing no distinction between angels and saints, Joan characterized what her intimate companions described as religious ecstasy as "comfort," a strikingly laconic report when compared with the overheated, lushly detailed, and erotically charged revelations of established mystics, validated through clerical channels Joan failed to consult. The sight of the rack only hardened her resolve. "Tear me limb from limb," she told her captors. "I would rather have you cut my throat than tell you all I know." Joan's refusal to part with the details of her most intimate experience, and her insistence that these were hers to withhold, expresses how absolute was her identification with virginity, a state of being unpenetrated and unplundered, the integrity of her body reflecting that of her soul.

Though mystical experience is ineffable, by definition outside mortal language's power to communicate, it was the custom of the period to narrate visions as if they were fever dreams come true. For Margery Kempe the "air opened as bright as any lightning" and left her "powerless to keep herself steady because of the unquenchable fire of love which burned very strongly in her soul." When Julian of Norwich was gravely ill, her body "dead from the middle downwards," she found herself plunged in darkness. Then the image of the crucifix began to burn before her blind eyes, her pain vanished, and her body was healed. Her holy "lover" appeared before her, and her vision lingered on the thorns pressed into his head, from which "the red blood trickl[ed] down . . . hot and freshly and right plenteously." Joined to Christ in mystical marriage, Catherine of Siena wrote of drinking the blood that spilled from his wounds. Said to have lived on the Eucharist alone for the last two years of her life, she died at the same age as had her bridegroom, thirty-three.

The preoccupation with blood that characterizes these saints is little different from a vampire's, an erotic thirst for life's essence, a thirst that, whether satisfied by God or Satan, dangled immortality. The early-twentieth-century playwright Charles Péguy cannot help but retroactively infuse Joan with a little private longing. "The Roman soldier who stuck his spear into your side had what so many of your saints, so many of your martyrs, have not had," she says to Jesus. "He touched you. He saw you . . . Blessed are they who drank in the look of your eyes," she says, where her contemporaries speak of the blood of his wounds.

The promise of revelation, dependably rendered in such fulsome, trenchant detail, made the genre a popular one, sensuous when not outright seductive. Julian of Norwich described the "malicious semblance" of the devil's face, as "red like the tilestone when it is new-burnt, with black spots therein like black freckles—fouler than the tilestone. His hair was red as rust, clipped in front, with full locks hanging on the temples." Devils and imps steal through the visions of the era's mystics, just as they leer from its artists' canvases, gleefully tempting the righteous and dragging off the damned. "Satan, in an abominable shape, appeared on my left hand," Teresa of Avila wrote. "I looked at his mouth in particular, because he spoke, and it was horrible. A huge flame seemed to issue out of his body, perfectly bright, without any shadow." But Joan never spoke of the devil. He seems to have had no place in her visions, occupied only by angels.

Still, as Anouilh's examiner reminds her, when the devil "comes to snare a soul . . . he comes with coaxing hands, with eyes that receive you into them like water that drowns you, with naked women's flesh, transparent, white . . . beautiful." Asked if she had the discernment to judge an apparition as either holy or demonic, Joan said she was sure she could distinguish between a real angel of God and a counterfeit. "I believed [in its goodness] very soon and I had the desire to believe it," she told the examiner; the word "desire" is sometimes translated as "will."

Frightened or not, Joan was waiting for what had happened to happen again. Not only had the experience continued to unfold in her mind; the visitation was hardly over before it had slipped between her and the life she used to have, and its influence didn't diminish but increased. She'd beheld a splendor that left mortal life little more than the taste of ashes in her mouth. She didn't tell her best friend, Hauviette, or her sister, Catherine, what had happened in the garden, not any more than she did the village curé or her kind, pious mother, who had introduced her to God and taught her to say the Paternoster and the Ave Maria and to recite what is known as the Nicene Creed, as first articulated in 325, when the Roman emperor Constantine I convened the Council of Nicaea. At this first of the twenty-one ecumenical gatherings recognized by the Catholic Church,* bishops representing all of Christendom stated the basic tenets of the Christian faith:

> We believe in one God, the Father Almighty, Maker of heaven and earth, and of all things visible and invisible. We believe in one Lord, Jesus Christ, the only-begotten Son of God, begotten of the Father, before all worlds, Light of Light, true God of true God, begotten, not made, being of one substance as the Father, by whom all things were made. For us men and for our salvation he came down from heaven: by the power of the Holy Spirit he was born of the Virgin Mary, and became man. For our sake he was crucified under Pontius Pilate; he suffered, died, and was buried. On the third day he rose again in accordance with the Scriptures; he ascended into heaven and is seated at the right hand of the Father. He will come again in glory to judge the living and the dead, and his kingdom will have no end. We believe in the Holy Spirit, the Lord, the giver of life, who proceeds from the Father, who with the Father and Son is worshipped and glorified. He has spoken through the Prophets. We believe in one holy catholic and apostolic Church. We acknowledge one baptism for the forgiveness of sins. We look for the resurrection of the dead, and the life of the world to come. Amen.

Instinctively, Joan protected herself from the critical regard that would follow her sharing such a confidence as her entertaining visits from angels bearing messages from the King of Heaven, and when the voice returned and spoke once more, again she kept it to herself. For all the years that remained to her, "a good seven" of her nineteen, she estimated, Joan's everyday companions, whose company she chose

---

* The most recent was Vatican II, 1962–65.

before that of mortals and whom she obeyed as she did not any mortal, were invisible and inaudible to everyone but her.

"They often come among the Christian folk and are not seen by any except by me," she told the examiner.

"Did you see St. Michael and these angels corporeally and in reality?"

"I saw them with my bodily eyes as well as I see you."

How could she have imagined them, she reasoned, when their voices came to her from outside her own consciousness, when they woke her from sleep to deliver a message? Standing trial, Joan complained that the clamor in the courtroom drowned the angels' voices out; she couldn't hear what counsel they offered. Sometimes the prison itself was so loud she couldn't hear them properly when they spoke to her in her cell.

"Who persuaded you to have angels with their arms, feet, legs, and robes painted on your standard?"

"I had them painted in the manner in which they were painted in churches."

"Did you yourself ever see them in the manner in which they were painted?" the examiner asked. It was among the questions Joan refused to answer.

Joan's evasiveness and the inconsistency of her testimony about the angels she heard and saw have drawn centuries of scrutiny and criticism. Vita Sackville-West observed that "her reluctance to discuss their personal attributes is manifest and consistent." On February 22, in the course of her second public interrogation, Joan said it was only after three visits that she recognized the angel as Saint Michael. On March 15, by which point the questioning had been moved to her cell, she said she saw him "many times" before she believed it was he. The discrepancy seems insignificant when Joan had established from the outset of the trial that she, and not those who presumed to judge her, would determine which questions she was bound to answer honestly, if at all. Her confidence in her vocation allowed her righteousness enough to warn her persecutors. "If you were well informed about me," she told them, "you would wish me to be out of your hands. I have done nothing except by revelation."

As the trial record shows, the longer and harder Joan was pressed to describe what couldn't be described, the more details she summoned to characterize a visitation she understood as angelic, in that it conveyed messages from God. The Old Testament term for angel, *mal'āk̲ 'ĕlōhîm*, means "messenger of God." Perhaps a single voice accompanied by a great light evolved into several voices Joan could distinguish from one another, and those in turn conjured beings who had lips with which to speak, crowned heads, and bodies she could see and touch and even smell. It's typical for visitations like Joan's to accrue definition and detail with each added encounter. She'd had an experience—thousands of them by the time she traded her mortal life for the eternal company of her angels—that required explanation. Perhaps she didn't so much invent details as relinquish them slowly. Perhaps she didn't invent but borrowed unconsciously. Familiar figures, holy and God-sent, angels and saints provided ready vessels in which Joan could safeguard what she didn't want to forget or deny, rapture so overwhelming and potentially disorienting that it required containment.

"A light came over the sun and was stronger than the sun," Joan tries to explain in *The Lark*, a light that entered and overcame what she calls "the shadow of me."

"How did you know it was an angel who spoke?" the examiner asked, the notary noted, and the judges allowed to remain in the trial record.

"By his angels' speech and tongue," Joan said.

"Born in the shadow of the church, lulled by the canticle of the bells, fed on legends," as the historian Jules Michelet described her. "Unawares, the young girl created, so to speak, her own ideas, turned them into realities, made them entities, powers, imparted to them, from the treasure of her virginal life, an existence so splendid, so compelling, that the paltry realities of this world grew faint in comparison."

Had Saint Michael not been clear as to the meaning of "good," he told Joan he was sending two female saints to be her daily, sometimes hourly, guides to furnish clear and dramatic role models.

"How do you know one from the other?" the examiner asked Joan.

"By the greeting they give me," she said. "I also know the saints because they tell me their names."

Saint Catherine was one of the Fourteen Holy Helpers,* powerful intercessors around whom cults developed during the plague years, their images displayed in churches and chapels Joan visited as a child. Born in Alexandria, Egypt, in 282, Catherine was the beautiful daughter of her people's pagan king, Costus. As a scholar, she penetrated a world largely claimed by men. By fourteen, Catherine had converted to Christianity, consecrated her virginity to her heavenly bridegroom, and become a convincing proselytizer. She left Alexandria for Europe, where she converted Valeria, the wife of the Roman emperor Maxentius, who had Valeria executed for the crime of practicing Christianity. Having removed the impediment that stood between him and the true object of his desire, Maxentius proposed that he and Catherine marry. Catherine, however, refused to accept an earthly bridegroom in Christ's stead. Maxentius ordered she be tortured, but the wheel meant to break her body fell into a pile of splinters at her touch. Undeterred, Maxentius had her beheaded, successfully.

A statue of another of the Holy Helpers, Saint Margaret of Antioch, stood just next door to Joan's family home, in the little church of Saint-Rémy. The second of Joan's heavenly guides, she was a daughter of royalty as well, if in a different sphere. Her father was a pagan priest who disowned her when she converted to Christianity and vowed to remain a virgin; she escaped his house disguised as a man. A Roman governor tried to make Margaret his wife at the cost of her faith, but she renounced him instead, defying a series of tortures by means of miracles, the most remarkable of which was her escaping from inside the dragon that swallowed her by using her cross to rake the inside of the beast's stomach until it vomited her back up. Eventually, Margaret's petitions went unanswered, or perhaps she saw more clearly what lay on the other side of mortal life and gave it

---

* The fourteen are Agathius, Barbara, Blaise, Catherine of Alexandria, Christopher, Cyriacus, Denis, Erasmus, Eustace, George, Giles (the only of the fourteen who was not martyred), Margaret of Antioch, Pantaleon, and Vitus.

up. Said to have been martyred in 304, she was declared apocryphal in 494, a finding that had no impact on her popularity or the reality accorded her by the faithful.

For Joan, as much as it had for the virgin martyrs of the early Church, being good meant being chaste, in mind and spirit as well as in body. Among the three acceptable modes of existence for a woman—virgin, wife, and widow—only a virgin escaped the pollution inherent to her sex. Three "orders of merit" clarified their relative worth: "Virgins would be rewarded a hundred times their deserts; widows sixty times; and wives thirty times." Within each of the three modes, "an explosion of female categories" betrayed a Linnaean determination to impose order on the gender held to be more primitive, lacking the moral restraint and cerebral capacity of men. Sexually immature girls, adolescents ready for marriage, married women, spinsters, late marriers, women past procreating: rankings observed from the perspective of something like animal husbandry were each subdivided according to a social hierarchy that reached from royalty all the way down through minor aristocrats, nuns, servants, and chicken dealers—prostitutes not worthy of inclusion, even in a group so universally disdained.

"Art thou not formed of foul slime? Art thou not always full of uncleanness? Shalt thou not be food for worms?" a medieval cleric ranted. Scholars of the period mined the classics for validation of the early Church's hostility toward women, which found an ideal target in menstrual blood, both tangible evidence and ready symbol of women's uncleanness. The "foul substance was blamed for preventing seeds from germinating, for turning grape mash bitter, for killing herbs, for causing trees to shed their fruit, for rusting iron and blackening brass, for giving dogs rabies." Aristotle taught that the gaze of a menstruating woman was so impure it would darken a mirror, stealing light from the other side of the glass, a conclusion rationalized by Galenic theories of harmful vapors, such as those that issued from menopausal women "because various excess humors no longer eliminated by menstruation now exited through the eyes." Tertullian memorably described a woman as "a temple built over a sewer," summoning Christ's image of "whitewashed tombs, which look beautiful on the outside but on the inside are full of dead men's bones and everything unclean."

But Joan, her squire reported, didn't menstruate. During all the months that he dressed and served her, Jean d'Aulon saw no evidence she was afflicted by the "female malady." "In her, the life of the spirit dominated, absorbed the lower life, and held in check its vulgar infirmities," Michelet wrote. "Body and soul she was granted the heavenly grace of remaining a child." Perhaps the fervor of her vow of chastity was enough to forestall menarche indefinitely. Perhaps the strain of warfare and imprisonment suppressed what would have been her natural reproductive cycle. The reason is irrelevant to the story. In memory, and then in biography and history, Joan would remain forever on the cusp of womanhood, not only chaste, but yet to fall under Eve's shadow or bear her stain.

Friends noted Joan's withdrawal from their company and must have wondered at her new solitary life. Perhaps they felt sorry for her, a girl too pious to have fun, but they'd never been visited by angels or shown the glories of paradise. They didn't know Joan had traded their company for a rapture that consumed her several times each day, and never more dependably than when she was in the woods and far from their company.

"I was only born the day you first spoke to me," Anouilh's Joan says to her voices, dismissing not only the childhood that hagiographers were so eager to fill with birdsong but the very notion of her ever having existed outside her vocation. "My life only began on the day you told me what I must do, my sword in hand."

Had Joan's conduct not been that of an exemplary Christian before the visitation, now her virtue was so intense it demanded her separation from earthly pastimes. As she herself put it, "Since I learned that I must come to France, I had taken as little part as possible in games or dancing." (Here and elsewhere in the trial transcript, Joan's use of "France" derives from the confusion inspired by Domrémy's ambiguous position on the border.)

"She gave alms gladly and had the poor of the village gathered together, and she wanted to sleep beside the hearth and to let them lie in her bed," testified Isabellette, an older girl who remained in Domrémy and married a farmer there. "One never saw her hanging about the streets, but she stayed in church to pray. She did not dance, and often we other young people used to notice that and talk about it. She was always working and spinning and digging the ground with her father," Isabellette testified for the nullification.

So devout she inspired gossip, Joan was derided as well. "She was deeply devoted to God and the Blessed Virgin," Colin, a childhood friend, remembered, "so much so that some other lads and I—for I was young then—used to tease her." One of those lads, Jean Waterin, said the same. "I and the others made fun of her," he admitted.

"I say my prayers, yes, Joan," Hauviette chides her friend in Péguy's *The Mystery of the Charity of Joan of Arc*, "but you, you never leave off saying them, you say them all the time, you say them at everyone of those crosses by the roadside, the church isn't enough for you. The crosses by the road have never had so much wear . . . You are our friend, but you'll never be like we are."

If Joan hadn't been a solitary soul before, she soon became one, her vision so firmly fixed on the glories and terrors of her vocation that she was immune to any pressure to conform to her peers' expectations, unaffected by censure from any mortal source. "She liked going to church and went often," her friend Mengette said. Joan confessed so frequently that the vicar commented on it, and others remembered seeing her on her knees at every opportunity. "She gave alms out of her father's goods, and she was so good and simple and pious that the other girls and I used to tell her that she was too pious." And, Mengette added, she was industrious. "She liked working and undertook all sorts of jobs."

She was holier, by far, than they, her only sin to evade chores so she could pray in the woods or visit a chapel "when her parents thought she was at the plough, in the fields, or somewhere else," her godfather Jean Moreau testified.

"When I was in the woods I easily heard the voices come to me," she told the examiner.

In fact, the dialogue between Joan and her voices was growing ever more urgent. Giving alms and devotedly caring for the sick were not enough for God, nor was a vow to remain a virgin for as long as he wanted. "Joan, Child of God," her voices called her, and they told her it would soon be time to leave her home and set out on a holy quest. And not only Joan was given presentiments of her leaving. "My mother told me several times that while I was still at home my father said he had dreamed of my going away with soldiers," Joan testified, "and my parents took great care to keep me safely."

Like most men of his era, Jacques d'Arc held dreams to be oracular and prophetic, and when he dreamed more than once that his younger daughter went off with men-at-arms at a time when the only women to do so were prostitutes, he received it as not only a dire warning but also a call to action.

"If I thought this thing would happen which I have dreamed about my daughter," Jacques said to his sons, "I should want you to drown her; and if you would not, I would drown her myself."

"They held me in great subjection," Joan testified.

"You were crying out to someone," Joan's father says in *The Lark*, when he catches her praying aloud. "The bastard fled before I could catch him. Who was it? Who was it? Answer me. Answer me or I'll beat you to salt marsh."

"I was talking to the Blessed Saint Michael."

Jacques strikes Joan. "That will teach you to lie to your father," he says. "You want to start whoring like the others. Well, you can tell your Blessed Saint Michael that if I catch you together I'll plunge my pitchfork into his belly and strangle you with my bare hands for the filthy rutting cat you are."

If Jacques d'Arc's recurring nightmare didn't prove him clairvoyant, it was disturbing enough that her family remembered and recounted something that delineated a significant conflict between Joan and her father. Years after the fact, when spies were plundering the memories of Joan's childhood friends and neighbors, they stumbled across what storytellers preserved not only for its drama but because it provides an element the virgin martyr's plot requires: a controlling father who intends to stymie her vocation, a forced betrayal typically the first obstacle to her glory. Chaste as she was, some aspect of Joan's behavior must have communicated insubordination, enough to eventually inspire Jacques's efforts to let another man take a turn at containing her. But, as Joan's father would discover, it's not easy to marry off a daughter who has given herself to God.

History is rarely kind to a heroine's antagonist, and Jacques d'Arc's misreading of his daughter's character amounted to perversion. She wouldn't follow an army but lead one, and the power she claimed would rest on her virginity, the most profound and closely guarded aspect of her identity, the one that provided the name with which she christened her reborn self: La Pucelle, the Maid, derived from the Latin *puella*, a girl yet to enter womanhood.

CHAPTER
III

A Small,
Nay, the Least,
Thing

When Joan was fifteen, her father was summoned to Vaucouleurs, some twelve miles north of Domrémy, to meet with the town's captain, Robert de Baudricourt, about the "escalating tensions between the warring factions." Aside from Mont Saint-Michel, and Tournai, both hundreds of miles to the west, Vaucouleurs was the single town north of the Loire to remain in France's possession, testimony to Baudricourt's grit and the tenacity of the men stationed in the garrison he oversaw. It was 1427, and Joan's voices were speaking no longer of virginity but of battle. She knew she was the chosen one and that there was, as she said, "no one on earth, be he king, or duke, or the King of Scotland's daughter, or anyone else, who can restore the kingdom of France." The "King of Scotland" wasn't a random allusion. Reflexively hostile toward England, Scotland was France's ally, and the king of the Scots' daughter had recently been betrothed to the dauphin's son Louis, who was not yet four years old. Only a girl who followed dynastic politics would have known of such a development, and only Joan, her voices made clear, could lead the dauphin's army to victory and him to his coronation at Reims, where all French kings were made.

"She was not so much warned by the oracle of the gods above," Alain Chartier recorded in his *Epistola de Puella* of 1429, "as threatened with a very harsh punishment unless she went swiftly to the King." Alain Chartier, of no relation to Jean Chartier, Charles VII's secretary, was one of France's two great poets of the era—the other was Christine de Pizan—and is unusual in identifying Joan's vocation as the product of divine coercion, perhaps intending to feminize his subject by ignoring a fervor satisfied only by making war. Similarly, Schiller's Joan bemoans her fate. "A terrible contract binds me to the spirit-world, powerful, invulnerable, and enjoins me to put to the sword and slaughter every living thing sent fatally against me by the god of battles."

But more than a few little girls must have imagined themselves as warriors striding into tales of fantastic chivalry, girls who dreamed of heroism—and martyrdom—for the Church, dreamed of destinies no man would grant them the authority to fulfill. The limited media of medieval Europe meant that very few trouvères, or writers of chansons de geste, achieved the popularity, and thus the cultural sway, of the twelfth-century poet Chrétien de Troyes, who enriched and enlarged the Arthurian cycle, bringing in ancient Celtic heroes, the theme of the Holy Grail, and Camelot as Arthur's capital. The extraordinary number of surviving copies of works translated and adapted throughout Europe, volumes replicated and illustrated by hand, proves the extent to which Chrétien de Troyes's vision saturated late medieval society. *Érec et Énide*, *Cligès*, *Lancelot*, *Yvain*, and *Perceval*: in each the knight-errant is the central character. He is courteous, generous, and of noble birth, a man who values his honor over his life and whose exploits are not confined to tournaments and warfare, but include fairy-tale elements like dragons, giants, and enchanted castles. The medieval imagination was crowded with the conventions of a literature not only written in the vernacular but also read and performed aloud, as were Easter passion plays and other liturgical productions. Every child knew heroism came in the form of a knight whose perfect virtue found its reflection in that of his lady, increasingly conflated with the Virgin Mary. As the medievalist Frances Gies observed, "The terms in which earthly women were flattered in troubadour poems were often borrowed—daringly—from those used to praise the Virgin Mary: the troubadour 'worshipped' his lady, there was 'no woman like her.'" Even in satire, Don Quixote's romantic delusions are centered on his peerless Dulcinea, so heavenly as to be forever out of reach.

Chansons de geste stimulated the cult surrounding the Virgin, whose popularity ascended steeply during the Middle Ages, perpetuated not so much by the Gospels' handful of references as by an extensive pseudepigrapha,* noncanonical texts that gathered miracles

---

* Unlike the apocryphal texts included in the Vulgate, pseudepigrapha, from the Greek *pseud*, "false," and *epigraphein*, "to inscribe," are not included in any scriptural canon.

and myths from a growing oral culture about the life of Mary, whom the theologian Jaroslav Pelikan stresses was "completely human in her origin, like all other human beings. Yet because she had been chosen by God to be the Theotokos [Greek, for Mother of God], her completely human nature had been transfigured." Virginity was the key to Mary's transfiguration, as it was for that of Joan, who described her vocation in terms familiar from *The Gospel of the Nativity of Mary* (today attributed to a ninth-century Carolingian scholar, Paschasius Radbertus). "Daily was she visited by angels," the gospel read, "daily did she enjoy a divine vision, which preserved her from all evil, and made her to abound in all good. And so she reached her fourteenth year."

Every Saturday, Joan went to Notre-Dame de Bermont, a hilltop shrine two miles north of Domrémy that was consecrated to the Virgin Mary, her devotion inspiring Schiller to replace bellicose Saint Michael as the bearer of Joan's vocation with an apparition of the Virgin, who, Joan says, "appeared in front of me, carrying a sword and a flag, but dressed in every other way like a shepherdess." When Joan protests she has no abilities as a warrior, the Holy Mother tells her, "a virgin without stain can accomplish all the good deeds in the world, if she withstands the love that's *of* the world. Only look at me. I was like you, a chaste maid, yet I gave birth to the Lord, the Lord Divine; I am myself divine!"

"And then," Schiller's Joan says, "she touched my eyelids, and when I looked up, the heavens were full of angels ... And as she spoke, the shepherdess's dress fell away from her, and she stood there, clad in the brightness of a thousand suns, the golden clouds lifted her up, slowly taking her from my sight, to Paradise."

Sword and flag notwithstanding, Mary's shepherdess costume is warning enough that Schiller's vision is romantic, reaching to feminize Joan, whose chastity did not mean she identified with passive divinity any more than she fantasized about giving birth to a messiah. She saw that role as her own. Probably, it was the remoteness of the shrine that attracted Joan more than its being consecrated to the Virgin, whom she mentions seldom and never with the fervor reserved for Saints Michael, Catherine, and Margaret. In the future, she wouldn't hesitate to seize a military advantage on the Festival of the

Blessed Virgin Mary, attacking Paris while its citizens were occupied by Masses and processions in the Virgin's honor. "Pass on," she said to the examiner who pressed her to admit the transgression, responding with the verbal equivalent of a shrug. Joan didn't speak of whom the shrine paid tribute to, only of the little pilgrimage required to reach it. The climb from Joan's house to the chapel is much the same today as it was when she made it, lovely in every season and especially so in spring, through high pastures divided by streams of bloodred poppies and along paths lined with a froth of Queen Anne's lace, and finally into the forest, carpeted in places with tiny strawberries. She carried a few sous* for a candle to light, as well as the flowers she'd picked on her way, and her angels kept her company. They assured her, she testified, that "God would clear a road for me to go to the lord Dauphin."

That road, however, was not immediately apparent. Joan's youth and gender held her captive to the supervision of any and every adult in Domrémy, and it was the spring of 1428, when Joan was sixteen, before she found a means of making her way to Robert de Baudricourt herself—for it was Sir Robert whom her voices told her to ask for assistance. Sir Robert, as Joan knew, had access to the dauphin, and according to her voices he "would give me men-at-arms" to accompany her west from the little pocket of resistance represented by the Duchy of Bar, which included Domrémy and Vaucouleurs, and through enemy territory to Chinon, where she would find the dauphin Charles.

Joan could have walked the twelve miles to Vaucouleurs, she could have started in the morning and arrived before noon, but there was little point in running away when she couldn't successfully navigate the world of men by herself. Both a girl and a stranger in a realm that allowed women no autonomy, she needed a man to provide her an introduction to the captain. But who? Willing as Joan was, she hadn't any idea how to accomplish what God asked of her. She should ask her uncle Durand for help, her voices said. At forty, Joan's mother's cousin's husband, Durand Laxart, was old enough to be Joan's uncle, and so she called him by that term of endearment and respect. But as

---

* There were twenty sous to the livre.

intimate as the two families were, they lived ten miles apart, and Joan had to wait for an opportunity to visit her uncle without alerting her father to a plan that could only further harden his heart against her.

By now Joan had determined that to align herself with God's will required the occasional earthly deceit and had reconciled herself to either hiding the truth or, when necessary, lying outright. "My voices would have been glad for me to tell them," she said of her parents, "had it not been for the difficulties they would have raised had I done so. For my part, I would not have told them for anything." Faith didn't allow Joan the luxury of mortal attachment. God claimed her devotion as absolutely as her voices directed her actions. "If I had had a hundred parents," she said to the examiner who had called attention to her failure of filial responsibility, "I would have gone nevertheless." She, like her judges, remembered Jesus's admonition to his would-be followers: "If anyone comes to me and does not hate his own father and mother and wife and children and brothers and sisters, yes, and even his own life, he cannot be my disciple . . . Whoever of you does not renounce all that he has cannot be my disciple."

"He'd been a good son to his father and mother, until the day he began his real task," Péguy's Joan says of Jesus. "Everybody was very fond of him . . . until the day he began his real task."

⊕

Laxart, a farmer who lived in the hamlet of Burey, just outside Vaucouleurs, was as rough in dress and manner as any peasant and equally reluctant to approach a member of the aristocracy. Joan might well have been, as he believed her to be, a "well-behaved, pious, and patient" hard worker who "confessed gladly" and went to church often, but what man of his station would agree to escort even such a paragon of virtue to one of the dauphin's captains, especially a paragon with so impudent a request?

A week of Joan's company taught Laxart how obdurate was her will. "Was it not said that France would be ruined through a woman, and afterward restored by a virgin?" Joan asked him. She was that prophesied virgin, she told her uncle, she was La Pucelle, and she told the examiner she had no choice but to go. Saints Catherine and

Margaret spoke of it continuously. "The voices told me I must leave and go to France." She could no longer stay where she was. "They said I was to go to the Dauphin, to have him crowned." As astounding as Joan's announcement was, Laxart received it as would a man typical of his time and place, who understood the world as subject to visits from God's emissaries, as well as of course from those of Satan. Joan was possessed, that was clear, but Laxart knew Joan, and he knew her goodness too well to imagine she might be possessed by a demon.

On May 13, 1428, Laxart brought Joan to Robert de Baudricourt, who, once he understood he was being asked to deliver a delusional peasant girl to the dauphin, suggested Laxart "give her a good slapping and take her back to her father." Joan's father was, of course, someone Baudricourt saw routinely, a man who had been made a village dean for his clear reason and good sense. Upon first hearing of Joan's mission, the captain must have taken pause at the idea of Jacques d'Arc having so mad a daughter—just as he would stop and wonder at every other thing he'd learn about her. For, by the following summer, all of Europe would know about the virgin warrior who had emerged from a remote village in Lorraine. One day she was a shepherdess, the next a knight on a charger. God's finger had brushed the earth, and no one, no matter his faith or lack thereof, could turn away from the spectacle. Some would say she was a witch, of course, and the finger Satan's. But as far as Baudricourt was concerned, for now Joan was no more than Jacques d'Arc's willful hoyden of a daughter, far afield from hearth and home, where she belonged, and a ready candidate for marriage and children—whatever it took to keep her tied down and too busy to think up such drivel.

Aside from Laxart, the only eyewitness on record to describe Joan's first confrontation with Sir Robert was Bertrand de Poulengy, a squire, or apprentice knight, stationed in Vaucouleurs. Immediately convinced of Joan's sanctity, Poulengy became a friend of her parents and often visited their home in the years after Joan's death. "I saw her there, talking to Robert de Baudricourt," to whom she said she had come "on behalf of her Lord, to ask him to send word to the Dauphin that . . . the Lord would send him help before mid-Lent."

Who, Sir Robert wanted to know, was this Lord?

"The King of Heaven," Joan said, and she explained that France belonged not to any mortal ruler but to God, who wished to entrust it to Charles and who "promised that the Dauphin would be made king . . . and that she herself would lead him to be anointed."

Sir Robert laughed. He had another idea. Why not, he said, "hand her over to the pleasure of his soldiers" instead? That was one way to disarm a presumptive virgin.

The Lark introduces Baudricourt as predator rather than procurer. After offering to "kick [her] in the place where it will do the most good," the captain negotiated terms for himself rather than his men, explaining his "rate of exchange" to the girl he called an "infernal nuisance" and "horrible mosquito." She could have her horse, man's clothes, and an escort, as long as he got what he wanted in recompense for his "benevolence." "The village girls have told you all about it, haven't they?" he asks Joan.

Of the confrontation, Jean Chartier, the royal historiographer from 1437 to 1450, said "they only laughed and mocked her for all this."

◈

"Don't get involved in earthly strife. It will engulf you. Your purity won't last," Bertolt Brecht's 1900 chorus warns Joan, offering medieval advice. "Your bit of warmth will perish in the all-pervading cold. Goodness departs from those who leave the comforting hearth." *Saint Joan of the Stockyards* is one of three plays Brecht wrote about Joan of Arc, and it unfolds in a mythical Dreiserian Chicago, where Joan, "at the head of a shock troop of Black Straw Hats"—as Brecht christened his Salvation Army—must make her way through the minions of Pierpont Mauler to approach the Meat King herself. She promises his already hungry workers she will convince him not to close his canning factory for his own financial gain. "In a dark time of cruel confusion, of ordained disorder, of systematic lawlessness, of dehumanized humanity," she cries to an agitated crowd, "we propose to bring God back."

Christian socialism underscored the antiestablishment, egalitarian message of Jesus, prefiguring Dorothy Day's Catholic Worker movement. Whether set in the fifteenth or the twentieth century, the war Joan brings is revolutionary. "This campaign of ours is undoubt-edly the last of its kind," Joan of the Stockyards tells the crowd of workers. "The last attempt to set Him up again in a crumbling world." The situation is apocalyptic, accelerating toward the Jesus who came bearing a sword of justice rather than a bleeding heart. "We are sol-diers of God," Joan cries. "Wherever conditions are unsettled and violence threatens we come marching with our drums and banners, to remind people of God, whom they've all forgotten, and lead their souls back to Him."

Discouraged if not defeated, Joan went home to find roving bands of looters circling Domrémy. By July, when Burgundian forces advanced on Vaucouleurs, Joan's family had been forced once again to take refuge in Neufchâteau, driving their herds into the fields as they left. For two weeks they stayed at an inn kept by a woman known as La Rousse—the Redhead. Joan "did not like living in those parts," she told a neighbor, "but preferred to live at Domrémy." Still there was much to be gleaned from wayfarers' conversation around a tavern's communal dinner table, information that fueled Joan's impatience to set off on her God-given errand. She didn't object to working in La Rousse's kitchen in exchange for room and board. She would rather pass the time doing chores than wait in idleness for her life to begin. But, as inquisitorial spies would later report, there were soldiers stay-ing at the inn, a sliver of information her judges used to fabricate the allegation that Joan, "of her own will and without the leave of her said father and mother, went to the town of Neufchâteau in Lorraine and there for some time served in the house of a woman, an innkeeper named La Rousse, where many young unguarded women stayed, and the lodgers were for the most part soldiers."

Having insinuated that La Rousse was a madam and Joan a pros-titute, the judges found an additional use for the slander. As stated in the ninth of the seventy "articles of accusation" brought against her, Joan, "when in this service, summoned a certain youth for breach of promise before the magistrate of Toul, and in the pursuit of this case, she went frequently to Toul, and spent almost everything she had.

This young man, knowing she had lived with the said women, refused to wed her, and died, *pendente lite* [pending litigation]. For this reason, out of spite, Jeanne left the said service."

The motif surfaces in every narrative genre of the time, including the minutes of a kangaroo court: a duplicitous, unchaste woman lures a trusting young man to his death as he struggles to free himself from her sexual stain.

No, Joan objected, she'd made no promise to any young man. She had consecrated all of her being to God, her chastity both symbol and proof of her faith. She would never wed, unless at God's command. "It was he who summoned me," Joan corrected the examiner. "Saints Catherine and Margaret assured me I would win my case." As they promised, the magistrate dismissed the suit and acquitted Joan, guilty of nothing but refusing to wed whomever her father had chosen to inherit the problem she'd become—a local boy, it's assumed. While parents commonly resorted to bribery, threats, and even violence to coerce a child to accept an unwanted spouse, by the fifteenth century Church law protected such children, and fathers no longer had the right to marry off daughters without their leave. Joan might have considered herself overprotected, but she wasn't chattel, not officially, and the ninth article was eventually dropped from the charges held against her. As for the maligned La Rousse, the innkeeper was a decent, proper woman, as several witnesses to Joan's childhood testified.

Had she not already, Joan would discover that to advertise her chastity was to ask for that claim to be challenged or, worse, rendered false, and for as long as she was in Neufchâteau, she remained always in the company of her parents, the whole family living among neighbors from Domrémy, insulated from strangers. There was no one more committed to guarding Joan's reputation than Joan herself, who had begun to perceive the lineaments of her future as a public figure and understood that rumor had power where truth did not. As soon as it was safe to do so, Joan's family returned to Domrémy to find, once again, most of their homes burned, the church left in ruins.

"Do you know," Péguy's Joan demands of those who counsel her to control her temper . . . "that the soldiers are attacking towns and breaking their way into churches everywhere? . . . And they shout all sorts of vile things at the Blessed Virgin, to our mother the Blessed Virgin, and they call names and blaspheme Jesus on his cross . . . [T]hey foul the bread and the wine, the body and blood of Jesus . . . Jesus's sacred body."

On October 12, 1428, the English laid siege to Orléans. As it was the single remaining bastion that prevented them from crossing the Loire and occupying what remained of France, there was talk of little else. The kingdom that had reigned supreme in Europe just a hundred years earlier now faced extinction. Should Orléans fall, all of France would follow it, and all who called themselves French would find themselves under the rule of the king of England. It grew ever harder to manufacture hope in the face of what appeared inevitable defeat. Soldiers too honorable to defect sank into the apathy of the condemned, and the French clergy found themselves marching circles around the army's frozen infantry, processing through the streets on a regular basis to demonstrate the constancy of their devotion in hopes of summoning a miracle. The dauphin, whose fear of illegitimacy inspired fatalism, was making plans to abandon his sinking kingdom for the castle of one of France's allies—Scotland or Spain.

By December, Joan was back in Vaucouleurs. Her voices promised her success; she had only to persevere, in this case by using Laxart's wife's advanced pregnancy as an excuse to travel north. Joan persuaded her parents to let her go with her uncle Durand to stay for a few weeks in his home and help her mother's cousin during her confinement, a ruse to which Jacques might not have agreed had he not been exasperated by the botched marriage plot that left Joan on his hands. He might reasonably have assumed his daughter would have given up her wild scheme after being dressed down by Sir Robert de Baudricourt in public and subsequently ridiculed. Not that Joan had disclosed what happened the last time she'd visited her uncle in Burey. In her parents' home, Joan had been as circumspect as always, continuing to cloak her preoccupation with her voices' demands. She'd practiced doing that for years. But the world in which Joan lived was small, and a grandnephew of Isabelle's had told Joan's brothers about her first meeting with Baudricourt. The report of so incongruous a transaction between their sister and the city's captain aroused Jean and Pierre's suspicions, as would any scenario involving Joan and men-at-arms, and they in turn told their parents about a spectacle that had already provided irresistible fodder for gossips.

For whatever reason—and perhaps it was nothing more than her own impatience—Joan left Domrémy in haste, a leave-taking remembered primarily for her cryptic good-byes. She left quickly but not in secret, bidding farewell to those she encountered as she was heading out of town. If she looked, she never found an opportunity to tell Hauviette that she was leaving, and Hauviette, who said she "loved her very dearly," had "cried very bitterly about her going." Mengette, with whom Joan spun and "did other household chores," did get a last embrace, perhaps due to proximity, as her "father's house was almost next door to Joan's father's."

"When she went away, she said good-bye to me," Mengette testified. "Then she departed and prayed God to bless me, and set out for Vaucouleurs."

"All I know," the farmer Gérardin of Épinal testified, "is that when she was about to go away, she said to me: 'Friend, if you were not a Burgundian, there is something I would tell you.'" It would appear Gérardin was the single enemy sympathizer in town, whose head Joan would have been happy to "take off," should God ask her to. As for Gérardin, he assumed Joan's secret was no different from that of any other girl of her age, "something about a lad she wanted to marry," he guessed.

"No eggs! No eggs!!" Sir Robert says to his steward in *Saint Joan*, by George Bernard Shaw. The play opens like a fairy tale, in a castle, and amplifies the apocryphal bird imagery that lifts Joan's story above those of other mortals and loans her the vantage of angels. "Thousand thunders, man, what do you mean by no eggs?" How can it be that all Sir Robert's hens—"the best layers in Champagne"—have stopped producing eggs?

"There is no milk," his steward tells him. "There are no eggs:

tomorrow there will be nothing . . . [T]here is a spell on us: we are bewitched . . . as long as the Maid is at the door."

Joan, however, wasn't waiting at the castle door. Nor was she staying outside town with her uncle in Burey, but lodging with friends of his, Henri and Catherine Le Royer, who owned a house within the walls of Vaucouleurs. She had no intention of returning to Sir Robert before strengthening the legitimacy of her request by attracting more and more powerful adherents to her cause. Word had spread in the eight months since Joan's earlier visit. Before the siege of Orléans, it had been easy to laugh off the odd girl in the homespun red dress, but news of the pivotal city's imminent fall delivered the French to a desperation that transformed Joan from the butt of a joke into a young woman who merited serious attention. Perhaps she really was who she claimed to be, the prophesied virgin from the marshes of Lorraine. "I heard it said many times that she was to restore France and the blood royal," her childhood friend Jean Waterin testified.

Joan had no sooner arrived in Vaucouleurs than the whole city knew of her return. Impatient for a first look at her, a throng gathered around the Le Royers' door.

"What are you doing here, my dear?" asked Jean de Metz, a squire stationed in the city garrison. "Is it not fated that the King shall be driven from his kingdom, and that we shall all turn English?" Jean asked her, his tone arch. A knight in training, like Bertrand de Poulengy, he was playing to an audience at Joan's expense, unprepared for sincerity so absolute it didn't acknowledge sarcasm.

"Before mid-Lent I must be with the King," Joan told him. "Even if I have to wear my legs down to the knees." The salvation of France had been ordained, and "for that she was born," she said to Henri Le Royer, identifying her messianic role as clearly as Jesus had to those who "sought him and would have kept him from leaving them" to minister to "other cities also, for," as Jesus said, "I was sent for this purpose." As it had been for Bertrand de Poulengy, the fervor of Joan's answer made Jean de Metz her friend for life, a man of good standing who became another of her instant adherents. "I had great trust in what the Maid said," Jean testified, "and I was on fire with what she said, and with a love for her which was, as I believe, a divine love."

"I believed in what she said," Catherine Le Royer testified, "and so did many others"—enough that Joan could gather together a party of companions and set out for Chinon without Baudricourt's blessing. But according to Catherine the mission was quickly aborted. "Joan said that this was not the way in which she ought to depart," and the party came back to learn that Joan's fortunes had shifted once again, just as they had the last time she'd returned to Vaucouleurs. But that was after an absence of many months, not the few days it took to get to Saint-Nicolas, a quarter of the way to Chinon, and back. As Saints Catherine and Margaret had promised, God had indeed cleared her way to the lord dauphin.

Of the two royal houses that supported Charles's hegemony, the Armagnac name dominates the pages of history books, but the house of Anjou was larger and more powerful. The "Queen of Four Kingdoms"—Aragon, Cyprus, Jerusalem, and Sicily—Yolande of Aragon was titular queen consort of Naples, Countess of Provence, and Duchess of Anjou (Fig. 7). The death of her elder sister, Joanna, in 1407, left the twenty-three-year-old Yolande the sole remaining heir to her father's crown, or would have, were she a man. Instead, she married Louis II, the Duke of Anjou, and after he died, in 1417, acted as regent for the eldest of their six children, Louis III. Her second son, René, was married off to Isabella, Duchess of Bar and daughter of the Duke of Lorraine, thus securing Yolande's influence in the north of France. As a noblewoman, Yolande had been tutored in those subjects considered appropriate to her gender—"reading and writing in French and Latin . . . music, astronomy, and some medicine and first aid." What she studied was political intrigue and maneuvering—the international relations of her day—and concluded she didn't necessarily need a crown to rule a kingdom, just a malleable king. In 1419, immediately in the wake of Agincourt, and five years before the Burgundians formalized their alliance with the English, Yolande cemented the houses of Anjou and Valois by means of that most popular and generally trustworthy form of political alliance, matrimony. Her daughter Marie was just ten when betrothed to the twelve-year-old dauphin Charles, whose father she'd persuaded to sign a decree claiming the dauphin as his son and heir. As Charles VI was known to have been Isabeau's sole sexual partner during the period of time when the dauphin was conceived, common sense supported his claim to the throne, but it couldn't rescue him from the effect of his mother's casting doubt on his birthright. When Isabeau demanded she return Charles to the French court, Yolande is said to have declared her unfit to raise the dauphin. "We have not nurtured and cherished this one for you to make him die like his brothers or to go mad like his father, or to become English like you. I keep him for my own. Come and take him away if you dare."

Sometimes depicted as a lazy dilettante without any interest in rule, or as a simpleminded playboy, the dauphin was neither stupid nor apathetic. Prior to his mother's betrayal he had been known for his theatrical military exploits, leading an army against the English when still a teenager. But Isabeau's betrayal left him prey to a psychic paralysis that made him vulnerable to scheming courtiers jockeying for power, some with allegiance to the Burgundian party. His marriage, in the spring of 1422, when the dauphin was nineteen and Marie seventeen, and the subsequent death of his father that fall resolved nothing. Seven years later, as Joan struggled to make her way to Chinon, the dauphin had yet to claim what was his, the throne of France remained empty, and Yolande had financed an army Charles didn't have the confidence to dispatch. She wasn't about to sacrifice the kingdom she'd secured for her daughter to his inertia, and her immediate concern was to keep the remaining houses of France united while fending off an advancing enemy. For months now she had been searching for a means to guide, or force, if need be, Charles into a war she wanted and he didn't. That a girl claiming to be the Virgin from Lorraine had arrived in Vaucouleurs to announce she'd been sent by God to lead France's army and escort the reluctant dauphin to be anointed king at Reims was news Yolande seized with excitement. Immediately upon coming into possession of so welcome a rumor, she dispatched her messenger, Colet de Vienne, from the court at Chinon to that of her son René, the future Duke of Bar and Lorraine and Baudricourt's immediate overlord.

Sir Robert, Yolande wrote to René, was on no account to squash or banish this peasant girl, not when his country needed the energy and confidence inspired by a prophecy fulfilled. René must contact Sir Robert immediately and tell him to have the girl evaluated and her words taken as those meriting serious attention.

Son obeyed mother; captain obeyed duke; Catherine Le Royer found herself with unexpected visitors. Baudricourt had done what Joan never thought to do: he summoned a Church authority to validate her mission, obliging Joan to participate in what she knew was a charade and considered a waste of time. "I saw Robert de Baudricourt, then captain of the town of Vaucouleurs, and Messire Jean Fournier enter my house," Catherine testified. "I heard Joan say that this man, who was a priest, had brought a stole, and that he had exorcised her in front of the captain, saying that if there was any evil thing in her, let it begone away, and if there was any good thing, let it come to them all." Since he had heard her confession, and thus already knew the state of her soul, "Joan said that this priest had done wrong." Promised success by her voices, Joan hadn't troubled to puzzle out how it might be realized, nor did she defer to earthbound clerics who ruled what they called the Church Militant, "all good Christians engaged in the struggle against the enemies of Christ," to distinguish it from the Church Triumphant, whose members inhabited heaven. Still, all the rest of the world, who lacked direct access to God, believed that to offend Church doctrine was a grave mistake, and it was only after Joan had Fournier's sanction that she received a summons from René's father-in-law, the old Duke Charles of Lorraine.

An invitation to the home of a nobleman was as good as an announcement that through the inaudible direction of her voices and the invisible hand of Yolande Joan had bounded out of the peasantry and into the highest echelon of society, an accomplishment rare enough to qualify as something of a miracle. Now her appearance needed to reflect her new station. "I asked her if she wanted to travel in those clothes," Jean de Metz said of Joan's dress of "the reddish-brown homespun material known as russet." If it was the typical farm girl's dress, it was long sleeved and ankle length, with a laced bodice. "She replied that she would rather have a man's clothes," Jean said.

"Then I gave her a suit and breeches belonging to my servants, so that she could put them on."

But, Joan's uncle Durand said, "some people of Vaucouleurs" determined that Joan should go off to see the duke in the clothes of a gentleman, not a servant, and had "everything that was necessary" made for her. As the clothing was offered as a gift, the citizens who outfitted their virgin warrior can hardly have found the idea of a woman wearing male clothing "abominable to God and man, contrary to laws both divine and natural and to ecclesiastical discipline . . . and prohibited under penalty of anathema." The trial record dilates this judgment with a description of Joan's dress so lingering in its specificity that it can only have been inspired by the delight taken in counting up the sins of others. Joan "wore shirt, breeches, doublet, with hose joined together and fastened to the said doublet by twenty points, long leggings laced on the outside, a short mantle reaching to the knees, or thereabouts, a close-cut cap, tight-fitting boots and buskins."

Joan, as it turned out, was—or she quickly became—something of a fop. The tailor-made clothes the citizens of Vaucouleurs gave her awoke a taste for the luxurious fabrics and flamboyant styles that sumptuary laws held out of a peasant's reach: velvet surcoats embroidered with gold thread; fur-lined mantles; colorful tunics bearing coats of arms; tight-fitting damask doublets with jeweled buttons and slashed sleeves that revealed contrasting silk linings; brightly colored hose; voluminous gowns—*houppelandes*—with sleeves that hung to the ground; *pigases* with their extravagantly long and pointed toes; chamois gloves; belts hung with bells and trinkets; an "infinity of hats . . . tam-o'shanters and furred caps, hoods and brims, chaplets of flowers, coiled turbans, coverings of every shape, puffed, pleated, scalloped, or curled into a long tailed pocket called a liripipe."

Joan could not have chosen a more dramatic moment to defy a dress code. Costume historians identify the high Middle Ages as the arrival of fashion in western Europe. Cotton from Egypt; silks from the Ottoman Empire; improved dyes and dyeing techniques; complex patterns and new fabrics, like brocade and velvet, made possible by Chinese innovations in weaving: crusaders went east bearing murder and returned home with the ingredients for haute couture. And the increased social mobility that accompanied the aristocracy's loss of power and conjured the ambitions of a man like Jacques d'Arc strengthened the yet ruling nobility's resolve to assign and maintain standards of dress that identified a peasant as a peasant, no matter how much money he had to spend on disguising himself as a lord. Etymology identifies *villein* as the progenitor of "villainous," as is *churl* of "churlish," suggesting the regard in which the aristocracy held a peasant, whose lowly stature was received as proof of his base character. The Burgundian chronicler Georges Chastellain "attributes sublime virtues only to the nobility," Huizinga observed of his *Chronique des choses de mon temps*, a history of the years 1417–74 that was written when "God, the theory went, had established an intangible order of which costume was merely the expression." The Third Reich didn't invent the yellow badge that announced its wearer as a Jew; it revived the idea from a decree made by Pope Innocent III in 1215 that Jews be "marked off in the eyes of the public from other peoples."[*] By the time Joan was born, two centuries of increasing social unrest had drawn the strictures of sumptuary laws that much tighter; never before or since has Europe insisted on so rigid and visible a classification of its citizens. Even were a prostitute successful enough to afford the fine clothes of an aristocrat, she could never be confused with a lady, required, as she was by law, to wear a striped hood or cloak. Within this context, Joan, whose dress revealed, in the opinion of her judges, "her obstinacy, her stubbornness in evil, her want of charity, her disobedience to the Church, and the scorn she has of the holy sacraments," refused to acknowledge the most basic and essential distinction, that drawn between male and female. "It was characteristic of the time, of the doctors' narrowmindedness, of their blind attachment to the letter without any consideration for the spirit," Michelet wrote, "that no point seemed more grievous to them than the sin of having assumed the garments of a man."

"Mark what I say," Shaw's inquisitor lectures, "the woman who quarrels with her clothes and puts on the dress of a man is like the man who throws off his fur gown and dresses like John the Baptist:

---

[*] Canon 68, Fourth Council of the Lateran, convoked by Pope Innocent III.

they are followed, as surely as the night follows the day, by bands of wild women and men who refuse to wear any clothes at all." Shaw's representation of the clerics' response isn't drawn from historical record, but it represents the Church's viewpoint well enough. As pronounced by an anonymous member of the University of Paris, "If a woman could put on male clothing as she liked with impunity, women would have unrestrained opportunities to fornicate and to practice manly acts which are legally forbidden to them according to doctrine . . . for example, to preach, to teach, to bear arms, to absolve, to excommunicate."

Jesus drafted his own death warrant in the temple when he upturned the tables of the moneylenders and berated those who sold doves for holy sacrifice, publicly challenging a corrupt social order that allowed the rich to purchase sacred power—an order swiftly reinvented by the Church that deified him. So now had Joan drafted hers by drawing the attention of both those who made and guarded rules she refused to obey and the multitudes governed by their misogyny.

With the example of Saint Margaret and other virgin martyrs before her, Joan sheared off her hair; by doing so, she announced she had removed herself from the company of other unwed girls, who were expected to leave their heads uncovered in public, their hair undressed and falling down their backs as an advertisement for prospective suitors. At a time when women didn't get their hair cut, ever, Joan's barely covered her ears. Hers was the original bob, the haircut assumed by flappers as a symbol of female liberation and still known in France as *la coupe à la Jeanne d'Arc*. It would have been possible for Joan to preserve her hair's length and still wage war, especially as women and girls often wore plaits coiled over their heads. Arguably, it would have been a comfort, or even a precaution, to have an extra layer of padding under a metal helmet designed not only to deflect arrows but also to preserve a knight's skull from the impact of a rock dropped on his head from a parapet.

But Joan didn't want a woman's hair any more than she wanted a woman's fate. By the time she accomplished her mission, Joan would have attended the highest state function mounted on a white horse, dressed in armor, and cloaked in red velvet as she processed before courtiers and nobles, escorting her *gentil dauphin* to the altar of Reims's cathedral, where he would be anointed Charles VII, his title secure, as no mortal could undo what God ordained. Unarmored, Joan wore clothes that befit a national heroine: conspicuously stylish and costly, as noted both by her worshipful, approving followers and by her enemies, who would call attention to her dress as evidence of decadence and, worse, pride. As they understood it, Joan had seized a set of symbols she didn't merit, and what delight they would take in the role a golden cloak would play in her capture and defeat, how outraged at the vanity and self-indulgence they saw in its rich weight on her shoulders.

What Joan wore—and what she didn't—announced what was more powerful for not being spoken aloud. Under interrogation, she said she dressed as a man as a practical concession to a life spent making war among men, but Joan wore male clothing under all circumstances, among soldiers or not. Schiller's Joan seizes a helmet before leaving home to embark on her crusade; from it "warlike thoughts" pour into her head and make her eyes flash, her cheeks red. The costly male costume in which Joan cloaked her virgin female body transcended the pragmatic. It was the physical manifestation—the announcement—of her refusal to abide by patriarchal strictures, a defiance that was absolute and uncompromising, and both Joan and her judges knew that. The extravagant attention the inquisitorial trial paid her clothing and the role her cross-dressing would play in the decision to execute her reveal how subversive and genuinely dangerous the clerics who ruled society considered Joan's assuming the right to wear male attire. No one, especially not Joan, thought her dressing as a man was "a small, nay, the least thing," as she dismissed the topic when under interrogation.

Womanly duties, as Joan thought of them, were fine for girls who imagined themselves as Cinderellas or Sleeping Beauties, good girls rewarded for menial housework and, in the case of Sleeping Beauty, a passivity so profound it was deaf, dumb, blind, and comatose. There were, as Joan observed, enough of those women already. Only shackles and a prison cell would halt the trajectory of a young woman who understood herself as the leader of a holy quest, summoned by the patron saint of the crusaders, Saint Michael—whose slaying of the dragon was considered "the primordial feat of arms" from which knighthood sprang—to join Perceval, Lancelot, and Galahad, especially Galahad, the Christ figure of medieval romance. When Galahad came to King Arthur's court, he saw that a single seat at the Round Table stood vacant.

"It belongs to one who hasn't yet come," the knights assembled told him. "It belongs to the Virgin Knight who will find the Holy Grail." Others had come before him, the knights told Galahad, they'd wanted to take the one seat left at the table, and all had died upon touching it.

Galahad sat down at the table and lived.

A sacred vessel borrowed from a Celtic myth about a magic cauldron, the Grail first appears in an unfinished romance, *Perceval le Gallois,* by Chrétien de Troyes, who used the vessel to represent and contain God's grace. Galahad wore flaming red armor when introduced to King Arthur's court on Pentecost, the feast that celebrates the descent of the Holy Ghost upon the apostles in the form of tongues of fire. Galahad does indeed fulfill Merlin's prophecy that it would be he, and no other, to find the Holy Grail, but before he can return to King Arthur's court bearing the Grail that is his alone to find, he is visited by Saint Joseph of Arimathea, who claimed Jesus's crucified body from Pilate and gave his own tomb for Jesus's burial. The rapture to which Galahad succumbs in the presence of the saint is so intense that he begs to die in its embrace and is taken up to heaven by angels.

Talk still turned to the crusades, as it did to any means of propitiating the divine, and the ideals described in *The Book of Chivalry* remained as influential as they were when first listed by Geoffroi de Charny in the middle of the fourteenth century: largesse, prowess, courtesy, and loyalty. Chivalry was a system of ethics that applied to both war and love, a system that governed all of noble life. That this code was, like the strictures of the Church, "about four parts in five illusion made it no less governing for all that." The trial record shows the reward Joan anticipated for her faith and service in the armies of God was the same as what Pope Urban II promised the sixty thousand crusaders he dispatched from Europe in 1095 to save Jerusalem from the infidels: absolution from sin and eternal salvation. She, too, believed that "the worst conceivable crime for a member of a Military Order was apostasy, denying the Cross, even to save his life." An army sixty thousand strong was extraordinary in its size; the sight of it was enough to inspire terror in a people for whom an army of five thousand was large.

Writing during the twelfth century, the prelate William of Tyre described the conditions that inspired the crusades, the first of which emerged during a period of violence and unrest analogous to that of the Hundred Years War. Eleventh-century Europe had yet to emerge from the anarchy that followed the collapse of the Roman Empire: raids were the rule; murder went unpunished; the Church presented the sole means of social cohesion. The only story that could be relied upon not to change was the one at the center of the Church, the Gospels that gave meaning to the sufferings of the Church Militant and pointed the way to paradise. In the name of Christ, crusaders took up their swords and rode east to reclaim Jerusalem, where the Son of God rose from the dead and where they practiced siege warfare little different from that of fifteenth-century Europe, waged for heavenly gain and characterized by "massacre and torture," "the mounting of heads on posts or even use of them as missiles." Raymond d'Aguilers, contemporaneous chronicler of the First Crusade, wrote, "Dismembered bodies lay in the houses and streets, trampled by knights and men-at-arms . . . Crusaders rode in blood to the knees and bridles of their horses." By the time the war was won, they had murdered thirty thousand Muslims, who still hear the word "crusade" as twenty-first-century Westerners do "jihad,"* an act of terrorism perpetrated by benighted barbarians living in a dark age of superstition and fear.

The Church Militant had officially endorsed mass murder, white-washing it as an act of piety.

---

* jihad: An Islamic term meaning "to struggle in the way of Allah" rather than a necessarily violent "holy war."

Dressed in her new finery, Joan was ready for her visit to the Duke of Lorraine, who, having heard of the divine company she entertained, summoned and provided her safe conduct because he was ill and wanted her to intercede with God on his behalf. For her part, Joan accepted the duke's invitation as an opportunity to campaign for his support and, as Marguerite La Touroulde, Joan's hostess for three weeks following Charles's coronation, testified, "told him she wished to go to France. And the duke questioned her about the recovery of his health; but she said she knew nothing about that . . . She told the duke nevertheless to send his son and some men to escort her to France, and she would pray to God for his health." The widow of Charles VII's financial adviser, Marguerite said Joan told the duke "he was sinning and that unless he reformed his ways he would not be cured. She urged him to take back his good wife," the notoriously pious Margaret of Bavaria, whom he'd abandoned for a mistress, Alison Dumay, in the town of Nancy, a quick coach trip to the south. If the duke knew anything at all about his outspoken guest, the caution to govern his lust could hardly have come as a surprise. He withheld the gift of his son-in-law's conscription, but Joan returned to Vaucouleurs the richer by four francs, "a horse with a black coat," and another ally among the aristocracy.

From the time she arrived in Vaucouleurs in early January 1429 until her departure for Chinon on February 13, subtracting two weeks for her visits to the courts of Bar and Lorraine, Joan was left with a month to fill, and it's assumed she received instruction in riding and carrying a lance from the knights stationed in the garrison there. "She was very bold in riding horses . . . and also in performing other feats and exercises which young girls are not accustomed to do," said Jean de Wavrin, a Burgundian who fought against Joan at Patay.

To master a knight's necessary skills, ordinarily acquired over years, Joan had the four weeks at Vaucouleurs and would be granted an additional three at Poitiers, when not being interrogated by the clerics assembled there to assess her claim of a divine vocation. Even a strong rider with native talent would be remarkable in achieving so high a level of expertise in six weeks. The girl who had protested that she "knew not how to ride nor lead in war" was praised universally—by comrades and enemies alike—for her adroit handling of a destrier. The expression Joan used for "ride" referred to a horse not as a garden-variety *cheval* but as a knight's courser: strong, swift, and bred for battle. A destrier was a specialized horse, as different from a harness animal as a Thoroughbred from a Clydesdale. It was a knight's deadliest weapon, plunging into the fray to rear up and come down kicking with forelegs powerful enough to kill an enemy with a single blow from an iron-shod hoof. Despite their relative prosperity, Joan's family was unlikely to have kept any but work animals. Oxen plowed; horses pulled wagons to market. Even an athletic girl who loved being outdoors and going off alone into the woods, a girl in the throes of chivalric fantasies, wouldn't have had the means to learn to ride a warhorse.

Joan's zeal for battle was apparent, but she knew better than to present herself to powerful men without a veneer of humility and a few words to suggest a reluctance to undertake so immodest a quest. Long before she was on trial for her life, she was careful to underscore her lack of personal ambition.

"It's no good breaking your heart to make men understand anything," Joan's mother tells her in *The Lark*. "All you can do is say 'yes' to whatever they think, and wait till they've gone out to the fields. Then you can be mistress in your house again."

But Joan didn't stoop to gather unacknowledged power. "If God didn't mean me to be proud, why did He send an Archangel to see me, and saints with the light of heaven on them to speak to me?" Anouilh has her ask her inquisitor. "He only had to leave me looking after the sheep, and I don't think pride would ever have entered my head."

"I would much prefer to stay with my poor mother and spin," Joan said to Jean de Metz, "for this is not my station. But I must go, and I must do it, for my Lord wishes me to perform this deed." Once her vocation had been fulfilled, however, Joan didn't return to the hearth but refused to relinquish her identity as a military chieftain. That she had been a child exemplary in her obedience speaks to her commitment to her voices' direction to be good, not to her embrace of domestic routine, to which she never intended to return.

"I am a soldier," Shaw's Joan declares. "I do not care for the things women care for. They dream of lovers, and of money. I dream of leading a charge and of placing the big guns."

DeMille's vision of his heroine's potency is even less subtle. "If thou comest from God," Sir Robert says to Joan, "show me what answer he would make to this!" Baudricourt rises from his throne-like chair to unsheathe and brandish his sword. Standing in profile, he points to its blade with his left hand, while with his right he holds its hilt just at the height of his pelvis; the length of it projects from his groin at an angle and rigidity suggesting tumescence. Provoked, Joan borrows a dagger-size knife from a page standing beside her and holds it up as if it were a chalice, her face tipped heavenward to receive the divine grace that infuses her little blade with miraculous power. With it she halves the much longer shaft of Sir Robert's weapon. Immediately, Sir Robert agrees to give Joan whatever she asks, but he cannot meet her eye as he speaks; his gaze is fixed on his severed sword. "I am convinced and will send thee to thy King," his unnecessary title card reads. If the scene provides unintended comedy for today's audience, it remains useful for the aggressive transparency of its symbolism, its release having preceded psychology's imposition of self-consciousness on popular culture. What could more obviously convey the nature of the fear Joan of Arc has always inspired than her unmanning her opposition with a supernaturally enhanced phallic weapon?

When she at last set out for Chinon, it was with six men, of whom at least one would admit to starting the trip contemplating her rape as a means of robbing her of the power she claimed.

CHAPTER
IV

The
King's
Treasure

The traveling party of seven included the two knights who financed the trip: Jean de Metz and Bertrand de Poulengy; Bertrand's servant, Julien; Yolande's messenger, Colet de Vienne; Richard the Archer; and the servant he shared with Vienne, Jean de Honecourt. "They were all knights and servants of Sir Robert de Baudricourt," Joan testified. "Sir Robert had sworn them to conduct me well and safely."

"Go," Robert said to Joan as she departed. "Go, and come what may." It was hardly a benediction, but Baudricourt was obeying orders, not acting out of faith. No matter his opinion, the price of getting rid of the obstinate girl had been to provide her an escort and a formal letter of introduction to the dauphin—a bargain, as it turned out. Even had Yolande not been scheming from afar, by now the citizens of Lorraine were traveling miles to get a glimpse of their Maid, thronging around her. Were Baudricourt to refuse to promote what they believed was her God-given mission, he'd risk an uprising.

With the formal introduction she needed, Joan and her six companions set out for Chinon on the night of February 12, 1429, "to go," as she said, "to the lord Dauphin, and for that I was born." Her phrasing often mimicked that of Jesus, as recorded in the Gospels, an echo here of Christ's admonition to those who tried to detain him from his vocation. "I was sent for this purpose."

Joan of Arc Leaving Vaucouleurs, Jean-Jacques Scherrer's monumental history painting, first exhibited in 1887 (Fig. 8), has insinuated itself into the origin myth of France much as Emanuel Leutze's equally narrative *Washington Crossing the Delaware* has shaped the vision of countless American schoolchildren. Life-size, regal, and handsomely attired in brown tunic, cape, and leggings, her yet-to-be-shorn hair falling over her shoulders and down her back—her transformation

incomplete—Joan pauses on the threshold of her magnificent and terrible fate. The Maid's horse lifts her to a heroic height. Like George
Washington towering over his seated rowers, she is more than head
and shoulders above the crowd around her, a sweep of caste from beg-
gar to courtier; "the mother of her country," history has judged her,
"the George Washington of France." She raises her left hand in farewell, her right reaches for the symbol of her vocation: a sword, its
hilt and blade divided by the hand guard, emphasizing its cruciform
outline and reminding us that her war is a holy one.

"No sword!" Sir Robert exclaims in Victor Fleming's 1948 film,
Joan of Arc. "Here," he says. "Take mine!"

Scherrer's painting has a focal point. The silver gleam of the
weapon being passed from the captain to the Maid captures the eye
and holds it on the critical moment, as a man of wealth and status
relinquishes the symbol of his potency to a much younger woman.
Just below that transaction is another reminder: painted in profile, the
pommel of Joan's armored saddle projects forward from her groin like
an abbreviated phallus. Sir Robert reaches over his head and past the
pommel to extend the tied scroll of a letter along with the weapon.
Behind him, a peasant woman weeps in the arms of a man whose eyes
beseech Joan. But Joan's gaze, like Washington's, is visionary, fixed on
what she alone can see.

The mourners are Joan's parents, of course, often inaccurately
included at the scene of her departure from Vaucouleurs, the painter's
sleight of hand reaching forward to the time when Joan's accomplishments and the awe they inspired would render her father's distrust
meaningless. During the nineteenth century the painting was exhibited internationally; Joan's canonization made it into an image recognized all over the world; it remains popular in reproduction. Maxwell
Anderson, who adapted his 1946 play within a play, *Joan of Lorraine,*
for Fleming's film, placed Joan's mother in the crowd around Joan,
mounted and wearing a man's traveling cloak.

"A mother bears children and she gives them to the world and she
thinks she knows them, but she doesn't know them at all," Isabelle
says. Before Joan can pass through the city's gates, before she exits
one world to enter another from which she cannot return, her mother
presses forward to give her the memento upon which her judges would

fix, the subject first raised during the preliminary trial that determined
the charges brought against Joan. By then she'd been in captivity for
a year, shackled for the last six months in the endless dusk of an unlit
cell, ill-fed, brutalized daily, and still obstinately immune to the efforts
of seventy judges to dismantle her resolve.

"Did you not have some rings?" the examiner asked Joan.

"You have one," she said. "Give it back to me. The Burgundians
have the other."

"Who gave you the ring now in the possession of the Burgundians?"

"Show me my ring if you have it."

"Who gave you the ring taken by the Burgundians?"

"My father or my mother, at Domrémy."

"What distinguished it from any other ring?"

"The names Jesus Maria were written on it."

"Who wrote them?" the examiner asked, and he repeated the
question, inspired by "a contemporary debate between the Francis-
cans, who encouraged reverence for the names of Jesus and Mary, and
the Dominicans, who urged the papacy to forbid it as a satanic cult."

The words did suggest a flight from orthodoxy. One effect of the
Papal Schism had been a proliferation of covert proto-Protestant
sects that wanted nothing to do with any pope. Joan's examiners
lingered over every conceivable means of implicating her in heresy
or witchcraft and pressed her in hopes of forcing her to admit the
names were an incantation of some sort. As they were throughout the
trial, trumped-up religious charges cloaked the political agendas of
the avaricious Sorbonne-trained clergy, just as they had hidden those
of the Sanhedrin who pronounced judgment on Jesus. Both tribu-
nals kowtowed to occupying forces while preserving what influence
they could. "Jesus Maria" was a device used by mendicant friars of
all orders: a means of identifying one another as separate from the
clergy they considered corrupt. Collette of Corbie, for example, the
visionary hermit and saint who founded the Poor Clares, is known to
have "traveled in Joan's region, using the emblem 'Jesus Maria' in her
letters." The judges who assembled in Rouen to try Joan, the majority of them creatures of the university, considered the use of sacred
names for any purpose outside the ordained celebration of the Mass

a crime of insurrection, of failing to submit to the ruling patriarchy's prescribed forms and traditions.

"Who wrote the names?"

"I have told you I don't know."

"Was there any stone set in it?"

"There were three crosses on it, and no other mark that I know of, except Jesus Maria. My brother gave me the one you have. Give it to the Church if you will not return it to me."

"Why did you look at this ring before going into battle?"

"Out of pleasure, and in honor of my father and mother."

"For no other reason?" the examiner asked.

"Saint Catherine appeared before me, and the ring was on my finger when I touched her."

"What part of Saint Catherine did you touch with the ring?"

"About that," Joan said, "you will get nothing more from me."

On the day of Joan's departure for Chinon, the French initiated hostilities with the English on a flat, barren plain some 150 miles southwest of Vaucouleurs to block the progress of a three-hundred-wagon convoy of munitions and barrels of salt-cured herring the English had requisitioned in anticipation of Lent's restriction on meat. According to the *Journal du siège d'Orléans* and Cousinot's *Chronique de la Pucelle*, Joan persuaded Sir Robert "to arm her because she knew, with clairvoyance, about the defeat of the French in the battle of Rouvray, near Orleans, the so-called Battle of the Herrings, in February and told him about it *before* the news reached Vaucouleurs."

"In God's name, Robert de Baudricourt, you are too slow about sending me," Joan says in Mark Twain's *Personal Recollections of Joan of Arc*, "and have caused damage thereby, for this day the Dauphin's cause has lost a battle near Orleans, and will suffer yet greater injury if you do not send me to him soon."

The governor was perplexed by this speech, and said—

"To-day, child, *to-day*? How can you know what has happened in that region to-day? It would take eight or ten days for the word to come."

"My Voices have brought word to me, and it is true. A battle was lost to-day, and you are in fault to delay me so."

That the French had initiated hostilities made the loss that much more ignominious. As the armies of France and their ally, Scotland, crossed the treeless plain on which the armies met, the English had been able to see the approach of the enemy and, under the command of Sir John Fastolf, stopped advancing and circled their wagons. Around the primitive fortification, they set spikes to discourage the charge of the French cavalry, a strategy that had served them well in earlier battles when they had been outnumbered. Time had proved the incompetence of "French knights [who] continued to see war as an arena in which to display their chivalrous qualities, not as an instrument of state policy." Perhaps even more costly, as military histories attest, was the inability of French commanders to work cooperatively with the commoners they disdained. "No member of the noble class trusted the local rural peasants enough to permit them to have weapons of such effectiveness as the longbow," whereas "the noble-born English knights and the common-born English longbowmen respected each other's skill and courage, and had long experience working together as a team." Over and over, the French—"individualistic glory-seekers . . . dilettantes" who "scorned . . . fellow soldiers in their own army, as social inferiors"—charged quixotically into a storm of arrows that assailed them before they were close enough to discharge their weapons effectively. Mounted on horses whose heads alone were armored, the cavalry corps trampled one another, as their destriers were more often maddened than incapacitated by enemy arrows. This time the leaders of the French and Scot forces failed to coordinate attacks and thus appeared to vacillate in their resolve to seize the convoy. Perceiving hesitance as cowardice, the English took advantage of the enemy's confusion and counterattacked from behind, putting the combined French and Scot forces, as many as four thousand men-at-arms, to flight.

Joan and her escorts waited for dusk to fall before venturing

beyond the gates of Vaucouleurs. While both contemporaneous narratives and later revisions explained Baudricourt's apparent change
of heart as accomplished by supernatural means, their authors were
either innocent of Yolande's offstage direction or intent on eclipsing it. Neither Joan nor any witness suggested Joan had foreseen the
battle's carnage, but she cannot have traveled far before she learned,
through mortal means, what four hundred fatalities made official: the
French had been decimated. Baudricourt died before the nullification
trial; we have witness only to his actions and words, but whether or
not the story of Joan's second sight is apocryphal, it was Yolande's
orders that determined Sir Robert's response. She would become one
of several figures critical to the advancement of Joan's career whose
influence has generally been ignored or downplayed because it under-
mines the conventions of the messianic narrative. Too, the story of
Joan of Arc tends to exonerate Charles's mother-in-law as it doesn't
his mother, Isabeau, because Yolande served Joan's mission. In truth,
the women were alike in ambition, each manipulating weak men to
gain political advantage.

Chinon, about 350 miles to the west, was at the end of an eleven-
day journey through English-occupied territory, the rivers in flood as
they were every February, "no roads and no bridges left." Even though
they took the precaution of proceeding only under cover of night,
that seven men-at-arms—or six, and one armed girl—traveled on
horseback undetected and undisturbed by soldiers guarding roads and
circling the towns along the way is often cited as the first miracle to
demonstrate Joan's uncanny powers. A story was told by "some soldiers who had gone to intercept her when she was on her way to find
the King," Seguin Seguin testified for the nullification proceedings. A
Dominican friar who provided the sole eyewitness account of Joan's
first formal ecclesiastical examination, at Poitiers, Seguin is considered by historians to have provided the most reliable of testimony.
They "had laid an ambush to capture her and rob her and her company," he said. "But at the moment when they were about to do so,
they had found themselves unable to stir from their positions; and

so Joan had escaped without difficulty together with her company." There would be other miracles, both less ambiguous and more dramatic. Still, whether it was accomplished with or without the grace of God, that so large a party eluded both enemy soldiers and the bandits spawned by anarchy was at least lucky and by no means expected. After all, Baudricourt had provided Joan a military guard for a reason.

What conflict emerged was internecine and came in the form of power struggles between Joan and those members of her escort who, like Baudricourt, were just following orders—except Sir Robert was safe within the walls of a fortified city and they were being asked to risk their lives for a girl who not only claimed she heard voices from God but dressed as a man. Husson Lemaître, a tinker from Viville, not ten miles from Domrémy, testified for the nullification that he'd "heard it said that while Joan was being taken from Vaucouleurs to the King, some of the soldiers of her escort pretended to be the enemy troops, and that those who were with her made a show of being about to take to their heels. But she said to them, 'In the name of God, do not run away. They will do us no harm.'" And, though Jean de Metz and Bertrand de Poulengy were firm defenders of Joan's holiness from the outset, her other companions plotted to undo the audacity of this inconvenient virgin, only to discover why it was that one of the king's squires, Gobert Thibault, heard "Joan's intimates say that they never had any desire for her. That is to say, that sometimes they had a carnal urge, but never dared to give way to it; and they believed that it was impossible to desire her . . . Suddenly their sexual feelings were checked." Whether the gift betrayed heavenly or, as her enemies would attest, demonic influences, and though her apologists would hardly have characterized it in such terms, Joan was believed to have safeguarded her virginity by using supernatural powers to emasculate would-be assailants.

"I afterward heard the men who led her to the King talking," Marguerite La Touroulde said,

and heard them say that at the outset they thought her presumptuous and that they meant to put her to the test. But once they were on the road, escorting her, they were ready to do anything that she wanted and were as anxious to bring her before the King as she was herself to get there. They could never have denied her anything that she asked. They said that . . . they wanted to make sexual advances to her, but at the moment when they were about to speak they were so ashamed that they dared not tell her their intentions or utter so much as a word.

"We escorted her to the King . . . as secretly as we could," Jean de Metz remembered. The need for cover prevented Joan from attending Mass as regularly as she liked; given the opportunity, she went more than once a day. "If only we could hear a Mass it would be a grand thing," Jean remembered her saying. "But, to my knowledge, we only heard the Mass twice on the way," once on the first night, when the party of travelers reached the town of Saint-Urbain and were invited to sleep in the abbey, and again a few days later, when they passed through Auxerre and Joan attended Mass in the principal church there. On February 21 the seven travelers paused at the village of Sainte-Catherine-de-Fierbois, a day's ride from Chinon, that much farther to the west. From Sainte-Catherine-de-Fierbois, Joan told the examiner, she'd requested permission to approach the dauphin at the castle. "I sent letters to my king telling him I had traveled a good hundred and fifty leagues to come to his aid, and I told him also that I knew many things to his advantage."

Once again, Joan's reputation had preceded her, and the dauphin's advisers were divided as to whether Charles should receive her. Members of the house of Anjou had little choice but to fall in line behind Yolande, although few if any other than René would have known it was she who arranged for the delivery of this living prophecy fulfilled. In Fierbois, Joan waited two days for an invitation to court. The idea of such a meeting between nobility and commoner wasn't as fantastic then as it would be now. Yolande was working within what was becoming the French kings' tradition of privatizing their relationship to the divine. Long before Joan was captured, the archbishop of Reims had started grooming Joan's replacement, Le Berger[*]—the

---

[*] Le Berger would suffer the predictable reversal and find himself reviled and condemned to death, although "Le Berger was spared the misery of long imprisonment

Shepherd—a genuine rustic chosen from among the ongoing pageant of mediums and prognosticators who had slipped into the widening breach between competing papacies. Ever since the election of Pope Urban VI in 1378, and the subsequent emergence of Clement VII, who left Rome and established a rival papacy in Avignon, the schism had aroused such intense animosity between opposing factions that families and tradesmen relocated to cities based on their allegiances to one or the other pope. Avignon might have been more accessible than Rome, but history has judged it "a virtual temporal state of sumptuous pomp, of great cultural attraction, and of unlimited simony." In other words, France's papacy was so palpably corrupt that the court had withdrawn its faith in popes and retrained it on visionaries like Marie Robine, whose access to political power had become more rule than exception. But Georges de La Trémoille, Charles's grand chamberlain and if not royal favorite then the most formidable among the dauphin's advisers, didn't want the help of a visionary complete with a train of hysterical followers, especially not a sword-rattling female one tricked out like a man. An opportunist devoted to protecting his own interests over any other, La Trémoille had a brother who served the Duke of Burgundy, and he wanted surrender, even at the cost of France's independence. He wasn't going to lose his hard-won control over Charles, whom he'd flattered, bribed, and browbeaten into submission, not without a fight.

Joan assuaged her impatience at another delay the only way she knew how: she went to Mass as often as the monks celebrated it and spent as many hours as she could within the sanctuary of the shrine at Sainte-Catherine-de-Fierbois, where Charles Martel was said to have left his sword as a trophy of his victory over the Muslims in 732. Martel was the grandfather of Charlemagne, who is recognized as the father of chivalry—from the French *cheval*, for horse—as his armies' increased dependence on cavalry gave birth to knighthood. Tales of miracles associated with Sainte-Catherine multiplied, and the shrine, on the pilgrim road to Santiago de Compostela, became

---

and the farce of a protracted trial, but was tied up in a sack and thrown into a river by the English without more ado."

the destination of countless knights who, having escaped their English captors, came bearing offerings of weapons and armor as well as "fetters, shackles, balls and chains, and other tools of imprisonment from which the saint had miraculously relieved her votaries." There would be many altars before which Joan kneeled in her short life, from the most humble to those in cathedrals of a size and splendor unimaginable to a rural peasant. By force of circumstance she paused longer at Sainte-Catherine-de-Fierbois than she would at others, on her knees among the ex-votos.

In its size and splendor, Chinon would have struck most small-town girls, few of whom traveled far from where they were born, as a vision from a fairy tale, an imposing stone structure complete with conical turrets whose bright, restless pennants advertised its occupants' coat of arms. The foundations of the castle were built at an altitude higher than any land in sight; its battlements rose from a ledge of rock that overlooked the river Vienne, a slab of shadow looming over any army so foolish as to try to scale its height. The Vienne is a major tributary of the Loire, its banks peopled ever since rivers were used as trade routes, in prehistory, and the strategic advantage granted by the château's height was joined by its unusual physical grace. Joan reached Chinon in the middle of the day on March 4, 1429, and lodged at a house belonging to a woman she characterized, in anticipation of her examiner's maligning her hostess, as having a good reputation. There she was forced again to do what she hated: wait.

"I was continually praying that God would send a sign for the king," Joan said, and at last he did. "I was in my lodging when the angel came, and afterwards we went together to the king." Joan and her angel had company as they climbed the steep switchback trail that led up to the castle's gates. Jean de Metz and Bertrand de Poulengy walked alongside them.

The confessor who traveled with Joan, Jean Pasquerel, testified that as Joan "was going into the royal lodgings that day, a man sitting on his horse near the entrance said, 'Is not that the Maid there?' swearing to God that if he had her for a night she would be no maid next morning. Then Joan said to the man, 'Oh, in God's name, do you take His name in vain when you are so near your death?' And an hour later that man fell into the river and was drowned." Pasquerel didn't join Joan's army until after their meeting at Tours, where she would be outfitted for battle, so he had not seen the event himself, but several eyewitnesses whom he considered trustworthy had confirmed it. Graham Greene's adaptation of Shaw's *Saint Joan* for Otto Preminger's 1957 film of the same title compressed the transaction into a single scene in which a loutish mercenary quits the company of a gaggle of whores to try to pull Joan down from the back of her horse. "You little slut," he says to her. "You think you're for the officers only, do you?"

"Let the poor man be," she scolds the squires who come to rescue her, "he's very near his end." The mercenary lunges toward Joan and falls to the ground dead as his fingers graze her cloak.

That a levelheaded pragmatist like Robert de Baudricourt had provided a guard for a girl who claimed to be the Virgin of Lorraine; that the captain had parted with knights and horses he could ill afford to sacrifice; that he risked his reputation by publicly supporting La Pucelle, as she called herself: La Trémoille knew the letter would have precisely the effect on Charles that his mother-in-law had intended. Simon Charles, the president of the Chamber of Accounts—considered among the dauphin's advisers as the courtier who, according to Régine Pernoud, "most faithfully records the reactions of the King, with whom he was intimate"—testified that it was "because of that letter the King was impelled to hear her, and Joan was accorded an audience."

But when Jean de Metz and Bertrand de Poulengy were admitted to the dauphin's chambers upstairs, they discovered that Charles wasn't expecting the arrival of the Maid from Lorraine. La Trémoille had intercepted the letters Joan sent from Sainte-Catherine-de-Fierbois, destroying hers and confiscating Baudricourt's, which, upon the dauphin's learning of its existence, he produced, demonstrating his duplicity.

"There is nothing in that court but evil," Alain Chartier warns in *Joan of Lorraine*. "A weak ruler draws evil to him as a dead dog draws buzzards."

Held downstairs in the guardhouse, Joan insisted she had a message for the dauphin and none other, but, "pressed in the King's name to explain the reason for her mission," and otherwise barred from his presence, she had no choice but to cooperate. There are "two reasons for which I have been sent by the King of Heaven," Joan said. "One is to raise the siege of Orléans, the other to lead the King to Reims for his anointing and coronation."

"When they heard this," Simon Charles testified, "certain of the King's counselors"—La Trémoille foremost among them—"said that he must put no trust whatever in Joan, and others said that since she claimed to have been sent by God and had something to say to the King, the King ought at least to hear her."

Schiller introduces a fictional knight from Lorraine to convince Charles of the validity of Joan's claim; he brings tidings of a battle never fought, with an army she had yet to command, prefiguring her victory at Orléans. "And while the generals discussed among themselves what or what not to do, and still unable to decide—before our eyes, a miracle! Suddenly a girl stepped out of the depths of the woods, a helmet on her head like some goddess of war, and beautiful yet at the same time terrifying. Her hair fell in dark curls around her neck; a sort of heavenly aura seemed to play about her figure." The knight describes how, struck dumb with wonder, and almost against their wills, her soldiers made such an onslaught against the terrorized enemy that "it was no battle—it was butchery! Two thousand dead lie on the field, not counting those the river swallowed up: on our side not a single man was lost . . . She calls herself a prophetess sent by heaven and promises to save Orléans before the moon has changed."

The precaution of a preliminary theological inquiry was undertaken immediately, before Joan was allowed an audience with the dauphin. The clerics assembled included, as one of Joan's comrades-in-arms would testify, the king's confessor, Gérard Machet, a University of Paris scholar, Pierre de Versailles, and a handful of bishops, including Jourdain Morin of Poitiers and Hugues de Combarel, all judged by history as "moral, serious, and ethical men," whose responsibility was only to "provide basic confirmation of her Catholic practices, morals, and purity." On the insistence of his advisers, Charles took the further precaution of soliciting "a respected but entirely independent opinion" from Jacques Gelu, who cautioned the yet-to-be-anointed king against any credulous embrace of Joan's claims. Charles must not, he wrote, "make himself ridiculous in the eyes of foreign nations, the French having quite a reputation for the ease with which their nature leads them to be duped." Joan came from Lorraine, Gelu reminded the dauphin, a region notoriously tolerant of witchcraft and one that shared a border with Burgundian sympathizers. Even were her motives pure, she was a gullible shepherdess. The wisest course was a slow one. Patience, Gelu advised, patience. Evil couldn't be hidden indefinitely; it would have to emerge from behind mortal attempts to hide it.

If Joan was daunted by her arrival in a world so unlike her own, where wealth had the power to banish the squalor of peasant life, she betrayed no discomfort. If she felt any awe at entering the castle of a king, she showed none to her companions. Chinon, to which Charles fled when the Duke of Burgundy's army seized Paris in 1418, was the pearl of the Loire valley, a favorite residence of kings and queens for centuries. Like the great majority of the castles in the region, it belonged to the house of Anjou—to Yolande—and had since the collapse of Roman rule, in the fifth century. Most of the structure was completed under the auspices of Henry II, who, having acquired France by marrying Eleanor of Aquitaine, died within its walls in 1189. Chinon was plumbed and heated. Its halls were hung with tapestries, and the coverlets over its down-filled beds were lined with ermine. The floors were marble; there were sconces and candelabra enough to banish the dark.

But Joan's attention was elsewhere, already beyond the château, galloping ahead of her. Long before she arrived at court, Joan had embarked on a prolonged visionary experience that would end only at her death; the ascension through social strata that delivered her to the highest level of aristocracy wasn't so ear popping for her as it would be for the average peasant girl. Still, having known only the beauty of nature, she discovered a new form, a shining man-made splendor she couldn't have imagined for herself: jeweled fingers and throats and hair that took more than one pair of hands to dress, clothes that required a lord have a valet and a lady a maid, and everywhere she looked silk gauze veils floating from the steeple-sharp points of the ladies' conical hennins, for the latest fad when Joan arrived at court was the headdress history has chosen as an emblem of the era's fashions. Crowns whose beauty couldn't match but necessarily informed her attempts to describe the ones her angels wore. The era's visual art betrays the conflation of earthly and heavenly riches, an equivalence introduced by the Bible. The book of Revelation's heaven is a city of pure gold, with foundations of precious stones, each of its twelve gates made of a single pearl.

Already, the citizens of Chinon were out milling in the streets, gossiping and waiting for a chance to see the Maid. Outside its walls were growing ranks of aspiring foot soldiers, as "French people of all ages and professions leave their homes to join the army and march towards Jeanne, like the Magi following their star." Multitudes of mostly simple folk walking with clogs on their feet, carrying axes, pitchforks, and pikes—farm implements that provided prototypes for weapons used in hand combat—"crowds of people along every road that leads from Lorraine to Chinon" came to volunteer their lives to serve in the army of the virgin warrior who had passed unmolested "through the territory of the King's enemies, and . . . almost miraculously, forded many rivers in order to come to the King."

"There is something strange about this girl," Yolande tells Charles in *The Lark*, "something remarkable. Or so everybody thinks, and that's what matters."

With Yolande overtly propping up his resolve, Charles defied La Trémoille and his cadre of Burgundian spies and sympathizers and demanded that Joan be brought upstairs. The scene in which Joan at last meets the dauphin claims a prominent role in every telling of her story, identifying her immediate discovery of the dauphin, who had hidden himself among a crowd of courtiers, as her first significant miracle, the one that ignited the fuse of her messianic trajectory. After all, she'd never seen him or his likeness before—what other than her voices could have tipped her off? Predictably, the scene grew more fantastic with every telling, although in the case of Joan the religious truth embraced by hagiography can't eclipse historical fact. The first meeting between Joan and Charles included only a handful of people. The second was a reenactment of the first and took place months later, after Joan had been thoroughly vetted by a Church tribunal.

"He came from on high," Joan said of the angel who accompanied her on her initial visit, and he "went with me by the stairs to the king's chamber."

"Who entered first?" the examiner asked.

"The angel went in first. He came by Our Lord's command."

"How?"

"He came in through the door," Joan said, and "from the door the angel stepped upon the ground and he walked towards my king."

"How far was the distance between this angel and your king?"

"The space of a good lance-length," she said, that distance being anywhere between nine and fourteen feet.

"And did anyone else see or hear this angel? Anyone other than you?"

"My king and several others heard and saw the voices which came to my aid," Joan said, a characterization that evinces how oblique and cryptic she became when interviewed about angels and saints and their properties. No witness for the nullification claimed to have seen, or heard, her voices, though they trusted they were real. Not one of Joan's contemporaries suggested she had ever lied about her experience of what she believed was a heavenly manifestation.

"Who were the others present?"

"Charles de Bourbon and perhaps three others"—Yolande, La Trémoille, and a handful of the dauphin's closest advisers.

"When the King learned that she was approaching," Simon Charles testified, "he withdrew behind the others; Joan, however, recognized him perfectly."

Among the courtiers, the grand master of the king's household and erstwhile crusader, Raoul de Gaucourt, remembered that Joan—he too called her a "poor shepherd girl"—"appeared before His Royal Majesty in great humility and utter simplicity. I heard her speak the following words to the King: 'Most noble Lord Dauphin, I have come and am sent by God to bring help to you and your kingdom.'"

Joan fell to her knees before the dauphin as she did before her angels and saints, Charles being one of the few mortals before whom she lowered herself in obeisance. She was wearing what she had on the journey from Vaucouleurs—"a black doublet with hose attached, a short tunic of coarse black material, black hair, cut round, and a black cap on her head." If she was surprised by the physical appearance of the man she had imagined countless times, she didn't betray it. Isabeau is reputed to have been beautiful in her youth, but her children, three of whom died in infancy, were an unprepossessing lot. Charles lived to be fifty-eight, longer than any of his siblings. If his official court portrait by Jean Fouquet (Fig. 10) is not of the warts-and-all school, then the dauphin must have been repellent. The lower half of his face, with its full-lipped, petulant mouth and fleshy chin, suggested sated appetites; the eyes above his bulbous nose were, as observed by his contemporaries, small and calculating. "If he can make three sous profit on any virtue you bring him he'll sell you out, and throw you in the corner like an empty sausage skin," Chartier observes in *Joan of Lorraine*. The dauphin's arms and legs were so spindly as to shock those who saw him when he was not upholstered in ceremonial velvet and fur but wearing his everyday green tunic. An inexpensive garment that wasn't discarded but repaired when the elbows gave out, it demonstrated well enough the poverty into which France's court had descended. Though Joan would find herself increasingly impatient with Charles's vacillation and what seemed like timidity, and he would sacrifice her life to his ambition, she never judged him. She saw no wrong in righteously criticizing most of the rest of the world, either collectively or one man at a time, but Charles was God's anointed. If she believed she could budge his resistance to undertaking military maneuvers he perceived as risks and she understood as opportunities, Joan would remonstrate with him for an hour, but she regarded Charles as she did the pope, both representatives of divine will who stood outside the reach of mortal censure—as did she.

Despite the protests of La Trémoille and Archbishop Regnault de Chartres, the dauphin agreed under pressure from Yolande to retire with Joan to a separate room. "The Maid talked with our lord the King in private," Joan's squire, Jean d'Aulon, wrote of the initial meeting, "and told him certain secrets that I do not know."

"After hearing her," Simon Charles added, "the King appeared to be joyous." By all accounts, the chronically indecisive and ineffectual dauphin emerged from the private audience radiating optimism and confidence, suddenly appearing as a man capable of rule.

Whatever transpired between the dauphin and the Maid has fueled six centuries of curiosity. Joan refused to discuss it at all, not even to save her life.

"What sign did you bring to Charles showing him you came from God?" the examiner asked repeatedly.

"Go and ask him," Joan said. "I have already told you that you will not drag this from my lips."

While Joan's testimony about her private audience with the dauphin fails to address the obvious point of her judges' questions—just how exactly had the divine manifested itself?—there's little sense in parsing each of her inconsistent responses to exhume a truth from their vivisection, not any more than in constructing rationales to explain the inconsistency of her comments, when Joan refused to make any other than a qualified oath to her examiner.

"You may well ask me such things, that to some I shall answer truly, and to others I shall not." She swore to tell the truth only about what she—not her judges—considered the subject matter of her trial for heresy and witchcraft and refused to divulge her private experience of God. Why would she when, as she said, she was "more afraid of failing the voices by saying what is displeasing to them, than of not answering you"? They were welcome to call other witnesses, she told them; those of her party knew well that the voice was sent to Joan from God, and they knew this voice.

If Charles gave any account of the sign Joan gave him, it was many years after the fact, and history is left with little more than sec- ondhand hearsay from the man Joan called her *gentil dauphin*.* Pierre Sala, a courtier and chronicler during the reign of Charles's son and successor, Louis XI, wrote that toward the end of his life the king had confided in his chamberlain Guillaume Gouffier, whose duties required him to sleep in Charles's bedroom. Gouffier told Sala that

---

* In this context, *gentil* is understood as an antecedent to the title of dauphin, an indication of caste, as in "gentleman," rather than its modern translation as "kindly."

Charles had made a "humble silent request in prayer to Our Lord . . . in which he begged him devoutly that if it were true that he was His heir . . . might it please God to protect and defend him." Otherwise, he asked that God allow him to escape to the court of one of his allies, in Spain or Scotland. Joan, Charles said, had known the prayer he made, known it in enough detail to convince the dauphin of her legitimacy. As all of France understood Charles's predicament, and suffered his indecision, any of his subjects might guess the nature of his prayers. Whether it was what Joan said, a repetition of his words so precise as to be miraculous, or the fervor with which she said it that convinced the dauphin is impossible to know. The atmosphere at court had been so long imbued with pessimism and anxiety that Joan's passionate certainty separated her from everyone else the dauphin knew.

Among the nobles summoned to court so that they might see and judge the Maid for themselves was Charles's cousin Jean II, the Duke of Alençon, a witness for the nullification trial. "When Joan came to find the King," Alençon testified, "he was at the town of Chinon, and I at Saint Florent," no more than a day's journey away.

> I was riding out on a quail hunt when a message came that a Maid had come to the King who maintained that she was sent by God to drive away the English and to raise the siege which these English had laid to Orléans. That is why I went to the King the next day, at Chinon, where he was, and I found Joan talking with the King. Just as I drew near, Joan asked who I was, and the King replied that I was the Duke of Alençon. Then Joan said, "You have come at a good time. The more of the blood royal there are together, the better it will be."

Alençon had assumed his title as a minor, in 1415, when he was six years old and his father died at Agincourt. Now twenty, the man Joan called her "Pretty Duke," presumably because he was handsome in the full flower of his manhood, was among Charles's intimates.

"After dinner the King went to walk in the fields," Alençon remembered of the day he arrived, "and there Joan ran at a tilt, and when I saw her do this—saw her wield a lance and run at a tilt—I gave her a horse."

Having navigated eleven nights on horseback under circumstances that demanded absolute control of her mount, Joan had proved herself better than an accomplished rider with remarkable stamina. She had a way with animals that people noted and that she would have been quick to identify as an expression of God's will. "I saw her completely covered by plate armor except for her head," a knight wrote to his mother from court. "A small axe in her hand," she was waiting for her page to subdue her "great black charger, which reared up fiercely at the entrance of her lodging and would not allow her to mount. Then she said, 'Take him to the cross,' which was in front of the church down the street. There she mounted without him moving, as if he had been tied."

Alençon's gift of a destrier was no small compliment but a costly tribute to the girl astride a galloping stallion, wielding a weapon twice as long as she was tall. A destrier could cost as much as fifty livres; now Joan had two.

"When the King had seen and heard her," Raoul de Gaucourt testified, "he wanted more information about her. So he put her in the care of Guillaume Bellier, who was the master of his house, the captain of Troyes, and my lieutenant at Chinon. His wife was a most devout woman with a very high reputation." A veteran crusader appointed by Charles as the grand master of his household and sent by him to the pope to initiate the nullification proceedings, Raoul de Gaucourt was careful to allude to the high reputation of Joan's hostess because it was she who, in her de facto role as chaperone, guaranteed the preservation of Joan's chastity, which had been confirmed by Yolande herself, attended by Lady de Gaucourt and Lady de Trèves.

"When Joan came to the King she was twice examined by women to discover what she was, man or woman, wanton or virgin," Pasquerel said, his recollection corroborated by Jean d'Aulon, who was chosen by Charles to serve as Joan's squire and "keep personal watch over Joan because he was the wisest knight and the man of the most approved honesty at his court."

"The Queen said and told the King that she and her ladies had found her beyond any doubt to be a true and intact virgin," Pasquerel testified, "with no signs of corruption or violation."

Joan had been lucky, some would say blessed, as well as chaste, at a time when the exploration of a girl's genitalia was an almost meaningless exercise, as it wasn't medically possible in the fifteenth century to determine with any certitude that a girl was a virgin, especially not if she was athletic and, like Joan, had been on horseback for a week and a half. She'd had more than enough physical activity to tear so delicate a membrane of flesh without her even knowing it had happened; a girl's hymen can easily be broken without pain or bleeding. In the course of three years, the young woman whose identity was inseparable from her virginity would endure one invasive inspection of her vaginal canal after another; if she ever voiced an objection, it was not recorded. Probably she was as stoic about the need to prove her virtue to those who would otherwise doubt her claim as she was about any other of the sacrifices her vocation demanded of her. And the blessing did hold, as even the exertions of warfare would leave the physical proof of virginity intact for her inquisitors to first double-check and then plot to destroy.

For the few days before Joan was sent to Poitiers for what would be a far lengthier and more thorough examination by clerics than she could have anticipated, the dauphin ordered that she be lodged in the Tour de Coudray, the keep embraced by the westernmost fortifications. "I lived in that tower with Joan," Louis de Coutes testified, he "and a certain Raymond" the two apprentice knights assigned to be Joan's pages. "All the time that she was there I was with her continuously, all day long," Louis said. "At night, she had women with her, and I well remember that during the time that she was in that tower of Coudray many of high rank came on several occasions to talk with Joan. What they said or did, I do not know, as I always ran off when I saw them coming; and I do not know who they were." Fourteen or fifteen at the time, Louis had been learning the art of war from Raoul de Gaucourt and was far more impressed by the status of courtiers than his lower-born mistress, whose piety struck him as exceptional. "I often saw her on her knees and praying, as I supposed. However, I was never able to hear what she said, although sometimes she wept."

A hundred and fifteen years earlier, Jacques de Molay, grand master of the Knights Templar, had slept in Joan's tower bedroom—as a prisoner, not a guest. By 1312, the Poor Fellow-Soldiers of Christ and of the Temple of Solomon, known informally as the Knights Templar, had been disbanded, its members accused of heresy, apostasy, and idolatry. For two centuries, the order had held Europe in the kind of thrall Joan would inspire, its history indivisible from that of the crusades, its heraldry still familiar: a bloodred cross on a white ground. Knights Templar were held to embody the valor of the knight and the chastity of the cleric; their embrace by the public adumbrated Joan's, as did their fate. In debt to the order and unable to wring enough taxes out of his people to finance an army, on Friday, October 13, 1307, King Philip IV sacrificed the Templars to the replenishment of his coffers. By then, the organization's high-minded vows of poverty had long yielded to the greed awakened by the sight of plunder, easy to perceive as recompense for the dangers and hardships of murdering infidels. Their tax-exempt status—granted by the pope—accelerated the Templars' arrival at wealth so fantastic that some became money-lenders and went into banking. But it was their autonomy that made it imperative to obliterate the order rather than seize its assets. To furnish the grounds for the arrest of some two thousand Knights, "the King's prosecutors dragged into the light every dark superstition and fearful imagining of sorcery and Devil-worship that lay along the roots of the medieval mind," suborned witnesses to provide false testimony, and extracted confessions under torture.

As Joan's trial would demonstrate, the injustice inherent in medieval ecclesiastical courts inspired the system's slavishly scrupulous maintenance of the appearance of justice. Sentencing required proof of guilt, even if that so-called proof was accessed by illegal and immoral means. Jacques de Molay, who had been Philip IV's friend and his daughter's godfather, was burned at the stake in front of the

Cathedral of Notre Dame, in Paris, after proclaiming his and the order's innocence. In the end, sixty-seven Knights Templar abjured their forced confessions and were condemned as lapsed heretics and burned alive before a crowd, satisfying the same need as would Joan's execution, for propitiation in the form of a human sacrifice that recast a violent crucifixion the Church had yet to convincingly package or contain within the mystery of the Eucharist. The symbolic reenactment of the Mass couldn't quench the Church Militant's thirst for real blood—not in the fifteenth century—and for as long as the Inquisition co-opted God's singular right to judge, and smite, it denied the power of Jesus's sacrifice to redeem mortal sin.

Jesus wouldn't have had to look as far back as 115 years to read his fate—only three, as it was immediately after the Romans executed John the Baptist for publicly denouncing Herod's incestuous marriage that Jesus assumed the Baptist's flock and his apocalyptic message. Warnings abounded, but they weren't warnings he needed to predict his martyrdom, as he was reported to have done in all four of the Gospels. The Sanhedrin set spies among Jesus's followers, spies whose livelihoods, if not their lives, depended on finding something useful, or just usable. "For many bore false witness against him," the Evangelist Mark wrote, adding that "their witness [testimony] did not agree." It took so little, really, to set a man on the road to Golgotha, an abandoned quarry immediately outside Jerusalem's city walls. Chosen for its elevation and visibility, Golgotha was a mound of barren rock the Romans forested with crucifixions, leaving the dead to hang for vultures to pick at until their bones fell to the ground for carrion beetles to polish. They served as a reminder of the cost of refusing to submit to an orthodox priesthood that asserted its exclusive right to mediate the most private among human experiences, that of the divine.

The record of Joan's examination at Poitiers has been lost. Once crowned, Charles might have had it destroyed because of its potential to embarrass and alienate those nobles who were identified as enemies in 1429 but had subsequently returned their allegiance to the French throne. More likely, its findings and opinions were inconvenient enough to the Inquisition that all copies were searched out and destroyed. But there were a few witnesses and chroniclers who described the proceedings. Alain Chartier, a political commentator as well as a poet, stressed Joan's unusual intellectual capacities—"she appeared to have studied at University rather than cared for sheep in the fields"—and though the Poitiers record itself is lost, a document accepted as the formal conclusions of the theologians who examined Joan was copied and distributed in the spring of 1429. While the Poitiers inquiry is generally understood to have been a far less formal hearing than the Inquisition's meticulously conducted trial at Rouen, it was undertaken by a formidable gathering of male clerics, many more than the hastily assembled Chinon tribunal, and was the third investigation into Joan's character—or the third invasive delay Joan would endure—before she was allowed to take up her quest. The dauphin and his retinue accompanied Joan to Poitiers, the provisional capital of what was left of France and the home of its royal parliament from 1418 to 1436. Joan was by now the subject of broadcasts given by town if not royal criers. Her entourage wasn't that of a king, hand-picked from among the highest echelon of society, but it was hundreds strong, the royal party dogged by crowds of peasants following Joan to what she knew was to be a test, but not the nature of that test. *Sola cum multis, infima de summis, indocta cum doctis, foemina cum viris,* Chartier called it: one against many, lowly against exalted, illiterate against scholars, a woman against men.

In reconstructing the examination from disparate documents, historians estimate eighteen clerics assembled to question Joan, representing members of the Dominican, Carmelite, Franciscan, and Benedictine orders. "Besides myself," Seguin Seguin testified, "there had been summoned Master Jean Lombard, professor of theology in the University of Paris, Guillaume Le Maire, canon of Poitiers and bachelor in theology, Guillaume Aymeri, professor of theology and a Dominican, Friar Pierre Turelure, Master Jacques Madelon, and several others . . . We were told that we had the King's orders to interrogate Joan and to report our opinion of her to the royal Council; and we were sent to the house of Master Jean Rabateau at Poitiers, where Joan was lodged, to examine her." Gobert Thibault, one of the dauphin's squires, remembered two more professors of theology who had been called to Poitiers: "Master Pierre de Versailles, and Master Jean Érault." In sum, they represented "a gathering of the finest clergy in non-occupied France." None was allowed to reserve judgment; each was obliged to either approve or disapprove of Joan's mission.

For some time, it was assumed that *De quadam puella* (Concerning a certain young girl), an undated treatise by Jean Gerson, the éminence grise among fifteenth-century French theologians, had been composed as a resource for the Poitiers commission. Included in the first edition of Gerson's collected writings, *De quadam puella* was probably not written by the University of Paris theologian himself; a later edition calls it the work of one of his followers. More problematically, it alludes to battles that took place under Joan's leadership, months after she had been given her army as a result of the Poitiers findings. No matter the document's date or author, it was Jean Gerson who established the criteria for *discretio spirituum*—the "discernment of spirits"—articulating what became the clergy's standard method of inquiry, employed at Poitiers as it would have been anywhere else in the realm. Despite his renown, Gerson wasn't so lofty in his erudition that he didn't abridge his treatise *De distinctione verarum visionum a falsis* (On distinguishing true from false visions) to a handy ditty:

Ask Who, What, Why.
To Whom, What kind, From where.

"By following Holy Writ [Scripture]," Joan would have to prove herself through her judges' "human prudence, inquiring about her life, her morals, and her intention . . . and through devout prayer, asking for a sign." Joan's "soul must be probed as to whether it be supernatural, as sacred writ expects it to be done," recorded the anonymous poet whose summary of the proceedings was included among the nullification trial's records. The "probing" of her soul, according to Jean, Duke of Alençon, was harsh—enough that she sought him out, distraught to the point of tears, but certainly not cowed. "Afterward, when she was taking her meal with me," he testified, "Joan told me that she had been very closely examined, but that she knew more and could do more than she had told her questioners." The poet, who is assumed to have been among the clergy present at Poitiers, bore witness to its being just as much a witch trial as the one that ended Joan's life in Rouen. Each time her fate lay in the hands of worldly men, with worldly ambitions. The difference would lie in their agendas, and thus their verdicts.

Scriptural guidance cited in *De quadam puella* amounted to twelve "propositions," of which six were offered in support of La Pucelle and six against. Old Testament prophets were summoned, and Old Testament female warriors as well, furnishing precedents against which to measure Joan. Christine de Pizan would include the same exemplary members of the female sex—Deborah, Esther, and Judith—in her panegyric "The Song of Joan." In fact, the fifth chapter of Judges, considered the "oldest remaining considerable fragment of Hebrew literature," is commonly referred to as the Song of Deborah, a prophetess whose militarist agenda neatly prefigures Joan's and whose exhortations to the general of Israel's army sound very like those Joan would use to rouse her battle-weary soldiers. Their plight mirrored that of the Israelites, who, having dependably once again done evil in the sight of the Lord, had subsequently been sold into the hands of the Canaanites. The fourth of Israel's pre-monarchic judges, Deborah went to the leader of the Israelite army, Barak, and said to him, "Up; for this [is] the day in which the Lord has given [the enemy general] Sisera into your hand. Does not the Lord go out before you?" The book of Esther was most likely conceived as "propaganda for the observance in Palestine of a festival brought home by Jews from the Dispersion" in the form of an origin myth for Purim, the holiday celebrating the Jews' escape from Persia. It's widely considered a historical novella, and its titular heroine is a Jewish orphan who marries the king of Persia and risks death to expose "a subtly planned anti-Semitic pogrom." An apocryphal text, Judith represents a nationalist, pragmatic religion that equated piety with patriotism, inspiring its protagonist to seek out Holofernes, the leader of the invading Assyrian army. After ingratiating herself into Holofernes's trust as well as his tent, Judith waits until he falls into a drunken sleep, then cuts off his head and takes it home as proof of God's enduring love for the Israelites.

"The Lord has struck him down by the hand of a woman," Judith tells her people when she shows them the Syrian general's head.

But scriptural precedents meant only so much in the face of Jesus's warning that his followers beware false prophets. "Many will come in my name, saying 'I am he,'" Jesus said, "and they will lead many astray." If Joan were a true prophet, the author of *De quadam puella* asserted, "she should be a person of excellent saintliness" and not a girl who was "inclined toward a certain indecency of youths, riding on horseback while dressed in the clothes of a man," having shorn off what, in the words of Paul—recalled as a witness for the prosecution—"had been given to her for a covering." It wasn't only sumptuary laws that forbade cross-dressing; in Scripture it amounted to taboo. Once Saul, a Pharisee who persecuted early Christians, Paul served laws as old as Moses: "A woman shall not wear anything that pertains to a man, nor shall a man put on a woman's garment; for whoever does these things is an abomination to the Lord your God."

Paul was spiritually a Jew, legally a Roman, and intellectually a Greek—an ideal passport for a proselytizer—and he not only spread the word but subjected it to his own revisions, including not only a pretext for misogyny but also its applications, even in a faith that promised, as he articulated it in his letter to the Galatians, "There is neither Jew nor Greek, there is neither slave nor free, there is neither male nor female, for you are all one in Jesus Christ." On earth, women were subservient and ever reminded that they were the sources of pollution and death. Adam was not the one deceived, Paul wrote to his disciple Timothy. "Adam was not deceived, but the woman was deceived and became a transgressor." Paul wrote a third of the New Testament; theologians consider his thirteen of the New Testament's twenty-seven books[*] to have had more influence on Christian doctrine than the contribution of any other of its authors. Church leaders continue to cite his exhortation "Let the women learn in silence with all subjection" to validate excluding women from positions of leadership. "I permit," Paul wrote to Timothy, "no woman to touch or have authority over men; she is to keep silent."

"I asked her again whether she believed in God," Seguin Seguin reported of the girl who spoke to angels. "She answered, 'Yes, more

---

[*] While Paul wrote nearly half of the New Testament's books, they represent just under a third of the text.

than you do.'" The dean of the faculty of Poitiers, Seguin recalled the Dominican professor of theology Master Guillaume Aymeri's challenge to Joan: "You said the voice told you that God wishes to deliver the people of France from their present calamities. If He wishes to deliver them," Aymeri said, "there is no need of soldiers."

The response Seguin described twenty-seven years after the fact was exasperated, indignant, and hardly the words of a girl overawed by her interrogators. "In God's name!" Joan said. "The soldiers will fight, and God will give them the victory." It was an application of what Joan's comrades-in-arms remembered as her favorite aphorism: "God helps those who help themselves." Included by Benjamin Franklin in his *Almanack*, the motto is often mistaken as a quotation from Scripture—even though it ignores or appears to discount the doctrine of grace and predates Christianity by at least six hundred years. The moral to Aesop's "Hercules and the Waggoner," it was used in a number of Greek tragedies, including *Philoctetes*, Sophocles's play set during the Trojan War, memorably resolved by Odysseus's idea to build a big horse and fill it with shock troops. "Heaven never helps the men who will not act," he says.

Trust in God and keep your powder dry. Praise the Lord and pass the ammunition. In one form or another, the motto has always appealed to soldiers—a natural call to arms from Joan's angels, who were no less impatient than she and equally irritated by hairsplitting.

"What language do your voices speak?" Seguin asked.

"A better tongue than you do," Joan answered. The dean testified that as he was from Languedoc, in the South of France, he spoke a vernacular heavily inflected by spoken Latin, and hence not as purely French.*

The girl who bristled at being called a simple shepherdess certainly didn't sound like one, and the letters she would dictate to the English betray the pugnacious relish with which they were composed, as well as the oratorical flair she'd exhibit under interrogation, the

---

* *Langue d'oïl* and *langue d'oc* were the two predominant medieval French dialects, each translated as the "language of yes." *Oïl*—now *oui*—was used as the affirmative in northern and central France, *oc* in the south.

pleasure she took in being "subtle with an altogether feminine sub-tlety," as one embittered Rouen judge characterized her ability to sway her listeners. In the end, the scriptural allusion that most effectively supported Joan's cause wasn't contributed by a Bible scholar but one she summoned herself.

"God cannot wish us to believe in you," Seguin said to Joan, "unless he sends us a sign, to show that we should believe in you. We cannot advise the King to entrust you with soldiers, whom you would run into danger, merely on your bare assertion. Have you nothing more to say?"

She did. "I have not come to Poitiers to make signs," she told all eighteen judges present. "But lead me to Orléans, and I will show you the signs I was sent to make."

It didn't take a cleric to recognize Joan's rebuke as an echo of Jesus's to the self-righteous Pharisees who asked him to prove his divinity with a sign sent from God. "An evil and adulterous genera-tion seeks for a sign," Jesus told them, a generation that served the let-ter of the law before its spirit and one whose wickedness he presented in terms of unlawful sexual conduct. Implicitly, Joan said as much to the sanctimonious priests who demanded a sign from her. By the time the discernment trial was over, the subject who had disingenuously warned the Poitiers examiners of her ignorance, assuring them, "I do not know A from B," had had occasion to remind them, "There is more in our Lord's books than in yours."

If Joan was guilty of anything, it was impertinence, and this the Poitiers commission forgave, concluding that "no evil is to be found in her, only goodness, humility, virginity, devotion, honesty, and simplic-ity." Beyond that, Joan inspired the people to "much pious belief, to the praise of God."

Or, as the Earl of Warwick, Joan's jailer in Rouen, summarizes for Anouilh, "In the end they agreed to use Joan as a sort of a flagpole to nail their colors to: an attractive little mascot, well qualified to charm the general public into letting themselves be killed."

Had Yolande determined the length—as well as the outcome—of the Poitiers deliberations? No gathering of French eminences could evade her influence, and, calculated or not, to withhold the Maid from the populace for a few weeks was an effective tease. Mobs are volatile. Most rulers fear them. And the violent uprising of the Jacquerie was well within the court's memory. Two generations earlier, the imposition of punitively high taxes on the underclass (whom nobles derided as Jacquerie for the padded vests, or *jacques*, that distinguished them as peasants) ignited riots directed at the lords who maligned and illtreated the peasants on whose labor they depended. Encouraged by Étienne Marcel, Paris's provost of merchants—a title equivalent to mayor—a group of agitators gathered one spring evening in 1358 in the cemetery at Saint-Leu, some twenty-five miles north of the city, to plan an attack on those nobles they judged so autocratic as to have withdrawn their allegiance to the king. The revolt was extinguished within three weeks, but the atrocities committed in the name of social justice provided an indelible reminder to the upper classes of how deep was the commoners' enmity and what savagery it could inspire—enough to capture and disembowel a knight before his family, winding his intestines on a spool while he was still alive, roast his gutted corpse on a spit, and force-feed him to his wife and children. It took a ruler like Yolande, whose confidence in her earthly power matched that of a messiah's trust in divine assistance, to cultivate so volatile a means of furthering her political agenda as mass hysteria. Without any other marvel to occupy its attention, let alone dangle a promise of salvation, the populace made do with spreading rumors, as ever more people streamed into Chinon, drawn to a swiftly widening pinprick of hope.

On March 27, 1429, Joan was officially presented to the wider court. No princess in all Europe has ever made so memorable a debut. The Count of Vendôme, one of Yolande's retinue, escorted Joan into the Grande Salle on the upper floor of the Château du Milieu, a "splendid apartment . . . some seventy feet long by twenty-five feet wide, with a vast hooded fireplace at one end, three large windows overlooking the gardens of the inner court, and one smaller window overlooking the town, the river, and the landscape beyond." Once the staring, hushed crowd had parted to allow Joan and the count to make their way to the throne, the count presented her to the man sitting there. It was not Charles. Before Joan's entrance, the dauphin had explained the ruse to all those assembled: as a means of testing the counsel of Joan's voices, he would change clothes with one of his courtiers, who would take Charles's place on the dais while the dauphin hid among the crowd. In Marco de Gastyne's *La merveilleuse vie de Jeanne d'Arc*, Joan herself suggests the challenge, conveyed to Charles by one of his courtiers, and in George Bernard Shaw's *Saint Joan* the dauphin exchanges clothes with Gilles de Rais, the notorious Breton knight who fought alongside Joan and whose career as a serial rapist and murderer of as many as two hundred children would inspire the creation of Bluebeard and end in his execution by hanging in 1440, at the age of thirty-six. There's no reason to imagine it was Gilles de Rais who pretended to be the dauphin—no evidence that Gilles de Rais was present or that the dauphin switched places with anyone, only that "he withdrew behind the others," as Simon Charles reported. But the conceit allowed Shaw, and others who followed his lead, to call attention to what had been a genuine and striking coincidence. Although he did not turn to the occult and the sacrifice of children until after Joan was executed—as if there were no lust so evilly ravenous that her proximity couldn't dismantle it—Gilles de Rais had in fact been one of Joan's comrades-in-arms, and as such invited their overt juxtaposition, as stark as black and white: the most vile and destructive manifestation of lust side by side with luminous, absolute purity. Joan's unquestioning acceptance of any soldier for God, no matter how burdened by sin, recalls the embrace of Christ, who turned no sinner away, a narrative flourish that sanctifies Joan and redeems one of the great villains of history.

Joan wasn't fooled by the impostor but went immediately to the dauphin. "Joan recognized him perfectly," Simon Charles remembered.

"I recognized him among many others by the counsel of my voice," Joan told the Rouen judges, "which revealed him to me."

"How do you come to know me?" Brecht's Meat King asks Joan of the Stockyards.

"Because you have the cruelest face," she tells him.

"Was there an angel over the dauphin's head when you saw him for the first time?" the examiner asked.

"If there was," Joan testified, "I did not see it."

"Was there a light?"

"There were three hundred knights and fifty torches, without counting the spiritual light, and I seldom have revelations but there is a light."

As Yolande intended, the crowd was thrilled and astounded by the immediate demonstration of Joan's supernatural power. Among them, only a handful knew Joan had already picked the dauphin out of a gathering so small it would be surprising if an intelligent and observant girl hadn't identified the dauphin, if only by virtue of the deference the others present were required to show him. That they kept silent bears witness to the force of Yolande's grip. Among that handful, only Raoul de Gaucourt, grand master of the king's household, testified for the nullification, characterizing Joan's presentation as a single event, rather than an original meeting followed by a subsequent, amplified reenactment. Gaucourt was eighty-five when he testified; the conflation was likely an innocent one. Twenty-seven years had passed, a long time for an old man to resist the impulse to revise the beginning of Joan's career to predict its subsequent glory, countless retellings and thus endless reimagining of his one claim to fame, which depended entirely on his proximity to "that poor shepherd girl."

The focus of every eye in the packed room, Joan fell to her knees to embrace the dauphin's legs, the same obeisance she made to her angels. Perhaps she had been coached to execute "the same bows and reverences customarily made before the King," as Jean Chartier recorded in *Chronique de Charles VII*, "just as if she had been brought up at court." She was wearing the rough black traveling clothes appropriate to Yolande's production, rather than the new finery she preferred. It's difficult to know if or how much Joan endorsed Yolande's use of creative deception. There's little reason to assume, and no evidence to suggest, she disapproved of what had been orchestrated to garner support for her mission or that she didn't understand by now that such demonstrations were useful, even necessary. After all, she'd been working assiduously for many months to enlist the support of a fraction of the number of courtiers Yolande convinced in an hour by staging and amplifying what had, after all, already happened. Joan's entrance was an announcement made to courtiers, an entirely mortal transaction; it was not a sign recklessly demanded of God. If Joan hadn't already understood the power of simple gestures and images to sway a multitude, she did now. Under interrogation, she conflated the original and the restaged versions; the composite included details from each meeting.

"Was any one else with you when you showed the sign to your king?"

"I think there was not, although many people were fairly near."

Asked again, two days later, after the interrogation had been moved from the public venue to Joan's cell—her judges' hostility that much more oppressive in close quarters—she changed her report, claiming that what had occurred privately during the original first meeting had been witnessed by the crowd assembled for her presentation to the court. "God willed that those of my party who were there should see the sign," she said, and thus take confidence in the divine assistance she promised. She added that it was not only her supporters who were impressed but also those who had called her motives or her sanity into question.

"The clergy ceased opposing me when they had recognized the sign," she told the examiner, a crown "so rich and precious that I do not know how to count or appreciate its riches. It signified that the dauphin would gain the kingdom of France."

"Does this sign still exist?"

"Yes," she said, "certainly, and it will last for a thousand years and more."

"Where is this sign?"

"Preserved with the king's treasure."

"Did you yourself see it on his head?"

"I cannot tell you without perjury," Joan said. "My voices have not given me leave to speak of it."

"Was it of gold or silver? Were there precious stones? What was this sign? Was it a crown?"

"It was a crown, yes, but no man could describe so rich a thing as this sign."

"Did the crown have a good odor? Did it glitter?"

"Yes, it was of good odor and it will always be so, as long as it is well and duly guarded."

To the medieval mind, Joan's characterization of a heavenly sign as having material substance, rather than confined to a mystical realm only she could see, wasn't nonsensical or even incredible. If devils and saints took on a convincing corporeal reality, so could a sign. Too, just as it was natural to express love, whether human or divine, in concrete material terms, so was it unavoidable to use mortal measures to communicate things of the spirit, splendid raiment "fully adequate to express spiritual purity." The crown, Joan said, had been carried to the king by "an angel from God, and from none other but Him. After I left the gathering I learned that more than three hundred people saw the sign," including Charles and his courtiers. If the examiner didn't believe her, he could send to the king to ask him.

"What reverence did you show the sign when it came to your king?" the examiner pressed.

"I uncovered my head, and I knelt down many times. I thanked Our Lord for my deliverance from the trouble arising from the opposition of the clergy."

"Of what appearance and size was this angel from God?"

"I have not leave to tell you that."

"Was he alone, or did other angels accompany him?"

"There were others as well."

"And these angels, were they all of the same appearance?"

"Some of them were fairly like one another, and some were not, as far as I could see. Some had wings or were crowned, others were not . . . And in their company were St. Catherine and St. Margaret who were with the . . . angels up to the very chamber of the king. Send to the king and he will tell you," she said.

The examiner didn't send to the king, not any more than he called any other witness to confirm or deny what was an unusual report from a mystic, that others present, and not just a few, had shared her visions. But what witness was needed to demonstrate that Joan believed a heavenly host appeared to bestow a mystical crown on Charles and thereby establish his birthright? That she asked for her testimony to be corroborated by the king of France, no less, was proof enough.

CHAPTER

V

Who Is This
Then,
That Wind
and Seas Obey?

On April 6, 1429, a week after her presentation to the court at Chinon, Joan arrived in Tours, about five miles northwest of Chinon, to be equipped for battle. She was accompanied by her squire, Jean d'Aulon, her page, Louis de Coutes, and the army's new bursar, Jean de Metz, to whom Charles's treasurer, Hémon Raguier, had entrusted nearly six thousand livres to disperse among the two dozen or so commanders in Joan's army to cover the expenses of waging war. While Joan is popularly imagined as the leader of a "peasant army," the core of her troops was "composed of the usual groups of aristocrats, mercenaries, municipal levies, and other typical elements." Joan did attract a great number of soldiers who had heretofore avoided joining a losing battle, but they were not different from the men-at-arms who typically volunteered. Knights were noblemen; they traveled with retinues that might include their wives, children, footmen, personal chefs, valets for the men, and maids for the ladies; a medieval army was followed by merchants eager to capitalize on the ready market it represented. Several entries in Raguier's 1429 account book relate specifically to Joan, the first being, "To the Master Armorer, for a complete harness for the Maid, 100 *livres tournois.*" As the armor was intended to protect the body of a girl, not a man, it was necessarily made to order, and thus costly. "She was armed as quickly as possible," Jean Chartier wrote, "with a complete harness such as would have suited a knight . . . born in the king's court."

To furnish context where no exchange rate exists, the armor worn at Agincourt by the Duke of Orléans had cost only eighty-five livres. Joan was outfitted in what was called "white armor"—not white in color but simple, lacking the decorative flourishes of ceremonial armor. Luster was determined by cost. Not all suits of armor were shining and silver, "the 'steel' used in the age of plate armor . . . quite different from the homogeneous refined material in use today. It was a very streaky steel that could vary from wrought iron to medium carbon steel in the same piece and often had a good deal of slag throughout." The work of a master armorer was "handed down from grandfathers and fathers to sons and grandsons."

From one fitting to the next, there was never a bride more excited by her gown than Joan was by her armor. Between her clothing and what was commonly called a "harness," Joan wore a heavy, quilted doublet, stuffed, like a mattress, with horsehair. A gambeson, as it was called, the vest cushioned the body and prevented the suit's metal plates from chafing and abrading the skin, offering just that much more resistance to arrows released with enough momentum to pierce plate. In fact, those who couldn't afford plate armor often wore a gambeson alone. Chain mail* sewn to the gambeson covered whatever plates of steel could not—the backs of the knees, for example—thus providing full-body protection. Contrary to the irresistible popular misconception, epitomized by the farcical image of a knight hoisted by a crane onto the back of his charger, a suit of armor no more immobilized the wearer than protective gear does a present-day firefighter. A harness consisted of enough individual elements to allow a nearly full range of motion, and the weight of well-crafted armor was distributed evenly over the body. Experiments with genuine fifteenth-century plate armor have demonstrated that even an untrained man can mount and dismount a horse, lie flat on the ground and get easily to his feet, run, and move his arms freely, all without discomfort—so long as his armor was properly fitted, as Joan's certainly was. The polished breastplate included a flange attached to its right side, an *arrêt de cuirasse*. This "arrest" stabilized the lance for better aim and allowed a mounted knight to hold the weapon firmly enough under his—her—arm to stop it from sliding backward on impact. With an *arrêt*, the entire breastplate and gambeson absorbed the shock of a successful strike and minimized injury to the right shoulder, elbow, wrist, and hand. A mounted knight required no codpiece, as the front

---

* Chain mail: A modern pleonasm, as both "chain" and "mail" mean the same thing, chain originally indicating mail with a chain-like appearance.

bow of a war saddle was armored to protect the groin. Three styles of helmet were available to Joan. The open-faced *bascinet* (Fig. 12) was no more than a steel skullcap with a pointed crown; the *sallet*, with a rounder crown, offered more protection and might include a visor; the *capeline*, with a brim, was best for scaling walls. According to her comrades, Joan "often went about with her head bare," as did many military commanders of high rank.

There is no teller of Joan's story, including—especially—Joan, who doesn't pay careful attention to her swords. Most biographers recognize the subject as inviolate and honor Joan's account of them. She'd arrived in Chinon carrying the weapon Robert de Baudricourt gave her when she left Vaucouleurs. It was a blade of no distinction, a concession to her need for protection while crossing enemy terri-tory—a place keeper for the sword that would identify Joan, just as Excalibur had King Arthur. While in Tours, Joan "sent for a sword which was in the church of Ste. Catherine de Fierbois, behind the altar," she testified. She'd known its location, she told the examiner, not because she'd discovered it herself during the hours she spent in the church but because she had learned of it "through her voices" months after she'd left Sainte-Catherine-de-Fierbois. "Immediately it was found there, all rusted over," she said. "It was in the ground, rusted over, and upon it were five crosses."

"You had been to Ste. Catherine de Fierbois?"

"Yes. From there I sent letters to my king, and from there I went to Chinon. In Fierbois, I heard Mass three times on the same day." Given her continual attendance, Joan must have come to know the monks to whom she wrote "asking if it was their pleasure that I should have the sword, and they sent it to me. It was not buried deep behind the altar. I believe I wrote saying it was behind.

"The local priests gave me a scabbard, as did those of Tours," Joan told the examiner, "one of crimson velvet, and the other of cloth of gold." As neither was practical for use in battle, she "had another made of very strong leather."

"Who brought you this sword?"

"I never saw the man who fetched it. But I know he was a mer-chant, an armorer of Tours. As soon as the sword was found, the priests rubbed it, and the rust fell off at once without effort."

Comparisons to King Arthur's sword are unavoidable, each a phallic blade possessed by the female earth and withheld until its rightful owner emerges, Arthur's embedded up to the hilt in stone,* Joan's hidden entirely, under dirt and rust. In the Middle Ages metallurgy was regarded as a sister art to alchemy, and a sword, like a saint's relic, was an object accorded reality in both natural and supernatural spheres. Metallurgy was magic that transformed matter, a power that in Scripture belonged only to God, who gave David the sword with which he slew Goliath. In the book of Revelation a "sharp, two-edged sword" of righteousness issues from the risen Christ's mouth.

"Do not think that I came to bring peace on Earth," Jesus said. "I did not come to bring peace, but a sword."

Luc Besson's *The Messenger: The Story of Joan of Arc* uses the shortcut of a mystical dream sequence to deliver a physical sword to the young Joan's side. Released in 1999, the film is laced with psychosexual trip wires, trimming Joan's vocation to fit a plot of mortal vengeance. The first to wield Joan's sword is a looting enemy soldier, who seizes it and gores her beloved sister to death before he rapes her, violating both blade and victim. The image isn't new or even repurposed. Martial d'Auvergnes's illustrations from the fifteenth-century *Vigiles du roi Charles VII* depict enemy soldiers goring women wearing the floor-length red dresses of peasants. In one, a nobleman, richly robed, thrusts his sword directly into the region of her groin; below them the cobbles are splashed with blood, a decapitated head turns its eyes away. In the other, an infantryman's blade enters a bit higher, into her lower abdomen; still, if the soldier's aim isn't as good as the nobleman's, his weapon is more impressive, with its unnecessarily distinct phallic outline. The *Vigiles*'s Joan presides over an attack on Paris while wearing a long red skirt, the phallic hilt of an oversized sword projecting from her groin (Fig. 26). The latter is missing in the scene of her being tied to the stake, the vanquished Maid unarmored as well as unarmed, her long hair restored. The delicate, mannered gestures of the genre can't mask the murderous fantasies Joan inspired, using

---

* In some versions of the Arthurian legend, Excalibur and the Sword in the Stone are one; in others they are two separate swords.

elements of an alphabet of ancient symbols we all recognize: a man's sword, a girl's long hair, her dress, presenting us with equally familiar equations between, for example, the loss of virginity and death.

If, as legend holds, the sword retrieved from Sainte-Catherine-de-Fierbois had once belonged to Charles Martel, he had buried it himself behind the altar, in secret, bequeathing it to whomever God chose as its next owner. Joan's physical description of the five crosses etched into its blade is consistent with decorative motifs typical of the eighth, rather than the fifteenth, century. If it was Martel's sword, it had been carried, used, and bathed in the blood of infidels by the first king of the Franks. To be given such a sword through mystical revelation was another sign that Joan was truly what she claimed to be: God's anointed and, thus, France's savior.

By the end of her military career, Joan would have owned five swords: Baudricourt's gift; the one retrieved from Sainte-Catherine-de-Fierbois; two she left on the altar of the church of Saint-Denis, outside Paris, as an offering of thanks for having been protected in battle; and one taken "as a prize of war from an Anglo-Burgundian leader." That one, Joan said, had been particularly useful for giving "de bonnes buffes et de bons torchons"—hard buffets and clouts. And yet the only witness who testified to ever seeing Joan using a sword was Jean, Duke of Alençon, who watched her "chase a girl who was with the soldiers so hard, with her sword drawn, that she broke her sword" (Fig. 16) over the prostitute's back, a significant blow as a battle sword typical of its time was a large weapon intended to be used with both hands and weighing as much as ten pounds. After that, in *Joan of Lorraine*, Dunois, the captain with whom Joan would relieve the siege of Orléans, tells La Trémoille that the whores left. "All of them. In a mess of tears and shrieks and bundles."

Jesus, too, was described as having used physical force just once, when he made a whip of cords and with it drove the moneylenders from the temple, chasing them off before overturning their tables. Like Joan's, his was a spontaneous, violent rejection of pollution, a righteous anger in hot pursuit of sin, protecting the sanctity of the temple—"temple" the word chosen by Paul as a metaphor for the body, especially a woman's. "Do you not know that your body is a temple of the Holy Spirit within you, which you have from God? You do not belong to yourself." In either case, architectural or physiological, the dwelling place of the Holy Spirit must be preserved from corruption.

"You think you have a right to set foot in the house of God just because of your filthy Mammon, but we know where and how you got it," Brecht's Joan of the Stockyards accuses a broker. "We know you haven't come by it honestly. This time, so help me, you've made a big mistake, and you're going to be driven out, driven out with a club."

"Where is that sword now?" the examiner asked Joan. "In what town?"

"I cannot say. I used it at Lagny. After, at Compiègne, I no longer had it with me," because, Michelet conjectures, the sword from Sainte-Catherine-de-Fierbois was the one Joan had broken over the prostitute's back, and "the virgin sword could not bear such a contact; it broke, and no smith could make it whole again."

"Was it lost?"

"That does not concern your case. Whatever I had when I was captured, my horses and swords and other things worth more than twelve thousand, is now in the possession of my brothers."

No matter where her arms ended up, she had never used them in combat. "I carried my standard into battle," she testified, "so as not to kill any one."

Charles VII's treasurer, Hémon Raguier, drained the coffers of another "25 livre tournois" to be given to "Hauves Poulnoir, painter living at Tours, to pay for fabric and paint a large and small standard for the Maid." The standard was about twelve feet in length, three feet at its widest, and tapered to two points. As chef de guerre, it was Joan who carried the great banner. Aside from preventing her from bearing arms, it allowed her to keep herself the focus of every one of the thousands of soldiers in her wake.

"Who told you to have the figure of Our Lord and the angels painted on the standard you carried?" the examiner asked.

"My saints told me, 'Take the standard in the name of the King of Heaven.' For this reason I had it painted so."

"Was there not something written on the standard as well?"

"The names Jhesus Maria," Joan said. "It was fringed with silk," she added.

"Where were these names? Were they written above or at the side or beneath?"

"At the side."

"At whose direction did you have it painted in this fashion?"

"I have done nothing except at God's command," Joan said. "And I have told you this often enough."

Its design conceived by angels and conveyed by Joan to the banner maker, Poulnoir, Joan's standard held the attention of her examiners, whose questions were precise enough to allow the creation of a reasonable facsimile (Fig. 13).

"What color was this standard?"

"It was white," Joan said, "of white linen or boucassin. The world was depicted on it, and two angels, one at each side. They were painted on a field of white sown with lilies"—by which she meant golden fleurs-de-lis, the heavily stylized flower that represented both king and country. Only a king could grant the use of a fleur-de-lis; the symbol harked back to Clovis, the first ruler of the Franks, who organized the informal and shifting alliances of the separate tribes of Gaul into a protonation, gathering chieftains loyal to his cause: rule by a single king whose successors would inherit the union. On Christmas day, 1496, seven years into his reign, Clovis converted to Christianity at the behest of his wife, Clotilde, who was visited by the Holy Spirit upon her husband's baptism at Reims. A dove descended from on high, bearing three white feathers representing the estates of clergy, nobility, and commoners, elements that would come together as three gilded petals, likely inspired by the yellow iris common to the area of Languedoc rather than by a white lily. Charles's official court painter, Fouquet, is the first known visual artist to record an emerging French nationalism. Many of Fouquet's history paintings survive; most include the motif of a field of gold fleurs-de-lis against a royal blue ground. Dunois remembered the standard somewhat differently, with "the figure of our Lord holding a fleur-de-lis in His hand."

Still, his version preserves the deliberate symbology of Joan's standard, which communicated a political message stressing Christ's role as king, rather than as shepherd or sacrificial lamb, thus underscoring the divine right of kings.

"And which do you prefer," the examiner asked Joan, "your standard or your sword?"

"I much prefer my standard to my sword," Joan said. "I prefer it forty times as much," she said, using forty as it is used in the Bible, as shorthand for a number too great to count, the number of days Noah floated on the face of the drowned earth, the number Jesus spent in the wilderness when tempted by the devil.

"Did you not throw or have others throw holy water on the pennons?"

"I do not know anything about that," Joan said. "If it was done, it was not at my instruction."

"Did not other men-at-arms have pennons made in the style of yours?"

"The Lords kept their own [coats of] arms"—as each knight would have to have done. Given the chaos of hand-to-hand combat, family crests were often the only means of telling friend from foe on the battlefield. "Some of my companions in arms had them made at their pleasure," she said, "others did not." If they did, she added, it was "merely to distinguish their men from others."

Heraldry provided an outward, readable sign of noble ancestry and advertised the wearer's right to bear arms. Once the king had granted a coat of arms to a family, it could be worn by no other, and given the medieval relish for symbol, collectively and individually they were fetishized to the point of cult worship. It was required of every knight to recognize the crest of every friend or foe he was likely to encounter in his career, a language that was highly specialized and visually dense, enough that it took years before most knights mastered what Joan picked up in a few weeks, acquiring what was her first alphabet as well as the ability to read combinations of its elements quickly. Myth insists on the simplicity of Jesus and Joan, but here simplicity might better be called single-mindedness. While their aims might appear uncomplicated—uncompromising—their intellects were without par. Many times the Evangelists cite the response of highly educated audiences to Jesus's radical interpretation of Scripture, listeners "astonished at his teaching, for he was teaching them as one who had authority, and not as their scribes." The Duke of Alençon was not the only one to marvel at Joan's exceptional gifts, her mastery of horsemanship and immediate understanding of weaponry. Like Jesus, regarded by some scholars as unlettered,* Joan had a memory good enough to obviate her illiteracy; she picked talents worth cultivating; she acquired mastery with unnatural speed and perception.

In Tours, Joan was approached by a young mendicant friar—an acquaintance of her mother, who had met him at Notre-Dame du Puy at Velay, some three hundred miles south of Domrémy. "Go to the shrine at Puy, Mother," Victor Fleming's Joan says to her mother as the two bid each other good-bye at Vaucouleurs, "and pray for us."

A major shrine, as Lourdes would become a few centuries later, Puy drew multitudes of pilgrims. Isabelle's prayers did of course focus on her daughter, as did much if not all the talk among a group of pilgrims from Lorraine, and Jean Pasquerel conveyed such saintliness that he appeared to Joan's mother as God's answer to those prayers. She and the other pilgrims pressed him to seek Joan out when he returned home to Tours, where he was a lector in the convent there.

An alternate theory holds that Yolande, in need of a reliable reporter from the front of the war she'd financed, arranged Pasquerel's introduction to the Maid. Yolande, whose own beauty taught her its value, was always busy behind the scenes and had groomed and placed beautiful women in courts all over France, with instructions to find their way into beds and make use of pillow talk—a network of

---

* While Jesus's relative poverty argues for his not having had the education lavished on boys from more affluent families, two scriptural references suggest he could read. Luke 4:17 tells of Jesus's reading from the book of the prophet Isaiah in the synagogue of Nazareth. In John 8:6, Jesus "drew in the dirt" to avoid being caught in the Pharisees' rhetorical trap, interpreted by some as an inability to write, although some versions of the book replace "drew" with "wrote," and later manuscripts refer to his having written the sins of the Pharisees in the dirt.

seductive spies to further her agendas by bringing home information and applying nudges where necessary. There's no reason to imagine Pasquerel might have fallen prey to feminine wiles, or any other temptation, but one of the men who brought him might have been less immune to pretty ankles and perfumed bosoms.

"Joan was lodged in the house of Jean Dupuy, a citizen of the town," Pasquerel testified. "I found Joan at his house, and the men who had brought me spoke to her like this: 'Joan, we have brought you this good Father. If you knew him well, you would like him exceedingly.'"

Joan did like Pasquerel exceedingly, so much so that she entreated him to join her holy army, as he did. "I served her as chaplain and heard her confession and sang her the Mass," he testified, remaining at Joan's side until she was captured and providing invaluable eyewitness accounts of the lifting of the siege of Orléans and of subsequent maneuvers.

Once Joan had been outfitted for battle, she and her army of twenty-five hundred set out for Blois, about thirty miles northeast of Tours, escorted, according to Jean, Count of Dunois, by the archbishop of Reims and Raoul de Gaucourt, who served as bailiff at Orléans. Blois was about halfway to Orléans; there Joan was met, Dunois continued, by "the men who were taking in the convoy of food, to wit the lord de Rais, and de Boussac, with whom were the lord de Culant, the admiral of France, La Hire, and the lord Ambroise de Loré, who has since become provost of Paris." Boussac was Jean de la Brosse, the marshal of France who would take part in all Joan's campaigns. La Hire, meaning "hedgehog," the nickname that recognized his prickly temperament, was the mercenary captain Étienne de Vignolles, infamous for the relish with which he undertook the pillaging of land and damsels. Invariably portrayed as loud, vulgar, and corpulent—larger than life—La Hire is a male incarnation of the prostitute with a heart of gold that can't be obscured by a tawdry costume or uncultured tone. "With all your sins you are like a bright new coin in the hand of God!" Joan exclaims to La Hire in *The Lark*. At Blois, he was the only captain to welcome Joan immediately, he and the Duke of Alençon the only two among Joan's comrades who would attempt her rescue after she was captured and sold. The rest of the guard wasn't so much following orders as following along for what promised to be a grand adventure if not a victory. Living prophecy or not, in an age when warfare was sanctioned recreation and knights crammed a furlough with jousting, brawling, and bullying, the Maid of Lorraine was marching toward the clash of real battle. If she had yet to establish her divinity, she still offered the excitement of a crusade.

At Blois, Joan paused to introduce herself to the enemy from a remove and warn them of her imminence. Just as she had first approached Charles and his court by means of a couriered letter from the remove of Sainte-Catherine-de-Fierbois, so did she send word to the English, telling them who she was and what they could expect from her arrival at Orléans. Even from a distance of six centuries, the salutation alone is a masterpiece of impudence, the repetition of the accusatory "you" and the "calling yourself" startlingly cocky forms of address coming from a peasant to royalty.

King of England, and you Duke of Bedford, calling yourself regent of France, you, William Pole, Count of Suffolk, John Talbot, and you Thomas Lord Scales, calling yourselves lieutenants of the said Duke of Bedford, do right in the King of Heaven's sight. [Surrender to The Maid] sent hither by God the King of Heaven, the keys of all the good towns you have taken and laid waste in France. She comes in God's name to establish the Blood Royal, ready to make peace if you agree to abandon France and repay what you have taken. And you, archers, comrades in arms, gentles and others, who are before the town of Orleans, retire in God's name to your own country. If you do not, expect to hear tidings from The Maid who will shortly come upon you to your very great hurt. And to you, King of England, if you do not thus, I am "chef de guerre"; and whenever I meet your followers in France, I will drive them out; if they will not obey, I will put them all to death. I am sent here in God's name, the King of Heaven, to drive you body for body out of all France. If they obey, I will show them mercy. Do not think otherwise; you will not withhold the kingdom of France

from God, the King of Kings, Blessed Mary's Son. The King
Charles, the true inheritor, will possess it, for God wills it, and
has revealed it to him through The Maid, and he will enter Paris
with a good company. If you do not believe these tidings from
God and The Maid, wherever we find you we shall strike you
and make a greater tumult ["hahay"] than France has heard for
a thousand years. Know well that the King of Heaven will send
a greater force to The Maid and her good men-at-arms than you
in all your assaults can overcome: and by blows shall the favor
of the God of Heaven be seen. You Duke of Bedford, The Maid
prays and beseeches not to bring yourself to destruction. If you
obey her, you may join her company, where the French shall
do the fairest deed ever done for Christendom. Answer, if you
desire peace in the city of Orleans; if not, bethink you of your
great hurt soon. Written this Tuesday of Holy Week.

Joan had composed the ultimatum six weeks earlier, when still in
Poitiers awaiting the result of a trial whose outcome she already knew.
Because the French were defending their land against an occupying
army, the rules of "just war"—determined by ecclesiastical tradition—
released Joan from the responsibility to formally declare war on the
English, as required of a leader who initiated hostilities. When war
was perceived as a form of propitiation, only those who undertook
to right a wrong could successfully appeal to God for aid. Joan didn't
have to warn the English, who knew of her advent in any case. As
leader of the army to which God promised victory, she could reasonably hold herself accountable to give the enemy a chance to retreat
in face of certain defeat, but her letter wasn't conceived as a merciful
gesture. It was a public platform from which to proclaim herself *chef de
guerre*—a title the French generals currently running the war would
certainly not have awarded her. For Joan, however, who traveled under
the protection of God, the advantage would never lie in stealth, and
she had no intention of collecting and maneuvering troops without
making the declarations her position entitled her to make—to those
at the very top of the English command hierarchy, two of whom were
too august to be present at Orléans. The Duke of Bedford was John of
Lancaster (Fig. 17), the third son of Henry IV, King of England and

acting head of state in France for his nephew Henry VI (Fig. 18), the seven-year-old King of England. John Talbot was Earl of Shrewsbury and constable of France, the commander in chief of the Burgundian army. As the Count of Suffolk, William Pole ruled what was settled in the fifth century as the kingdom of Anglia, north of London on England's east coast; Thomas, Lord Scales, a Knight of the Garter, the highest order of English chivalry, served as the Duke of Bedford's lieutenant. These were the men to whom she threw down the gauntlet of what "can be read as a mere license for aggression and violence."

"Surrender to the Maid . . . the keys of all the good towns you have taken and violated in France." Joan's enemies used sexual slurs to invalidate her claim to power; she called the English occupation an act of rape. "She comes in God's name to establish the Blood Royal." Here was the exalted blood necessary to counteract the polluted flow that had first issued from between Eve's legs—blood that was sacred, as holy as menses were base. Blood at one with that of the immaculate Christ, both mortal and divine, the antidote to Isabeau's wanton betrayal. Here was Joan, announcing herself as God's anointed, his messiah: La Pucelle. In naming herself the Virgin, Joan made "a preemptive strike against being seen as a camp follower," because it wasn't only Jacques d'Arc who presumed prostitution was the sole purpose of a woman among soldiers.

"If you obey her, you may join her company"—words spoken down from a considerable altitude—"where the French shall do the fairest deed ever done for Christendom." Joan's prose galloped on ahead of her, as mannered and romantic as that of any chanson de geste, switching suddenly to passages whose language and cadence harked back to the God of the Old Testament, demanding his chosen people make genocidal war on those who would occupy their land. "I am sent here in God's name, the King of Heaven, to drive you body for body out of all France. If they obey, I will show them mercy." As with other of her letters, Joan refers to herself as both "she" and "I," reserving the exalted, decorous third person for the Maid, and not adopting the familiar first person but quoting the most exalted of all voices. "Now you shall see what I will do to Pharaoh," God promised Moses. "For with a strong hand [I] will send them out, yea, with a strong hand [I] will drive them out of [your] land." "I will drive them out," Joan warned the occupying army, "if they will not obey, I will put them all to death."

The letter was unsigned; it would be another six months before Joan took the time to learn to sign her name. That a maid, generally understood as booty to be seized by conquering soldiers, would so thoroughly subvert the accepted order of things as to declare herself *chef de guerre* to the king of England and promise to mete out God's retribution was a presumption previously unimagined—unimaginable—to those who received the missive and in turn released only one of the two messengers who had been dispatched with it. The Armagnac whore had better go home before they caught and burned her, the English replied to Joan's challenge. They'd already set tinder under the stake they'd prepared for the messenger they hadn't released, debating whether or not burning him would break the charm she'd used to bewitch her army. Joan sent the herald who had been released back with her response.

"Go and tell Talbot that if he takes up arms I shall do likewise . . . Let him have me burnt, if he can catch me."

❖

Maxwell Anderson, whose *Joan of Lorraine* premiered in 1946, slides the responsibility for what remains, five hundred years later, an unladylike broadcast from a girl whose delusions included her equality to men over to her brothers Jean and Pierre, who take it upon themselves to teach their hand-wringing, timorous sister how to behave like a man, with authority. Joan's first lesson in what is "not girl's work," as Pierre refers to what Joan's angels call "speaking boldly," inspires not confidence but lament.

"Oh, if I could speak large and round like a boy, and could stand that way and make my words sound out like a trumpet—if I could do that, I could do all the things God wants me to do. But I'm a girl, and my voice is a girl's voice, and my ways are a girl's ways." And her lines were written in the aftermath of Rosie the Riveter's 1942 eruption into the culture as the icon representing all the wives and daughters who selflessly took on jobs their husbands and sons had left to join the army. By the play's premiere, World War II was over, and the men had come home to discover that once freed from domestic chores, not every woman could be enticed, or coerced, back to the hearth. Just as disturbing, the ones who refused to relinquish agency that had belonged to men held on to their identities as women. The girl in the "We Can Do It!" poster wears red lipstick with her blue coveralls and glares through movie star eyelashes while showing off her flexed bicep. It's a war effort poster; Rosie's pose is confrontational, but the Axis powers aren't the enemy. The fist she holds up is as blatant a symbol as the sword in the hand of her World War I predecessor. "Joan of Arc Saved France. Women of America, Save Your Country, Buy War Savings Stamps" (Fig. 36). The 1917 Joan's gaze is tender, rapturous, and, like her sword, directed up, toward heaven. Her red lips part, a blaze of white light pours over her head: here is the heroine of *Joan of Lorraine*, whose shining armor protects her "girl's ways" and whose creator's vision of Joan was retrospective and romantic. Born in 1888, Anderson was twenty when Joan was beatified, America innocent of world wars to come, and the only war effort a woman was expected to make was as a consumer, spending what was presumably her husband's money. Not Rosie: she's discovered what it's like to have her own, lips closed in what might be a seductive pout if the jut of the bottom one didn't make her point clear. Rosie's men's clothes hide a truer Joan than does the shining armor, a woman who rolls up the sleeve of her coveralls as a warning: a fight stands between her and anyone who might take away her place in the world.

❖

It isn't numbered among Joan's miracles, but that a girl of seventeen successfully denied thousands of soldiers the solace of swearing, gambling, and fornicating—every anodyne to the strains of war—is by any measure extraordinary. As described by Louis de Coutes, whose "personal recollections" Twain used as a narrative device, the camp at Blois was filled with "brigands" like "wolves and . . . hyenas. They went roaring and drinking about, whooping, shouting, swearing, and entertaining themselves with all manner of rude and riotous horse-play; and the place was full of loud and lewd women, and they were no whit behind the men for romps and noise and fantastics."

Secular culture tends to judge profanity a failure of manners when it judges it at all, but Joan and everyone she knew understood that to take God's name in vain was a serious transgression, the sort that invited capital punishment. According to Jean Gerson, "the whole of France, for all her Christianity, suffers more than any other country from the effects of this horrible sin, which causes pestilence, war, and famine." The severity of these perceived punishments demonstrated how absolute was the medieval belief in God's inclination to smite any who offended him. Joan "told La Hire, whose habit and custom it was to swear frequently, to swear no more," Seguin testified, "and when he was tempted to swear by God to swear by his staff" instead—an amusing recommendation to an audience alert to the phallic references that saturate narratives of the Maid. Twain's Joan suggests that "he might swear by his bâton," calling it "the symbol of his generalship." As for gambling, Marguerite La Touroulde remembered Joan "had a horror of the game of dice." It was a horror that demonstrated Joan's familiarity with the Gospels' account of the Roman soldiers who, when they were done crucifying Jesus, divided his clothes among themselves by throwing dice. The sword broken over the camp follower's back suffices to underscore Joan's determination that her soldiers conduct themselves as chastely as their leader. Under her command, she announced, any soldier caught with a prostitute would be forced to marry her, a punishment that was never imposed, as, Dunois explained, "when we were in her company we had no wish or desire to approach or have intercourse with women," adding, "That seems to me almost a miracle." Promising victory only to an army that demonstrated its faith by living it, she required her chaplain to hold twice-daily services for worship. "Joan bade me assemble all the priests twice a day, in the morning and the evening," Pasquerel testified, "and when they came together, they sang anthems and hymns to Saint Mary, and Joan joined them. And she would not let the soldiers mix with the priests unless they had confessed, and she exhorted all the soldiers to confess in order to come to this gathering; and at the gathering itself all the priests were prepared to hear anyone who wanted to confess."

Though she didn't conceive them as such, the rites of the Church gave Joan the means to summon her soldiers, thwarting male authority as she sidestepped the army's chain of command by seizing the clergy's. Even more subversive and dangerous, Joan was controlling men by censuring their sexual behavior, promising with authority greater than a pope's that only soldiers no longer burdened by pollution would ascend to heaven. The rest, by implication dirty and un-absolved, were damned. Perhaps it would have been tolerable for a woman to clothe and armor herself as a man, had she not claimed the arena of a man's power as well as his costume. A hundred years earlier, when Jean de Montfort, the Duke of Brittany, was captured by the English, his wife, Joanna of Flanders, took up his sword and rode from town to town gathering forces to lead "a heroic defense in full armor astride a war-horse in the streets, exhorting the soldiers under a hail of arrows and ordering women to cut short their skirts and carry stones and pots of boiling pitch to the walls to cast down upon the enemy. During a lull she led a party of knights out a secret gate, and galloped by a roundabout way to take the enemy camp in the rear, destroyed half their force, and defeated the siege." Joan would have been familiar with the heroics of "Jeanne la Flamme," as Joanna was known throughout France for incinerating the tents and supplies of the enemy. "Le feu! Le feu! Amis, fuyons! C'est Jeanne-la-Flamme qui l'a mis! Jeanne-la-Flamme est la plus intrépide qu'il y ait sur la terre, vraiment!" one popular Breton ballad proclaimed. "Fire! Fire! Friends, flee! It's Jeanne-la-Flamme who set them! Jeanne-la-Flamme is the bravest on earth, truly!" Though she was dressed and armored as a man, Joanna had undertaken a female war of defense—against a male incursion; once her husband had been killed, she went on fighting, offering her life in trade for that of her son. Her actions might have suggested to some little girls that a woman's life offered more than domestic servitude, but Jeanne la Flamme was hailed for her devotion as a wife and mother in spite of her possessing the courage and ingenuity reserved for men. For that she was forgiven, not praised.

In contrast, Joan would prove as much a demagogue as Jesus, whose radical departure from law to love demanded social justice. A refusal to remain within the confines imposed on gender was a potentially even more disruptive departure from convention than a commitment to embrace the underclass, especially a refusal that was broadcast to ever more people. "Whoever listened to the voice and looked into the eyes of Joan of Arc fell under a spell," Twain explained, "and was not his own man any more."

"When Joan departed from Blois to go to Orléans," Pasquerel testified, "the priests marched in front of the army, . . . singing the *Veni Creator Spiritus*," a ninth-century Latin hymn (we would recognize it as a Gregorian chant) sung a cappella whether in a chapel or on a military campaign. Its first verse translates "Come, Holy Ghost, Creator blest, and in our hearts take up Thy rest. Come with Thy grace and heavenly aid, to fill the hearts which Thou hast made." As the vanguard of priests parted the air with sacred song, preparing the way for the promised Virgin from Lorraine, Joan moved before her troops at a more stately pace than she would ever allow them again, through an expanse of moor and forest known as the Sologne. There, Pasquerel remembered, "they camped that [first] night in the fields and did the same on the night following." As able a horsewoman as Joan was when armored, she was unused to sleeping in armor and, according to her page, Louis de Coutes, "awoke bruised and weary" and dismissed the pain, which had no place in her vision of the quest on which she'd embarked. It wasn't, after all, a battle wound, which would prove less easy to deny. Just as the Templars had regarded Jerusalem as a holy city possessed by infidels, so did Joan see Orléans, the city she and her crusaders were to save in the name of God. This was the quest's picturesque aspect, not consciously choreographed as a romance but informed by the stories Joan knew so well, among them that of Lorraine's own Baldwin and Godfrey, leaders of the First Crusade, the elder dubbed Baldwin I of Jerusalem for his holy courage, the first among crusaders to bear the title King of Jerusalem.

A great marshy basin inadequately drained by the Loire, the Sologne was uninhabited at the time, its population sparse and migratory—a landscape claimed by spies who would have quite a scene to report back to the English. Joan and the convoy emerged from the woods at Chécy, just five miles east of Orléans, where they were met by the famed and noble Bastard of Orléans, Jean, Count of Dunois, who was, as he testified, "in charge of the city, being lieutenant general in the field." The son of Louis I—Duke of Orléans and Charles

VI's younger brother—the Bastard of Orléans (Fig. 15) would fight alongside Joan at Orléans and for the rest of the Loire campaign, one of only two of her comrades who proved unwaveringly loyal to her to the very end.

Not surprisingly, long before Joan arrived, Dunois had ferreted out all he could about the girl who was coming to win the war he was losing. His envoys "the lord de Villars, seneschal of Beaucaire, and Jamet du Thillay, who was afterward bailiff of Vermandois," had returned from Chinon to confirm that whoever she was, she had the Church's approval and the dauphin's army, augmented by corps of fanatical followers, a "rough band of looters and libertines," according to one source, from which "Joan forged a disciplined army of soldiers." The count "immediately collected a great number of soldiers," Jean d'Aulon testified, "to go out and meet her" and discovered the Maid in command of far more reinforcements and provisions than he had expected. Tethered to a city whose debilitated citizens fixed on one religious cure after another, Dunois had seen them come and go, all of them, flocks of self-scourging, nearly unclothed penitents, wailers and keeners rubbing ash into their wounds, whole monasteries processing through the streets with banners and crucifixes, chanting prayers purchased by those who could afford them. The siege wrung insanity from the city, squeezing zealots out onto the streets until every corner had its own harangue. Naturally, the people of Orléans were fixed on the Maid, but here was evidence of her sway beyond the city's walls. Not only had the bankrupt dauphin clearly gone further into debt to outfit Joan for battle, but he had also sent her in the company of captains of high rank. Joan's grip on the whole of France's imagination was proved by the number of soldiers who enlisted to fight under her command—twenty-five hundred was a large army by medieval measure. Dunois noted that she had convinced a great number of clerics to join her army as well—enough chaplains, Joan informed him, to have confessed every last one of her soldiers. They were ready to fight, and she to allow them to face death.

Between Blois and Orléans, however, were Beaugency and Meung, both occupied by the English, who also controlled all major roads on that (west) side of Orléans. The only reasonable course was to make a wide berth around the two towns so that they could approach the city from the east, which was less heavily guarded, "instead of going straight to where Talbot and the English" were, as Joan had assumed.

"Was it you who advised me to come here, on this side of the river?" Joan demanded of Dunois when she discovered in which direction she had unknowingly been led. Her squire, Jean d'Aulon, testified that Dunois answered yes. "I answered that I and others, who were the wisest, had given that advice in the belief that it was the best and surest."

Joan had approached Orléans under the assumption that she was off to wage war, leading an army intended to drive off the English, but "in actual fact it had as its immediate aim the revictualing of the city," a mission conceived, according to Charles's counselor, Guillaume Cousinot, "as a test for Joan." To deliver a convoy that included, according to Jean Chartier, "many wagons and carts of grain and a large number of oxen, sheep, cattle, pigs, and other foodstuffs" required a circuitous approach that couldn't accommodate the thousands of soldiers under Joan's command. They would have to wait while the convoy crossed the Loire at Chécy, just east of Orléans, as Chécy presented the advantage of unguarded access to the river's right bank, on which Orléans lay. Here the river was about four hundred yards wide, "shallow, rapid, but navigable, with many sand banks and islands." Unfortunately, an unexpected obstacle had presented itself. An adverse wind, blowing east instead of west, now prevented the use of barges to transport provisions to the estimated twenty thousand hungry citizens waiting within the city's walls. The situation, as Dunois presented it, was beyond mortal control. That was exactly why she had been sent, Joan argued. As Dunois and his captains noted, her assumption that she was being led directly to the enemy—on the other side of the Loire—betrayed a profound lack of understanding of the geography she'd covered.

"In God's name," Joan said to all members of the war council that had excluded her, "the counsel of the Lord God is wiser and surer than yours . . . It is the help of the King of Heaven. It does not come through love for me, but from God himself who, on the petition of Saint Louis and Saint Charlemagne, has had pity on the town of Orléans and has refused to suffer the enemy to have both the body of the lord of Orléans and his city"—the Duke of Orléans having been captured at Agincourt. As the leader of the Armagnac party, the duke, who was Dunois's legitimate half brother,* was literally priceless—not offered for ransom—and had been incarcerated across the channel for more than fourteen years. This was the only time Joan was observed to have mentioned Charlemagne or Saint Louis, invoking earthly and immortal powers and conflating kings with saints, a confusion that wasn't hers alone but inspired by the divine right of kings, which granted the anointed immunity to mortal judgment, thus dangling the temptations of tyranny. Charlemagne, never canonized, reigned as the first Holy Roman emperor from 800 to 814; it was his protection of the papacy that first married church to state. Saint Louis, the only king of France to be canonized, reigned from 1226 until 1270 and led two crusades. A petition to undertake a holy war couldn't have found a more likely, and ultimately ironic, voice: it was Saint Louis who, in pursuit of the Cathars (who believed the material world was the work of Satan and rejected the Eucharist, arguing that Jesus's body could not be contained in a piece of bread), established the Inquisition's power and reach, thus sanctioning an indefinite state of holy war, its first target a sect free from gender bias. Catharism placed no value on one sex over the other; not only did it attract women as converts, but it invited them into the clergy.

"You thought you had deceived me," Joan said to the captains who had sidelined her, "but it is you who have deceived yourselves, for I am bringing you better help than ever you got from any soldier or any city."

"Immediately, at that very moment," Dunois recalled of his initial collision with Joan, "the wind, which had been adverse and had absolutely prevented the ships carrying the provisions for the city of Orléans from putting out, changed and became favorable." On the river's bank, the beech saplings' slender trunks righted themselves and then pitched their limbs to the west. Immediately, the barges were loaded, their sails raised, and the provisions borne across the river. From this

---

* Jean Dunois, Count of Dunois (and later Count of Longueville), was the illegitimate son of Prince Louis d'Orléans and his mistress, Mariette d'Enghien.

point forward Dunois remained convinced of Joan's sanctity and the divine source of the aid she brought. "That is the reason why I think that Joan, and all her deeds in war and in battle, were rather God's work than man's," he testified, "the sudden changing of the wind, I mean, after she had spoken."

Pasquerel's version was a little different, and no less marvelous: "Now the river was so low that the ships could not ride up or touch the bank where the English were; and suddenly the water rose, so that the ships could touch land on the French side."

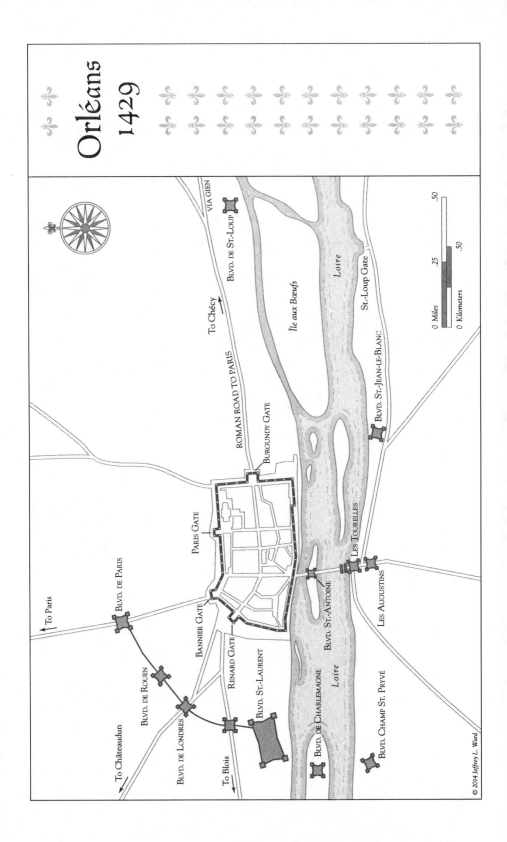

Orléans
1429

© 2014 Jeffrey L. Ward

To Paris
To Châteaudun
BLVD. DE PARIS
BLVD. DE ROUEN
BANNIER GATE
BLVD. DE LONDRES
RENARD GATE
To Blois
BLVD. ST.-LAURENT
PARIS GATE
BLVD. DE CHARLEMAGNE
Loire
BLVD. CHAMP ST. PRYVÉ
BLVD. ST.-ANTOINE
LES TOURELLES
LES AUGUSTINS
BLVD. ST.-JEAN-LE-BLANC
ST.-LOUP GATE
Loire
Île aux Bœufs
BURGUNDY GATE
ROMAN ROAD TO PARIS
To Chécy
BLVD. DE ST.-LOUP
VIA GIEN

0 Miles   .25   .50
0 Kilometers   .50

CHAPTER
VI

Surrender
to the Maid

*e*ven without a magically rising river or fortuitous shift of wind, the convoy's entry into Orléans proceeded with the unnatural ease of parting seas. "The Maid immediately boarded the boat, and I with her, and the rest of her men turned back toward Blois," her squire, Jean d'Aulon, testified, "and we entered the city safe and sound with my lord Dunois and his people."

Joan's page reported an equally uneventful arrival. "Joan, I, and several others were conveyed across the water to the city side, and from there, we entered Orléans." To approach the city from the east required passing unimpeded before the bastille of Saint-Loup, occupied by the enemy, before which was the boulevard of Saint-Loup. In this context the word "boulevard" means not a road but a bulwark* intended to provide cover from gunpowder artillery. Constructed of earth and wood, the boulevard's walls were both low enough to fire over easily and yielding enough to absorb cannon strikes without breaking or crumbling like the stone walls they protected. The French had used them for about twenty-five years—for as long as they'd had bombards—and the English, seeing their effectiveness, adopted the practice. As Dunois had sent most of Joan's army and all the clergy except Pasquerel back to Blois, the provisions traveled under a minimal guard of about two hundred soldiers in expectation of minimal interference. There was no hope of transporting so much food stealthily, or any more quickly than an ox moved.

As it happened, the English didn't do little; they did nothing. Witnesses for the nullification called this miraculous and didn't offer the pedestrian explanation for their inaction reported by the *Journal du*

* From Dutch *bolwerc*.

siège d'Orléans: the English, who had been strangling the city for six months, systematically starving its citizens, would not have allowed a great caravan of provisions unobstructed entry into the walled city had they not been successfully distracted by the people of Orléans. No more than five thousand of the estimated twenty thousand citizens of Orléans were men capable of doing battle, and prepared to guard the convoy, they "sallied out in great strength, and went charging and skirmishing before Saint Loup" with the result that "there were many dead, wounded, and captured on both sides." The convoy rolled and clopped and squealed slowly past a churning mass of soldiers so intent on killing one another that they didn't so much as check to make sure a guard remained on the Burgundy Gate.* By the time the living were counting up the dead, it was too late. Slow as it was, the convoy had entered the city as if there were no siege to lift.

Untroubled as she was by the imperatives of mortal warfare that preoccupied Dunois—forces, weaponry, munitions—Joan was so intent on making an immediate frontal attack on the English that she didn't want to be delayed by gratitude. As far as she understood it, she'd yet to accomplish anything for which she deserved to be thanked, and Dunois had "begged her to agree to cross the Loire and enter the city of Orléans, where they were most eager for her." He managed to separate Joan from her army only by ordering its captains to return to Blois and await reinforcements there. Having "succeeded in rendering them 'well-confessed, penitent and of goodwill,' a state of affairs which might suffer erosion in her absence," Joan wanted to make war immediately, before her men had a chance to sin their way out of God's grace and die unconfessed. While she bristled at his not receiving her as an equal, Dunois, as convinced of Joan's holiness now as he had been suspicious before, held himself responsible to protect her, from herself as much as from others.

Jean Luillier, a merchant, remembered how ardent was the people's response to Joan when she at last materialized, rumor made flesh, on the evening of April 29, 1429. "Her entrance was greatly desired by

---

* The single gate on the east side of the city, also known as the Saint-Aignan Gate, and accessed directly by the Via Agrippa.

all the town's inhabitants, because of her renown and of the rumors abroad," and, Luillier added, because "they did not know where to turn for help except for God." Accompanied by a detail of knights, Joan entered the Burgundy Gate astride a white charger, armored and carrying her white standard with Dunois at her side, and was received "with as much joy and enthusiasm as if she had been an angel of God." Thousands, "men, women, and small children," the *Journal du siège d'Orléans* reported, strained toward the Maid and the white horse that lifted her above the crowd and showed her to the far edges of the craning multitude. It was eight in the evening, the sun low enough in the sky to flare off armor, conjure flames on a breastplate. The heads and shoulders of the people around her horse were packed so tight she couldn't see the ground below, and the clamor pressed in. "There was a very extraordinary rush to touch her or even to touch the horse on which she sat." At some point, "such was the press around her, as they tried to touch her or her horse, that a torch set fire to her pennant. At this, Jeanne struck spurs into her horse, turning it with great skill and herself extinguishing the flame."

For six months a rain of punishments had fallen on the people who now surrounded Joan and her captains. Siege warfare was a waiting game, and the moment the English had surrounded Orléans, they began cultivating an atmosphere of dread fatalism to accelerate what physical deprivation couldn't accomplish on its own. Water mills had been destroyed as soon as possible to prevent the French from grinding any grain they had stored. Without any means to remove waste from within the city's walls, sanitary conditions deteriorated and encouraged the spread of disease. Rumor of betrayal was constant, both from within and from without, especially after a hole was discovered in the city's north gate the previous month. Either French traitors had been poised to allow the enemy in, or the English had already penetrated the city. Caught within the walls that protected them, hungry enough to cook rats, driven, some of them, to infanticide, the citizens had endured everything from a sudden unexpected cannonade to random arrows falling from the sky, dipped in pitch and set alight in hopes of striking tinder. What used to be a marketplace was empty now, supplanted by a black market's secret barter. But for months even the rich had found little to buy or trade, and they stood among the commoners reaching for a touch or even the secondhand touch of someone whose fingers brushed Joan's armored thigh, caste having done nothing to free them from want. Whoever didn't feel it himself could see it all around him; whatever Joan kindled in the thousands of eyes fixed on her was little different from that burning in those fixed on a messiah whose impossible multiplication of loaves and fishes to feed a hungry mass thousands strong is held among his greatest miracles, a messiah who taught his followers to pray for their daily bread.

I have "been sent for the consolation of the poor and destitute," Joan said of herself. As a warning to her enemies, and thus the enemies of God, Schiller gives her an additional line, plucked from Isaiah, the prophet of apocalypse from the eighth century BC quoted by all four of the Evangelists: "The day of vengeance is near at hand."

Charles Péguy, a socialist with a mystical bent, emphasizes Joan's preoccupation with the poor, "who are starving and who get nothing to eat." She watches two children fall upon the bread she gives them "as if they were animals" and feels sick at "them being as glad as they were." She's a prisoner to her guilt over their suffering. "I thought of all those in misery who get no comfort, I thought of the worst off of all, those who come last, those who are really cast off.

"Who is going to give them their daily bread? Lord, I can't give it to them all the time. I can't give everything. I can't give to everybody."

"Who was it that touched me?" Jesus cried when the multitudes pressed upon him, grasping for him. "Someone touched me for I perceive that power has gone forth from me."

"Jesus, your people are hungry today, and you don't satisfy your people," Péguy's Joan accuses Christ. "Will it be said you won't multiply fishes and loaves any more? Will it be said you won't weep for this multitude?"

"If their baseness is beyond measure, so is their poverty," Joan of the Stockyards accuses a corrupt broker. "You have shown me not the baseness of the poor but *the poverty of the poor*."

When the crowd at last fell quiet enough that she could be heard, Joan "exhorted everyone to trust in God," Luillier testified, and thus "be delivered from our enemies." It took the combined efforts of the Count of Dunois, La Hire, Jean d'Aulon, and Louis de Coutes to usher Joan out of the boiling sea of people, allowing her to break away, at which point—accounts differ—she went either to the cathedral to receive Communion or straight to the home of an accountant named Boucher and there took the Eucharist before retiring for the night. Her page remembered she had been "most exhausted when she arrived, for she had not taken her armor off to sleep the night before she left Blois." Boucher was "one of the important citizens of the town, who had married one of its most important ladies." The couple's combined rank measured how great an honor it was to play host to the Maid, as it had been for those who gave shelter to the equally itinerant Jesus, who chose his companions from among the destitute and the outcast, those destined, as he told them, to inherit the earth. A messiah is an exalted mendicant, depending on the kindness of strangers. "Foxes have holes, and birds of the air have nests, but the Son of man has nowhere to lay his head." Encamped, Joan slept on the ground among soldiers; when inside a besieged city's walls, on her host's bed. Once she left her earthly father's home, she claimed no mortal place.

Immediately upon rising, perhaps woken by the citizens of Orlé- ans, "still in so great a state of excitement about her that they almost broke down the door of her lodging in their desire to see her," Joan sent two messengers to the English demanding the release of the her- ald they had yet to free. If they did not, she promised, as the *Journal du siège d'Orléans* reported, "she would kill with a brutal death all the English who were prisoners in Orléans, and also those who were held among the lords of the English who were being held as ransom for others." Outraged to discover no battle plan under way, Joan "went to see the Bastard of Orléans and spoke with him," her page testified, "and she came back very angry as there were no plans to attack that day," April 30. No further plans at any rate. While Joan argued with Dunois, La Hire and a small party of knights led a charge of ragged infantry, townsmen bearing improvised weapons, on the English occupying the fort that guarded the city's two northern gates. Though they forced the enemy back behind the portcullis of their stolen tower, the victory was so minor as to have escaped the notice of Joan, who was on the other side of Orléans, surrounded by townsfolk.

A night's rest having restored her restless energy, once Joan and Dunois parted company, she answered her impatience by learning her way around the walled city, taking directions from the worshipful throng that followed her wherever she went—until she found "a certain bulwark that the King's men held against the bulwark of the English and from there," as recorded in the *Journal du siège d'Orléans*, "she addressed the English opposite, requesting them in God's name to retire, otherwise she would drive them away." The bulwark was that of Belle-Croix, on the French-controlled side of the bridge that spanned the Loire between Orléans and the river's left bank. One of the lords she addressed, "called the Bastard of Granville," her page testified, "answered Joan most abusively, asking whether she expected them to surrender to a woman and calling the French who were with Joan 'unbelieving pimps.'"

In trying to pull together the factions of the increased forces, Dunois confronted a similar outrage on the part of his unconvinced captains. An "absence of echeloned units" characterized France's still-feudal armies, another instance of progress stymied by French hauteur, as without any system of rank no captain was accorded military command over another. As the grandiloquent Lord of Gamaches made clear, the social hierarchy was supreme, untrumpable. "Since you pay more heed," Gamaches said, "to the advice of a little saucebox of low birth than to a knight such as myself . . . I lower my banner and am no longer anything than a simple squire. I prefer to have a noble man as my master, rather than a hussy who may once have been God knows what."

If being called a whore by the enemy provoked her to tears of rage, Joan found the accusation that much more offensive and unacceptable from someone she presumed a friend, or at least a civil comrade, and it required Dunois and the cooler-headed among his captains to effect a reconciliation between noble knight and lowborn saucebox, one as loath as the other to bring mouth and cheek together in a forced kiss of peace. But the Battle of the Herrings remained in recent memory; the French army had succumbed to fatal disorganization even when its members were enthusiastically allied. With or without divine assistance, Dunois wasn't going to squander lives by initiating hostilities when his captains were feuding and demoting themselves out of responsibility. But the Maid and her effect on the people teetering toward mass hysteria within the besieged city's walls and on the increasingly nervous English without—but not beyond hearing distance of a crowd thousands strong—made it difficult to prevent an uncontrolled conflagration. By now Joan had provoked the English in a second letter Dunois described as "written in her mother tongue, in very simple language. The substance of the letter was that they, these English, must agree to give up the siege and return to the kingdom of England, or else she would attack them so strongly they would be forced to retire." He went on to identify the enemy's receipt of Joan's letter as the point at which their former power evaporated so that "four or five hundred soldiers and men at arms could fight against what seemed to be the whole force of England," unnerving the English so that "they dared not leave their strongholds and bastilles." Luillier, too, remembered the English's reaction to Joan's second letter as a tipping point: "From that moment the English were terrified and no longer had the powers of resistance that they had previously had." Even so, they did send the message that they would catch, "torture and burn her, and that she was nothing but a rustic, and that she should return to herding her cattle."

Though he was reluctant to leave her outside his direct supervision, Dunois was concerned that, either by intent or as a result of her helpless militancy, Joan would provoke a conflict before he could receive and organize his reinforcements, and on May 1 he "left Orléans for Blois to confer with the Count of Clermont and to collect other troops who were waiting there," as many as 4,000 soldiers, as Blois's garrison had swelled by then to 2,000, and "the town militia may have added another 2,000." The English, forced to divide their limited forces among the French cities they'd seized and now occupied, typically did not capture a city by means of a surprise attack meant to deliver it into their hands with a single coup de main. Instead, they took over outlying structures that controlled passage through the walls' major points of egress, thus preventing the delivery of food and supplies to the people within, who made do, starved, and finally surrendered. In the case of Orléans, these satellite fortifications were the Tourelles, freestanding turrets that flanked the bridge over the Loire, the river serving as a moat that extended along the stretch of wall protecting the city's south side, and the bastille of the Augustins, a fort made from the abandoned ruins of a convent that squatted at the end of the bridge. Both were on the far side of the river, the bastille of Saint-Loup squatting by the road to the Burgundy Gate, in its east wall. There were three smaller gates, two in the city's north wall and one in its west, but without access to the Loire they were of less tactical import. Too, medieval warfare was as mannered as any other social interaction of the age. A knight threw down his gauntlet to challenge an enemy, who picked it up to accept the invitation to fight. A captain declared war with a grandiose dispatch asserting his army's just cause for attack. It was easy enough for a single captain or small party to come and go unannounced without reprisal, and Dunois would have had little trouble leaving to organize forces to move in and retake the critical towers and bastilles, reopen the city, and break the siege.

It was a Sunday; Joan went to Mass and then rode through town with her squire and her two pages. Inspecting the battlements, she made slow progress as everywhere she went crowds pressed thick around her and her horse. The next day, she left everyone behind to reconnoiter outside the city's walls and discover the environs' blind spots and strongholds, and on Tuesday, May 3, the people of Orléans held a formal citywide procession in Joan's honor and "presented money and gifts to the Maid and her companions, and asked them to deliver their town from its siege." As was her habit, Joan ended the day in prayer, this time in the cathedral, and from there went back to the Bouchers' and to bed.

The next morning, "as soon as she learned we were returning and bringing the reinforcements we had gone to fetch," Jean d'Aulon testified, "the Maid immediately mounted her horse and rode out with some of her men to meet and help us," adding that "if it had been necessary she would have rescued us." With the aid of her own and better counsel, she escorted Dunois and the augmented army back to Orléans "before the enemy's eyes," ushering every soldier from the nearby garrisons of Gien, Montargis, Châteaudun, and Château-renard through the Burgundy Gate without incident. She was eager to tell Dunois how much she'd learned about the city's fortifications, and he to confirm that rumors of Sir John Fastolf's approach were true. Fastolf and his army had reached Janville, no farther north than a day's march, at which point the French could assume they'd join the English forces already gathering at Saint-Loup. It seemed to Jean d'Aulon that "the Maid was highly delighted with this news," for she immediately prevailed upon Dunois to mobilize for an attack.

"Bastard, Bastard," he remembered her saying, "in the name of God, I command you to let me know as soon as you hear of Fastolf's coming. For if he gets through without my knowing it, I swear to you that I will have your head cut off."

"I do not doubt that," Dunois said, exhibiting the courtly patience he'd be called on to use in many if not most of his dealings with the Maid, "and I will be certain to let you know."

Joan and Jean returned to the Bouchers', where they intended to rest in preparation for combat. Joan lay down on a bed with Charlotte, the Bouchers' daughter, who was nine and a child "much-honored" by such intimacy and who, Sackville-West hoped, "observed the rules that children were then taught to observe when sharing a bed: to keep to their own side, not to fidget, and to sleep with their mouths shut." Jean was dozing "on a couch that was in the Maid's room," when Joan was roused by her voices' strident call, and Pasquerel, who was lodged with the others, remembered her leaping from Charlotte's bed and crying, "Where are the men who should be arming me? The blood of our men is flowing on the ground!" She woke Jean. "In the name of God!" she said. "My counsel has told me that I must attack the English, but I do not know if I should go to their bastille, or against Fastolf, who is to revictual them." While Jean was being armed, there came a great tumult from the street outside the Bouchers', "a great noise and loud cries from those in the city, who shouted that the enemy were doing great harm to the French."

"Oh wicked boy!" Joan said when she found her page awake and therefore accountable. "Why did you not tell me that French blood is being spilled?"

"She urged me to go and fetch her horse," Louis de Coutes testified. "In the meantime, she had herself harnessed by her hostess and her hostess's daughter." They began at her feet, with the leather shoes worn under the armored boot, called *sabatons*, identified by their exaggeratedly long and memorably pointed toes, and then, one to a leg, moved up to the greaves, or shin plates, followed by a plate for each knee and thigh, followed by the gambeson—worn under the shirt, like a bulletproof vest—over which went a tunic of chain lined on top with a layer of leather, the hauberk, the cuirass (breastplate), spaulders (which protected the shoulders), gauntlets, and at last the helmet. In sum, a lot of buckling.

"When I had harnessed her horse," Louis said, "I found her ready in her armor" and highly irritated to discover that in his agitated rush her page had forgotten her standard, which he had to run inside to fetch and pass to her through the window. Immediately, "Joan galloped off in the direction of the Burgundy gate, and her hostess bade me run after her, which I did." As she passed through the gate, she saw a gravely wounded French soldier being carried into the city and began to weep, telling Jean d'Aulon, who had caught up with her, that "she never saw French blood without her hair standing on end." By now it was clear the battle was at the boulevard of Saint-Loup, and she hurried east on the Via Agrippa to join the charge. En route, "she found many wounded, which distressed her greatly," Pasquerel testified.

Joan rode with the cavalry, a medieval army's assault troops, her presence exciting them to giddy bloodlust. The battalion of mounted knights led the charge, galloping full tilt with foot soldiers following in their wake, ranks of archers proceeding under the cover of a shield wall carried by infantry, followed by pikemen and hand-to-hand combat soldiers armed with axes, hammers, maces, and morning stars (spiked clubs). Knights used lances only for the initial strike and often broke and discarded them upon penetrating the enemy line. Once past that line and into the melee, they switched to hand-to-hand combat with swords. Illustrations from the period, validated by archaeological evidence, allow for a reasonably accurate picture of siege warfare, not only the combat formations and the structures under attack, but the weaponry as well. Gunpowder artillery was as yet crude, but it was effective. "By 1429 purchases of gunpowder by the French royal treasury were in thousands of pounds rather than the hundreds of the previous century." A culverin, or hand cannon, was an inexpensive weapon—no trigger, just a barrel and a muzzle loader—its projectile more likely to penetrate plate armor than a longbow's arrow was, but far less accurate. The big cannon, however, didn't need to be accurate to knock down heavy fortifications, making doors of walls, and the combustion of gunpowder brought the fire-and-brimstone smell of sulfur and a hellish level of noise that was in itself a weapon against both man and beast, testing the skills of seasoned knights. Reserved for battle, destriers were restless, charged stallions that demanded a much higher level of horsemanship than any other mount. A well-timed series of blasts could dismantle an otherwise organized charge of riders mounted on horses unprepared to be terrorized by the din.

Chansons de geste couldn't have warned Joan of the reality of combat, not any more than the plundering of *écorcheurs* had approximated warfare. If it had been difficult for her to reconcile the chaste knights of romance—"protectors and defenders" who were "the big and the strong and the handsome and the nimble and the loyal and the valorous and the courageous, those who were full of the qualities of the heart and the body"—with lesser men of lower morals, it was far worse to learn that picturesque skirmishes conceived by troubadours to fit the niceties of assonance had hidden the filth and degradation of battle. "The Franks there strike with vigour and with heat, / Cutting through wrists and ribs and chines in-deed," *The Song of Roland* sung, "Through garments to the lively flesh beneath; / On the green grass the clear blood runs in streams." In reality, no more than one in four cavalry forces was of noble birth or manners. The weight of mounted horses with infantry underfoot rendered marshy land, like that on either side of the Loire, into a slippery muck of dirt and blood and excrement that made it a rough slog, when not an impossibility, to drag heavy artillery—cannon, counterweight trebuchets, or catapults, and bombards—and its equally heavy ammunition within range of enemy boulevards. Still, three hours of hard fighting delivered the French to a decisive victory, and having emptied the ramparts of Saint-Loup, the soldiers set about destroying them. According to the author of the *Journal du siège d'Orléans*, by the time it was done, 140 Englishmen had been killed, and another forty taken prisoner—representing all the enemy forces, Jean d'Aulon testified, the French having carried out the "assault with very few losses." Had the Maid's entry into the war been met with failure, it would have punctured and deflated her army's confidence, made evident by the fierceness of their

attack. While her comrades celebrated what was a critical if small victory, Joan, sickened by the carnage she'd inspired, wept.

"They're dead," she says to Dunois in Anderson's *Joan of Lorraine*. "Horribly dead . . . In the midst of evil. And it was I that killed
them . . . I have been the death of many men . . . I thought victory
would be beautiful. But it's ugly and bloody and hateful."

"The voice of Heaven drives me on," Schiller's Joan bemoans,
"not my own will—rage like an angry spirit . . . no joy to me, dealing
out death."

According to Pasquerel, Joan refrained from fighting on May 5,
as it was Ascension Day, and made do with warmongering on paper.

> You men of England, who have no right to this Kingdom of
> France, the King of Heaven orders and commands you through
> me, Joan the Pucelle, to abandon your strongholds and go back
> to your country. If not, I will make a war cry ["hahu"] that will
> be remembered forever. And I am writing this to you for the
> third and final time; I will not write anything further.
> Jesus Maria
> Joan the Pucelle
>
> [In postscript] I have sent my letters to you in an honest
> manner but you are holding my messengers [or "heralds" in
> French], for you have kept my herald called Guyenne. If you
> are willing to send him back to me I will return you some of
> the men captured at the fortress of Saint-Loup, for they are not
> all dead.

"She took an arrow," Pasquerel testified, "tied the letter with a thread
to the tip and told an archer to fire this arrow at the English," crying,
"Read, this is news!"

"News from the Armagnac's whore!" they shouted upon reading
the letter. "When she heard this, Joan began to sigh and weep copious
tears, invoking the King of Heaven to her aid." She would always be

quick to tears and equally quick to dry them. This time she had been
comforted, she later reassured Pasquerel, "for she had had news of her
Lord." Too, once she considered the transaction, she saw it made little
material difference that the English had taunted and insulted her.
Whatever they said, they hadn't ignored or even dismissed her; in
fact, the prompt return of her herald suggested that they took her seriously enough to proceed with caution.

Like Schiller, Joan's confessor downplayed the bloodlust—in service to a cause for which Joan would readily lay down her own life,
but bloodlust nonetheless—that inspired her remorse and made sure
to testify as to Joan's punctilious observation of a holy day, an over-
due riposte to her inquisitors having made much of those occasions
on which she chose war over worship. Still, her squire and her page
remembered that she didn't allow the previous day's euphoria to fade,
but, as Jean d'Aulon told it, "when the Maid and her people saw how
great a victory they had won over their enemies on the day before,
they came out of the city in fair order to attack a certain other bastille
in front of the place, called the Bastille of Saint Jean le Blanc."

The boulevard of Saint-Jean-le-Blanc was on the riverbank opposite Orléans and required Joan and her forces to "cross to a certain
island," the Île aux Boeufs, "that lay in the Loire, where they would
assemble" and from there launch an attack by using two barges to
create a bridge to the shore. From there the troops charged over the
boulevard—ramparts—to the fortress, only to find it deserted. In
that retaking the bastille of Saint-Jean-le-Blanc was accomplished
without active combat, Pasquerel was technically correct that Joan
hadn't engaged in battle on May 5, but she had been looking for one.
Still, it was hard to be disappointed in a bloodless victory when the
English, with their superior forces, had turned and run to hide in the
stronger battlement of the bastille of the Augustins, one of the two
great bridgehead fortifications blocking the main entrance to the city.
Along with the Tourelles, immediately to its north, it squatted at the
end of what functioned as a drawbridge does over a moat; to cross the
Loire and enter Orléans, one had to get past both fortifications. Even
had the French chosen to move on from the small wins of Saint-Loup
and Saint-Jean-le-Blanc to the equally winnable skirmishes required to
chase the English from the northern and western avenues, they would

eventually have had to attack the choke hold on the city represented by the Augustins and the Tourelles, considered by military historians among "the most imposing fortifications ever built": twenty meters long, twenty-six meters wide, surrounded by a ditch eight meters deep.

Dunois and the other captains argued for the kind of conservative gambit favored by Bertrand Du Guesclin, a national hero whose military career Joan had admired. Like Joan, Du Guesclin was one of a handful of military leaders throughout the Middle Ages whose extraordinary victories catapulted them from middle-class anonymity to knighthood, a process analogous to making a silk purse from a sow's ear, as it required ennobling a commoner and endowing him—or, in the case of Joan, her—with a coat of arms. Among European countries, France was the most inflexible in requiring irrefutable proof of noble ancestry from the would-be knight. *Lettres d'ennoblissement* were issued rarely and didn't deliver Joan or her hero Du Guesclin to the aristocracy so much as remove them from the hierarchy of social strata, freeing them to form bonds of attachment with all people. Joan's ability "to use the power of her charisma to persuade Frenchmen of all social classes to serve the higher cause of France with little or no pay" would prove key to her success. "Perhaps as true a knight as a real-life man of the fourteenth century could be," Joan's hero was, like her, a figure of "extraordinary popularity"—a man revered as a true-life Galahad, his reputation that of "being 'the most courteous' and 'the least covetous' knight as well as a terrific fighter and born leader."

As the constable of France—commander in chief of its armed forces—from 1370 to 1380, Du Guesclin "managed to subordinate French notions of chivalrous conduct to intelligent planning and execution." He characteristically avoided frontal assaults to carry out a battery of separate minor attacks that guaranteed expeditious and definitive victories, fracturing the attention of the enemy's military captains and destroying the morale of their forces. The Roman emperor Fabius Maximus, who delivered Rome's 202 BC victory over Carthage during the Second Punic War, is credited for instituting what came to be called the Fabian strategy and earned him the title "Father of Terrorism." Dunois's council, to which he had not invited hotheaded Joan, determined that the numerical inferiority of the

French forces demanded they use diversionary tactics as well as incite the general populace to undertake acts of sabotage. To follow a course of uncloaked aggression could only end in slaughter and defeat, they reasoned, an invitation for the enemy to cross over the Loire and obliterate the whole of France. Joan picked the direct strike as the only feasible strategy for an army that trusted in the protection of God: a course of stealth and surprise implied a failure of faith.

According to the testimony of Simon Charles, as reported to him by Raoul de Gaucourt, grand master of Charles's household and captain of Chinon, "Any attack or charge was out of the question." Gaucourt was deputized to watch at the city's gates "and prevent anyone from breaking out." Joan ignored the command.

Finding her way blocked, she called Gaucourt "wicked," as she had her page, a word reserved for anyone, friend or foe, who frustrated her cause. "Whether you like it or not," she said, "the soldiers will charge, and they will win as they have done in other places." Backed by the town's garrison and the citizenry, largely in agreement with Joan, the army she'd infused with her impatience "broke out" of Orléans, and Dunois girded himself for what he expected to be a costly and unavoidable disaster. No matter what inexperienced nonsense Joan planned, the soldiers were behind her, and the captains' council was left with no choice but to align their focus with hers. The dreaded imminence of Fastolf and fresh enemy forces allowed them to produce a face-saving rationalization as they set out with Joan, La Hire, "and many other knights and squires and around four thousand soldiers," as the *Journal du siège d'Orléans* reported.

"La Hire and the Maid," Jean d'Aulon testified, "who were always in the van[guard] to protect the rest, swiftly couched their lances and were the first to strike out at the enemy." The French army crossed the Loire east of the city and made a westerly charge along the boulevard of the Augustins, where they met the English, who "sallied out of the Tourelles in great strength, shouting loudly, and falling on the French." On both sides combat was "strong and harsh," but, the *Journal* continued, "the Maid and La Hire all of their army joined together and attacked the English with such great force and courage that they caused them to recoil all the way." The bastille of the Augustins was taken, the English locked inside the Tourelles, the "majority of the enemy . . . killed or captured," Jean testified, "and the lords with their men and their Maid remained beside [the bastille] all that night," sleeping armored on the ground, Joan happy for the excuse to stop limping. When she'd dismounted to enter the Augustins on foot with her jubilant infantry, mostly commoners like herself, she'd stepped on a *chausse-trappe*, a little bit of mischief designed to sprain an ankle or pierce a foot. Known today as a "caltrop" (from the Latin *calcitrapa*, or foot trap), the weapon was a simple one, four iron spikes arranged so that three formed a tripod base and one projected upward, waiting for the tread of man or beast, penetrating that much more deeply when a foot or hoof struck it while running. Intended to slow the advance of both infantry and cavalry, *chausse-trappes* were strewn over battle-fields, not so lowly a contrivance that images of them weren't included in coats of arms as a symbol of resistance.

"Get up early tomorrow, earlier than you did today," Joan told Pasquerel before retiring. "Keep close to me all the time. For tomorrow I shall have much to do, more than I ever had, and tomorrow the blood will spurt from my body above my breast."

Having decided that their unexpected success rested on what had turned out to be a surprise attack, in that the English would never have expected the French to take such a suicidal gamble, the captains met to review their position at the end of the day, again excluding Joan. Given the size of the English army relative to the French, whose one significant victory was so impossible that only a fool would expect another like it, the council decided that the French would pause to rest and send out spies and then fine-tune their battle plan with the secrets they gathered, the only way to match the might of a larger army. "Seeing that the city is well-stocked with provisions, we shall very likely be able to hold Orléans until the King sends aid," they told Joan. "The council does not think it needful for the soldiers to sally forth tomorrow." The captains ought to have guessed Joan's response to their temporizing; they'd heard it often enough.

"You have been to your council, and I to mine," she said. "And believe me, the counsel of my Lord will be put into effect, and will endure, while your counsel will perish."

"Behold you scoffers, and wonder, and perish," the Evangelist Luke wrote, summoning the seventh-century BC prophet Habakkuk's apocalyptic message, which resounds throughout the New Testament, proclaiming a cornerstone of Christianity: "The just shall live by his faith," the faithless perish.

The soldiers did believe the Maid, and the dissenting captains were left again with no choice but to follow the lead of an army that would mutiny at their failure to fall in behind her. They saw no point in hurrying a conflagration that was in any case guaranteed, as the English would eventually have to burst from the Tourelles. Caught between Orléans's hive of fevered citizens, every hour more of them, women and children included, swarming over the ramparts with their helmet-splitting rocks and pots of boiling oil or lime, and a French army under a spell of energetic savagery that made their numerical disadvantage irrelevant, the English could wait to make a move until hunger decided their fate. If they could wait for a few days before attacking, Dunois and the others had reasoned, reinforcements might arrive. Still, better to join the Maid in acting rashly than to allow her to publicly pull rank on them by assuming all of their soldiers. Whether or not they were to prevail, the French would trade their lives to outrun the dishonor of failing to keep up with a girl, even if she had bewitched the horse she sat on.

✦

Joan was up by sunrise on the morning of Saturday, May 7, preparing for what would prove the "bloodiest military engagement of the Hundred Years War since Agincourt" just as she would any other day. She made her confession to Pasquerel, she heard Mass, and she received the Eucharist. As the French army had slept in the field, clothed and armored, she had her forces mobilized by dawn and had charged at the English before they'd had a chance to even inspect, let alone repair, the bulwark around the Tourelles, and the *Journal du siège d'Orléans* reported a "spectacular assault during which there were performed many great feats of arms . . . [T]he French scaled the different places adeptly and attacked the angles at the highest of the strong and sturdy fortifications so that they seemed by this to be immortal." Having nowhere to run, the English fought back as desperately as the situation merited, and the French losses were severe as well.

"I myself was the first to plant the ladder against the said fortress of the Bridge," Joan told the examiner, under a rain of arrows, rocks, and cannonballs. "I was raising the ladder, and as I was raising the ladder I was wounded in the neck by a crossbolt"—distinguished from the crossbow by the projectile it launched, which looked more like a dart than an arrow and was discharged by a bow mounted on a stock. The bolt, shorter and heavier than an arrow, fell from above and penetrated the mail between her harness's breast and shoulder plates, its impact great enough to stun and fell her. According to the *Histoire du siège d'Orléans*, the Lord of Gamaches, the same who had called Joan a "little saucebox," "rode up hastily to defend her with his axe, seeing that the English were about to descend from their walls to surround her. 'Take my horse,' he said, and added a generous apology." The *Histoire* was written by J. B. P. Jollois in 1833; Gamaches's vindication may reflect a chivalrous impulse rather than the historian's discovery of fact. Whether or not the captain resigned himself to the peculiar power Joan represented, he would never know that his toehold in history would rest on his proximity to a girl who seized control of not just one but two armies.

The wound did bleed copiously enough to merit Joan's prediction that it would "spurt from my body," and as she was carried to safety, English soldiers were exulting, screaming that they'd "killed the witch!" Once she had been released from her harness to allow for the removal of the bolt, it was clear that, though its head had, as Dunois remembered it, "penetrated her flesh between her neck and her shoulder for a depth of six inches," it had stopped fortuitously short of puncturing a lung or severing a major artery. No eyewitness remembered Joan pulling the bolt from her own breast, and reports of her doing so, like that in the *Chronique de la Pucelle*, are likely apocryphal, Joan's valiant defense of her inviolate body amplifying her virginity. Her confessor wouldn't have replaced heroism with tears, not any more than Dunois would relate the depth of the wound without mentioning that she had taken hold of the projectile's shaft and extracted it herself. Probably, she endured its removal by a medic, whose arsenal of curatives was limited, in the case of flesh wounds, to olive oil and pig's grease. "When some soldiers saw her thus wounded, they wanted to lay a charm on her," Pasquerel testified, "but she refused it, saying,

'I would rather die than do what I know to be a sin, or to be against God's law.'"

Having established Joan's punctilious observance of a scriptural command, her confessor added that "she said she knew she must die one day, but she did not know when, where, how, or at what hour." Joan allowed the wound to be bandaged and afterward confessed to Pasquerel "with tears and lamentations," for each time she returned from battle her conscience carried a new burden of casualties and deaths. Refusing to rest after the bleeding had slowed under the bandage's pressure, she demanded to be re-armored and, despite what would have been an incapacitating if not fatal injury for any other mortal, returned to the front for another six hours of combat, appearing to the enemy as having been resurrected by a supernatural means. Then she told her soldiers "that when they saw the wind blowing in the direction of the fortress, then they would capture it," her page testified.

"Glasdale, Glasdale, give in, give in to the King of Heaven!" she shouted at the captain in charge of the eight hundred or so English occupying the Tourelles. "You have called me a whore, but I have great pity for your soul and for your men's souls." Below them, the river burned, the people of Orléans having dragged one of the city's barges under the bridge and set it on fire. "Then," Pasquerel continued, "Glasdale, armed from head to foot, fell into the Loire and was drowned, and Joan, moved to pity, began to weep bitterly for the soul of this Glasdale and of all the rest, who were drowned there in great numbers." The *Journal d'un bourgeois de Paris* provided a funereal epilogue: "Afterwards [Glasdale] was fished up, cut in quarters, and boiled, and embalmed." It was in this reduced and disassembled state that the vanquished waited a week for passage home, to a cemetery across the channel.

What few English survived the battle were taken captive, and the French remained in control of the smoking bridge when Dunois called off hostilities, as beyond the bridge the two armies had been locked in indecisive combat for hours. It was eight o'clock in the evening, and he told the exhausted army to retreat for the night into the city, where they would be fed and allowed to rest.

"Then the Maid came up to me," Dunois testified, "and requested me to wait a little longer. Thereupon she mounted her horse and herself retired into a little vineyard at some distance from the crowd of men, and in that vineyard, she remained at prayer for eight minutes." When she came back, she promised her soldiers, "In God's name, tonight we shall enter the city over the bridge."

"Immediately," Dunois said, Joan "took up her standard and placed it on the edge of the ditch. As soon as she was present, the English trembled and were seized by fear; the soldiers of the King recovered courage and began the ascent, delivering the boulevard by assault without meeting any resistance. The boulevard was thus taken and the English found there were put to flight and all killed."

Jean d'Aulon described the battle's final charge in greater complexity. Retreat had been sounded and was under way, he said, when Joan returned from prayer and saw her standard in the hands of a knight to whom she hadn't entrusted it—as that knight had offered to take a turn carrying what had by then become a heavy burden for her page. When the knight failed to immediately release the banner's staff, Joan, in the ensuing tussle, "shook the standard so vigorously that I imagined others might suppose that she was making a sign to them." According to Jean, the Maid's soldiers had seen a signal where there was none and "rushed together and immediately rallied, and they attacked the bulwark so sharply that within a short time they had taken both it and the bastille, from which the enemy retired."

"The she-warrior," Alain Chartier wrote, "had destroyed the conquered fortresses like a tempest . . . [L]ike lambs to the slaughter, they [the English] were all defeated and finally killed." Clément de Fauquembergue, the same parliamentary scribe who doodled a long-haired girl armed with a sword in the margin of his register, summarized the critical battle as "a maid all alone holding a banner between the two enemy forces."

The English might have decided to relax their hold on Orléans only briefly, expecting Fastolf and reinforcements; they might have decided to refocus their efforts on towns with stone fortifications that couldn't be burned away from under their feet. They might have attributed their failure to overcome the French to exhaustion and concluded that there was no choice but to allow the army to recover its strength. But the Duke of Bedford's memorandum to his nephew Henry VI, England's seven-year-old king, for whom he acted as regent, made what had inspired their flight clear enough. "There fell by the hand of God a great stroke upon your people assembled there," caused by "unlawful doubt aroused by a disciple and follower of the fiend, called the Pucelle, who used false enchantment and sorcery, and drained the courage of the remaining soldiers in ways that were marvelous." The Duke of Alençon, who wouldn't join the French fighting under Joan's influence, if not her official command, until she moved on from Orléans to Jargeau, said from what he "heard from the soldiers and captains who were there, they all regarded almost everything that happened at Orléans as a miracle from God; they considered it to have been the work of no human hands but to have come from on high." No matter the source, as one military historian summarized, "the myth of English invincibility was shattered."

It was midnight and the streets were thronged when Joan and her captains did, as she had promised, enter Orléans over the bridge, hastily restored to allow a party of knights to pass through the city's main gates, as no French citizen had done since before the siege. "Paid, forty sous for a heavy piece of wood obtained from Jean Bazon when the Tourelles were won from the English, to put across one of the broken arches of the bridge," the city's 1429 account book records. A fisherman, Jean Poitevin, received "eight sous for having beached a chaland," or barge, under the bridge, and the team of carpenters who had feverishly repaired what they could of the bridge were rewarded with sixteen sous "to go and drink on the day the Tourelles were won."

Every church bell in Orléans was ringing as Joan materialized from out of the dark, she and her white standard polished by torchlight. Night had fallen to lend the spectacle a theatricality impossible in daylight hours. Again the populace exalted her, straining toward the light that fell on their virgin warrior astride her white horse, "giving wondrous praise . . . especially above all to Joan the Maid," as recorded for posterity the *Journal du siège d'Orléans*. So many bells, enough ringing even for Joan. When they fell silent, the clergy led the people in singing "Te Deum laudamus"—a fourth-century hymn of praise. "All the earth doth worship thee . . . To thee all Angels cry aloud; To thee Cherubim and Seraphim continually do cry, Holy, Holy, Holy."

⊕

"He was transfigured before them, and his face shone like the sun, and his garments became white as light," "glistening . . . as no fuller on earth could bleach them." "And when they lifted up their eyes they saw no one but Jesus only."

The transfiguration is singular among the Gospel miracles. In every other instance, it is Jesus who effects change in others: people, a herd of swine, a fig tree cursed and "withered away to its roots," water changed to wine, and wine to blood. In this one instance, Jesus himself is changed, anointed with light before—or by—his onlookers' eyes. It was dark, past nightfall on the mountaintop where he had taken his disciples to pray and where, with their willing spirits and weak flesh, they'd fallen asleep. Suddenly awakened, they saw "the appearance of his countenance was altered, and his raiment became dazzling white." The unnatural brilliance is associated with mystical experience in both New and Old Testaments, blinding Saul and remaking him into Paul on the road to Damascus, when "suddenly a light from heaven flashed around him. And he fell to the ground and heard a voice saying to him, 'Saul, Saul, Why do you persecute me?' And he said, 'Who are you, Lord?' And he said, 'I am Jesus.'" When Moses received the Ten Commandments, a cloud descended over Mount Sinai. From it God spoke, and when the prophet returned to his people, "Moses did not know that the skin of his face shone because he had been talking with God." On the mountain of Jesus's transfiguration, "lo, a bright cloud overshadowed them [the disciples], and a voice from the cloud said, 'This is my beloved son, with whom I am well-pleased; listen to him.'" As he did for John the Baptist, God identified Jesus to his followers as the Messiah, bathed him in unearthly radiance, and bade them take heed. Jesus was a holy messenger, and so was the Maid of Orléans, resplendent in her circle of light.

"O unique virgin, worthy of all glory and praise, worthy of divine honors, you, pride of the kingdom," Alain Chartier wrote, "you lamp, you light, you pride not only of the French but also of all Christians."

Intent as she was on how her deeds were received by God and his angels, Joan hadn't paused to consider the mortal response, which in any case her vocation rendered irrelevant. "Master Pierre de Versailles," one of Joan's examiners at Poitiers, "was once in the town of Loches in the company of Joan," where he observed "that the people threw themselves before the feet of her horse to kiss her hands and feet." Pierre "said to Joan that she did wrong in allowing such things which were not suitable for her and that she ought to distrust such practices because she made men into idolaters."

"In truth," Joan replied, "I would not know how to protect myself from such things, if God does not protect me."

Jesus inspired the same hunger; his steps were dogged; his clothes were unraveled by countless hungry hands. "And all the crowd sought to touch him," Luke wrote, "for power came forth from him and healed them all."

People came to her home, Marguerite La Touroulde remembered, "bringing paternosters [rosaries] and other holy objects for her to touch." Joan laughed at the requests. "You touch them!" she said to Marguerite. "They will be as good from your touch as from mine."

Jesus not only attracted but cultivated his followers' attention and feverish adulation with public miracles. Each crossed the threshold from gossip to that of broadcast—an earthbound mortal confined and magnified by celebrity, a leader summoned from the underclass in fulfillment of prophecy, a peasant without regard for mortal measures, moving among the power elite, undaunted, cloaked with the arrogance of the consciously anointed. Jesus, like Joan, was a messiah as political as the prophecy that summoned him, promising salvation, deliverance from an enemy, and preaching love and violence. A king, humble and riding on an ass, a girl leading an army from the back of a charger, each possessing royalty that cannot be conferred by any hand but God's. Figures of purity, free from sexual stain. Impossible people, alien architects of their own destruction.

The people of Orléans couldn't relinquish her; they had to touch her, lay their charms and beads and rings against her, kiss, if she allowed it, her hands, her feet. By the time she extracted herself from their grasp, her mud- and blood-spattered armor shone again, like new. The reach of countless fingers had polished it as bright as the night was dark.

CHAPTER
VII

A Leaping
Stag

Once Joan escaped adulation, she returned to the Bouchers', where a surgeon dressed her wound and, Dunois recalled, she "had her supper, eating four or five toasts soaked in wine heavily watered, and she had taken no other food or drink that day."

With the single exception of a gift of poisoned carp, the only food Joan is reported to have eaten is the meal commemorated by the Eucharist: the Last Supper at which Jesus broke bread, directing his disciples, "Take and eat; this is my body," and "Drink, all of you," the wine that is his "blood of the new covenant." It seems unlikely that a girl of such vigor and stamina could exist for years on the few mouthfuls of bread and sips of wine reported by Dunois and also Louis de Coutes, who called her eating habits "very abstemious" and remembered that she "often ate only a morsel of bread in a whole day and it was astonishing that she ate so little." What, and how much, Joan ate was significant. "In the Middle Ages," Huizinga wrote, "the choice lay, in principle, only between God and the world, between contempt or eager acceptance, at the peril of one's soul, of all that makes up the beauty and the charm of earthly life. All terrestrial beauty bore the stain of sin." Jesus demanded his disciples choose between him and all the rest of life. Dunois and Louis de Coutes gave testimony more than twenty-five years after the fact, each having told and retold his adventures with the Maid to countless curious listeners, each convinced of the divinity of the girl who every day had called upon them to confess sins redeemed by Christ's blood, to partake of the Eucharist. Any of Joan's comrades might easily associate her most powerfully, or even exclusively, with bread and wine, sparingly served.

When Joan rose, a little after dawn, she learned that the remaining English had already assumed battle formation outside the city's walls. As her wound and its bulky dressing prevented her from putting on plate armor, when she left the city in the company of La Hire, Gilles de Rais, and a few other captains, she wore only a *jasseran*, or light coat of mail fashioned entirely of small rectangular steel plates that overlapped like fish scales. It was a Sunday, and thus permissible for an army to defend itself but not initiate an attack, and Joan didn't even bother to line up her soldiers, but instead held them at bay, "as a trainer holds back a pack of eager dogs." The English, unsure what to make of what looked like a trick, held their ground but didn't advance. Standing at attention, they watched as Joan asked that a portable altar be fetched and saw how, under her direction, the French all bent their heads under the ministrations of her priests, who invested them with fiendish powers of invincibility. Not one of her men was bothering to stand guard, all of them chanting now, voices too distant to discern their sinister meaning. Among the English, rumor had it that her soldiers stole the host and she washed it, as Satan decreed, in menstrual blood.

The *Chronique de la Pucelle* cited the deposition of a French soldier, Jean Champeaux. "Look back and see whether the English are turning their backs or their faces," Joan said to her men and, on hearing they were in retreat, ordered her army, "Let them go, it is not the Lord's pleasure that we should fight them, today; you will get them another time."

"Oh God! What do I see!" an English soldier cries in Schiller's *Joan of Arc*. "She's there, the horror's coming! Rising, glowing darkly, out of the flames of fire, like a spirit from the night, out of the jaws of Hell. Where can I run away to? She holds me in her eyes of fire already."

The English, Jean d'Aulon testified, "departed discomfited and in confusion," leaving behind any artillery that was likely to slow their retreat—not just their heavyweight cannon, but their crossbows and arrows as well.

Suffolk took his corps to Jargeau. The greater part of the army left under the command of Lords Talbot and Scales for Meung, where they expected to meet Fastolf, about whom the most recent intelligence indicated he hadn't left Paris, where he'd gone after the Battle of the Herrings to collect reinforcements, a task that would grow ever more challenging. Though Fastolf provided inspiration for the figure of vanity and cowardice that Shakespeare made of Falstaff, adjusting the real man's name to suggest impotence, his military career was exemplary. No evidence suggests that Sir John, who would finally clash with Joan at Patay, was anything but a great knight and feared leader. Upon hearing rumors of his marching south from English-occupied Paris with reinforcements, the citizens of Orléans had—before Joan arrived—considered abandoning the city. Still, no one wanted to sign up for an unfair fight whose outcome was predetermined by the hand-maid of Satan.

Joan remained in Orléans for two days, resting and allowing her wound to heal. Because frontal attacks were as bloody as they were successful, costly to victor and vanquished alike in terms of fatalities, the French army had been reduced to an estimated two thousand soldiers, not nearly enough to continue to defend Orléans while recapturing all the cities along the Loire currently occupied by the enemy. The violence of the direct charge was part of what terrorized the English, used as they were to haggling over ransoms while pinching off shipments of wine and chasing down spoils of war. If Joan never, as she swore, killed a man, she did inspire a single-minded savagery, and her reputation among the English was as a leader of what both she and her judges termed "massacres."

The *Chronique de la Pucelle* reported that on May 13 Joan left for Tours, where she met the dauphin to extract money and victuals to replenish her forces. Dunois testified that he and some other captains had accompanied Joan to Loches, some ninety miles southwest of Orléans, to convince the dauphin with the mended sleeves to finance the reinforcements they needed. Dunois's is the more credible account, not only because it was given under oath. For Dunois the scene at Loches was less an event of military historic interest than the context of his observing, as few others reported having done, Joan in thrall to her voices. When, upon arrival, the traveling party found the dauphin closeted with his confessor and his advisers, Joan refused to wait for an audience. She knocked on the door of his private quarters, entered before any response was given, and fell on her knees before Charles. "Do not take such long and copious counsel," she beseeched him, "but come as quickly as you can to receive a worthy coronation."

Observing the extravagance of her supplication, Charles's confessor Christophe d'Harcourt, Bishop of Castres, asked Joan if she would "say here in the presence of the King how your counsel appears when it speaks to you." Blushing, she replied to him, "I know enough of what you wish to know, and I will tell it to you willingly."

Dunois said that she answered, in so many words, that "when she was at all unhappy because what she said on behalf of God was not believed, she went aside and prayed to God, complaining to him that the people to whom she was speaking did not readily believe her, and as soon as the prayer to God was over, she heard a voice say to her, 'Daughter of God, go, go, go, I will be your aid.' And, when she heard this voice, she was thrilled and also wished to remain in that state forever. And," Dunois added, "what is more, in repeating the words of her voice, she had surges of wonderful joy, raising her eyes to heaven."

Dunois's is the sole account of what Joan's direct experience of the divine might have looked like. She said her voices spoke a tongue that wasn't human, and they spoke only to her; no one other than she heard them. Outside of hurried appeals for God's protection in battle, or his attention to the mortally wounded begging for absolution, Joan prayed in privacy. Pressed to divulge what it felt like to be consumed by grace, she refused, and the single report of her visions other than Dunois's offered even less description than the Bastard's. The 1643 *Martyrologie des chevaliers* (Martyrology of knights) recognized a resident of Chécy, Guy de Cailly, at whose home Joan spent the night before escorting the convoy of food into Orléans, as having "shared in the visions of Joan of Arc." Though Guy appears to have offered no details about the experience, Sackville-West grants the account "some verisimilitude," based on Charles's having ennobled Guy "a few months later (June 1429) in a document couched in," as she described it, "the strangest language of fantasy and heraldry combined."

Predictably divided on the subject of how to proceed now that Orléans had been retaken, Charles's advisers argued among themselves while Georges de La Trémoille set to work furthering his own agenda, which, at the moment, was to take a little shine off the armored Maid. Under La Trémoille's direction, the dauphin sent out a notice dated May 10, 1429 (preserved among the records of a number of towns), calling upon all citizens of France to give thanks to God for the great victory at Orléans that had been accomplished by captains who, "through their great prowess and courage in arms, and always by means of the grace of our Lord, . . . captured the whole of this fortress," the Tourelles. At the letter's close, Charles gave Joan a perfunctory acknowledgment that left the impression of an afterthought: "Let us also honor the virtuous deeds and wondrous things . . . regarding La Pucelle."

The apparent truth of Joan's outlandish claims had its effects on everyone. If it frightened the English to oppose the Maid, it worried the French to have a supernatural advantage. No matter his personal feelings toward her, La Trémoille was certain the wisest public course was to minimize the Maid's presence in the battles she'd won. By now Joan knew better than to count on the embrace of aristocrats whose vantage allowed them to see her power unfold in earthly terms, unlike the uniformly worshipful commoners who lacked the altitude required to see beyond their infatuation. The nobility's tight embrace of the chivalric code made the idea of retaking Normandy, lost at Agincourt, very tempting, but honor is expensive. Having satisfied the first demand of her vocation, Joan immediately redirected her attention to the second. The way to Reims had to be cleared, and first in line was Jargeau, on the Loire just twelve miles east of Orléans, to be followed by Meung and Beaugency, twenty and twenty-five miles downriver, respectively. Still a commoner, if an uncommon individual, Joan understood better than the nobility how important it was for the dauphin to claim the throne as the indelibly anointed king of France. The people put stock in such rites.

Whether from Tours or from Loches, Charles "commanded the

nobles of all his lands," the *Chronique de la Pucelle* reported, accurately this time, "to provide men and arms for the army which was mustered 'for the cleaning up of the Loire River.'"

The advantage given by the lift of the siege boosted recruitment for the French and did the opposite for the English. Unaccountably, the ever-imminent-never-materializing Fastolf had yet to leave Paris with his army of four thousand, dallying there from May 4 until June 8, and, once his reinforcements had mobilized, approached the front very slowly, "fatigued, demoralized, and defeated" by an adversary he hadn't even seen. Joan's rumored power was as critical to a battle's outcome as Fastolf's had once been, and she would discover that on her ascendency there was more chasing than fighting.

On May 22, Joan was in Selles-en-Berry (now Selles-sur-Cher), a day's journey closer to her target. There she met Guy and André de Laval, sons of Anne de Laval, the widow of Joan's hero, Bertrand Du Guesclin. From Selles, Guy wrote to his mother on June 8, telling her that Charles had introduced him to the celebrated Maid, stirring his friends to envy at his good fortune. She "seemed entirely divine" to him, "her deeds, and to see and hear her." He closed his letter with a reference to a ring Joan had sent his mother three days before their meeting, a gesture Joan had called "a very small thing and that she would willingly have sent you something better considering your recommendation." Probably he referred to a letter Anne de Laval had written to their cousin La Trémoille, affirming her good character. Joan left Selles-en-Berry on May 27, and by the end of the month she was with the Duke of Alençon at his home in Saint-Laurent, where she met her pretty duke's mother, Mary of Brittany, and his wife, Jeanne, whose father was the imprisoned Duke of Orléans. Alençon's wife told Joan that she was "very much afraid" for her husband. By the age of twenty-three, he had already spent five years as a prisoner, having been taken at the Battle of Verneuil and held captive in the tower of Le Crotoy, where Joan would find herself the following year, no ransom high enough to buy her freedom. Joan remained with Alençon and his family until June 6, before at last decamping for Jargeau.

All but one suburb of Jargeau was fortified by a wall surrounded by a deep ditch; the city was a miniature of Orléans. Within was the Duke of Suffolk, William de la Pole, and an estimated seven hundred soldiers. Contemplating the town's five towers from across the Loire, the captains of the French army, among them Dunois and La Hire, debated whether they should attack at all. It was June 10; trustworthy spies reported that Fastolf was at most two days away; the five towers were said to be packed with gunpowder and artillery. Joan pressed for an immediate charge across the city's one fortified bridge, Alençon testified, telling her men "not to fear the numbers or hesitate about attacking the English because God would lead their enterprise."

Having learned of Joan's high-handed manner toward seasoned captains and the resulting conflicts with Dunois, Charles had put his cousin Alençon in command of the forces at Jargeau, which, as Alençon ceded all military decisions to Joan, did put an end to squabbling among the various *chefs de guerre*. Joan tore across the bridge with her troops to recapture the outlying, unprotected suburb, expecting little if any resistance. But the English intercepted, coming out from behind the fortifications in such force that the French fell back—all except Joan, who took up her standard and, as Alençon testified, "set off to the attack, exhorting the men-at-arms to have good courage," and filling them with such purpose and optimism that they quickly drove the English back into their powder-packed towers and installed themselves in the suburb. Upon rising, Joan fired off a bulletin to the English, who could, she said, "surrender this place to the King of Heaven and to the gentle King Charles, and then you can go, otherwise you will be massacred." The message didn't inspire the derision it had in Orléans, the idea of the French entrusting their army to a witch no longer a joke, nor did it result in retreat. The French initiated an intensive bombardment, firing cannon and other gunpowder artillery from across the river and the suburbs until they'd destroyed one tower completely and so compromised the city's walls that by the end of the day Suffolk was asking La Hire to arrange surrender. The parlay excluded all the other French captains, including Joan and Alençon, both of whom lambasted La Hire for presuming to take it upon himself to speak on behalf of France. Both refused to honor the English's terms, which were to remain unmolested in Jargeau for fifteen days, at which point they would leave if the elusive Fastolf hadn't yet relieved them. Joan's conditions were that unless the English left immediately, with their horses, they would remain under attack. The

English stayed; Joan launched a direct assault on what remained of the city's walls and dismissed Alençon's hesitation by reminding him of their unfair advantage. "Oh gentle duke, are you afraid?" she chided. "Do not doubt. The time is right when it pleases God. And one ought to act when God wishes. Act and God will act."

"Terrible and very magnificent," Enguerrand de Monstrelet said of the attack that began on the morning of Sunday, June 12. By dawn the French soldiers, having "placed themselves in the ditch with ladders and other tools necessary to make an assault, attacked marvelously those who were inside," who, the *Journal du siège d'Orléans* reported, "defended themselves most virtuously for a long time."

Joan fought, as before, with her standard. And, as she had at Orléans, she charged forward with the army, climbed a siege ladder, and was knocked to the ground—this time from a blow to her head from above. Fifteenth-century paintings, such as those that constitute Auvergne's *Vigiles du roi Charles VII*, painted c. 1470, depict the type of helmet Joan wore as a *capeline*; it had no visor attached to its domed crown, and its brim was longer in back, to protect the neck, as does a firefighter's. On hitting her helmet, the stone fell to pieces like Saint Catherine's wheel—in some accounts it's the helmet that shatters— and Joan popped up from the ditch calling for more blood. "Our Lord has doomed the English," she exhorted her army. "At this very hour they are ours." Reminded of the source of their commander's fortitude, the French captains dismissed Suffolk's second call for a meeting to establish terms of surrender, and the soldiers redoubled their efforts, and "at that moment," Alençon testified, "the town of Jargeau was taken."

Alençon, who had been enthralled by the Maid from the moment he'd met her, found himself that much more overawed when Joan made good on her promise to his wife. "During the attack on the town of Jargeau, Joan told me at one moment to retire from the place where I was standing, for if I did not 'that engine'—and she pointed to a piece of artillery in the town—'will kill you.' I fell back, and a little later on that very spot where I had been standing someone by the name of my lord de Lude was killed. That made me very much afraid, and I wondered greatly at Joan's sayings after all these events."

The French left Jargeau with a "large garrison of their own soldiers on the bridge," Jean Chartier explained, to keep the remaining enemy trapped within the city they no longer owned and thus prevent Scales and Talbot's forces from joining with Fastolf's four thousand, whenever they arrived. With the addition of twelve hundred troops from Charles, Joan and Alençon commanded an army of about six or seven thousand, recruitment no longer a problem as, according to the *Journal du siège d'Orléans*, "lords, knights, squires, captains, and valiant men at arms," many of whom had avoided battle until the raising of the siege, now clamored to join the crusade. Among the new captains was Arthur de Richemont, the constable of France and thus captain of them all, in name anyway. Raised for the most part in the ducal courts of Burgundy, Richemont was effectively orphaned before he turned ten, when his widowed mother married the English king Henry IV. Still, his fealty was not to the Burgundians, as his bosom boyhood friend was the Valois dauphin, Louis of Guyenne, who died of dysentery in 1415—the same year Richemont was taken prisoner at Agincourt and commenced a five-year exile in England. His mother's marriage to the king granted him uncommon privileges for a hostage, one of these being his marriage to Margaret of Burgundy, the widow of his best friend, Louis, and daughter of John the Fearless. It would be hard to identify a noble whose loyalties were so thoroughly divided, granting him perpetual license to make war from either side. Richemont's only allegiance was to active combat, and in 1424, when the Duke of Bedford refused to grant him command of an army, Yolande found it easy enough to seduce him across the channel. That he was the king of England's stepson married to the daughter of John the Fearless didn't present any ethical or emotional obstacle to his accepting the title constable of France. Upon his arrival at the French court, however, Richemont discovered that La Trémoille, whom he'd counted among his friends, was now an enemy. Yolande hadn't poached France's new constable from the other side to make peace. She'd been shopping for a warrior, and La Trémoille wanted to be rid of warriors once and for all and commit to a course of diplomacy—surrender, in Joan's terms—in which he could control

Charles, easily exciting him to paranoia. By 1427, La Trémoille had convinced the dauphin to ban Richemont from court and, by extension, from joining forces with the army maintained by that court.

Alençon, necessarily loyal to his brother-in-law, the dauphin, testified that just as he told Joan he refused to fight in the same army as Richemont, "news came that the English were approaching in great numbers . . . Then Joan said to me—for I was about to retire because of the lord constable's arrival—that we had to help one another."

It was June 17, 1429, and the dreaded Fastolf and his four thousand soldiers had arrived just outside Beaugency in the Beauce region. To retake the town, another with a strategically important bridge, Joan needed Richemont's troops, and she was innately attracted to a commander as energetically hawkish as she was herself. As Alençon remembered, she introduced herself with what was, for her, admirable tact.

"Ah, my good constable, you have not come by my will, but now that you are here, you are welcome." The two dismounted, and Joan, with her signature chivalric flourish, fell to her armored knees and embraced the captain's.

Guillaume Gruel, Richemont's personal chronicler, recorded the dialogue from his employer's perspective with an evident taste for the dashing. "Joan, it has been said that you wish to fight with me. I do not know if you are from God or not. If you are from God, I do not fear you because God knows my good will. If you are from the devil, I fear you even less."

Though Joan couldn't have known it, not yet, she had already begun to demonstrate the Faustian bargain she represented to the dauphin. It was hardly possible to regret the enemy's flight, but the English hadn't surrendered as a justly beaten enemy—not on mortal terms—and they made it clear to the French that they interpreted their change in fortune as having been accomplished by sorcery, which, as La Trémoille underscored, would invalidate any diplomatic overtures France's improved position might encourage it to make. To enter into a friendly alliance with a powerful captain who had fallen out of Charles's favor was neither wise nor avoidable, but whether or not she knew the cost of disobeying earthly kings, she served a higher liege. Joan needed Richemont's soldiers, an estimated one thousand to twelve hundred reinforcements collected and salaried by Yolande. Charles, whose irrational suspicions La Trémoille continued to cultivate as a matter of habit, regarded Richemont as a foe until 1433, two years after Joan was executed. Yolande, whose grandson the future Louis XI would describe as having "a man's heart inside a woman's body," had at last swept the fat spider away from the throne and out of the castle.

Fastolf arrived at Beaugency to find the French in battle formation—"6,000 soldiers of which the leaders were Joan the Maid, the duke of Alençon, the Bastard of Orléans, the Marshal of La Fayette, La Hire, Ponton [de Xaintrailles], and other captains," according to a Burgundian soldier, Jean de Wavrin.

"Many of the King's men were frightened" of the battle that awaited them, Alençon testified, "and said that it would be a good thing to send for the horses," but, "as I very well know, the English were routed and killed without great difficulty.

"The next day," Alençon continued, "we took the Beaugency road, and in the fields we found more of the King's soldiers, and there an attack was made on the English who held Beaugency. After this attack, the English stripped the city and went into the castle. And guards were placed in front of the castle to prevent their coming out. We were in front of the castle when news came to us that the lord constable was approaching with some soldiers." At the prospect of being barricaded inside a tower until they became desperate enough to walk out into Richemont's army, the English requested a treaty of surrender. In return for safe conduct and a promise not to engage in battle for ten days, the French gave them leave to retreat. Fastolf, whose failures in the face of Joan of Arc represent the single stain on an otherwise exemplary military career, would be remembered here for attacks that were "poorly timed . . . incredibly ineffective . . . badly organized and completely unassisted by archery or gunpowder weapons." Cannon was one thing, its weight challenging transport, but when the English archers hadn't picked up their bows, whether out of fear or disorganization or mutiny, a profound shift had occurred.

It wasn't fifteen years since their mastery of the swift and accurate longbow had determined the outcome of Agincourt, England salting French earth with French blood.

The troops whose command preceded Joan's would have let the English go all the way back to Paris, but Joan, her single-minded focus fixed on Reims, wasn't inclined to let an army she'd trounced, one town after another, escape without attempting to demoralize them even further, thus easing the journey to Reims that much more. "In God's name!" Joan exhorted any captain who hesitated chasing after the English. "We must fight them. If they were hanging in the clouds we should get them. For God has sent them to us for us to punish them. The gentle King shall have the greatest victory today that he has had for a long time. My Counsel tells me that they are all ours."

Her captains might have hesitated, but Joan, the de facto constable of France, had their allegiance and, increasingly, their respect for her abilities. Several spoke of what struck them as the remarkable, even miraculous, rate at which she acquired the expertise of seasoned knights. Thibault d'Armagnac, who fought under Joan at Patay, testified that "in the leading and drawing up of armies and in the conduct of war, in disposing an army for battle and haranguing the soldiers, she behaved like the most experienced captain in all the world, like one with a whole lifetime of experience." Alençon, who had been convinced of Joan's genius upon meeting her, echoed Thibault d'Armagnac. "In the conduct of war she was most skillful, both in carrying a lance herself, in drawing up the army in battle order, and in placing the artillery. And everyone was astonished that she acted with such prudence and clear-sightedness in military matters, as cleverly as some great captain with twenty or thirty years' experience; and especially in the placing of artillery, for in that she acquitted herself magnificently."

What should they do? Alençon asked Joan.

"See that you all have good spurs!"

"When those present heard this," Alençon testified, "they asked her, 'What did you say? Are we to turn our backs on them then?' 'No,' answered Joan, 'it will be the English who will put up no defense. They will be beaten, and you will have to have good spurs to pursue them.'"

Joan ordered a line of march determined by the speed at which individual corps could travel, placing La Hire in the vanguard with the fastest of the cavalry. Along with Dunois, Alençon, Richemont, and Gilles de Rais, she rode with the main body of cavalry and infantry—in sum, six thousand men, according to the *Journal du siège d'Orléans*, all of whom answered to Joan. The English had been marching resolutely north for nearly four hours and had stopped to rest just a few miles south of Patay when their army's rear guard sighted the French cavalry coming up fast on their heels, Joan's heralds galloping before it with a warning for Fastolf.

Perhaps, as a commander whose expertise was field—rather than siege—warfare, Fastolf felt an echo of his former confidence at the prospect of combat on terrain no different from the flat farmland on which he had trounced and humiliated the French just four months earlier. With Talbot under him, he commanded five thousand men, and he knew the military weaknesses of the French. He'd been at Agincourt, called "one of the most lopsided killing orgies in military history . . . that epitomized the recurring pattern of almost all the battles of the Hundred Years War: English discipline and skill ruining mindless French valor." At Agincourt, ten thousand of France's twenty-four thousand soldiers were slaughtered, while England lost only a few hundred men from an army one-quarter the size of France's.

He wasn't running, Fastolf told Joan's heralds; she could expect the English to stand their ground just where they were, about four miles south of the actual town of Patay, neither advancing nor retreating. Reserving the main body and rearguard of his forces, Fastolf sent the "vanguard, supplies, artillery and non-combatants to hide in the woods" adjacent to the field he'd selected for battle. Talbot, according to Jean de Wavrin, was dispatched with "five hundred elite mounted archers" to secrete themselves "between two strong hedges through which he felt that the French would pass." His orders were to hold them off until Fastolf had determined a plan of attack and arranged his soldiers. The ambush might well have granted victory, even to a smaller army, but for a stag flushed from the woods by the rank clamor of the lathered French cavalry, La Hire in the lead, having ridden the French corps hard all the way from Meung, fifteen miles to the south. As soon as the stag discovered itself in a clearing, unprotected, it bolted back under cover and, as fate had it, into the formation of English archers. The animal would have been a red deer, whose habitat spreads across Europe. Among the largest of the deer family, the bull's height approaches that of an elk, and at an average weight of five hundred pounds, the momentum generated by its charge would have provided its antlers with enough thrust to pierce armor. Moving at top speed, the stag couldn't have stopped even had it wanted, and it "uttered a great cry" as it plunged, hooves thrashing, into the formation of English archers. The military glory of England, their nerves on edge at the approach of the witch, dropped their bows and scattered screaming into the woods, where they collided with their own army's hidden vanguard and supplies, the ensuing chaos summoning Fastolf from the field, his troops following in disarray. Among those taken prisoner, Alençon testified, was Talbot, who had accompanied Bedford to France in 1427 and had been forced to give up the boulevard of Saint-Loup at Orléans, after having presided blindly over the skirmish before which Joan ushered her parade of bounty.

Were it not for eyewitness testimony, French and English both, it would be tempting to gather the stag into Joan's flock of undocumented sheep, birds, and butterflies—another creature that migrates across cultures as an archetype that travels between mortal and immortal realms. It is the stag that pulls Artemis's chariot through the clouds, changing sky to heaven. In one Christian legend, a stag draws a hunter away from his companions and deep into the woods, where the sacred beast confronts him, a crucifix emerging, like the single horn of a unicorn, from the center of its head, between its antlers. Illustrated medieval bestiaries identify the stag as an incarnation of the avenging Christ who tramples and destroys the devil, a manifestation of purity and nobility that dates back to the psalms of the Old Testament. The anonymous *Ballade du sacre de Reims*—a coronation ballad—echoes Christine de Pizan's *Ditié de Jehanne* in summoning prophecies of a noble *cerf volant*, a "Flying Stag . . . arising from the pure roots of the beautiful garden of the noble fleur-de-lys," she wrote, tidily sowing the soil of Eden with the royal flower of France.

A military history of the Battle of Patay might diminish the stag's role by lumping it among lightning bolts and other developments beyond mortal influence: "the unplanned, that turns the tide of a battle." One creatively presents the victory that followed its charge as a default. The English soldiers' attention having been diverted from sacred responsibility to irresistible sport, they took off after the animal on an impromptu hunt. Whether the stag was temptation or antagonist, its significance lies outside the study of waging war and belongs to the uncanny. The violent trajectory of an animal chosen to represent Christ precipitated a peculiar chain of events that resolved a decisive battle in under an hour, with minimal losses to the French. As to the enemies of God's chosen, Alençon testified, "four thousand men in dead and prisoners," a tally that included the capture of Talbot, Scales, and other English captains: in sum, a catastrophic loss. And the typical, and typically superstitious, medieval Christian could not help but regard the stag as a manifestation of the divine—or the diabolic.

Although it was almost twenty miles north of the Loire, and although Joan continued to make war after it was won, the Battle of Patay was the decisive victory of the Loire campaign, the culmination of what Orléans's war cry had begun. At its conclusion, the citizens of Janville refused to allow the battered English army back within their city walls, seeing the prudence of giving in to the Maid before she did to Janville what she had done to Jargeau. Because something had happened at Jargeau, where Joan had made her customary offer of clemency upon the surrender to her king, after having promised, according to Perceval de Cagny, Alençon's "master of the horse," a "massacre" to any who dared resist. When her men faltered, Alençon testified, she told them to take heart, for God had damned the English. At the conclusion of what was a definite rout, many more enemy troops had been executed than taken captive for ransom, and, more unusual still, executions continued after the cease-fire. Although it's unlikely Joan had condoned the unnecessary carnage, the bloodlust she aroused wasn't easily switched on and off. As it was her habit to retire after battle to confession, Mass, and the counsel of her voices, she might have been enjoying the company of angels as her men celebrated victory by succumbing to one sin they weren't denied. "Whatever the relationship of religious fanaticism to the savagery," one medievalist summarized, "it did not repress the knightly proclivity for turning war into sport."

From Patay, Joan took her troops to Orléans, where she awaited permission to approach Gien, to which Charles had abruptly moved his court. Within what had very recently been enemy territory, Gien presented a single advantage: its location offered a more direct route to Reims than did Loches—the reason, Joan naturally presumed, for the dauphin's unexplained relocation. Her impatience gathered for nearly a week, during which Charles was closeted with his advisers. When, on June 24, she at last arrived in Gien, she didn't, as she expected, meet the dauphin and from there continue with him directly to Reims but was immediately hobbled by the usual intrigues, each courtier proposing a plan tailored to his own greedy agenda. La Trémoille warned Charles that there were too many cities and towns controlled by the Burgundians, the journey to Reims too risky to undertake. But Joan's argument for making haste to Reims was a pragmatic one. As she said, once Charles "had been crowned and consecrated, the power of his enemy would steadily decline, until in the end they would not be able to harm either the King or the kingdom." She promised Charles that, contrary to La Trémoille's dire predictions, the towns between Gien and Reims would surrender without resistance. How dangerous could the journey be with an escort of twelve thousand soldiers, not counting the limitless forces under Saint Michael?

Charles temporized; Joan assuaged her impatience by composing an announcement of her triumph. The letter was distributed to many cities in the realm, like the one Charles had disseminated after Orléans was freed. A copy remains; it was brought to the city of Tournai, in present-day Belgium, some twenty-five miles east of Brussels. Carried by Thierry de Maubray, a messenger bearing news of the realm, it was "copied and transmitted to the thirty-six 'Banners,' or sections of the city." Referring to herself in the third person, Joan proclaimed to each citizen in the land that within eight days, La Pucelle had "chased the English out of all the places that they held on the river Loire by assault and other means." She listed the enemy captains her army had either killed or captured and closed with a threat couched as an invitation, not so much asking as commanding the recipients' presence at the coronation. "May God watch over you and grant you grace to uphold the just cause of the kingdom of France."

Under the spell of Joan's cockiness, Dunois sent the Earl of Suffolk, taken prisoner at Jargeau two weeks earlier, a note from Gien, "a small piece of paper," he testified, "four lines that made mention of a maid who would come from the oak wood, riding on the backs of archers." All Frenchmen knew the prophecy, and now they knew its fulfillment, but it couldn't hurt to remind an English captain that his losses were ordained, there was no point in struggling.

Joan and her army set out for Reims with the dauphin and his retinue on Monday, June 27, 1429. Cravant, Bonny, Lavau, Saint-Fargeau, Coulanges-la-Vineuse, Auxerre, Saint-Florentin, Brinon, Saint-Phal: all the Loire towns "welcomed the soldier and the Maid, and all made homage to the dauphin," as if years of enemy occupation were instantly undone—a transformation that often required nothing so cumbersome as the movement of troops. The English army had been too small for it to garrison each town it conquered, and those it did were given minimal manpower. As Joan's army approached, sources including the *Chronique de la Pucelle* suggest that most English-occupied towns surrendered without resistance, let alone bloodshed. But Troyes, where Charles's mother had publicly disowned and humiliated him, proved harder to convince. The city's identity was informed by the treaty that bore its name, and it had prospered under Anglo-Burgundian rule. One of the few occupied cities that had been garrisoned, Troyes had time to wait on rescue from the English forces, the dauphin's guarantee of amnesty insufficient to woo its citizens to relinquish the city's keys.

Initially, Troyes's garrison of five to six hundred soldiers inspired the conceit that the town might resist Joan and her army. Like everyone else in the realm, the people of Troyes knew of Joan's victories and their unnatural accomplishment, but not of the magnitude of her

forces, thousands strong, and when they sallied out to discover themselves surrounded by a sea of enemy soldiers, they made an about-
face and drew the drawbridge up behind them. Having been "told
continually by their Anglo-Burgundian leaders that she was led by
a force other than God," after some deliberation they dispatched an
envoy to examine Joan in the form of Brother Richard, a mendicant
friar and disciple of Saint Bernard of Siena. Brother Richard was one
of countless turn-or-burn preachers who emerge from societies whose
apocalyptic beliefs warn of imminent extinction. Jesus was as well.
Cultures preoccupied with death cannot help but dwell on rewards
and retribution, and in Paris a popular preacher could summon a mob
twenty thousand strong, the frenzy of devotion predicting an equally
fierce rejection. In April, Brother Richard had been run out of Paris
and refused entry by several towns between Paris and Troyes, where
he'd found asylum and then adulation. The citizens of Troyes, too,
would send him packing, but for now he retained their faith, and as
Joan testified, "The people of Troyes sent him to me. They said they
were afraid I was not a thing sent from God."

"Come boldly!" Joan said when he drew near her. "I shall not fly
away." Just as a witch could fly, so could holy water set her flesh afire,
and Brother Richard sprinkled it liberally over Joan, who faced him
defiantly in her indecent clothing, feet planted on the earth as firmly
as his own. Joan, on whom the spray of water fell without a sizzle, was
unconvinced of the sanctity of Brother Richard and galled by his presuming to judge her. Still, she didn't waste the opportunity to use him
for what he was worth, "since it was he who was entrusted with the
delivery of the letter that she addressed to the people of Troyes during
the march on Reims, the letter that won their surrender."

> Joan the Maid commands and informs you in the name of
> the King of heaven, her rightful and sovereign Lord, in whose
> service she is each day, that you should render true obedience
> and recognition to the gentle King of France . . . And if you do
> not I promise you and certify upon your lives that we will enter,
> with God's help, all the towns that should belong to the holy
> kingdom and establish a good firm peace there, whoever comes

against us. I commend you to God, may He watch over you if
it pleases him.

Reply soon.

As did every crisis or impasse, the obduracy of the people of Troyes
fractured the dauphin's council. Archbishop Regnault de Chartres,
who would perform the coronation, felt the king's forces had wasted
enough time on Troyes and ought to proceed directly to Reims before
Joan seized the opportunity to make another stop on her bloody road
show, picking up that many more fanatical hangers-on. The Lord of
Treves, Robert le Maçon, accorded the wisdom of his years, said Joan
should be summoned for her advice, as they owed the past months'
victories to her aid.

"In God's name," Dunois remembered Joan telling Charles,
"within three days I will lead you into the city of Troyes, by love, force,
or courage, and that false Burgundy will be quite thunderstruck." No
amount of gallantry could seduce La Trémoille and his fellow leeches,
but Charles granted Joan's request to answer the Troyens' resistance
with military action. Her troops at the ready, she did indeed amaze
the enemy, who watched her forces immediately "set up all of the
French gunpowder artillery against the walls and prepared for its use,"
moving at what looked like unnatural speed. Beyond the walls, hundreds of other soldiers were making a production of bundling sticks
into a rising mountain of fagots to cast into the city's moat, inviting Joan and all her mortal army to walk over water and position
themselves for attack. Recognizing the folly of continuing to hold out
against what Joan was advertising as the imminence of one of her
infamous massacres, the Troyens delayed capitulating for a single day
before sending an envoy to negotiate surrender. Charles entered the
city with Joan not behind but next to him, carrying her standard, as
they headed up the victory procession, after which "the dauphin dealt
mercifully and without punishment with the Troyens, who quickly
resupplied his army."

According to Alençon's master of the horse, Perceval de Cagny,
the towns between the cities of Troyes and Reims fell with provi-
dential ease. Joan sent her standard ahead of her as the premature

announcement of what was an assured victory for the French, followed by Charles's offer of amnesty to those who submitted to his rule. One of these towns was Châlons-sur-Marne, as near to Domrémy as Joan had drawn since undertaking her quest, and a few of her old neighbors and friends made the ninety-mile journey to see their famous daughter. Among them were her godfather Jean Moreau and Gérardin of Épinal, the Burgundian whose decapitation Joan had nonchalantly suggested as a gesture of leave-taking. One of the citizens of Domrémy who made the effort required to testify on her behalf at her nullification trial, he recounted her warm reception of him and his traveling companions and remembered what in retrospect he considered a prophecy. But it didn't require clairvoyance to see that no matter how great her volunteer army, Joan had enemies at court; or that Charles was as devious as the courtiers who curried his favor. She feared but one thing, she told Gérardin, and that was treachery.

Schiller gives Joan's presentiment the form of a sinister Black Knight, who, she says, "enticed me from the battlefield."

"Look over there!" the Black Knight says, his face hidden behind his visor. "There rise the towers of Reims, the goal you fought for and your journey's end. The vast cathedral glitters in the light, which you will enter in triumph, and where you will crown your King, and so fulfill your vow. Do not go in there! Turn back! Hear my warning!"

From Châlons-sur-Marne, Joan set out with Charles and his cortege for Sept-Saulx, the château of Archbishop Regnault de Chartres, just fourteen miles southeast of Reims, as close as the archbishop had drawn to the city since its occupation by the Burgundians and his subsequent attachment to Charles's court, where he found an ally in La Trémoille. Regnault's flock hadn't seen him for twenty years when, on Saturday, July 16, they opened the gates of Reims for him, along with Charles, Joan, and an army in want of food and lodging. Upon entering the city to the frenzy of curiosity and welcome she'd come to expect, Joan discovered that the Burgundians, foreseeing the unavoidable, had done their best to strip the cathedral of its sacred objects. Joyeuse, the legendary sword of Charlemagne, identified by

The Song of Roland as the "lance, which wounded Our Lord on the cross," a relic of inestimable value traditionally present at a coronation, was missing. From vestments to chalices and candlesticks, anything of value that wasn't nailed down or too heavy to carry had been snatched as spoils of war. But, "secreted away by monks loyal to the dauphin," the single artifact essential to the transfer of divine right had been hidden and preserved. The Sainte Ampoule had descended from heaven, on Christmas Day 496, transferred from the hands of angels to those of Saint Rémy, bishop of Reims and patron saint of Joan's parish church: Domrémy. With it, he baptized Clovis the first Christian ruler of the Franks, redefining the crime of Christianity as the mandatory state religion. In the miraculously multiplying manner of loaves and fishes—or the Brothers Grimm's "Magic Porridge Pot"—the Sainte Ampoule had never run dry, the vial's contents having hallowed nearly a thousand years' worth of coronations thus far.

A full midsummer moon gave the citizens of Reims that much more time to prepare for an occasion usually months in the planning, and "all night long the city resounded to the blows of hammers and mallets." If it wasn't the pomp of a time of plenty, there was more than enough sparkle and heraldry to gratify Joan and dazzle her parents, who had come to bear witness to their daughter's transformation from disgraced runaway to exalted virgin and *chef de guerre* of all France. At nine in the morning, the exuberant celebrants poured into the cathedral after the dauphin, himself under a guard of eight hundred soldiers. No report includes a description of the day's weather, but it was almost certainly a fine day, bright and clear, as any among Joan's detractors would have pounced on so obvious an indication of heavenly displeasure as lowering, storm-laden clouds. So the sun shone through the great rose window, spraying coins of colored light over the hushed congregants, whose state costumes were typically "ornamented by hundreds of precious stones" and other furbelows. Perhaps La Hire wore the red velvet cape that impressed itself on his comrades' memories: it was covered all over with tiny silver bells. Immediately behind Joan and Charles walked the four appointed guardians of the chrism—the admiral of France, the Lord of Graville, the marshal de Boussac, and Gilles de Rais—followed by Dunois and Alençon, carrying crown and scepter. Joan had petitioned Charles to relax his exile of Arthur de Richemont, who as constable should have been present to bear the ceremonial sword that stood as a surrogate for Joyeuse, but Charles refused, suggesting how tenacious was La Trémoille's hold over him.

Upon reaching the altar, Charles prostrated himself on the floor, and the archbishop did as well, and then the archbishop rose from the dauphin's side to dab the holy oil on his head, chest, shoulders, elbows, and wrists—points of intelligence, passion, and command. "I anoint you for the realm with holy oil," Regnault said, "in the name of the Father and the Son and the Holy Spirit," and the congregants cried, "Long live the king for eternity!" The archbishop prayed that Charles prove himself worthy of the power with which he had been entrusted, and the consecrated king replaced the simple shift he had worn for his anointment with regalia befitting his role as earthly representative of God's rule. "Three gentlemen from Anjou . . . were charged with reporting the ceremony to the Queen, Marie of Anjou, and her mother," Yolande, as Charles had sent his wife instructions from Gien "to return to Bourges since the operation he was launching was a dangerous one." Too, "the royal entourage judged that it was the king alone whose coronation then mattered." Marie would be crowned later in Paris, as were all French queens, in a ceremony to which far less importance was attached. After the crown was placed on the new king's head, "Everyone cried 'Noel!'" the unnamed trio wrote, "and the trumpets sounded in such a manner so that it seemed as though the vaulting of the roof would be rent."

"When the Maid saw that the king had been consecrated and crowned," the Journal du siège d'Orléans recorded, "she knelt before him in front of all the lords standing around them, and she embraced his legs, saying as she cried warm tears, 'Gentle king, the pleasure of God has been executed. He Who wished that I relieve the siege of Orléans and Who brought you into this city of Reims to receive your holy consecration, demonstrated that you are the true king and the one to whom the kingdom should belong.' And there was a great pity from all who saw this." It was a friendly account and ignored expressions inspired by feelings other than sympathy, feelings of those for whom "questions of precedence and etiquette" assumed a "religious significance."

"Was your standard not made to wave above the king's head when he was crowned at Reims?" the examiner demanded.

"No," Joan said. "Not so far as I know."

"Why then was your standard carried into the church at Reims at the consecration? Why yours rather than those of the other captains?"

"It had been present in the perils," Joan said. "That was reason enough for it to be honored."

Called a commoner by men, Joan bore divine heraldry, advertising a status beyond the highest of mortal honors. The spot she claimed was an unprecedented disruption in what was, to the medieval mind, the crucial order upon which human existence depended: an inalterable hierarchy decreed by God. The *scala naturae*, a Neoplatonic concept of a great chain of being, ranked all of creation down "from the infinite Creator to the smallest of his Productions" by way of angels and demons, mortal princes, both lay and ecclesiastical, nobles, and commoners. Below them fell animals, plants, and minerals in order of their ability to answer human needs and desires. The rite of anointing was symbolism choreographed to amplify and make manifest the sacred transaction that cemented a king in his rightful place in the great chain, as most exalted among mortals. *Joan of Arc at the Coronation of Charles VII at Reims* by Jules Eugène Lenepveu (Fig. 22), an academic painter of the same era as Jean-Jacques Scherrer, illustrates how radical a breach Joan had effected. Lenepveu elevates Regnault, Charles, and Joan above the mass of lesser knights and nobles, all three on a blue dais decorated with gold fleurs-de-lis. To the left of the canvas's center, the archbishop places the crown on Charles's head, his eyes cast down on the kneeling king and the king's eyes fixed on the floor below his knees. Joan, armored and wearing a rich red and gold surcoat, stands slightly to the right of the canvas's center, which is claimed by the sword in her right hand, the weapon tilted at the familiar suggestive angle and sanctified by a hilt that transforms its shaft into a cross. She is a solitary figure in the packed cathedral. Her placement on the dais separates her from archbishop and king, removes her from the company of all mortals, and lifts her toward the ranks of stained-glass saints overhead. Her eyes are fixed on three beams of light from a source outside the canvas, a symbol of the trin-

ity, and her surcoat falls aside to expose a perfectly round and seemingly nippled plate of armor—like a single, Amazonian left breast.
The standard whose staff she grasps with her left hand reaches above
all the earthly regalia, and the drape of its white fabric falls behind
her shoulders, its outline suggesting a pair of great white-feathered
wings. Before all of Europe, a virgin dressed as a man and armored as
a knight stepped into the most sacred ritual of her people, fracturing
the patriarchal triumvirate of mortal king, divine king, and the high
priest who provided the liaison between them, a performance that on
a popular level invited the awe reserved for a Demiurge, while igniting
fury in Joan's multiplying enemies among the aristocracy.

"My lord," La Trémoille warns Charles in Anderson's *Joan of Lorraine.* "This girl is ambitious and unscrupulous. She intends to rule
France. In your place." He reminds Charles that her victories on the
battlefield have nothing to do with "tactics, relying entirely on her
personal prestige, the fanatic enthusiasm of her followers."

⊕

Miracles and those who perform them are by definition unnatural, and Joan attributed hers to a god whose favor depended on the
virginity she wore like a badge. By calling herself La Pucelle and wearing men's clothes, Joan directed attention to her veiled genitalia and
held it there. European men's fashion during the late Middle Ages
was both revealing and suggestive. Doublets, short jackets that terminated above the pelvis, were in style, the uncovered groin protected
by a codpiece (the word *cod* is Middle English for scrotum) that not
only accentuated the size of a man's penis but also, as both Brueghel's
genre paintings and courtiers' portraits make clear, suggested tumescence. The fifteenth century marked the height of these accessories'
popularity, as well as their size and decoration, which often verged on
the pornographic. Codpieces were everywhere a girl looked, and only
Joan's richly colored and finely tailored silk velvet *chausses,* or hosen,
conspicuously lacked the addition. As described in the fourteenth of
the seventy articles of accusation initially brought against Joan, she
wore "short, tight, and dissolute male habits" that advertised her singular sexuality, flaunting her power to both summon and crush desire.

Her transvestism was dramatically different from that of the typical cross-dressing martyr, a woman who assumed male dress to pass as a man undetected and thus preserve her chastity. Usually, this attire was a cassock, intended to cloak the entire body of a celibate. Thomas Aquinas pardoned such brave women who, "as a means of hiding from enemies, . . . protected themselves by total, not partial, sex masquerade." Joan was different.

Complete in the androgyny she invented for herself, lifted above hunger, lust, and fear, and beyond the reach of physical laws mortals obey, Joan emerged in an era when all extraordinary manifestations were interpreted and understood only inasmuch as they could be placed within the context of Scripture, a time when the abnormal was regarded with terror and read as an oracle. Contemporaneous chronicles of the Black Death, for example, placed its arrival within the context of the ten plagues God visited on Egypt as punishment for enslaving his chosen people. A letter from the papal court in Avignon explained "how terrible events and unheard of calamities had afflicted the whole of a province in eastern India for three days. On the first it rained frogs, snakes, lizards, scorpions and many other similar poisonous animals. On the second . . . thunderbolts and lightning flashes mixed with hailstones of incredible size." On the third, a "stinking smoke, descended from heaven and consume[d] all the remaining men and animals and burnt all the cities and settlements in the region."

Henry Knighton, an Augustinian canon writing at the end of the fourteenth century, specified cross-dressing as a catalyst for plague, as "whenever and wherever tournaments were held, troops of ladies would arrive dressed up in a variety of extraordinary male clothing . . . Mounted on chargers . . . they abused their bodies in wantonness and scurrilous licentiousness. They neither feared God nor blushed at the criticisms of the people, but were . . . deaf to the demands of modesty." Like Joan, they made manifest what women were directed to hide. Whether wanton or virgin, each parodied, and thus dishonored, men, not only destabilizing their sexual identity, but attacking the foundation of a religion whose adherents were instructed to pray to God as "Father"—for God was not woman but man.

"You stand alone, absolutely alone," Archbishop Regnault warns

in Shaw's *Saint Joan*. "Trusting to your own conceit, your own ignorance, your own headstrong presumption, your own impiety in hiding
all these sins under the cloak of a trust in God." The simple people,
he tells her, "will kiss your hands and feet . . . and madden you with
the self-confidence which is leading you to your destruction. But you
will be nonetheless alone: they cannot save you. We and only we can
stand between you and the stake."

At the closing of the coronation ceremony, "the Maid," Dunois
testified, "who was riding between the Archbishop of Rheims and
myself, said these words, 'Here is a good people. I have never seen
a people rejoice so much at the coming of so noble a king. May I be
lucky enough, when I end my days, to be buried in this soil.'"

"Where do you expect to die?" the archbishop asked Joan, yank-
ing her attention back to what he intimated might be her imminent
demise.

"Wherever God pleases," Joan said. "For myself, I do not know the
time or the place, any more than you do."

"I sometimes heard Joan say to the King that she herself would
last a year and scarcely more," Alençon testified, "and that they must
think during that year how to do their work well."

⊕

Portents of her doom abounded, but Joan didn't stoop to curry
favor. Covert and temporizing, trending toward a gray realm of compromise, politicking was a degrading mire into which she wouldn't
deign to set her armored foot, not for fear of treachery nor fire. It
grew ever clearer, both to Joan and to those who would take it upon
themselves to destroy her, that the coronation had invested the Maid,
not the dauphin, with a new identity, the anointing having "produced
an extraordinary perception of Joan of Arc in France and beyond."
Voices speaking of betrayal to come were not exclusively angelic, but
it was too late to consider what fantasies of revenge an archbishop,
prince among clerics, might conceive in response to Joan's having
upstaged him during a moment of glory that had belonged to him as
much as it had to Charles, each of them outshone, and the king just
about pilloried by the national troubadour.

"You Charles, King of France, seventh of that noble name," Christine de Pizan wrote, "who have been involved in such a great war before things turned out at all well for you, now, thanks be to God, see your honor exalted by the Pucelle who has laid low your enemies . . . in a short time, for it was believed quite impossible that you would ever recover your country, which you were on the point of losing . . . A little girl of sixteen . . . in preference to all the brave men of times past . . . must wear the crown." Christine dated her *Ditié de Jehanne* July 31, 1429. By then, "after an illustrious career," the poet had been in retirement for eleven years and only broke her silence because she couldn't resist celebrating, as one historian put it, "the proof Joan offered of Christine's consistent defense of women from misogyny."

The entire culture of fifteenth-century France was possessed by Joan. As her stock fell with the court, it rose with the populace. The adulation she had already identified as idolatrous, and a danger to her soul, had force enough by now to elevate her beyond the reach of any earthbound bishop. "The famous holy oil they talked so much about was rancid," Charles complains in Shaw's *Saint Joan*. Too old to be of use, it's a dead symbol of a bygone order, while Joan herself has become the object of worship. From pamphlets distributed in Paris to papal broadcasts nailed to church doors in Avignon, from epic poems, sermons, and treatises across the Continent, Charles of Valois and all his court melted away in the heat of Joan's radiance.

After the ceremony, Charles and his entourage and "many other high nobles" retired to the archiepiscopal palace. Joan's name wasn't listed among those who attended the reception. The single source of the guest list is the pro-Burgundian *Chroniques d'Enguerrand de Monstrelet*, whose author might have succumbed to the temptation to deny Joan the sliver of posterity conferred by an invitation to the archbishop's residence. She might have been there, but it would have been easy enough to exclude her, as her status as a commoner provided an excuse for Regnault to bar her from so august a gathering. In either case, Joan had enjoyed enough of the court's costumed spectacle. Knowing she might not have another chance to be with her parents, she was ready to put aside her cloth-of-gold surcoat in exchange for the company of her family and wouldn't have squandered an opportunity to resolve whatever ill feeling remained between her and her father, who was staying, as Hémon Raguier recorded in Charles's account book, as a guest of the king at an inn called the Striped Ass. Sources differ as to whether Isabelle made the journey to Reims; whether she did or did not, her cousin Durand Laxart accompanied Jacques.

Having planned to march on Paris immediately after the coronation, Joan had announced as much to the Duke of Burgundy (Fig. 19) in a grandiose letter sent the morning of the ceremony, when it was clear he would not witness the anointing, a communication in which Joan swung from politesse to insolence and back again, inadequately cloaking her presumption in hollow formalities and suggesting the distraction of a foreign crusade to satisfy an itch for battle: "Great and mighty prince, Duke of Burgundy, Joan the Maid calls upon you by the King of Heaven . . . If you want to make war, wage it against the Saracens."

Medieval Europeans referred to Muslims as Saracens, originally understood to be a dark-skinned people originating in the Sinai Peninsula—Arabs. By the fifteenth century, the term had become a xenophobic catchall for non-Christian peoples, idolaters who worshipped Muhammad and Termagant, a genderless god invented not by Muslims but by Christians, who believed Termagant's rise to be a harbinger of apocalypse. Capitalized, the name was given to the antagonist in popular mystery plays based on familiar Bible stories; by the late sixteenth century, when Shakespeare used it without an uppercase *T*, it had come to mean a shrewish, overbearing woman, another instance of the inescapable urge to associate the female with the diabolic.

Joan's reference to a group of infidels awaiting righteous genocide predicted another letter, one she would send two months before her capture and address to the "heretics of Bohemia," whom she promised annihilation for their apostasy—a maneuver entirely outside the jurisdiction of her vocation, which, as the following months would demonstrate, was where she was headed.

"I pray, beg, and very humbly request rather than demand that you no longer wage war in the holy kingdom of France." The implication that Joan had the right to demand anything of the duke rendered the request considerably less humble, especially as she went on to suggest that his well-being hinged on obeying her, the self-proclaimed messenger of God. "And I would have you know, by the king of Heaven, my rightful and sovereign lord, for your good, for your honor and upon your life, that you will not win any battle against loyal Frenchmen, and that all who wage war against the holy kingdom of France, wage war against King Jesus." She followed the implicit threat by chiding the duke for failing to attend the coronation, which as one of the six peers of the realm he was obliged to do. "I wrote to you and sent letters by a herald, that you should be at the consecration which today, Sunday the seventeenth day of this present month of July, is taking place at the city of Reims."

The other conspicuous absence was that of Pierre Cauchon, bishop of Beauvais, who had visited Reims a few weeks earlier to take part in a Corpus Christi procession, on May 26. When he left the city to return to his diocese, he discovered it in the hands of the Armagnacs, having been swept, during his brief absence, into the wake of victories that followed Joan from Orléans to Reims. Expelled from Beauvais, along with all the rest of the Anglo-Burgundians and those loyal to their cause, he was forced to flee to Rouen, the capital of English-occupied France and the city in which he would preside over the trial that condemned Joan to death.

Cauchon was fifty-eight. His nature was calculating; he'd always known whom he could use. Having followed a conspicuously outstanding academic career as a law student at the University of Paris, he'd ascended the hierarchy of the Church Militant with dispatch and efficiency by cultivating every powerful man he encountered. Appointed *vidame*, or "temporal lord," of the Reims Cathedral in 1412, from that height he gained access to the Duke of Burgundy and began making himself first useful and then indispensable to Philip, through whose influence he would acquire Beauvais's bishopric. The same year Joan was born, the man who would be revealed as her archenemy started acquiring the power he'd need to destroy her. Cauchon, whom Michelet identified as "among the most violent in the violent party of the Cabochiens"—revolutionaries whose 1413 coup d'état aimed against the Armagnacs briefly delivered them control of

Paris—"went straight to where wealth and power were to be found, in England, with the bishop of Winchester, Henry Beaufort, who was the half-uncle of King Henry V. He became English, he took to speaking English," and when Beaufort, who recognized Cauchon's ambition and greed as a reflection of his own, needed an arm long enough to reach into French intrigue, he had its owner firmly under his sway.

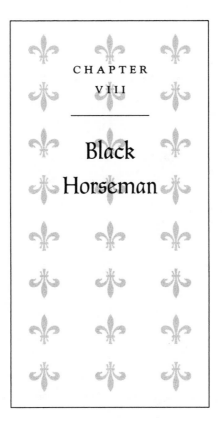

CHAPTER
VIII

Black
Horseman

While Charles lay prone on the floor of Reims Cathedral, the Duke of Burgundy and the Duke of Bedford were conferring in Paris on how best to respond to the most recent stunt by the French, especially given its having been accomplished by so dangerous a means as sorcery. Reims was less than a hundred miles from Paris, whose citizens were growing increasingly restless at the approach of the virgin witch and her fatal spells, a topic that summoned less hilarity and more hysteria with each mile she drew closer to their walls. It had been six weeks since Jargeau fell "in a frenzied and gory assault," and rumors had traveled as they do, more sensational with each retelling, alleging atrocities that much more atrocious.

As the English had installed their bureaucracy in Rouen, an attack on France's former capital wouldn't compromise the administrative arm of the occupation, but even so, to lose Paris, the uncontested jewel of Europe, would be a morale-destroying reversal. To lose it to a witch would be an unprecedented abomination, a manifestation of the devil's might. English-occupied Paris was preparing for a battle it couldn't afford to lose, Joan's plan to immediately take the city stymied first by the newly crowned king's obligatory round of fetes and then by his departure on Thursday, July 21, for Corbeny. Seventeen miles northwest of Reims, Corbeny was the site of the abbey of Saint Marcouf, patron saint of the scrofulous. The king and his retinue remained there through July 23, when Charles fulfilled his duty in "touching for scrofula," known during the Middle Ages as the King's Evil because the power invested in a new sovereign's freshly anointed hand was believed to cure the unsightly tubercular infection of the lymph nodes in the neck. Inevitably, hundreds of other ailing pilgrims came as well, bearing other diseases. All received a "touch piece" as a souvenir of Charles's ministration and were directed to keep the medals hung where they'd been placed, around their necks. The implicit message was that to remove them was to sever contact with the life-sustaining divine, even when that contact was a degree removed, as more than a few post-plague monarchs avoided communing with an unwashed populace and chose instead to touch the coins to be distributed or pass a jeweled hand and mumbled prayer over a sack of the things. Typically stamped with an image of Saint Michael slaying Satan in the form of a dragon, touch pieces were in essence amulets to ward off disease, their origin in what James Frazer called "sympathetic magic," a system of superstitions whose "law of contagion" assures those who practice it that holy properties are transferred by touch. The misapprehension is so primitive as to predate logic—a limbic wish universal to the species. Though the Church would have objected to the analogy, aboriginal peoples in Polynesia and elsewhere practiced the converse of the Christian rite, believing that were a tribesman to accidentally brush against a sacred chief and fail to perform a subscribed ceremony "for the purpose of removing this sacred contagion," he would "swell up and die, or at least be afflicted with scrofula or some other disease."

Touching for the King's Evil guaranteed a long day, not so much for Charles, inclined to linger wherever he was the center of attention, as for Joan, restless whether in or out of the public eye. Increasingly desperate to embark on the remainder of a vocation she now saw, and presented, as unfulfilled, she told Alençon she'd "had four missions: to expel the English; to have the King crowned and anointed at Reims; to free the Duke of Orléans from English hands; and to raise the siege the English had laid to Orléans town." The duke remained in England; the English remained in France: she had much to accomplish in a year Charles was forcing her to fritter away. Alençon's testimony was given from a remove of twenty-seven years, by a man overwhelmed by his first sight of the Maid, under whose command he remained until forcibly removed by the king, a man who had heard Joan say innumerable things for months on end. With respect to Joan's stated vocation, he is a less reliable source than Seguin Seguin, the consistently clear witness from Poitiers, whose firsthand experience of Joan was limited to the beginning of her public career. Seguin identified only "two reasons, for which she had been sent by the King of Heaven: one was to raise the siege of Orléans, the other to lead the King to Reims for his anointing and coronation." When she was examined at Poitiers—only four months earlier—Joan had yet to raise the siege or escort Charles to Reims. She hadn't looked beyond the two mortally impossible challenges that lay before her. Now, having accomplished what God asked, she had no defined quest on which to fix her purpose, and she was not only uncomfortable without a concrete goal but also unmoored at the apex of her fame. Joan's voices had banished the girl who'd lived the simple, anonymous life of a farmer's daughter. That girl had been thoroughly and irretrievably eclipsed by the identity Joan forged to answer God's call: the Maid, a virgin heroine whose narrative hinged on making holy war on France's enemies and winning with the force of heaven on her side. She still had France's enemies to fight, but the path to victory wasn't illuminated by the bird's-eye view of angels. Saints Catherine and Margaret no longer came to her with names of people who would aid her cause or places where sacred swords were hidden. An intimate of the king's, she'd outgrown such help, and the discourse between Joan and her voices had changed. What began as her responding to their direction had become her appealing to them for advice and for permission the king withheld.

"If my Voices do not answer, if no injunction is laid on me, then I cannot stay here. I must arm again, and find the enemy, and fight as before," Joan says to God in Anderson's *Joan of Lorraine*. "I have courage to die, but not to die thus, in small, sick ways, daily." Shaw portrays her as an addict of war, seeking its thrills. "Oh, dear Dunois, how I wish it were the bridge at Orléans again! We lived at that bridge . . . it is so dull afterward when there is no danger: oh, so dull, dull, dull!"

"You will miss the fighting," La Hire agrees. "It's a bad habit but a grand one, and the hardest of all to break yourself of."

As "the medieval Western European conception of the ideal military commander placed far greater stress on the commander's moral qualities than on his technical competence in planning and fighting battles," Joan's rectitude afforded her the deference of the majority of the French captains. In the case of Paris, there wasn't one captain who didn't share her conviction: retaking Paris was key to cementing Charles's rule. Once France's rightful capital, Paris, had been restored, the English would be forced to retreat across the Channel. The key was to mobilize and attack swiftly, before the English had time to pack a few thousand more longbowmen within its city walls, recognized throughout Europe as the largest and strongest—almost thirty feet high, topped with wall walks, and punctuated by rectangular towers that rose high above the walks. A population of 200,000 made Paris an enormous city, with six points of entry protected by "massive gate houses . . . with angular towers, arrow slits, gun-ports, murder-holes, portcullises and drawbridges built into them" and enough room to accommodate hundreds of soldiers within them. France had but one advantage to seize—time.

"What voices do you need to tell you what the blacksmith can tell you," Shaw's Joan demands of the feeble sybarite the playwright makes of Charles, "that you must strike while the iron is hot?"

From the abbey at Laon, king and courtiers decamped to Soissons, where they lingered, twenty-five miles closer to Paris, until July 28. Unable to wait even a day longer before underscoring Charles's arrival at legitimate rule with a show of force, on the twenty-ninth Joan secured permission from the king to line up her soldiers, as many as six or seven thousand, at Château-Thierry, about halfway along the sixty-mile route from Reims to Paris, where she kept them at the ready all day, in battle formation, in hopes that "the duke of Bedford would come to do battle." He never did, as the king, who had gone on to Provins, must have known he would not. La Trémoille had been negotiating an armistice, if not the indefinite peace that would require Charles's capitulation, since June 30—two and a half weeks before the coronation. On that day, well in advance of Joan's bellicose letter to the Duke of Burgundy, La Trémoille had arrived at the duke's court in Dijon to begin talks that resulted in the duke's dispatching an envoy to the coronation with a letter intended for Marie and Yolande "expressing optimism that the King would conclude a treaty." Had Joan, who understood the cost of even a day's inaction, any presentiment that she'd embarked on "eight months of drifting about with the King and his council, and," as Twain called it, Charles's "gay and showy and dancing and flirting and hawking and frolicking and serenading and dissipating court—drifting from town to town and from castle to castle," she would have been that much more impatient with the fairy-tale procession described by Michelet: "The expedition seemed but a peaceful affirmation of ownership, a triumphal journey, a prolongation of the celebration at Reims." With magical ease, "the paths were made smooth before the king, the cities opened their gates and lowered their drawbridges," and Joan complained.

While La Trémoille finagled offstage, composing ententes in anticipation of forthcoming signatures, the king did his diplomatic best to avoid conflict with Joan by means of conciliatory gestures intended to distract her from warmongering. On July 31, Charles forever exempted the citizens of Domrémy and Greux from taxation, an entitlement they enjoyed until the French Revolution swept away all such indulgences, and in early August, after following the wide berth Charles made around Paris to Provins, still fulminating over a putative truce about which she, *chef de guerre*, was not consulted, Joan received the much better consolation of René of Anjou, Yolande's son, at last joining the French army. Whatever small internecine coup had delivered René to Joan suggests Charles's mother-in-law had not withdrawn her support of the Maid in response to the unwelcome communication she received from the duke.

Having received René's arrival as a portent that God remained with her army, Joan couldn't resist letting off a war whoop in the form of an open letter to the people of Reims. "Joan the Pucelle sends you her news and prays and requests that you do not have any doubt about the merit of her cause that she is waging for the blood royal. And I promise and certify that I shall never abandon you so long as I live. And it is true the king has made truces with the duke of Burgundy," she wrote, but "no matter how many truces are made like this, I am not at all happy, and I do not know if I will keep them. But if I do it will only be to protect the honor of the king, and also that they do not take advantage of the blood royal." Whether or not an accord had been signed—and there was every reason to keep Joan in the dark with respect to statecraft—for as long as she was kept from active military engagement, the unofficial truth was as good as a truce. After reassuring the citizens of Reims that her first allegiance was to the blood royal—albeit a qualified fealty that allowed her to ignore the court's political efforts—Joan closed by asking them to "let me know if there are any traitors who wish to harm you, and as soon as I can I will drive them out . . . Written this Friday, 5th day of August, near Provins, in a camp in the fields on the way to Paris."

On August 7, the Duke of Bedford—John of Lancaster, regent of France—responded to news of the coronation for both himself and the Duke of Burgundy by issuing a challenge to Charles and his forces to meet them on the battlefield. The letter was not a pro forma provocation to war. Its value was as propaganda; for this reason the dukes dispatched it from Montereau, the town on whose bridge the Duke of Burgundy's father had been assassinated ten years earlier. Charles did, the two dukes announced, "without cause entitle yourself King" and "wrongfully made new attempts against the crown and lordship of the most high and excellent prince, my sovereign lord Henry, by the grace of God natural and rightful king of the kingdoms of France and England . . . And you are seducing and abusing ignorant people, and you are aided by superstitious and damnable persons, such as a woman of disorderly and infamous life, dressed in man's clothes, and of immoral conduct, together with an apostate and seditious mendicant friar . . . both of them . . . abominable to God." Charles was to meet the English "in the field in the country of Brie," or anywhere in the Île-de-France, "in person, bringing the deformed woman and the apostate cited before, and all the perjurers and other force that you wish and can muster." Until now, they told Charles, they had shown uncommon generosity to a pretender whose "fault and connivance" were to blame for "that most horrible, detestable and cruel murder . . . committed, against every law and the honor of chivalry, against the person of our late very dear and well beloved father"—John the Fearless.

That the dukes threw down the gauntlet even as they negotiated for a cease-fire suggests that events were unfolding as Joan predicted. The English weren't looking for peace. They'd vacillate, contradict, haggle, and protest to prolong the cease-fire and buy as much time as possible for Paris to ready itself for attack. As Joan told Charles, "Peace was to be found only at the tip of a lance."

Joan and her army reached Montépilloy on August 14, having passed through Coulommiers, La Ferté-Milon, Crépy-en-Valois,
Lagny, and Dammartin, confirming each town's fealty to Charles
without having to resort to force. At Dammartin, however, Joan had
the opportunity to observe the English army "ordered in a good formation and placed in an advantageous position," as reported by the
Journal du siège d'Orléans, and she saw as much as she could of them
the next day, August 15, when the French awoke to discover Bedford
had mobilized his troops in the dark, anticipating a battle with the
French army on the flat, dry fields between Montépilloy and Senlis,
where the French were bivouacked, about thirty miles north of Paris's
walls. Bedford had also made Philip, Duke of Burgundy, the governor
of Paris, "so that a prince of the blood royal could be said to exercise political authority over the capital of France." The English had
assumed the same formation as they had at the Battle of the Herrings,
but the day was so hot and the earth so parched that neither army
could see the other for all the dust hanging in the air between them.
Joan had but six or seven thousand soldiers to Bedford's eight or nine
thousand, but the outsize confidence of her army made up for the difference, and a few peripheral skirmishes couldn't obscure the fact that
the opposing armies were at a stalemate. The English squatted behind
their defenses, waiting for Joan to lose her patience, order a charge,
and impale her cavalry on their portable rampart of spikes. Charles
and La Trémoille "rode about the battlefield with the duke of Bourbon," and Joan lost her patience and used herself as bait to tempt the
enemy. Knowing how much they would prize her capture, she placed
herself at the very front of her army's vanguard, leading her men "as
close as the shot of a culverine [cannon]," according to an eyewitness account from the Berry herald, Gilles Le Bouvier. Given Joan's
repeated insistence that she'd rather die than fall into the hands of
the English—as both the trial record and the nullification witnesses
attest—and given what happened once she did fall into those hands,
Joan's decision, perhaps more impulsive than strategic, to insert herself into so needlessly perilous a situation betrays how desperate she
was growing. "A bad habit," Shaw calls Joan's thirst for war, but it

was worse than that. She wasn't just addicted to battle; she was adrift without it.

But the English left her unmolested. She announced she would allow them the privilege of drawing up their lines while she and her troops withdrew until such time as they said they were ready. And still they didn't venture out from behind their defenses. The day's single gratification was that La Trémoille fell off his horse, and such was his girth that it took his entire entourage to get him back in the saddle of the unfortunate beast below it. Two years after Joan was executed, his enemies at court failed to assassinate him when "his assailants' daggers cut only fat."

Joan waited until dusk to release her men to return to camp for the night, unaware of the betrayal the following day would bring. On August 16, the archbishop of Reims came to Paris with Raoul de Gaucourt and other dignitaries to greet Philip in person with the news that Charles was willing to accept responsibility, and make reparations, for the murder of John the Fearless. In return for Burgundy's neutrality, Charles agreed to surrender four cities that had only just promised him fealty: Compiègne, Senlis, Creil, and Pont-Sainte-Maxence. By the time he arrived, all that remained of the English was a circle of holes where spikes had been pulled up and a river of hoofprints and wheel tracks hastening toward Rouen, where Bedford had taken his army. Joan celebrated the outcome of Montépilloy as a rout, presenting it as a partial fulfillment of her promise that the king's approach to Paris would be like that to Reims, the enemy one by one relinquishing all those cities that belonged to their rightful king. If she understood that her king had betrayed her, she didn't disclose it to any witness. But she couldn't help but recognize how gingerly was the Armagnacs' approach to Paris, especially measured against the accelerated pace of their victory march to Reims. August 17 predicted further frustration, when Charles discovered how luxurious were the royal apartments in Compiègne, whose citizens welcomed him, unaware that he'd only just offered them up in a negotiation returning them to the enemy. Newly ensconced, Charles made no effort to bring himself to leave. "The Maid," Perceval de Cagny, Alençon's master of the horse, reported, "was deeply grieved that he wished to extend his stay."

"We have feasted in Campiegne [sic], Senlis, and Beauvais, and we must feast in many more if the plans hold," she prays in *Joan of Lorraine*. "But, O King of Heaven, the food is bitter. It is bought with money the King has accepted for provinces and cities . . . And my Voices have said nothing . . . they have not spoken, they are silent."

While Charles enjoyed the privileges of his new status, the English purchased Brittany's neutrality with "the unprecedented offer of the county of Pitou" and held out the title constable of the army to Richemont, along with the honored position's clout, an invitation that, had he accepted it, would have included the distinction of having become the highest-paid mercenary in the Hundred Years War. Though he refused the English, he also "stayed away from the new king and even, unfortunately for her, from Joan," who appealed to Alençon when Charles evaded her requests to initiate hostilities. "My fair duke," she said, "equip your men and those of the other captains. By my banner, I want to go see Paris from closer than I have ever seen it." On August 28, Charles signed a truce of four months with Philip, Duke of Burgundy, and Joan was now just seven miles north of Paris, at Saint-Denis, where she had been for two days, with the three or four thousand men accompanying her and Alençon. Joan's refusal to wait for a command from the king had effectively split the French army. Captains were unwilling to follow her if it meant La Trémoille would arrange for their exile from court: Richemont's case had provided an instructive example. Six weeks had passed since Charles's coronation, and Joan, the instrument of God's will, had lost at least half of her men, and most of the faithful who remained were soldiers whose bankrupt king hadn't ever paid them wages to join his army. They fought under Joan in the expectation that God would reward their valor and service.

By the time Joan approached her target, Charles had been crowned for seven weeks, and "the defenses of Paris were strengthened . . . boulevards were constructed in front of the gates, houses built next to the walls were knocked down, gunpowder weapons were mounted and stones were gathered . . . 1,176 cannonballs . . . delivered to the gates of Paris . . . and placed near the city walls." Between Joan's forces, stationed at Senlis, and the walls was a moat, the moat surrounded by a trench. The English army, eight or nine thousand strong, stood between this trench and their characteristic fence of sharpened stakes aimed at the cavalry's advance, a liberal peppering of *chausse-trappes* awaiting the foot soldiers.

Joan spent nearly two weeks skirmishing around the walls of Paris, whose fortifications were built, as one military historian put it, "as much to intimidate any enemy into *not* attacking as . . . to defend against any onslaught." Without Charles's permission to mobilize, it was all the fighting she could get away with, and in any case its purpose was to provide an excuse to reconnoiter. By September 8, when Charles at last gave his wan go-ahead, she was poised to attack the point she'd determined most vulnerable, the Saint-Honoré Gate, on the Seine's right bank, some sixty feet wide and thirty feet high, based on archaeological evidence. "They began by bombarding the walls with their gunpowder weapons and by throwing large bundles of sticks, wood, carts, and barrels into the moat," over which Joan was the first to walk, entering "near to the Pigmarket," Alençon's master of the horse, Perceval de Cagny, wrote. "The attack was hard and long and it was a marvel to hear the sound and noise of the cannon and couleverines which those inside fired at those outside." The Armagnac Perceval claimed "not any man was killed or was wounded who was not able to return to his side and his tent without aid," which was almost certainly untrue. Clément de Fauquembergue reported a great number of casualties, and fatalities, by gunfire. The *Journal d'un bourgeois de Paris* "happily estimated the Armagnac casualties at 1,500." The men of their party were "so full of great error and foolish trust that on the advice of a creature . . . in the shape of a woman—who this was, God knows"—they believed "they would certainly win Paris by assault" and "would all be made rich with the city's goods." They made what the Bourgeois described as "a very savage attack," during which they "said many vile insults to the Parisians: 'You must surrender to us quickly, for Jesus's sake, for if you do not surrender yourselves before it becomes night we will invade you by force,' Joan said, 'willing or not, and you will be put to death without mercy.'"

"'See here, you whore, you slut,' said one. And he shot his crossbow right at her and it went right through her leg, and she fled. Another went right through the foot of the man who carried her standard, and when he felt himself to be wounded, he lifted his visor to see to draw the bolt from his foot, and another man shot at him and hit him between the eyes and mortally wounded him." If Joan fled, it wasn't far. Monstrelet, a Burgundian chronicler, reported that she was so gravely wounded she "remained the whole day in the ditches behind a small mound." Both Joan and the standard under which she fought were down; "the attack was very violent . . . and lasted until four hours after noon," when "the Parisians became confident in themselves" and fired "their cannon and other artillery so many times that the army charging at them recoiled." Against the protests of Joan, who had to be dragged away from the trench into which she'd fallen and carried back to camp, Alençon took the opportunity to call a cease-fire and "stopped their attack, and they left." As the French retreated, the Parisians "fired into their backs, which was very terrible. Thus it was put to an end."

But on September 9, "encouraged by the arrival of the count of Montmorency and fifty to sixty" knights, all of whom had "defected from the city, wishing to fight with her and the French army against their former allies," Joan sent for Alençon and prepared for battle, despite what was a significant wound, which took, she testified, five days to heal, by which she meant that it had stopped bleeding; weeks later she was still suffering the injury's effects. But they hadn't a chance to assemble for battle before René of Anjou and the Count of Clermont arrived, both envoys of Charles, who demanded Joan and Alençon report to him in Saint-Denis, where, "over the vehement objections of Joan, Alençon, and others," Charles said there were to be no further attacks, as he "saw that the town of Paris was too strongly fortified." "And thus," Perceval de Cagny wrote, "was broken the will of the Maid and of the king's army."

⊕

"If I had not been wounded, I would not have left. I was wounded in the trenches before Paris, after I left Saint-Denis."

"Was that not the feast day of the Holy Nativity of Our Lady?" the examiner asked Joan of the day she initiated the assault.

"I think it certainly was."

"Do you think it was right to attack the town of Paris on the day of the Festival of the Blessed Mary?"

"It is good to observe the Festival of the Blessed Mary."

"Do you think it was a good thing to do, to make war on a holy day of obligation?"

"Pass on," Joan said.

"My Father is working still, and I am working," Jesus said to the Jews who condemned him for healing on the Sabbath.

"And this was why the Jews persecuted Jesus," the Evangelist John explained. "This was why the Jews sought all the more to kill him, because he not only broke the sabbath but also called God his own Father, making himself equal with God."

For "he said to them, 'The Sabbath was made for man, not man for the Sabbath; so the Son of man is lord even of the Sabbath.'"

The basilica at Saint-Denis protected the burial vaults of nearly every French king and held an embarrassment of relics, the bones of earthly rulers who in death, as in life, were petitioned for political favors. The site—rather than Reims—of queens' coronations, the abbey church had great significance for France, and thus for Joan as well. Saint-Denis's heraldry, a blue ground sown with fleurs-de-lis, would provide the background for the coat of arms she would be given upon her knighthood; hers included a sword and crown (Fig. 25). Not surprisingly, Joan withdrew into its sanctuary, where she remained far longer than the average supplicant, long enough to draw the attention of bystanders and thereby offer her persecutors another opportunity to make use of rumors spread by her enemies.

"What arms did you offer to Saint-Denis?"

"It was a whole black suit of armor,* for a man-at-arms, with a sword. I wore the suit at Paris."

"To what end did you make an offering of these arms?"

"It was an act of devotion, such as soldiers perform when they are

---

* Black armor, like white, indicated rank. The less refined the metal composing its plates, the blacker it was considered to be. Joan's own armor was white not only for its lack of ornamentation but also because its plates were made of metal pure enough to sustain a polish, and thus more expensive to maintain as well as purchase.

wounded. I had been wounded before Paris, and so I offered them to Saint-Denis."

"You did this so that the arms might be worshiped."

"No. Because it was the war-cry of France—"

"At Saint-Denis in France you offered and deposited in the church in a high place the armor in which you had been wounded in the assault on Paris, so that it might be honored by the people as relics."

"I denied this once before," Joan said.

"Further, in the same town, you had waxen candles lit, and from them poured melted wax on the heads of little children, foretelling their fortune, and making by these enchantments many divinations about them."

"No," Joan said. She'd stayed at the altar for as long as she had to for the counsel she needed and eventually received. "My voice told me to remain at Saint-Denis in France, and I wished to remain."

"But you did not remain."

"No. Against my will my lords took me away."

The failure to take Paris, the wound she sustained in her thigh, and the unfortunate timing of these two incidents, on a holy day of obligation she failed to honor, all suggested a rupture between Joan and God; they inspired doubt. As one military historian summarized her predicament, "While Joan had been victorious, others had been able to replace La Trémoille in Charles's favor, but after she had lost . . . and had been badly wounded in the process, the former king's favorite returned to his chief counselor position with even greater power and influence." An unfortunate result of La Trémoille's holding Joan away from the stage of battle, "where he could balk and hinder her," as Twain put it, was that it removed her far enough from the eye of the public that fewer and less detailed sources follow Joan's movements from the fall of 1430 until the spring of the following year, when her capture reignited her celebrity.

In October 1429, Joan was recuperating from the wound in her thigh at Bourges, the capital of Berry, where she was the guest of René de Bouligny, the king's finance counselor, and his wife, Marguerite La

Touroulde, and where she encountered a rival visionary, Catherine de La Rochelle, dismissed by the medievalist Pernoud as a "member of a vagabond lunatic fringe." Without a military operation to occupy her attention, Joan was irritated enough by Catherine's claim of intimacy with a "White Lady covered in gold" who visited her at night that she challenged Catherine to produce the White Lady and sacrificed two nights' sleep to prove Catherine to be the "very uninteresting fraud" Vita Sackville-West judged her. "On the first night, Jeanne, having stayed awake till midnight, evidently got bored and went to sleep. In the morning, when she asked if the 'white lady' had appeared, Catherine assured her that she had indeed appeared," prophesying the discovery of hidden treasure to pay an army that would oust the English, "but that she, Catherine, had been unable to awaken her, Jeanne, adding that the 'white lady' would surely appear again next night."

For this, Joan told the examiner, she prepared by sleeping all day, "so that she might stay awake the whole of the succeeding night. And that night she went to bed with Catherine, and watched all night; but saw nothing, although she often asked Catherine whether the lady would come, and Catherine answered: 'Yes, presently.'" When the White Lady failed to appear, Joan advised Catherine "to return to her husband, to run her household, and to nourish her children," in essence pushing her offstage to join the ranks of the "plenty of other women" who shaped their lives in answer to the demands of men rather than God. "The business of this Catherine is nothing but folly," Joan wrote to Charles—folly that proved expensive to expose, however, as "Catherine later reciprocated by testifying to the ecclesiastical court at Paris that 'Jeanne would have left her prison by the aid of the Devil if she had not been well guarded.'"

From Bourges, Charles sent Joan on the fool's errand of besieging Saint-Pierre-le-Moûtier, more village than town, but an expertly fortified village that he didn't expect to buckle under her weakened charge. "Her army, of which she was only a minor commander, was woefully undersupplied," and her commission an ignominious one. What La Trémoille identified as the first strike in an upper Loire campaign was a match not only to settle a personal grudge but also to pit Joan against a purely mercenary foe, as the area was controlled by Perrinet Gressart. Currently in service to the Burgundians who paid

FIG. 1 (ABOVE LEFT). Drawing, 1429, Clément de Fauquembergue. A clerk's doodle in the margin of Paris's parliamentary record is the single extant contemporaneous image of Joan of Arc. Likenesses made in her lifetime were destroyed upon her being condemned as a witch, rendering them dangerous devil's currency.

FIG. 2 (ABOVE RIGHT). Miniature, fifteenth century, artist unknown. Having protected Joan's modesty by leaving her legs out of the image's frame, the artist feminizes her armor into an impregnable steel bodice and peplum that emphasize a woman's build.

FIG. 3. Domrémy. The house in which Joan was born and lived until she was seventeen has been restored and is now maintained as a museum.

FIG. 4. The interior of Joan's childhood home. Between the front door and the window is the hearth before which she sometimes slept.

FIG. 5. *Joan the Woman*, 1916, Cecil B. DeMille. Though Joan (Geraldine Farrar) insisted she had never been a shepherdess, the urge to align her career with Jesus's messianic trajectory has proved impossible to resist by artists in all media.

FIG. 6. *Joan of Arc*, 1879, Jules Bastien-Lepage. Bastien-Lepage resolves the controversy around Joan's angels by hanging them behind her, over her abandoned loom and out of her sight. Perhaps, the painter suggests, they are creatures of her imagination.

Fig. 8. *Joan of Arc Leaving Vaucouleurs*, Jean-Jacques Scherrer (1855–1916). Before setting out on her God-given mission, Joan pauses at the city gate. A spindle representing women's menial work lies discarded in the foreground.

Fig. 7. *Yolande of Aragon*, fifteenth century, artist unknown. Yolande parades behind the future king of France, wearing the crown she would help Joan set on his head.

Fig. 9. *Joan the Maid*, 1994, Jacques Rivette. Joan (Sandrine Bonnaire) uses the polished breastplate of a suit of armor for her first haircut, shearing off what the Apostle Paul said God had given women "for a covering" to preserve their modesty.

FIG. 10. *Charles VII*, c. 1450–1455, Jean Fouquet. The king's portrait, as executed by the official court painter, confirms descriptions by his contemporaries, which were unanimous on the subject of his homeliness.

FIG. 14. Orléans, woodcut, fifteenth century, artist unknown. The city of Orléans as it looked during Joan's lifetime. The bridge across the Loire, heavily fortified on either side, was the scene of the final and decisive battle of the lifting of the siege.

FIG. 11. *Joan of Arc*, 1948, Victor Fleming. Though no portrait of La Trémoïlle (far right) exists, the director has remained faithful to contemporaneous chronicles that present him as an enormously fat, insidious, and successful manipulator of Charles. (From left to right: José Ferrer, Ingrid Bergman, Gene Lockhart)

FIG. 12 (RIGHT). *Bascinet*, iron, fifteenth century. Tradition holds that this is the helmet worn by Joan at the lifting of the siege of Orléans. If not hers, it is typical of her time and place.

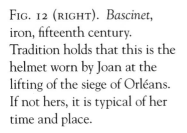

FIG. 13 (FAR RIGHT). Although Joan's original standard and pennons have been lost, she described them (under interrogation) in sufficient detail to create these facsimiles.

Fig. 15. Jean, Count of Dunois, fifteenth century, artist unknown. As the commander of Orléans's struggling forces, Dunois expected Joan to prove more hindrance than help. When he resisted her God-given authority, she overcame his reservations with a demonstration of the power she claimed.

Fig. 16 (ABOVE). *Vigiles du roi Charles VII*, 1493, Martial d'Auvergne. Astride her white charger, an armored Joan brandishes her sword at the prostitutes following her army. The red fabric draped around her thigh echoes the sweep of the camp followers' skirts and parts, like a labial curtain, to reveal her armored phallic leg.

Fig. 17 (RIGHT). *John of Lancaster, Duke of Bedford*, engraving, George Vertue (1684–1756). The third surviving son of England's King Henry IV, Lancaster served as France's regent for his nephew Henry VI, who assumed England's throne as an infant.

FIG. 18. *Henry VI,* c. 1535, artist unknown. Henry was not yet eight years old when he became king of England on November 6, 1429. He assumed rule in 1437, endured bouts of insanity throughout his reign, and suffered a complete mental breakdown when England lost the Hundred Years War.

FIG. 19. *Philip the Good, Duke of Burgundy,* Rogier van der Weyden (1399–1464). Pragmatic as it might have been, Burgundy's traitorous alliance with England served the duke's personal agenda as well. Philip's father, John the Fearless, was assassinated by order of the dauphin Charles in 1419.

Fig. 20. *The Entrance of Joan of Arc into Orléans*, Jean-Jacques Scherrer (1855–1916). Slicing through the shadowed world of mortals, golden light from on high makes it clear: The army Joan leads is God's.

Fig. 21. *Joan of Arc at the Coronation of Charles VII*, 1851, Jean Ingres. Plate armor suggests rather than obscures Joan's female form, preserving her femininity. Spaulders, or shoulder guards, converge into breasts over a wide-hipped steel peplum that covers her groin. A red skirt opens to reveal only so much of one armored leg.

Fig. 22. *Joan of Arc at the Coronation of Charles VII at Reims*, 1889, Jules Eugène Lenepveu. A nippled, breast-like plate peeks out from under Joan's gold surcoat, underscoring the gender of this warrior.

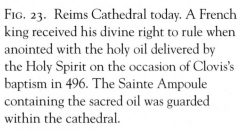

FIG. 23. Reims Cathedral today. A French king received his divine right to rule when anointed with the holy oil delivered by the Holy Spirit on the occasion of Clovis's baptism in 496. The Sainte Ampoule containing the sacred oil was guarded within the cathedral.

FIG. 24. *Saint Joan*, 1957, by George Bernard Shaw, directed by Otto Preminger. Once in possession of the throne, Charles stymied Joan's attempts to rejoin the war, testing her obedience. "It's so dull afterward when there is no danger," Joan (Jean Seberg) complains to Dunois (Richard Todd).

FIG. 25. Joan's coat of arms. During the Middle Ages it was exceedingly rare for a peasant to be invited to join the French aristocracy. Even rarer was permission to use the fleur-de-lis, a symbol reserved for royalty.

FIG. 26 (ABOVE). "Joan
Outside the Gates of Paris,"
Vigiles du roi Charles VII,
1493, Martial d'Auvergne.
A demure androgyne with
a man's torso grafted onto
a woman's hidden hips and
legs, Joan contemplates
action she is not dressed
to join.

FIG. 27. *Joan of Arc,* 1948,
Victor Fleming. Maxwell
Anderson's romantic script
ignores the capture of
Joan (Ingrid Bergman) at
Compièigne. The prayers she
offers when free, costumed
as though she were a priest,
deliver her directly into
English captivity and the
martyrdom that awaits her.

Fig. 28 (ABOVE).
The Messenger, 1999, Luc
Besson. Vanquished, Joan
(Milla Jovovich) falls not into
the enemy's hands but into a
mystical consummation with
a Jesus only she can see.

Fig. 29 (RIGHT). Rouen
tower today. The keep in
which Joan spent the last five
months of her life, fettered in
an unlit cell, was restored in
the nineteenth century.

The Passion of Joan of Arc, 1928, Carl Dreyer.

Fɪɢ. 30 (ᴀʙᴏᴠᴇ). The director captures the inquisitor Cauchon's spirit, or lack thereof. (Eugene Silvain as Cauchon)

Fɪɢ. 31 (ʟᴇꜰᴛ). Joan (Maria Falconetti), like Jesus, is mocked and crowned before being executed for blasphemy.

Fɪɢ. 32 (ʙᴇʟᴏᴡ). As described by Matthew, "When they came to a place called Golgotha, they offered [Jesus] wine to drink, mingled with gall"—a sedative he refused. Here, as Joan is led to the stake, an old woman steps forward with water for the condemned.

FIG. 33 (ABOVE). *The Trial of Joan of Arc*, 1962, Robert Bresson. Joan's executioner complained that her stake had been set too high for him to cast a rope around her neck and strangle her, a mercy routinely extended to those about to be burned. (Florence Delay as Joan)

FIG. 34 (RIGHT). *Joan the Woman*, 1916, Cecil B. DeMille. The director does a handy job of uniting Joan's nationalism with her piety, using light to nail her to a great fleur-de-lis.

FIG. 35 (BOTTOM). *Jeanne d'Arc*, 1900, Georges Méliès. Not even in his playful rendition can Joan (Jeanne d'Alcy) escape her messianic destiny.

Fig. 36. World War I poster, 1918, Haskell Coffin. Sword aloft, bathed in the light of her vocation, a rapturous Joan casts her eyes up toward heaven. As though glowing through the carapace of her armor, two orbs of light at the level of her hidden breasts suggest a female bosom that cannot be obscured by the trappings of war.

Fig. 37. *Classics Illustrated* comics cover, 1950. Shining armor and white horse, banner and sword, and a phallic leg sheathed in red: From medieval manuscript to comic book, Joan's iconography remains consistent.

his bills, Gressart had made himself known to La Trémoille when he captured him en route to a negotiation and failed to honor his guarantee of safe passage, demanding an extravagant ransom of fourteen thousand ecus to release him. The siege of Saint-Pierre-le-Moûtier was to be the first in a series of smoldering conflicts that eluded decisive outcomes; the upper Loire campaign was designed to exhaust Joan's forces' morale along with her patience. On November 8, "the French were forcibly compelled to retire," when, Jean d'Aulon testified, Joan told him she had "fifty thousand men in her company and would not leave that spot until she had taken the town.

"Whatever she might say," Jean continued, "she had not more than four or five men with her, which I know for certain as do several others who also saw her." Apart from what sounds, even coming from Joan's ever-awed squire, like a delusion on Joan's part and hyperbole on his, Joan did take the town with her handful of men, ordering them to bring "faggots and withies to form a bridge over the moat" so that it might be possible for her army of five earthbound and who knew how many celestial forces to scale Saint-Pierre's wall.

"They were immediately brought and put into position," Jean testified. "The whole thing utterly astonished me, for the town was immediately carried by assault . . . there was no great resistance." He went on to avow his faith that "all the Maid's exploits seemed to me rather divine and miraculous than otherwise."

Joan celebrated her victory by arranging for an encore. In a letter to the nearby city of Riom, she asked its citizens to demonstrate their loyalty to the king by sending supplies to La Charité, the town to which she was to next lay siege. She wanted "gunpowder, saltpeter, sulphur, arrows, heavy crossbows and other military supplies" and advised the letter's recipients to be quick about it "so that no one may say that you were negligent or unwilling," chasing her threat with a benediction. "May our Lord God protect you." Beneath the words is the first, and shakiest, of the three surviving examples of her signature.

The siege of La Charité lasted a month and was abandoned on Christmas Eve, as the French could make no effective attack on the heavily fortified town, with its large garrison and stockpiles of artillery and ammunitions. The gift of 1,300 ecus from the citizens of Bourges to the king's forces couldn't hire and provision enough soldiers to prevail in a contest that, Joan made clear to her examiners, she had undertaken not upon counsel of her voices but at the behest of "men-at-arms," who "told her it was better to go first against the town of La Charité," when she herself had eyes only for Paris. The diversion La Trémoille conceived for Joan had been expensive and effective. The Berry herald characterized the defeat as shameful, accomplished as it was, "even without any relief having come to the aid of the besieged." The French "lost their bombards and artillery." Upon her retreat to Jargeau, on Christmas Day, Joan received letters from Charles conferring nobility on her and her family in "thanks for the multiple and striking benefits of divine grandeur that have been accorded us through the agency of the Maid" and in consideration of "the praiseworthy, graceful, and useful services already rendered by the aforesaid." Joan already possessed the equivalent of a coat of arms, bestowed by a ruler far more august than Charles, who, in conferring knighthood, had, as Régine Pernoud put it, "acted like a minister of state granting a decoration to a functionary he is about to send into retirement."

The Maid's ascent to the nobility cannot have aligned with any fantasy inspired by chansons de geste. As described in L'ordene de chevalerie, the investiture was a public sacrament that began in ritual purification. "The candidate [for knighthood] first was bathed, the bath symbolizing the washing away of his sins. Then he was clothed in a white robe symbolizing his determination to defend God's law, with a narrow belt to remind him to shun the sins of the flesh. In the church, he was invested with his accoutrements: the gilded spur, to give him courage to serve God; the sword, to fight the enemy and 'protect the poor people from the rich.' Finally, he received the colée, a blow of the hand on the shoulder or head, 'in remembrance of Him who ordained you.'" It almost appeared that the paper dubbing had been timed to vanish in the blur of feasting and drinking and dancing between Christmas and Joan's posthumously conferred birthday: Twelfth Night.

A bleak winter was setting in, bitterly cold and clouded with disappointments for Joan, who spent the greater part of it cooped up in Sully-sur-Loire, La Trémoille's family château some thirty miles upriver from Orléans, to which, on January 19, she traveled to attend a banquet given by the city council. The thirty miles between village and city included a stop midway, at Jargeau, and gave Joan the opportunity to note that "the activity of royalist 'partisans' was seen everywhere," a grassroots shiver of awakening nationalism that inspired their allegiance to the Maid who championed their independence. Charles had moved with such eager dispatch in concluding the truces with England and Burgundy that he "crushed the élan of the royal army, which began to show signs of discontent."

As Joan had prophesied without aid of her heavenly counsel, the Duke of Burgundy continued to avoid the peace conference that had been the truces' alleged aim, and Joan spent much of February and nearly all of March looking forward to military action she hadn't been given leave to undertake, pacing Sully's courtyard under a rectangle of gray sky as she dreamed of battles to come, retiring for long hours into its chapel, the ringing of the Angelus inviting her to her knees and the possibility of the comfort that first arrived on the notes of church bells. From Sully, Joan sent a second letter to the citizens of Reims, dated March 16. "Joan the Pucelle has received your letters mentioning that you fear being besieged," she wrote, reassuring them that she would intercept any army that marched on their city.

"If it should so happen that I do not encounter them coming to you, shut your gates, because I will be with you shortly. And if they are there I shall make them put on their spurs in such haste that they will not know where to put them."

A week later, on March 23, Jean Pasquerel sent a letter on Joan's behalf to the Hussites of Bohemia, the predominantly Czech followers of Jan Hus, a priest and university master in Prague whose theology reprised that of the English heretic John Wycliffe. From the pulpit the Church had awarded him, Hus was so brazen as to attack what he called the corrupt clergy, and he made a point of taking no side in the schism as he considered one pope as depraved as the other. Hus was condemned for his social consciousness, which not only allowed women to assume priestly roles, including teaching, but also denounced the practice of selling indulgences, by which only the moneyed could purchase sacred power; this was no different from Jesus's reviling those who sold sacrificial doves in the temple, and its

outcome was as fatal. Hus was burned at the stake in 1415, galvaniz-
ing his followers to take up his campaign to separate church and state
and inspiring the Church to make bounty hunters of crusaders willing
to capture or kill its detractors. The Hussite Wars, as they were later
called, continued from 1419 until 1434, bracketing Joan's career and in
their viciousness betraying how serious a threat Hus's teachings presented to the Church. Panegyrics like Christine de Pizan's, published
only two weeks after Charles's anointing, not only congratulated Joan
for fulfilling her original vocation but also suggested future ones. Both
loud and respected, Christine's voice was unavoidable by anyone, like
Joan, who moved among the knights and courtiers who were the
paean's intended audience. "She will restore harmony in Christendom . . . She will destroy the Saracens, by conquering the Holy Land."
Probably, Joan's impatience to engage in active combat had inspired
fantasies of setting off on what was unambiguously a pilgrimage, with
an objective that seemed from her remove to be purely divine, beyond
the reach of mortal politics, and firmly within the mandate of the
Church.

   "For some time now," Joan dictated to Pasquerel, "rumor and public comment has reported to me, Joan the Pucelle, that from true
Christians you have become heretics. Like the Saracens you have
blighted the true religion and worship, embracing a disgraceful and
criminal superstition . . . What rage or madness consumes you?"
she demanded of the Hussites. "Do you believe that you will remain
unpunished for it? . . . To tell you frankly, If I was not occupied with
these English wars, I would have come to see you a long time ago."
If the Hussites did not reform, she promised to "set off against you so
that, by the sword if I cannot do it any other way, I may eliminate your
mad and obscene superstition and remove either your heresy or your
lives." Because this letter was unique for having been written in Latin,
its style different from Joan's other communications, its authorship
has been questioned. But a cleric would naturally compose an ecclesiastical communication in the language of the Church, especially if
he couldn't assume its Czech recipients would be literate in French.
Too, any translation of Joan's spirited vernacular into Latin's formal
confines would necessarily sacrifice its distinctive cadence.

   In *Saint Joan*, Shaw gives Joan of Arc credit for what was in truth

John Wycliffe and Jan Hus's challenge to ecclesiastical authority, using one of his characters to identify Joan's defiance as "the protest of the individual soul against the interference of priest or peer between the private man and his God. I should call it Protestantism if I had to find a name for it." But Shaw's characterizing Joan as a Church reformer is a flight of imaginative projection, as she hotly defended all that Wycliffe, Hus, and their intellectual heir Martin Luther abhorred: veneration of the saints and holy images, confession to and absolution by clerics, intercession for the dead, anointing the sick, the sale of indulgences, and the conferring of last rites, none of which, they argued, had scriptural basis.

The Hussites presented a safety risk and international scandal serious enough that in July, Beaufort, the bishop of Winchester and the Duke of Bedford's uncle, had little trouble financing an army of 350 mounted archers to set on the distant heretics, and less trouble still marching them from the docks of Calais straight to Paris, with no thought of saving Bohemia—uncle and nephew being of like mind and scruples.

It's not only Shaw who imagined Joan as a social reformer or retroactively credited her with ideas she would have found foreign. Brecht gave his Joan, not of Arc, but of the Stockyards, a socialist agenda and magnified the populism she borrowed from Jesus until it eclipsed the far greater part of the historical Joan's vision. "Slums breed immorality, and immorality breeds revolution," she preaches to the stockbreeders who are driving up the price of meat, appealing to their self-interest with a bleeding heart's naïveté. It is another three scenes before she understands. "I know their money, like a cancerous growth, has eaten away their ears and human face." The judgment would have more likely issued from Hus than from the girl who couldn't resist velvet tunics and cloth of gold.

No matter what topics Joan fulminated about in her correspondence, her focus hadn't wavered from recapturing Paris, where in March bourgeois factions within the city's walls, including "clerks, artisans, and merchants," had organized under the leadership of Carmelite monks and were planning a revolt. But when one of them was arrested and tortured until he gave up the others, she retrained her attention on Compiègne, for whose people she said she "always prayed with her counsel." Having been squabbled over by Armagnacs, Burgundians, and English, the citizens of Compiègne had been besieged eight times in the previous fifteen years. Joan's was the single command they followed. For the Maid they had pledged their allegiance to Charles and sent him the city's keys before his coronation, and for her they refused to obey Charles's subsequent order that they surrender to the Duke of Burgundy, "resolute to undergo every risk for themselves, their children, and their infants, rather than be exposed to the mercy of the duke." The citizens of Compiègne reflected Joan's own stubborn courage back at her and reignited her determination to prevail over the enemy or die trying.

To expire in battle was to enter eternal glory, and after writing one final letter to the people of Reims, Joan marshaled her troops. It was the last letter she would ever send; in it she warned the people of Reims of a traitorous alliance within its walls, its purpose "to betray the city and let the Burgundians inside." Promising Charles's aid were the city besieged, Joan left Sully "without the knowledge of the king, and not taking leave from him," as Perceval de Cagny wrote. "She went to the town of Lagny-sur-Marne because those of that place were making good war against the English in Paris and elsewhere," a battle half won even before Joan arrived. Her movements were not covert; once she and her small army of zealots reached Lagny, she sent word to Charles, requesting reinforcements. Of the exultant tide of twelve thousand soldiers that accompanied her to Reims the previous July, only five hundred men remained; the rest had ebbed and vanished, her army so reduced she couldn't maintain even a rudimentary military household and had no page or herald, upon which communication depended. Still, far better to take on a small battle with a small army than to forgo fighting.

Joan spent three weeks in Lagny and from there made war on Anglo-Burgundian troops under the command of Franquet d'Arras, easily chasing off the infamous mercenary. With or without a sizable army or adequate entourage, she retained the reputation of a sorceress who bent the odds of battle, and Lagny was just twenty miles outside Paris, the hub of medieval media. The witch was drawing closer and had recovered whatever she had lost back at the Saint-Honoré Gate. Recruiting was a problem for the English, desertions so common that the Duke of Bedford was forced to issue an edict on May 3, 1430, against captains and soldiers who refused to embark for France. "Each and every captain and soldier in the city of whatever rank or condition who has been retained to make the voyage" to France, he announced in the name of the boy king Henry VI, "who are found delaying in London will be seized immediately and arrested with their horses and armor kept as surety and they shall be imprisoned," a penalty that stopped just short of death.

By this time Charles had yet to admit having been duped by Bedford, and Joan took Franquet prisoner and held him hostage in hopes of trading him for Jacquet Guillaume, who had been captured in the plot recently uncovered in Paris and whom Joan hoped to use as a means of mustering forces within the city. Once she learned Guillaume had been executed along with all the others who had been arrested for treason, she surrendered the now worthless Franquet to the jurisdiction of the bailiff of Senlis. "As the man I wanted is dead, do with this fellow as justice demands," she told the bailiff. Such exchanges and negotiations were routine, and in this case the public was satisfied by what was regarded as the just execution of a known rapist who, she said, also "confessed himself a murderer, a thief, and a traitor." Still, Joan's examiners presented Franquet's execution as evidence of a bloodthirsty vengefulness outside the confines of battle, and they accused her of bribery.

"Did you not send money, or have money sent, to him who had taken the said Franquet?"

"What am I, Master of the Mint or Treasurer of France," Joan said, "that I should pay out money?" Had she had any, it would have been spent on provisioning her army.

The victory at Lagny returned luster to Joan's trajectory, and she was embraced by the fervid crowds she'd grown to expect, and perhaps even need, as they demonstrated a confidence in her prowess that official sources now withheld. Excited at their having joined those citizens of France lucky enough to be rescued by the Maid, the people of Lagny mustered all they could for public celebrations in Joan's honor, enough that anyone who wanted to see or touch her would have had the chance. During the three weeks she remained in town, a bereaved family approached her for intercession on behalf of a child who died at birth and, having not been baptized, was doomed to suffer purgatory.

"How old was this infant?" the examiner asked Joan.

"Three days old. They told me three days had passed with no sign of life in the child, which was as black as my coat of mail."

She was in church, kneeling before an image of the Virgin, when the boy's mother and sisters came to her with his corpse, and she prayed with them, and, as she testified, "at last life appeared in the child, which yawned thrice, and was afterwards baptized, and immediately it died and was buried in consecrated ground. But when it yawned, the color began to return."

"Was it said in the town that the resuscitation was due to your prayers?"

"I did not inquire about it," Joan said, although she knew better than any that "the incident was trumpeted as a miracle."

If Joan, like others present at the baby's fleeting return to life, believed she had raised him from the dead, she knew better than to admit such a thing. She was praying with the baby's family when "life appeared in the child." That was all. Her judges could make what they would of it.

Fixed as it was on the ever-looming torment of death, the medieval imagination was possessed by the story of Lazarus of Bethany. John is the only Evangelist to tell the story, characterized by the single instance of Jesus's use of the word "dead" to describe the person he subsequently raised, a miracle he orchestrated to prove his divinity.*

"But if I do them [perform miracles]," Jesus said of his plan for a spec-

---

* This was different from the story of Jairus's daughter, found in the Synoptic Gospels and not in John. "Why do you make a tumult and weep?" Jesus asked Jairus, after banishing an eager, heckling audience. In private he took the girl's parents to her bedside. "The child is not dead but sleeping." Near death but not dead. "Taking her by the hand, he said to her 'Tal'itha cu'mi,' which means 'Little girl, I say to you, arise.' Immediately the girl got up and walked (she was twelve years of age) and they were immediately overcome with amazement. And he strictly charged them that no one should know this" and (mis)interpret it as a resurrection.

tacle, "even though you do not believe me, believe the works, that you may know and understand that the Father is in me and I am in the Father."

"I know," Lazarus's sister Martha said to Jesus, "that whatever you ask from God, God will give you." By then, Lazarus had been entombed for four days. Before a great crowd of mourners and onlookers, Jesus called upon God for help.

"'I have said this on account of the people standing by,' he said aloud, 'that they may believe that thou dist send me.' When he had said this he cried with a loud voice, 'Lazarus, come out.' The dead man came out, his hands and feet bound with bandages, and his face wrapped with a cloth. Jesus said to them, 'Unbind him, and let him go.'"

The miracle prefigured Jesus's resurrection and caused so much public unrest that, according to John, "the chief priests and the Pharisees gathered the council and said 'What are we to do? For this man performs many signs. If we let him go on thus, everyone will believe in him, and the Romans will come and destroy both our holy place and our nation,'" and it was "from that day on that they took counsel how to put him to death."

"Never," Péguy's Joan says of Jesus, "had a man stirred up so much hate in a man."

Historians generally finesse Joan's revival of the infant in Lagny as that of "a newborn baby on point of death" or dismiss it as "a curious incident" that "demonstrated Joan's growing cult." Joan didn't equivocate; the baby she saw was as black as her coat of mail—not her "white armor," but chain with a dark, bluish cast—and had been described by family members as lifeless for three days.

"Have you cured people with those rings?" the examiner asks Joan in Robert Bresson's The Trial of Joan of Arc, its script based on French trial minutes and witness testimony for the nullification. He speaks in particular of the one she received from her mother and father, bearing the suspiciously heretical joining of the names Jesus and Maria.

"No," Joan says. She pauses, eyes cast down, considering the question before looking up at the judges ranged before her. "Not by means of the rings," she says.

The incident at Lagny was different from Joan's previous miracles, as winds do shift and waters rise and men fall to their deaths without a divine nudge. Until Lagny, Joan had been associated with highly unlikely but not impossible events. Raising a child from the dead was beyond the reach of reason and partook of the greatest of God's powers. Once perceived as having triumphed over death, Joan, like Jesus, had arrived at the moment in her career when it was clear to her enemies that there was no longer any time to waste in eliminating her influence.

"Are you so tired already of the visible presence of God," Schiller's Joan asks Charles, "that you seek to smash the vessel that contains it, and drag down into the dust, the virgin that God has sent you?"

A week after she left Lagny, "Easter week," Joan told the examiner, "when I was in the trenches at Melun, I was told by my voices, by Saint Catherine and Saint Margaret, that I would be captured before St. John's Day," which followed Midsummer eve. Joan's voices repeated the warning "several times, nearly every day," and they told her this suffering was inescapable: "'It had to be so,' they told me, and they said I should not be distressed, but take it in good part. They said God would aid me."

On May 14, Joan was in Compiègne, at a reception given in her honor, by which point the Duke of Burgundy had "amassed a large army and artillery train" and "begun his move on Compiègne in earnest." It was the "greatest gunpowder weaponry arsenal" that existed among the powers at war, and "almost all of it was directed entirely against Compiègne and Joan."

Like Orléans, Compiègne was on the bank of a river, its main entrance accessed by a bridge over the Oise, diverted to fill a moat enclosing all the city's walls, which boasted an unusual number of towers, forty-four of them in just the length running along the river. "Every day," Jean Chartier recorded, Joan "fought large skirmishes against the English and Burgundians" besieging the town. As she was not a defensive fighter but an aggressor who didn't like being confined within city walls, she made sallies on all the towns within a twenty-mile radius of Compiègne, marching first on Choisy-au-Bac, a strategically important site, located as it was on the Aisne River. To keep Choisy was to prevent the Burgundians from controlling the town's bridge and, once over it, surrounding Compiègne, little more than three miles to the southwest. Combat was harsh and bloody, and Joan's troops, protected only by hastily assembled makeshift bulwarks, hadn't the ability to withstand the firepower at the duke's disposal. By May 16 she was forced to withdraw her little army back within the walls of Compiègne, from which she set out with the Count of Vendôme and the archbishop of Reims for the town of Soissons, in hopes of enlisting the support of the town's garrison and using its bridge to cross the Aisne River.

The Count of Vendôme was a friend, Regnault an enemy in cahoots with Soissons's captain accompanying Joan in anticipation of what Vita Sackville-West called "the pleasure of seeing the fresh discomfiture which there awaited her," one rendered "more bitter by treachery." Soissons had pledged its loyalty to Charles, but the city's captain, Guiscard Bournel, "refused to allow Jeanne and her followers to enter, and persuaded the citizens that they had arrived with the unavowed intention of remaining there as a garrison." Uncharacteristically, and despite the fact that she and her troops were forced to bivouac in the fields outside the city's walls, Joan made no attempt to gain access to the bridge by either force or persuasion; instead, she moved on to Crépy-en-Valois to round up "300–400 more soldiers who had come to fight for the freedom of Compiègne."

"About Soissons, and Guichard Bournel," the examiner asked, "did you not deny God and say you would have the captain drawn and quartered if you got hold of him?" The question was based on hearsay, one of many attempts to illustrate what her judges presented as an unnatural thirst for blood and violence.

"No," Joan said. "Those who said I did were mistaken."

On May 22, spies reported Philip's troops were converging on Compiègne, and Joan set off hurriedly, at nightfall, the new moon but one day old and the stars hidden by clouds.

As DeMille envisioned the expedition, Joan rides before her army, unaware of the dark angel on horseback moving ahead of her, ghostly, transparent. His black wings shimmer among the leaves of the forest that presses in on the shadowed road. The pace of the winged figure is resolute and stately—funereal, as if timed to a dirge. Just outside Compiègne, the dark angel halts his black mount and turns to face Joan, raising one arm to point the way to her doom. Surprised by the specter, Joan lays one hand on her armored breast and pulls up her mount, reeling, inasmuch as a body astride a horse can reel.

"Does thou not see the Black Horseman!"* her title card cries. But Joan's confused comrades can't see the fate that awaits her.

"I have not long, . . . I have not long!" her next card laments.

---

* The Black Horseman is traditionally interpreted as the famine that follows upon war. Revelation 5:6.

CHAPTER
IX

The
Golden
Cloak

After a hard night's ride, Joan and her army, now no more than four hundred strong, reached Compiègne at "a secret hour of the morning" "and entered the town without having encountered any resistance" and "without confusion nor disturbance from either herself or her men." The ease with which she accomplished the operation recalled her equally unhindered entrance into Orléans under siege. Perhaps she took this as auspicious, as she anticipated an efficient triumph over "a small and unsuspecting garrison, with an open bridge and a friendly town behind her . . . child's play," Sackville-West judged it, "for the victor of Orléans and Patay." It was the eve of the Feast of the Ascension, and as usual Joan heard Mass at dawn and only then approached the captain of Compiègne's garrison, Guillaume de Flavy, to learn what she could of the present situation. She and her men had spent the night armored and on horseback, but Compiègne was in danger of falling to the enemy, and she hadn't time to spare. The "young, violent and formidable de Flavy . . . told her that the bridge at Margny"—immediately across the river Oise—"was held by the advance guard of the Anglo-Burgundian army." The Duke of Burgundy waited five miles to the north, with the larger part of the enemy forces. What Guillaume de Flavy did not tell Joan was that while she was slipping through the dark after her Black Horseman, the Duke of Burgundy's vassal Jean of Luxembourg-Ligny was leading his forces downriver from Clairoix to Margny to meet with the Duke of Burgundy and "eight or ten other gentlemen" to orchestrate the tightening of the siege around the weakening city.

"Not to worry, Charles," Yolande says in Luc Besson's *The Messenger.* "If God is still with her, she will be victorious."

"But her army is so much smaller," Charles says, suffering a spasm of conscience.

"Then her faith," Yolande answers, "will have to be bigger."

It was easy for those who betrayed Joan to comfort themselves. No one needed to worry about rescuing a girl with heaven on her side. If Joan was vanquished, she had fallen from the grace she had once summoned.

"He trusts in God," the chief priests and elders said of Jesus, "let God deliver him now, if he desires him; for he said 'I am the son of God.'"

Not anticipating an attack by French troops, the Anglo-Burgundians had laid aside their weapons to attend to their boulevard and other defensive maintenance, when, at nine in the morning, "mounted on her horse, armed as would be a man," Georges Chastellain wrote, Joan sallied out from Compiègne's main gate, "adorned in a doublet of rich cloth of gold over her armor. She rode a gray steed, very handsome and very proud, and displayed herself in the armor and manners that a captain who leads a large army would. And in that state, with her standard raised high and blowing in the wind, and accompanied by many noble men, around four hours before midday, she charged out of the town" and set out to join a "large and forceful skirmish [that] was being fought on the meadows outside of town. She armed herself and had her men armed [*sic*] themselves." Though it was no longer the fashion for knights to wear rich coats into battle, Joan had acquired so many gifts from grateful burghers with their bolts of velvet and satin. God's *chef de guerre* should look her part.

Joan and her small army "mounted their horses, and went out to join in the mêlée," and had already moved across the bridge toward Margny before the Anglo-Burgundians ran to rearm themselves.

"Did your voices order you to make this attack from Compiègne?" the examiner asked Joan.

"I had no order to go forth. With my company I crossed over the bridge of Compiègne and through the boulevard. I attacked the forces of lord Jean de Luxembourg, and twice drove them as far as the camp of the Burgundians, and the third time to the middle of the highway."

Behind her were Guillaume de Flavy and ranks of "archers and men with crossbows and culverins at the gate of Compiègne, and more archers and crossbow men in little boats bobbing on the river." As Joan wasn't known to deviate from her characteristic forward-in-the-name-of-God approach, the Duke of Burgundy was waiting for her arrival, and the third time she "charged forward strongly into the Burgundian army," she was ambushed.

"The English who were there [in the middle of the highway] cut off the road from me and my company," Joan testified. "I retreated to the fields, on the Picardy side near the boulevard. And there was nothing but the river and the boulevard with its ditch." The enemy "turned toward the Maid in such a great number that those of her company could not hope to save her" and, frightened for her safety, begged her to hasten back within the walls of Compiègne. "But," Anatole France explained, "her eyes were dazzled by the splendor of angels and archangels."

She spoke to her men furiously, Perceval de Cagny reported. "'You be quiet!' she told them. 'Their defeat depends on you. Think only of striking at them.' Even though she said this, her men did not want to believe it and by force they made her return directly to the bridge," where she didn't hasten back to safety but remained, a target toward which every soldier came running, so that "there was a great clash of arms." "The situation," according to Sackville-West, "was really beyond redemption." Joan's men in flight came "pouring back across the bridge into the town" as she "went after the fugitives, fighting desperately to defend their rear . . . Her last moments under arms were worthy of her gallantry." At the sight of a stampede of Burgundians and English tearing across the river after the French, Guillaume de Flavy ordered the bridge raised and the gate shut, leaving Joan and a few of her men locked outside the city walls, outnumbered and soon surrounded. In a field just a short gallop from safety, "an archer," Chastellain wrote, "a rough and very sour man, full of much spite because a woman, who so much had been spoken about, should have defeated so many brave men, as she had done, grabbed the edge of her cloth of gold doublet, and threw her from her horse flat to the ground. Never was she able to find refuge nor to receive help from her soldiers, though they tried to assist her to become remounted." It was six thirty in the evening and bright, as the sun wouldn't set until nine. Captured with Joan were her brother Pierre, Jean d'Aulon, and Jean's brother.

Perceval de Cagny was not one of the chroniclers who suggested Guillaume de Flavy had, in closing the gate, carried out an order intended to deliver Joan into the hands of her enemies, but Compiègne's main gates had remained closed all along, and there was no reason for the captain to imagine the city might be in enough danger to merit closing a small, auxiliary gate on Joan, whose purpose was to save his city and garrison. As documents prove the Duke of Burgundy used what Kelly DeVries calls "bribery to achieve the surrender of towns in 1430, the case of Guichard Bournel and Soissons being the perfect example," it's quite likely Compiègne would have been included among those towns. Joan, who provided what turned out to be the sole eyewitness account of her capture, didn't mention any of the gates of Compiègne at all.

"If your voices had ordered you to make this attack from Compiègne, and had signified that you would be captured, would you have gone?"

"If I had known when I was to be taken, I would not have willingly gone. Nevertheless, I would have done their bidding in the end, whatever it cost me." The standard of faith to which she held herself was that of Jesus, who, in Gethsemane, after his disciples had fallen asleep and left him to contemplate his fate, "fell on his face and prayed, 'My Father, if it be possible, let this cup pass from me; nevertheless, not as I will but as thou wilt.'"

"When you made this attack from Compiègne, did you have any voice or revelation to go forth and make it?"

"I did not know I was to be captured that day, and I had no other order to go forth. But I had always been told that I must be taken prisoner."

"Why didn't you take special precautions on the day when you were captured," the lieutenant to the bailiff at Rouen asked her, "since you suspected this would happen?"

"I knew neither the day nor the hour," Joan said, as she had to the archbishop of Reims when he asked where she expected to die, again borrowing from Jesus's parable about the imminence of death and salvation, which the Gospels characterize as a consummation between Christ, the holy "bridegroom," and the faithful, who wait in expectation of his coming to "bear them away to the marriage feast."

"Of that day and hour no one knows, not even the angels of heaven, nor the Son, but the Father only," Jesus said, and Joan focused less on her mortality than on the eternal salvation she expected in reward for her service, hedging the bet by traveling in the company of a priest to whom she turned whenever she found a sin to confess, which, under the commandment-bending contingencies of war, was frequently.

In Luc Besson's mystical interpretation of Joan's capture, the violent, dirty clamor of battle vanishes as Joan is pulled backward from off her high horse, her right arm holding her cruciform sword aloft. The ground on which she falls isn't the blood-laced mud of a battlefield but the lush, otherworldly meadow where she first received the sword of her vocation and where the breath of God now tears over Joan like "the rush of a violent wind," as the apostles described the descent of the Holy Spirit, ravishing her. "My Lord," she whispers to a vision of a white-robed Jesus. "My Lord" (Fig. 28).

Victor Fleming is guided by a similar impulse to sanctify what he, too, reveals as the fulfillment of vocation rather than a tumble from grace; his, however, is chaste. Costumed in a priestly black tunic, complete with white collar, Joan places her armor on the altar at Saint-Denis (Fig. 27) and is delivered into captivity immediately, in the very next scene, the Battle of Compiègne excised from Anderson's script, as it is from Shaw's.

Every telling of Joan's life pauses, as it must, at this threshold between her freedom and her captivity, the point at which her trajectory as a crusading knight shifts toward the passion of Christ. "We will draw down the curtain, now," Twain writes, "upon the most strange, and pathetic, and wonderful military drama that has been played upon the stage of the world. Joan of Arc will march no more."

"Holy and terrible one, hard is your hand," Schiller's Joan cries as she is taken. "Am I cast out forever from your grace? No angel comes, and miracles have an end: Heaven's gates are shut; God turns away His face." A century later, her lament assumes, in Péguy's voice, a chill, nihilistic cast. What happens, she says, "when you see that your prayers are useless" and "the whole of Christendom is plunging purposely, plunging steadily to the losing of all souls"?

In the days following Joan's fall into enemy hands, rumor amplified the role her rich cloak—or doublet, depending on the source— had played in her capture. It was a detail that Perceval de Cagny didn't include in his description of how five or six foot soldiers unseated Joan, "the one putting his hand on her and the others on her horse," and that Georges Chastellain might have been tempted to invent as a glamorous accessory to a scene he hadn't witnessed. From the moment Joan assumed the attire of an aristocratic male, her every lace and seam had been the object of scrutiny and gossip; her extravagant taste was common knowledge, the cloak too irresistible a symbol to discard.

Joan had been defeated, the archbishop of Reims announced to his flock, because "she did not wish to pay attention to any counsel and did everything at her own [authority] . . . full of pride due to the rich garments she had begun to wear." He hadn't the courage to admit the observation was his own, attributing it instead to Le Berger, the shepherd who had yet to have been drowned in a sack, to suggest the words had been pronounced by a mystical cognoscente. "She often dressed in rich and sumptuous habits, precious stuffs and cloth of gold and furs," reads the thirteenth article of accusation Regnault's cronies drew up preparatory to Joan's trial. "It is notorious that when she was captured she was wearing a loose cloak of cloth of gold."

Like the shepherdess's crook, the golden cloak proved impossible to strip away from the account. "Have I not been punished for my vanity?" Shaw's Joan asks the inquisitor. "If I had not worn my cloth of gold surcoat in battle like a fool, that Burgundian soldier would never have pulled me backwards off my horse; and I should not have been here."

The "tremendous and immediate excitement" occasioned by her capture was enough to remind anyone who might have forgotten the degree to which Joan possessed the imagination of all Europe. The English exulted; the French worried that so unambiguous a defeat cast doubt on Joan's claim of a divine vocation; the rest of the world watched to see what would happen next.

The archer who pulled Joan down from her horse was in the service of the Bastard of Vendôme, a vassal of Jean II of Luxembourg, who was himself a liege of the Duke of Burgundy. Vendôme, "more joyous than if he had a king in his hands," escorted her immediately across the Oise River to Margny, just at the end of the bridge that connected the town to Compiègne. There, in the manner of a noble—and thus announcing her noble status—Joan formally surrendered to Jean of Luxembourg, as she had refused to do to the Bastard of Vendôme. Luxembourg was not only a vassal of the Duke of Burgundy's but also, as demonstrated by England's royal account books, in the service of King Henry VI and had carried out a number of *chevauchées* against the French—raids like those that had blighted Joan's childhood. Immediately upon gaining a prize of such magnitude, the impoverished count found himself pulled into a glare he hadn't known before. Joan wasn't in captivity for more than a few hours when the Duke of Burgundy came calling, accompanied by Monstrelet. Though present at a meeting that was by any standard historic, the great Burgundian chronicler reported only that "the Burgundian and English partisans were very joyous, more than if they had taken five hundred combatants, for they did not fear or dread either captains or any other war chief as much as they had up until that day this Maid," and he conveniently forgets what the Maid and Philip the Good said to each other—"some words that I do not remember very well." Whatever transpired had evidently shown either Joan in too flattering a light or the duke in too unflattering a one. In any case, the duke left in a state of elation and went immediately to where he was quartered to compose an exultant circular, preserved among the records of the town of Saint-Quentin.

"The woman called the Maid has been taken," he crowed, "and from her capture will be recognized the error and mad belief of all those who became sympathetic and favorable to the deeds of this woman."

Under heavy guard, Jean of Luxembourg transported Joan, her brother Pierre, her squire, Jean d'Aulon, and his brother some two miles upriver from Margny to the fortress of Clairoix, where they remained until Sunday, May 28, by which time the Duke of Burgundy had already received a letter from Jean Graverent, the pro-Burgundian vice-inquisitor of France. On behalf of the University of Paris, Graverent demanded that Joan be turned over to his jurisdiction "as soon as it can be done safely and conveniently . . . since she is strongly suspected of various crimes smacking of heresy." The letter was dated May 26, and as Paris's street criers could not have broadcast the news of Joan's capture before the previous evening, he'd responded so immediately as to suggest he was poised to pounce—not for himself, but for the man who would act as his deputy, Pierre Cauchon. Graverent was conducting another inquisition and would arrive in Rouen only in time to observe the trial's second, private phase of interrogation, limiting his involvement in what he wasn't as confident would be the certain success Cauchon anticipated.

From Clairoix, the prisoners were removed to Beaulieu-les-Fontaines, another twenty miles northeast of Compiègne, where Jean of Luxembourg had been quartered since early 1430, when he had taken the town. Joan was valuable, the ransom he anticipated high, and he wasn't going to risk her escape or rescue by bewitched fanatics. Beaulieu's fortress was secure; her cell was small, stone walls and stone floor with a single square window. He kept her locked in it for six weeks as negotiations between England and France broke down once again. Impatient to be freed and anticipating her ransom, Joan knew Charles had Talbot with which to bargain, and other English captains, too, as well as gold to gather to sweeten the deal. Guileless as she was, she never imagined her king hadn't already started to negotiate for her release, and preoccupied with enemies in the French court angling to thwart her ambition, she hadn't considered what her capture might be worth to the English. Nor did it occur to her that whoever proved her a sorceress could destroy not only the Valois line but also the French monarchy, dependent as it was on a drop of chrism over which the devil had now swept his foul paw. Joan had been called a witch, many times, but she gave the epithet as little credence as she did any other—after all, being called a whore hadn't tarnished her virginity. Joan was a visionary; she had friends, but she understood her quest in terms of roles rather than individuals with personalities that complicated outcomes. She didn't see Charles, for example, as Georges Chastellain did: "There were frequent and diverse changes all around his person, for it was his habit . . . when one had been raised high in his company even to the summit of the wheel, that then he began to be annoyed with him, and, at the first occasion that could provide some sort of justification, he willfully reversed that person from high to low," not so much hardening his heart as taking active pleasure in his sadism; from such cruelties he "savored all the fruit all he could suck." He was a fearful person, without the moral fiber to resist demonstrating what power he had, and Joan's vision of her anointed Christian king was so convincing that it eclipsed the actual man, whom she defended on the eve of her execution as "the noblest Christian of all Christians," who "loves the faith and the Church better than any."

There was only one person as eager as Joan to resolve her predicament, and as it happened, Pierre Cauchon, the bishop of Beauvais, was in Calais, as was the Duke of Bedford, when news of Joan's capture reached him. He could prove Joan was a sorceress, Cauchon told his old friend. Too, he pointed out, Joan had been taken prisoner in what was rightfully his diocese, which he'd served loyally, *in loco*, until forced by the French to seek asylum in Rouen. It was "not actually in the diocese," Michelet pointed out, "but it was hoped that people would be easily deluded on that point." Deluded or not, no one objected to the claim. On June 22, when the University of Paris again demanded the Duke of Burgundy relinquish Joan for trial, the letter was signed not by Graverent but by Cauchon.

Joan, however, was not in the duke's possession, at least not yet, as Jean of Luxembourg, torn by competing influences, stalled for time. For her second meeting with the Duke of Burgundy, this time accompanied by his wife, Isabel of Portugal, Joan was transferred from her tower room to the Episcopal palace next to the cathedral. The meeting included Jean of Luxembourg and his wife, Jeanne of Béthune. Again, no record was made of the conversation among the five, but the result was that while husbands plotted the Maid's fate, wives found themselves swayed by her fervor and convinced of her innocence. Joan remained at Beaulieu until July 10. She was allowed to keep Jean d'Aulon in her service, she had the company of her brother, and Jean of his, and she nearly managed to set all of them free.

"How did you expect to escape from Beaulieu?"

"I had hidden myself between two pieces of wood. I would have shut my guards up in the tower, had it not been for the porter, who had seen and encountered me. It did not please God to have me escape on this occasion."

Maintaining that it was the prerogative of all prisoners to attempt escape, she would try again from a different tower. On July 11, as troops moved south toward Compiègne in anticipation of renewing the siege, Joan was moved to Jean of Luxembourg's grander residence, at Beaurevoir. Jean's wife, Jeanne of Béthune, might have influenced "the choice of a more suitable residence for the prisoner . . . rather than a mere fortress made especially dangerous for a woman by the comings and goings of soldiers."

Joan was chaperoned by three women for whom she "conceived a great devotion": Jean's aunt the Demoiselle of Luxembourg; his wife, Jeanne of Béthune; and his stepdaughter, also named Jeanne. As the first step in securing any sympathy for Joan was to get her out of men's clothing, the two older women were "greatly distressed by her obstinate refusal to abandon her masculine clothes, and tried by every means to persuade her into a more feminine frame of mind." When she rejected the dresses they offered, they appealed to her vanity and brought fine fabrics for her to consider, hoping to tempt her into accepting female attire tailored to her wishes.

"You were told to change your habit at Beaurevoir," the examiner said. "Were you not?"

"Yes."

"But you refused."

"If I had had to do it, I would rather have at the request of these two ladies than of any other ladies in France, save my queen. But I had not God's permission."

"When do you cut your hair?" Jean's stepdaughter asks Joan in Jacques Rivette's *Joan the Maid*, as she watches her hack away at it with scissors.

Joan pauses before answering; the hand with the scissors is still. "When I look too much like a girl," she says. "My hair goes with my clothes. I've been wearing them for so long. I have done and seen so much with them. I could not leave them." It's unlikely Joan's "black hair, cut round," would have received any less meticulous attention than the rest of her appearance, but scriptwriters, unhampered by conflicting evidence, prefer she cut her own hair with a knife, a pair of crude shears, whatever she can find, sawing at it while she watches her transformation in a makeshift mirror. For Joan's first haircut, Rivette chooses the polished breastplate of a suit of armor as a mirror (Fig. 9).

The old Demoiselle of Luxembourg moved on from dresses to extortion and "cast herself at [her nephew's] feet; in vain did she plead with him not to dishonor himself" and threatened to withhold his inheritance should he sell Joan to the English. "But what power had this good dame against the Norman gold of the King of England, and against the anathemas of the holy church? For if my Lord Jean had refused to give up this damsel suspected of . . . crimes against religion," Anatole France explained, he would find himself exposed "to heavy legal penalties." Jean of Luxembourg was among the bankrupt nobility, and as "the younger son of a younger son, he could not even count with any certainty on succeeding to his aunt's fortune, which he fully expected his elder brother to dispute." He needed whatever money he could get for the Maid's ransom. Beyond that, the Duke of Burgundy was his feudal lord; he could not withhold Joan without fear of reprisals. For as long as his aunt was alive, he remained under her sway, but the facts remained: Jean of Luxembourg had Joan in his custody and would be forced to relinquish her to the Duke of Burgundy, who was in service to the king of England, who "had a lien on French prisoners . . . Therefore he had a lien on Jeanne."

Traveling from court to court, secular and ecclesiastical, all that summer of 1430, Pierre Cauchon lobbied tirelessly, an impresario assembling the performance of a lifetime. The bishop needed a venue, a cast, scriptwriters, prompters, backstage support. The beauty of it was that the hardest part, publicity, had already taken care of itself. What European wasn't awaiting the "beautiful trial" Cauchon promised? As for its prophesied verdict, whoever burned the most notorious and dangerous sorceress ever known would catapult himself into the kind of fame and power that could set him on the path to the papacy. The first reward Cauchon had picked out for himself was the archbishopric of Rouen, recently vacated. Among the unlucky witch's fatal mistakes had been evicting him from his diocese, not only for incurring his enmity, but also because it was partly in consideration of the loss of that position and its advantages that the English "placed him in charge of special missions in England, Paris, and elsewhere," one of those missions being the trial of Joan of Arc. According to the chatty account book of Normandy's receiver general, Pierre Surreau, who recorded that 765 *livres tournois* were given to Cauchon in consideration of his tireless diplomatic service, "for 153 days, 'Pierre Cauchon took leave of the king, our lord, to do his business, as much in the city of Calais as in many trips to my lord the duke of Burgundy or to my lord John of Luxembourg in Flanders, to the siege before Compiègne, and at Beaurevoir in the matter of Joan called the Maid.'"

Joan, too, grew increasingly expensive, and Jean of Luxembourg had the right to turn her back over to the French for a ransom rather than selling her to the English. But only England was collecting the funds to pay for her. "In August 1430, a special tax was levied by the estates of Normandy to raise 120,000 *livres*" to cover the expense of what would be a protracted trial involving scores of justices, "of which 10,000 was set aside for Joan's purchase" from Jean of Luxembourg, whose brother Louis of Luxembourg, the bishop of Thérouanne and councilor to the English king Henry, had negotiated the price. Louis—the rich older brother whom Jean expected to contest any will that favored him—was an intimate of both Bedford and Cauchon. As the dean of the church of Beauvais from 1414 until 1430, he divided his time between Beauvais and the archbishopric's palace in Rouen. A year after Joan's execution, Henry ordered his treasurer general in Normandy to pay Louis 1,000 livres in consideration of "the great expenses which in the cause of our service he has had and has to pay."

On September 18, 1430, the Demoiselle of Luxembourg expired, and her nephew's conscience along with her, a crisis from which Joan averted her face by focusing obsessively on the fate of Compiègne, whose every skirmish she followed. When the city at last fell, on October 24, "a kind of frenzy seems to have taken possession of her," as Sackville-West described it. For the first time, Joan and her voices were at odds, and "the argument continued daily for some time, Jeanne beseeching, the Voices refusing their permission" for her to attempt to escape from her captors. No matter how desperately Joan begged them to allow her to rush to the aid of Compiègne in an exultant, quixotic last act, she must not jump, Saints Catherine and Margaret said.

But without the distraction of war, the months slid silently by, each day as slow as emptiness could make it. She knew she had but a year; what consolation did she have but to look forward to her arrival at redemption? "I yearn to breathe the airs of heaven," Galahad, a "maiden knight" as chaste as Joan, prays in Alfred, Lord Tennyson's "Sir Galahad."

I muse on joy that will not cease,
Pure spaces clothed in living beams,
Pure lilies of eternal peace,
Whose odours haunt my dreams;
And, stricken by an angel's hand,
This mortal armour that I wear,
This weight and size, this heart and eyes,
Are touch'd, are turn'd to finest air.

Like Galahad, like Roland, Joan was to be borne up from the battlefield by the wings of angels. Roland "offers his right-hand glove to God, and Saint Gabriel takes it . . . God sent his angel cherubin down to him . . . Saint Michael . . . Saint Gabriel . . . they bear Roland's soul to Paradise." Joan knew God's heroes died in rapture, in glory, not in a dank cell, exiled from combat. The claustrophobia of prison made her wild and reckless, she who was so impulsive by nature, to the point that "she ceased to listen to her Voices, who forbade her the fatal leap." As Beaurevoir's tower was typical of medieval fortresses, with arrow slits rather than windows, a guard was posted only at the bottom in the reasonable presumption that no one would try to escape from the top. Joan could not have jumped from a point lower than the tower's crenellated rampart, which is estimated to have been seventy feet high, a measurement based in archaeological fact rather than hagiographic hyperbole. There was nothing that might have broken her fall—no tree limb or anything else that might encourage escape, no hillock of grass or cushion of undergrowth. She landed in the castle's dry moat.

"Why did you jump?" the examiner asked.

"I had heard that the people of Compiègne, all of them to the age of seven, were to be put to fire and to the sword. I would rather die than live after the destruction of such good people." As Michelet saw it, the problem was a simple one. "Her body was at Beaurevoir, her soul at Compiègne."

"Was that the only reason?"

"The other was that I knew I had been sold to the English, and I would have died rather than fall into their hands."

"Did you expect to kill yourself when you leaped?"

"No, because as I leaped I commended myself to God and Our Lady."

"Hadn't your voices forbidden you to jump?"

"I begged their pardon afterward. I admitted I was wrong in jumping, and my angels forgave me. They saw my need, and that I could in no way hold myself back, so they lent aid to my life and prevented me from being killed."

The line of questioning aimed at two capital crimes. If Joan had attempted suicide, she'd condemned herself, like Judas, who turned away from the limitless grace of a god who forgave everything—except rejection. If she'd expected her angels to soften her landing, she'd committed the antithetical sin, equally dire, of presuming God would save her from the mortal consequences of her acts. That she never considered seeking forgiveness and receiving absolution from an earthly cleric, rather than supernatural beings only she could see, was by definition heretical.

"Did you receive any great penance?"

"A large part of my penance was the hurt I did myself in falling." The hurt Joan did herself was significant enough that she didn't know where she was when she regained consciousness; her Burgundian captors had to tell her. "For two days she neither ate nor drank nor moved," and the physician who attended her feared she'd broken her back.

⊕

"The devil took him [Jesus] to the holy city, and set him on the pinnacle of the temple," the Evangelist Matthew wrote. "If you are the Son of God," the devil said, "throw yourself down; for it is written: 'He will give his angels charge of you, and on their hands they will bear you up, lest you strike your foot against a stone.'"

The devil has a good memory for Scripture, too—as good as Jesus's, when given the opportunity to speak, quoting here from Psalm 91.

Jesus answered him, "Again it is written: 'You shall not tempt the Lord your God.'"

⊕

"You presumed upon the grace of God," the examiner said. But Joan admitted only disobedience—not the presumption that her angels would loan her wings. It seemed obvious to her that if they had, she wouldn't have been injured. And were she the author of such blasphemy, why would they have come to aid and soothe her?

"St. Catherine told me the people of Compiègne would have succor before St. Martin's Day in winter without fail. And she told me to confess and ask God to forgive me.

"So I was comforted and began to get well, and to eat, and soon afterwards recovered." Joan's account of her leap was given on March 6, 1431, four and a half months after Compiègne fell—long enough to countless times review what she'd done, as she must have, filling the dark of her cell and its sleepless nights with memories of past deeds, this one followed by unconsciousness, disorientation, and days of death-like torpor. Given the friable nature of human memory, and her fixation on redemption, it's possible she attempted a suicide she later denied. Joan's vigor and her tolerance for physical injury and pain were unnatural enough to inspire her confidence in superhuman strength, but could her sense of invulnerability have been strong enough to make leaping from an altitude of seventy feet, the average height of a six- or seven-story building today, seem survivable?

As the Church's grip on the people's collective imagination loosened, Joan would increasingly be perceived as a young woman who, once her active trajectory was halted by her capture and incarceration, fell prey to doubt. *The Messenger* replaces Joan's voices with a hooded presence claiming to be God—or is it the devil, so adept at impersonation? In either case, Besson suggests the apparition, which only Joan sees and hears, is evidence of her decompensating under the crush of guilt inspired by the mass murders for which she was responsible. Hadn't she, the 1999 film asks, suffered what psychoanalysis would term a delusion of grandeur? Isn't God the internalized fantasy of a terrorizing and inconsistently benign patriarch? The film poses questions from a vantage medieval Europeans never had and dismisses the comfort Joan received from her voices. She admitted instances in which they failed to provide the direction she sought. She argued with them sometimes. Before her life ended, she would have disobeyed and even briefly betrayed her voices, but she was never heard to say, as she does in Anderson's *Joan of Lorraine*, that her voices abandoned her, leaving her to "wait here alone, in the darkness and in silence," asking if she "made an error that was not forgiven."

She hadn't been beaten, stripped of her clothing, or scourged. She didn't fall under the weight of the cross on which she would be crucified, but Joan had her Via Dolorosa. Sold to the English, she endured a punitive reversal of Christine de Pizan's portrait of her victorious sweep through the spring countryside in the wake of Charles's coronation: "As he returns through his country, neither city nor castle nor small town can hold out against them. Whether he be loved or hated, whether they be dismayed or reassured, the inhabitants surrender." She wouldn't fulfill Christine's prediction that she would go on to save all Christendom from heretics and unbelievers, hers an unstoppably glorious trajectory. Instead, she was "paraded throughout many of the lands of France occupied by the Burgundians and then the English."

From Beaurevoir to Rouen, she was the single irresistible exhibit of a traveling sideshow that crawled out of dark November and on into December and its darker Christmas, a six-week pilgrimage guaranteed its share of rain and sleet, two weeks' worth anyway, as Joan and her retinue of guards and hecklers followed the circuitous route necessary to skirt French-held territory, moving over flatlands low enough to dip, here and there, into marsh.

The vanguard of such processions was traditionally given to the spoils of war. Joan would have taken the lead under heavy guard, wearing not armor but shackles, mounted on a horse, perhaps, or pulled in a wagon, even held in a cage, at last cut down to mortal size, a maid returned to her proper state: booty. She never spoke of the journey. After a year spent surrounded by throngs of worshipful well-wishers, Joan was learning what it was like to be an object of public loathing, ridicule, and censure, a symbol not of France's victory but of its loss. People spat at her because she was French, they threw things at her because she was a witch, they called her a dirty cunt because the Church told them female wickedness wore a sexual stain and they hadn't the imagination or independence of mind to think of anything else. Long separated from her brother and Jean d'Aulon, and now from the kind women around Jean of Luxembourg, Joan had only her voices to comfort her. "I asked that when I was taken I might die quickly without long suffering in prisons; and the voices told me to be resigned to everything, that it must so happen." They said it often enough that she knew her suffering was ordained and that a "great victory" awaited her. "Take everything peacefully," they said to her. "Have no care for thy martyrdom. In the end thou shalt come to the Kingdom of Paradise." A victory unlike Roland's or Galahad's, but deliverance and paradise nonetheless.

From Bapaume the party moved north, out of the valley of the Somme and into the plains of Flanders, to Arras, whose felicitous placement on the Scarpe River presented a strategic advantage that had purchased centuries of strife. Courts as far-flung as that of the Spanish Hapsburgs had claimed the city, which became a famed center of troubadour culture, the cosmopolitan home to poets' societies and host to countless recitals of chansons de geste, whose audiences were as eager as a barn filled with bumpkins to see a witch, as they would be a dragon or any other outright manifestation of the devil's work. If seeing Joan was frightening, it was in equal measure reassuring. To the English and the Burgundians she presented a mortal vessel into which they could project and contain their fear of evil, just as she had given the French one in which to safeguard their faith. Like all messianic leaders, she fulfilled an essential psychic need for both her enemies and her adherents; thus she possessed multitudes, all of them fixed on her unlawful example.

"When you were in Arras, did not my lord Jean de Pressy and others offer you a woman's dress?"

"Yes. He and many others also asked me to take an outfit of that sort."

"And it was Captain Baudricourt who had a male costume made for you, with arms to match?" the examiner said, adding that the captain had done so "reluctantly, with great repugnance."

"It was not Sir Robert who gave me clothing but the people of Vaucouleurs. I was armed by order of my king."

While in Arras, Joan was confined in one of the Duke of Burgundy's many châteaus, where a sympathetic guard slipped her a file, or a would-be savior slipped it past a guard, but it was discovered and confiscated before she had a chance to use it. By the time the victory parade left for Avesnes-le-Comte, the days had grown significantly shorter than they had been upon the party's arrival in Arras, enough to startle and disquiet anyone who'd spent two weeks in a cell. Every day the sun's light drained away a little sooner, a little faster, as she was drawn ever farther from any source of mortal rescue. Fields and pasture claimed what wasn't wooded or settled, and the apple orchards of Normandy were falling under winter's shadow as Joan passed by land she and Alençon had dreamed of reclaiming, co-commanders of an army out of reach of court politicking. How starkly frail a branch looked without leaves or fruit, nothing more than a dark scribble against a pale, chill sky. The procession visited ten cities, in which Joan spent a night or two in the town keep, probably in hearing of a public sermon devoted to her grievous sins, for what preacher would squander the opportunity to edify his flock with a morality tale inspired by a visit from the fallen Maid? By now, Joan had been called a witch and a whore so many times, as often as she'd been threatened with rape, that the words themselves had lost their power to summon tears, and the same angels who had protected her from the idolatry she recognized in her followers diminished the impact of her abrupt arrival at universal revilement. Though the torments that awaited her were extraordinary enough to be the object of fascination six centuries after her birth, the company she kept was even more so. Her fate was sealed; the face with which she met it remained her own. Still, the clamor of battle would have been preferable, even less disorienting, than her passage through an endless gauntlet of staring peasants. The dread her presence aroused muffled the jeering that would otherwise greet a war prize of her magnitude, and only those curious enough to overcome their fears drew close. The rest hung back; they didn't want to see the sorceress who'd led the armies of France so much as they wanted to be able to tell their grandchildren that they had.

Le Crotoy, in whose prison Alençon had spent five years awaiting ransom, lay twelve days to the west, through Avesnes-le-Comte, Lucheux, and Drugy, and offered a respite of three weeks on the Normandy coast, protected from the eyes of all the people, some of whom traveled a considerable distance to join the restless clots gathered around the castle in which Joan was housed. Not every pilgrim was hostile. "She received the ladies of Abbeville, who had arrived by boat down the Somme, and who came to see her as a marvel of their sex," and she was allowed to go to Mass—the last she would ever attend—celebrated by a fellow prisoner, Nicolas de Queuville, a priest who also heard her confession. It was a hiatus she'd look back on as presenting comfort, if not freedom.

There was this, too: She'd never seen a beach before; she'd never seen the sea. She hadn't seen any body of water wider than a river, its right bank visible from its left. At Le Crotoy, only the marsh grass underfoot was familiar, footprints filling rapidly with water. But look west, where the sun set, and the grass disappeared, and the land as well. The bay of the Somme spread out flat, shallows and sandbars sliding almost imperceptibly into the sea, a desolate scene in December, as there was no water deep enough for a port of any kind. If she admitted its beauty, she must have seen its menace as well. The land on which she stood ran out; there was no more.

They left Le Crotoy on December 20, a three-day caravan along the Normandy coast. Joan was in irons, watching through bars to see how it was that sometimes there was no line drawn between sky and water, and the water wasn't any color at all, none she could name. If she was lucky, she saw a sunset pave the sea with fire, a straight path burning like a fuse toward another day's end. Joan spent one night at Saint-Valéry-sur-Somme, and then it was December 21. The cell she slept, or tossed, in still stands, built just inside the ruins of the old city walls. Eu had a prison, too, as did Argues, once the home of William the Conqueror. From Argues, the party quit the coast and turned south to Rouen, where Joan arrived on December 23, 1431.

The
Tower
Keep

A cage had been made to measure for the girl once fitted for the best armor money could buy. "I have heard from Étienne Castille, the blacksmith," Jean Massieu, the trial's usher, testified, "that he made an iron cage for her, in which she was held in a standing position, secured by the neck, the hands, and the feet, and that she was kept in it from the moment when she was brought to Rouen until the opening of her trial." No eyewitness claimed to have seen Joan caged, so it might have been used as a threat rather than the actual physical trap for which it was intended. The weeks of Joan's approach to Rouen had allowed time to prepare for the incarceration of so dangerous a sorceress, one with untested powers, an individual who leaped off ramparts and survived falls that would kill a mortal: a witch with the ability to fly. No one saw her in the cage, but the mason Pierre Cusquel, one of the few local craftsmen to own a massive scale, saw it soon after it was built. "I saw it being weighed at my house," he testified—probably to determine its price.

By the time Joan arrived, some of the Rouennais had been waiting near the city's gates for as long as a day, protecting what turf they'd claimed, elbowing and pressing forward, taking courage in numbers and jeering and profaning freely where smaller crowds just gaped and pointed. Rouen wasn't a town but a city, the second most populous in France, with throngs to fill its streets and squares. When Joan arrived, it had been occupied for more than a decade, since January 1419, when it surrendered to the English after a merciless six-month siege. Henry V had marched on the city in July 1418 to discover its fortifications had been augmented in the three years since Agincourt. Now Rouen had one of the largest garrisons in France, and, with seventy thousand citizens, it was a prize Henry was set on acquiring, and with it the rest of Normandy. As he hadn't enough troops to make an assault on the freshly buttressed walls, he made do with surrounding them and their sixty towers bristling with crossbows. Resigned to starving them into submission, he cut off all means of getting food into the city, and by the time winter arrived, the Rouennais had eaten their dogs, cats, and even rats before at last, inevitably, they began slaughtering their horses. In December, the city's leaders made the decision to push all the old, the ill, and the orphaned—twelve thousand people, nearly a fifth of the population—outside the city walls. Henry, recognizing a wicked and dishonorable advantage he was not above seizing, refused to allow the would-be refugees to cross the line of siege, so there they remained, trapped in the frozen ditch between the city walls and the enemy forces, huddled together. On Christmas Day, Henry allowed the Church to distribute bread to the living, but the gift did no more than awaken hunger and forestall an inevitable end. The clamor they made died one voice at a time. No one survived. Rouen's was the story of Orléans, without the Maid.

"Joan was brought to this city of Rouen by the English and imprisoned in the castle of Rouen," a Rouennais remembered, "in a room beneath the staircase on the side looking out to the open country"—a tower cell on the north side of Bouvreuil castle, built by Henry upon his victory over Rouen and named for the hillock on which it stood. Bouvreuil overlooking the city with its deep stone gutters running with color from the dye works, staining the Seine blue one week, orange the next. The boy king, Henry VI, had been living in Bouvreuil castle since June 1429, save a trip to England for his November 6 coronation. He would have a second, in Paris, on December 16, 1431, six and a half months after Joan was executed.

The room in which Joan was held for the last five months of her life was eight steps up from the castle's oval courtyard, "lined with buildings constructed against the walls: the great hall, where governmental functions took place; kitchens and servants' quarters . . . and . . . in the middle of the courtyard . . . a chapel." She wasn't underground, but with no source of light other than its one barred window her cell was "very dark," and it was barren, although large enough to allow room for as many as half a dozen visitors when Cauchon called on her with a cadre of examiners. The trial's usher, Jean

Massieu, who accompanied Joan back and forth from her cell to the chambers in which the trial was conducted, testified that there was "a great bed in it, on which she slept," always in leg irons. "I know for certain that at night she lay chained by the legs with two pairs of irons, and tightly secured by another chain which passed through the legs of her bed." That chain was "attached to a great block of wood five or six feet long, by means of a lock." Night and day she was left in the care of five "guards of the lowest sort . . . common torturers"—*houssepailliers*, the usher called them. In medieval French the word was the equivalent of "ruffian," increasingly used in place of "abuser." As usher, or in the words of Cauchon, "executor of the commands and convocations emanating from our authority," Massieu overheard them mock her cruelly at every opportunity. Pretending to have overheard information critical to her case, they purposefully raised her hopes of release one day and told her she'd surely be burned on the next. Three of these ruffians remained locked within her cell and were with her at all times. They moved about freely; chains rendered her "unable to stir from her place." Should she need to use the latrine, with which all such keeps were furnished, a guard unlocked and accompanied her to the closet-size room with a hole in the floor through which waste dropped directly into a cesspit or moat. In winter months, it would have been gelid. Typically, the atmosphere that filled such privies was so saturated with ammonia gas that they came to be called *garderobes*, or cloakrooms, where guests could expect their coats to be hung, as the caustic smell was believed to kill vermin.

The latrine wasn't directly annexed to the cell like the cell's two ancillary spaces. One was a landing for the stairs with hidden access to the other, used by spies: a room large enough to accommodate several men at once, from which it was possible to spy on Joan in her cell and eavesdrop on conversations that unfolded between her and those, like her false confessor, sent to extract useful admissions. Because the English were "desperately afraid that she might escape," the single room had but three keys. One was in the possession of the bishop of Winchester, identified by Régine Pernoud as the "real manager of the trial"—the same bishop who had embezzled funds earmarked for stamping out Hussites to raise an army of archers to fight the French.

A second key was entrusted to the man determined to please Cardinal Beaufort, Bishop Cauchon; the third to the bishop's henchman, Jean d'Estivet, the trial's promoter, or lead prosecutor.

That all three of her keepers were clerics allowed them to collectively preserve the conceit of Church custody, but Joan was in a military prison maintained by her enemies, which, as Jean Fabri, one of the few assessors, or assistant judges, to take Joan's part, reported, "greatly displeased some of the assessors" . . . as it was not "proper procedure . . . since she had been handed over to the Church . . . But no one dared raise the subject." For a month, Joan asked that she be moved, as was her right, and placed in Church custody under the guard of women. The worst that had happened at Beaurevoir was that a knight, Haimond de Macy, had come calling and, as he testified for the nullification, "tried several times playfully to touch her breasts. I tried to slip my hand in, but Joan would not let me. She pushed me off with all her might." This aborted assault on the fortress of Joan's unpolluted body was repeated in Rouen by a tailor sent to measure her for clothes she wore once before choosing flames over a dress. She slapped him forcefully, too. Initially held under relentless threat of attack, Joan "complained to the Bishop of Beauvais, to the sub-Inquisitor, and to Master Nicolas Loiseleur that one of her guards had tried to rape her," as the scribe Guillaume Manchon testified. Other witnesses heard, on other occasions, the same complaint, finally answered by a woman—the last who would be in a position, like Yolande and the old Duchess of Luxembourg, to intercede on her behalf.

"It's grotesque," Bedford whispers to Cauchon in Bresson's *The Trial of Joan of Arc*. They eavesdrop through a chink in the wall as she is questioned in her cell. "She's lived with soldiers and slept on the straw with them and she's still a virgin?"

"You're not a maiden," Jean d'Estivet says to Joan on the other side of the wall.

"I say I am. If you don't believe me, too bad."

"You don't belong to God but to the Devil."

"I belong to our Lord, Jesus Christ," Joan says, calm in her defiance, calm and arrogant.

In Rouen, it was Joan who appealed for a vaginal examination to prove her virginity. The procedure was conducted under the authority of the Duke of Bedford's wife, Anne of Burgundy—Philip's sister— and necessarily accomplished within a few weeks of Joan's arrival, as the duke and duchess are known to have departed from Rouen on January 13, 1431. A notary for the trial passed on the unsubstantiated report that Bedford secreted himself in the spies' annex and peered through the chink in the wall at Joan as she was examined by the matrons, who subsequently attested that the Pucelle was a true maid, uncorrupted. Fortuitously if not miraculously, her hymen remained intact despite evidence of an "injury from riding horseback," a conclusion that didn't exonerate Joan but predicated Cauchon's changing tack by swapping in one superstition for another. If, as she claimed, her power lay in her virginity, it stood to reason that "if she were robbed of it, she would be disarmed, the spell would be broken, she would sink to the common level of women."

"These women confirm that she's a virgin," Bresson's Bedford tells Cauchon.

"Yes," Cauchon says, "that's what gives her strength."

"If it's her virginity that gives her strength we'll make her lose her virginity." Bedford is matter-of-fact, as if speaking of prying the lid off a box.

Joan had taken what measures she could against assault. Period illustrations allow costume historians to augment the descriptions culled from the trial record:

> two layers of hosen securely fastened to the doublet, the inner layer being waist-high conjoined woolen hosen attached to the doublet by fully twenty cords, each cord tied into three eyelets apiece (two on the hosen and one on the doublet), for a total of forty attachment points on the inner layer of hosen. The second layer, which was made of rugged leather, seems to have been attached by yet another set of cords. Once this outfit was thus fastened together by dozens of cords connecting both layers to the doublet, it would be a substantial undertaking for someone to try to pull off these garments . . . The use of twenty cords on the inner layer was an excessively large and exceedingly awkward amount for this type of clothing, which

normally had no more than half that number, indicating that she was deliberately taking measures to further increase its protective utility at the cost of her own convenience.

Once her virginity had been confirmed—once it had been established that there was something of value to guard—Joan complained she couldn't tie all her laces tightly enough to defend herself from the unrelenting predation of her guards. Anne of Burgundy went to the Earl of Warwick, captain of Bouvreuil castle. What member of the English peerage would allow so disgraceful an incident as a prisoner's rape, knowing how such a contemptible crime would reflect upon the English, the English who were working so hard to dishonor the French? For that matter, how would it reflect on Cardinal Beaufort?

Warwick ordered his commander of the guard, John Gray, "a gentleman in the service of the duke of Bedford," to arrange for Joan's guards to be replaced by a putatively less uncivilized team.

Having discovered that threats and bribes weren't enough to marshal troops in terror of a sorceress, the English wasted no time in getting the trial under way. Soon after Joan's arrival in Rouen, a chorister who was often in the cathedral where the judges gathered overheard a handful speaking among themselves. "A case must quickly be framed against her," one said, and, as soon as it was feasible, "an excuse . . . found for putting her to death." A Dominican friar, Jean Toutmouillé, testified that "they reckoned that while she was alive they would have no glory or success in the field of war."

Eager as they were to recapture Louviers, fifteen miles south of Rouen, and check the accelerating decline in their fortunes, the English decided they "would not besiege the town until the Maid had been examined"—and executed. On January 9 the trial's preliminary phase began. It continued for a month and was dedicated to the appointment of Cauchon's immediate underlings, the selection of the sixty or so assessors, and the dissemination of muckraking spies to gather what they could about Joan. Cauchon named Jean Le Maître, the sub-inquisitor for Rouen, as his reluctant co-judge. Le Maître's assistant, Isambart de la Pierre, testified that, like many others, Le Maître had been "moved by fear." He attended only some of the trial's sessions and "took no part in the interrogations."

"There was no one who was not afraid," Guillaume Manchon testified for the nullification. As one of the trial's three official notaries, Manchon was "present at all that has been said and done," an eyewitness to everything that unfolded during the proceedings, his memory aided by the act of writing and rewriting the minutes. "The English instituted the prosecution, and it was at their expense that it was conducted. I do not think, however, that the Bishop of Beauvais was compelled to prosecute Joan, nor was the promoter Jean d'Estivet. They did what they did voluntarily. As for the assessors and other counselors, none would have dared to refuse."

When Isambart was discovered to have counseled Joan, prompting her when she was being interrogated, he was advised to be silent or be drowned.

"We only gave our opinions and took part in the trial out of fear, threats, and terror, and it was in our minds to run away," one of the assessors, Richard de Grouchet, testified.

Some sixty assessors, of whom at least forty attended each day of the trial's public sessions, were drawn from the University of Paris, mostly Dominicans. (The Inquisition recruited and trained judges almost exclusively from Franciscan and Dominican orders.) Some "came of their own free will, some to win English favor, some because they dared not refuse," and some sought vengeance; it wasn't only Cauchon that Joan's victories had chased out of their dioceses and away from their sources of power and revenue. All summoned were required to sit in judgment: none could abstain from offering his opinion, for example, on whether or not to put Joan to the rack, which was decided by vote. If the cowed collaborators outnumbered the chop-licking prosecutors, they had no strength in their numbers. The few brave enough to raise objections became immediate cautionary tales. Nicolas de Houppeville, a bachelor in theology at the University of Paris, was thrown out on the second day when a notary told Cauchon he had overheard the man say the trial presented a number of serious risks. Having noted the unseemly slavering of the bishop at Joan's arrival in Rouen, how he "spoke exultingly with great joy" of the "beautiful trial" he had planned, a day's worth of the proceedings was sufficient to confirm Nicolas's suspicion that the trial would amount to a disgrace. The bishop, he pointed out, was a member of the opposition party. The trial was being financed by the opposition; the prisoner jailed by their military. Joan had already been rigorously and officially examined by the Church at Poitiers—by Cauchon's superior, the archbishop of Reims. Cauchon had no ecclesiastical right to serve as her judge. Incensed, Cauchon demanded Nicolas de Houppeville appear before him, as he did, but only to declare that as Cauchon was not his superior the bishop had no jurisdiction over him, any more than he did over Joan. Technically, this was true, but it didn't impede Cauchon's having him thrown in prison. To betray any sympathy for Joan or allow her the smallest comfort—let alone be caught offering counsel to a girl alone, accused, and unrepresented—was to defy the bishop and, as several assessors made clear, place oneself "in danger of death."

Jean d'Estivet was confirmed in the position he'd filled for Cauchon before, as promoter of the ecclesiastical court of Beauvais. Witnesses to his behavior betrayed surprise at his venom, but Cauchon, having worked closely with him before, knew exactly whom he'd chosen. A vindictive sadist subject to seizures of rage and fixated on the subject of female pollution, Jean took every opportunity to defame and castigate Joan, calling her "a wanton and a whore" even after her chastity was verified, a "loose woman and a filthy creature."

As Joan stood in her cage, or lay on her block of wood, or paced as much as fetters allowed, which was only to make shuffling circles like a hobbled dog on a chain, spies were dispatched to Domrémy, Greux, Neufchâteau, Vaucouleurs, Sainte-Catherine-de-Fierbois, Chinon, Poitiers, Tours, Orléans, Jargeau, Troyes, Patay, Reims, Senlis, Saint-Denis, Lagny, Compiègne, and any other place Joan was known to have stayed for so much as a night. "Somebody important from Lorraine came to Rouen," Jean Moreau, a merchant (a different Jean Moreau from Joan's godfather), testified. This person had been "specially commissioned to gather information in Joan's country of origin, to find out what reputation she had there." But the information he brought back to Cauchon—"nothing that he would not have liked to hear about his own sister"—earned him only calumny. The bishop called him "a traitor and a sinner and told him that he had not carried out his instructions properly" and refused him compensation for his expenses in visiting six parishes, as well as the agreed-upon fee for his labor. Another former spy, Nicolas Bailly, a "scrivener" (equivalent to a notary public) who with the provost Gérard Petit collected information about Joan, was similarly abused, even after having gone to the trouble to have a dozen witnesses appear in person to certify the accuracy of the reports made. Both were accused of being in league with the Armagnacs; neither was paid. There was nothing bad to be found in Joan, but there was a tissue of rumor and speculation from which to create the single precondition required by an inquisitorial trial: *diffamatio*—a bad reputation, the kind men invent to destroy women brazen enough to claim powers men consider theirs alone.

All three notaries, Guillaume Manchon, Guillaume Colles, and Nicolas Taquel, testified to the corruption of what was presented as a trial that hewed to every letter of the law. Two auxiliary and unnamed notaries were hidden in an alcove behind a curtain in the room where the interrogations were conducted, writing and eliding as directed by a prelate. Manchon, Colles, and Taquel's official French notes were sometimes redacted rather than translated into Latin by Thomas de Courcelles, a "zealous university man and rector of the faculty of law" who was ultimately so ashamed of his involvement in the trial that he "suppressed his name wherever it occurred in the French minutes." Courcelles testified for the nullification with the intent to vindicate himself along with Joan. Bedford's confidant, the Rouen canon Nicolas Midi, a rabid exponent of the University of Paris, reduced the redacted notes to seventy articles of accusation, which were subsequently reorganized into twelve, excluding redundancies and some, but not all, of the more absurd false charges—the one, for example, that Joan kept a mandrake hidden in her bosom as one of the tricks of her trade, a magic tuber that was held to summon money. She'd heard that near her village there was one, she told Midi, though she'd never seen it. Whatever it was, she knew it was held to be "an evil and dangerous thing to keep."

Twigs of fairy trees and trumped-up breaches of marriage contracts never made, unuttered blaspheming of God, and never-witnessed rituals with the devil: there was enough kindling to set below a stake. Hadn't her own father dreamed many times of her disgraceful conduct with soldiers and, upon waking, instructed her brothers to drown her should they come true? A century of public burnings preceded the trial of Joan of Arc; still, many historians consider hers the first great witchcraft trial, catalytic in its effects across Europe, as high-profile political inquisitions like Joan's yielded to those of countless unknown and mostly destitute women who lived outside the cold shoulder of society. Some were midwives, some were prostitutes, some were mentally ill or unfortunate enough to have been raped and ruined for decent society; all made the wrong enemy. None had the protection of father, uncle, brother, or son. Like Joan, they were judged by slander and called whores, filth, the devil's handmaidens. Society had arrived at a kind of democracy, if not one that suggested the ethical evolution of the species: it was the right of every citizen to watch a witch burn, in person, for himself. The widespread demand for live performances of atrocities and live sacrifices—scapegoats on which to pin their accusers' sufferings—meant witches were found everywhere.

For one year, from May 1429 to May 1430, Joan presided over a handful of battles resulting in a loss of fewer than ten thousand men, in total. Her trial, its verdict, and the publication of her example united as a catalyst for the three centuries' worth of zealous, often hysterical, witch hunts amounting to the theatrically cruel execution of as many as a hundred thousand women—a "vast holocaust," in the words of one historian.

While her family, friends, and comrades were being interrogated, Joan was "subjected to the Inquisition's tactic of the prison informer," of whom two are known. A canon of the Rouen Cathedral, Nicolas Loiseleur, one of Cauchon's cherry-picked cronies "very highly regarded by Bedford's government," "pretended to be a man from the

Maid's country and so succeeded in getting writings, conversation, and confidences from her (in prison) by giving her news from home, which was pleasing to her," the notary Manchon testified. Loiseleur gained Joan's trust before he revealed himself to be a priest and asked to be her confessor. Joan accepted, and whenever Loiseleur visited, Manchon said, spies in the hidden annex listened through the peephole wall of her cell and recorded all they said for Jean d'Estivet to pore over in pursuit of incriminating evidence. As none existed, none could be extracted. Disguised, Jean d'Estivet himself visited Joan, pretending to be another prisoner, without success.

Loiseleur adapted his function to that of provocateur and encouraged Joan "to defy the court and resist attempts to induce her to modify her statements . . . and [said] that she must not trust the judges," who sought to destroy her. While Joan didn't need encouragement to speak her mind, often impudently, rarely with deference to those who considered themselves her betters, the one man she reflexively considered an ally—she, at least, held confession too sacred to cloak perfidy—didn't caution Joan to still her sharp tongue. Instead, Loiseleur advocated her impertinence, and thus the enmity of those who heard it.

Joan's first public examination was held on a Wednesday, February 21, 1431. The sun had yet to rise when Jean Massieu retrieved her from her cell, and though it was but a short distance to the castle's chapel, it was long as well. Joan couldn't be marched, or even walked, through the courtyard. The ankle cuffs of her leg irons, connected to each other by only a few links of chain, made it impossible for her to advance more than a few inches with each step. Joan could hobble forward at a torturously slow pace, but not walk. The two moved under cover of armed guard, Massieu's job to watch she didn't stumble and fall. From the time of her capture, in May, nine months earlier, Joan had refused women's clothes from her captors. By the time she left Arras, perhaps sooner, she encountered no one inclined to risk offering her a change of male attire. Having not been captured with a portmanteau, she appeared before her judges, some richly robed, in clothes she had worn every day for months. Whether she was allowed to attend to personal hygiene or had the means to launder her clothes was the prerogative of her captors, who answered to the demands of the English tribunal. She was as pallid as a life spent entirely indoors predicted; she was, undoubtedly, gaunt.

Perhaps, as it had been when she approached the gates of Chinon, Joan had an angel by her side with—as Anouilh described Saint Michael—"two white wings reaching from the sky to the ground." Maybe "the light that comes in the name of the voice" fell around her as she walked, bright enough to burn away faces that spat at her. If the tongues of angels stopped up her ears, maybe she didn't hear all the cries of "Death to the witch!"

"Tell us if you are the son of God," the high priest Caiaphas demanded.

"You have said so," Jesus said.

Caiaphas tore his robes. "Now you have heard him blaspheme," he told the crowd of scribes and elders assembled in the dark, an unofficial predawn hearing, as the Sanhedrin could take formal action only by daylight. In either case, the verdict preceded the trial. "What is your judgment?"

"He deserves death," the crowd said. "Then they spat in his face, and struck him and some slapped him."

To rid himself of the rabble collecting around Jesus, Caiaphas, the power-hungry high priest who "sought false testimony against Jesus that they might put him to death," had to convince the Romans that in declaring himself messiah, a temporal king anointed by God, Jesus challenged the Romans' authority. Just as Cauchon seized the opportunity to satisfy his ambitions by proving Joan a witch, so had Caiaphas assumed the responsibility to provide the occupying Romans with a verdict demanding Jesus's execution. Scriptures used to contextualize and explain human experience were also legal divining rods, and in the trials of both Jesus and Joan they were a source of sacred vocabulary. "You will see the Son of man seated at the right hand of power, and coming on the clouds of heaven," Jesus said, drawing on the second-century BC prophet Daniel, who wrote, "There came one like the son of man . . . and to him was given dominion."

The isolated answers Jesus gave to the Sanhedrin were drawn from Old Testament apocalyptic prophecies he claimed as validation of his kingship, and they were used as evidence of the capital crime of blaspheming. Joan's answers and the Scripture summoned to condemn her for blasphemy were drawn from New Testament accounts of the life and death of Jesus and were used similarly by and against her.

Cauchon began the proceedings by explaining to Joan that she was before the Inquisition because she had a *diffamatio*: "Considering the public rumor and common report and also certain information already mentioned, after mature consultation with men learned in canon and civil law, we decreed that you be summoned to answer interrogations in matters of faith and other points truthfully according to law and reason."

She would willingly appear before him, Joan said, and requested Cauchon "summon in this suit ecclesiastics of the French side equal in number to those of the English party." No answer to the request was recorded, and no cleric representing Joan's political side came forth.

On paper, the trial appears orderly; in the moment it was not so much uncontrolled as purposefully disorienting and disrespectful, one assessor interrupting another, firing questions so fast at Joan that "just when one of them was asking a question or she was replying to it, another would interrupt her; so much that several times she said to her interrogators, 'My dear lords, please take your turns!'" Massieu was only one among many who were "surprised to see how well she could reply to the subtle and tricky questions that were asked her, questions that an educated man would have found it difficult to answer well" under more civilized proceedings. Not only did the assessors interrupt one another, but "they often asked Joan questions in several parts, and several of them asked her difficult questions at the same time . . . The examination generally went on from eight to eleven hours," so long that some of the assessors complained of the exhaustion following their participation in what "proceeded in an atmosphere of 'the greatest tumult.'" That neither Joan's spirit nor her mental acuity flagged as she resisted the combined force of dozens of opponents who protested they were being overburdened by what was, for nearly all of them, the passive role of sitting in judgment attests to her unnatural fortitude even more powerfully than her stunts on the battlefield.

Cauchon and Joan clashed immediately over a point they would continue to argue on subsequent days of interrogation. "Will you place your hands on the holy gospels, and promise to speak the truth in answer to all questions put before you?"

"I do not know what you wish to examine me on," Joan said. "Perhaps you might ask such things that I would not tell."

"Will you swear to speak the truth upon those things which are asked you concerning the matter of faith and about what you know?"

"About my father and mother and what I have done since I had taken the road to France, I will gladly swear. As for my revelations from God, I will say nothing, not to save my head."

"Will you or will you not swear to speak the truth in those things which concern our faith?"

"Once again and on many occasions," Cauchon admonished Joan to swear to tell the whole truth and nothing but the truth, and over and over she refused. In the end they made a tacit compromise when "Jeanne, kneeling, and with her two hands upon the book, namely the missal," made a qualified oath. She'd tell the truth, but only so much of it.

The interrogation followed a basic chronological order but often returned to topics covered during earlier sessions or verged into non sequiturs intended to disorient Joan. The first day's questioning opened on a pedestrian note. Joan was "alone, sitting on a high chair" and facing forty-two clerics, over whom Cauchon presided. The master of ceremonies on this inaugural and self-consciously historic occasion, Cauchon examined her himself, as he wouldn't for most of the subsequent sessions.

"Where were you baptized?"

"In the church of Domrémy."

"Who were your godfathers and godmothers?"

"One was named Agnes, another Jeanne, another Sibylle. My godfathers were Jean Lingué, another Jean Barrey. I know there were others, as my mother told me there were."

"What priest baptized you?"

"Master Jean Minet, as far as I know."

"Is Master Minet still living?"

"I believe so."

"How old are you?"

"Nineteen, I think."

"Recite the Paternoster for us."

"I will gladly, if you hear me in confession."

"Two clerics of the French language will hear your Paternoster."

"I will recite it in confession, not otherwise."

"If we are to believe you know your prayers, you must recite them."

"I said I would, in confession." On this point Joan did not compromise. She would not say her prayers before the tribunal. "She said also that she came from God," the record states, "and that there is nothing for her to do here, and asked to be sent back to God, from whom she came."

Cauchon summarized the first day's accomplishments:

Whereupon we, the aforementioned bishop, forbade Jeanne to leave the prison assigned to her in the castle of Rouen without our authorization under penalty of conviction of the crime of heresy. She answered that she did not accept this prohibition, adding that if she escaped, none could accuse her of breaking or violating her oath, since she had given her oath to none. Then she complained that she was imprisoned with chains and bonds of iron. We told her that she had tried elsewhere and on several occasions to escape from prison, and therefore, that she might be more safely and securely guarded, an order had been given to bind her with chains of iron. To which she replied: "It is true that I wished and still wish to escape, as is lawful for any captive or prisoner."

The trial record shows that forty-eight clerics joined Cauchon for the second day of public interrogation, relocated to the castle's great hall, with room enough for an audience as well as seventy clerics. Joan, of course, missed the proximity of the sacraments and the altar. Over the following two weeks, while "leading Joan from her prison to her place of trial," Massieu "several times passed the castle chapel," and "let her, at her request, stop there and say her prayers." When Jean d'Estivet caught him, he threatened the usher with prison for "having let that excommunicated whore come near [t]here without permission."

The sentence might have been a foregone conclusion, but Joan had not been excommunicated—not yet. To assemble the justification for her punishment would require another three months. As it was the second day of questioning, Joan had an additional objection to the oath: she'd taken it the day before.

"Not even a prince, Joan, can refuse to take an oath when required in matter of faith."

"I swore yesterday; that should be quite enough. You overburden me."

The deadlock was resolved, as it had been the previous day, with Joan's taking a qualified oath, swearing "to speak the truth on that which concerned the faith"—*the*, not *her*, faith.

The judges' interrupting each other and speaking all at once made it difficult to accurately record all that was said, let alone who said what, and while each day's proceedings began with a roll call of those judges who attended the session, the trial record rarely identifies particular prosecutors other than Cauchon and his deputy, "the distinguished professor of sacred theology, Master Jean Beaupère." The canon of Rouen Cathedral, Beaupère, who had already decided Joan's voices had "natural causes" arising from "the malice inherent in the nature of women," commenced the day's examination by "exhort[ing] her to answer truly, as she had sworn, what he should ask her."

"You may well ask me such things," Joan said, "that to some I shall answer truly, and to others I shall not . . . If you were well informed about me, you would wish me to be out of your hands. I have done nothing except by revelation."

Beaupère took revelation as the focus of that day's examination, from the arrival of the voice and accompanying light, to what advice Saints Catherine and Margaret had given her, and how they had paved her way to Robert de Baudricourt.

"Was it Captain Baudricourt who advised you to take the clothing of a man?"

This question, the record states, "she refused to answer many times. Finally she said she would charge no one with this; and she changed her testimony many times." In fact, though the question was rephrased many times, in many ways, on many days, the topic of cross-dressing not so much an occasional digression as a routine jam in a cul-de-sac, Joan's answer was consistent. She had assumed the clothing of a man in service to her vocation; it was a choice ordained by God and none other. Not even for the privilege of attending Mass would she agree to put on women's clothes.

On the trial's third day, sixty-two clerics watched as Joan and the bishop recapitulated the previous days' stalemate. After Cauchon had, as the record states, "thrice admonished her to take the oath, the said Jeanne answered, 'Give me leave to speak,'" and when the great hall had quieted enough that she could be heard, Joan said, "By my faith, you could ask me things such as I would not answer. Perhaps I shall not answer you truly in many things that you ask me, concerning the revelations; for perhaps you would constrain me to tell things I have sworn not to utter, and so I should be perjured, and you would not want that. I tell you, take good heed of what you say, that you are my judge, for you assume a great responsibility, and overburden me. It should be enough to have twice taken the oath."

"When did you last take food and drink?" Beaupère asked Joan.

"Since yesterday noon I have not taken either."

"Has your voice come to you?"

"I heard it yesterday and to-day."

"At what hour yesterday?"

"Three times: once in the morning, once at vespers, and once in the evening, when the Ave Maria was rung."

"What were you doing yesterday morning when the voice came to you?"

"I was sleeping, and the voice awakened me."

"How did it wake you? Did it touch you on the arm?"

"It woke me without touching me."

"Was it in the room with you?"

"I don't know, but it was in the castle."

"Did you not thank it and kneel down?"

"I was sitting on the bed, and I put my hands together. I asked for help, and the voice told me to answer you boldly."

Joan turned on her chair to accuse Cauchon once more directly. "You say that you are my judge," she repeated. "Take care what you are doing for in truth I have been sent by God and you put yourself in great danger." The assessors knew well enough to maintain an unreadable expression, but the audience packed into the gallery felt no such responsibility, and, like Joan's previous warnings to the bishop, her words inspired a communal gasp released in a static of whisper, anxious and amused. Cheekiness was one thing; to upbraid the bishop by claiming an intimacy with God that was not available to him, another.

"Do you know if you are in God's grace?" Beaupère asked, hoping to trick Joan into admitting the capital crime of presuming on God's generosity, and silencing the gallery. As it happened, the question provoked one of Joan's most often cited and admired parries.

"If I am not, may God put me there," she said, "and if I am, may God so keep me." Here, Joan's genius lay not in the words—they weren't her own—but in the uncanny speed at which she arrived at a response that allowed her to avoid making an original statement about so dangerous a subject as God's grace. Instead, she used a scrap of a prayer validated by the Church for many years. She had a memory that was not only capacious but also well organized, its function unimpeded by sleep deprivation, hunger, and the relentless abuse by her captors.

"I should be the saddest creature in the world if I knew I were not in His grace," Joan added for Beaupère. "If I were in a state of sin, I do not think that the voice would come to me."

The examination arrived at the infamous fairy tree by way of an interrogative stroll through the Domrémy of Joan's childhood, passing by the fields where, Joan emphasized, she "did not go with the sheep and the other animals" and pausing to consider the ragged bands of children who trailed home "much wounded and bleeding" after a day spent warmongering in Maxey. Try as it might to maintain a cordon sanitaire between its doctrine and secular culture, the Church has never been able to comb faith apart from fantasy. No church ever has. Joan's accusers were as heterodox as they were high-minded, giving credence to the very things Joan dismissed with a curt "I put no faith in that."

"I heard from my brother that it is said I received messages at the tree, but that was not so, and I told him I did not, quite the contrary. The sick, when they can rise, go to the tree and walk about it," and they drank from a spring beside it, "to restore their health. I have seen them myself, but I do not know whether they are cured or not."

"Is there not in your part of the country an oak-wood?" the examiner asked Joan.

"Yes."

"And do fairies not repair there?"

"I do not know," she said. "I have never heard that they do."

"What of the prophecy that out of this wood would come a maid who should work miracles?"

"I put no faith in that." The prophecy with which Joan was familiar said France would be saved by a maid from the marshes of Lorraine, not one who emerged from the oak wood behind her father's house.

Though the late-nineteenth-century illusionist and filmmaker Georges Méliès typically remained faithful to the plots of familiar folk and fairy tales he chose as subjects for his short silent films, for *Jeanne d'Arc* he scrambled what was known of Joan's real life. Released in 1900, the film begins with an apparition of three tinted pastel figures, more fairy godmother than angel, that emerge, hanging in mid-air beside the trunk of a great tree standing, like a sentinel, at the entrance to the tangled heart of a forest. Joan's sheep scatter; she falls to her knees before Saint Michael, beseeching him, as if to release her from her vocation. Behind her, the shadowed forest looms, and she staggers from her knees to her feet, pressing her hands to her head in operatic fright inspired by the looming terror of the task at hand. The angels vanish after the first seventeen seconds of the ten-minute film and return for a single ambiguous visitation in the eighth minute: twelve seconds of what might be a memory or a dream.

The sensibilities that characterize Méliès's body of work—sin, redemption, rebirth—and his obvious delight in devilry and mischief are distinctly medieval, a fin-de-siècle *danse macabre*. Like chapbooks, his films unfold in silence, without title cards, a medium for the illiterate that draws no distinction among supernatural manifestations—not any more than the average man or woman of the Middle Ages. Imps, ghosts, angels, mermaids, a talking moon, Satan in the role of innkeeper: fancy animates a world lighter than the one Méliès places reverently on the shoulders of France's national heroine. Not only does his careful, sanitized script for *Jeanne d'Arc* eliminate the supernatural from his heroine's mortal life; it returns Joan to female dress when not armored for battle, demonstrating how long-lived and universal is the unconscious response to those aspects of Joan that challenge patriarchal rule.

As if he had siphoned the religion from Joan's plot into Bluebeard's, Méliès saturates the seventeenth-century fairy tale inspired by atrocities committed by Gilles de Rais with enough Christian symbology to recast a fairy tale of original sin as a parable of redemption. "La Barbe-Bleue" offers a screen onto which Méliès projects Christian interpretations of the bride's disobedience and its results. After handing his newest wife a huge, phallic key to a forbidden room, Bluebeard leaves her without a chaperone to save her from her weak nature. Immediately, the bride succumbs to a spell cast by an antic devil that capers around her, out of her sight. When she slides the key into the forbidden lock's hole, she discovers the wives who predeceased her, murdered and hanging on hooks. In horror, she drops the key into a pool of blood that has spilled, menses-like, from their ravished corpses. No matter how hard the bride tries to wash the phallic key to remove evidence of her transgression, the stain of its profane baptism is indelible. Before this fatally curious Eve can be rescued from her base nature, the Virgin Mary must fight the devil for her soul. Virtue triumphs; the dead wives are resurrected; the film's last frame gathers the saved under the wings of a great white dove.

The unpolluted Maid of *Jeanne d'Arc*, however, ascends to her reward unaided by the Virgin. Dressed in bright, virginal white—forever beyond the reach of sexual sin—Joan rises from the flames of her pyre in a phoenix-like resurrection and arrives in a heaven over which the Eye of Providence (the same that tops the dollar bill's green pyramid) beams from out of its triangle: a tidy reduction of the Trinity. When she raises her arms to form a cross, the audience understands: the Maid's white gown isn't a bride's but a messiah's: Joan is the Christ. God the Father and God the Son would be out of place in Méliès's paradise, which, as it turns out, includes only women and might not be any more heavenly than being placed on a limitless pedestal (Fig. 35).

⊕

As was true of all medieval institutions of higher learning, the University of Paris, "surpassing all others in the fame of its masters and the prestige of its studies in theology and philosophy," employed a method of critical thought that came to be known as Scholasticism, its labyrinthine dialectical methods and preoccupation with Christian orthodoxy the original source of the question of how many angels can dance on the head of a pin. As conceived by Thomas Aquinas, Scholasticism undertook to answer questions of faith rationally, by the application of logic, a quixotic pursuit if ever there were one. And once reason had demonstrated it couldn't justify God or his universe, Scholastics didn't abandon what had revealed itself as a specious effort but clung more intently to "only a hard shell of argument by logic, practiced, as Petrarch said in disgust, by 'hoary-headed children.'"

The fourth and fifth days of Joan's public questioning were attended by fifty-four and fifty-six clerics, respectively, and by however many illustrious guests Cauchon had summoned. After the obligatory conflict over the oath, this time terminated by Joan's telling Cauchon, "You ought to be satisfied, for I have sworn enough," Beaupère, identified on these two days as the lead prosecutor, asked Joan how she had been since the trial's previous session, three days earlier.

"You see well enough how. I have been as well as possible."

Had she heard her voices? he wanted to know.

"Yes, truly, many times."

The interrogation that followed was devoted to hairsplitting over Joan's angels, a topic the canon could not in its inconsistency settle.

Angels assume a corporeal presence throughout the Old and New Testaments. They stand in roads and block the passage of man and beast; they sit under oak trees, wrestle, climb up and down ladders, and brandish swords. They also speak through the mouths of donkeys, go up in flames over altars, carry the virtuous up to heaven,

and smite the wicked from above. From the Greek *angelos*, for "messenger," angels most often assume no more than a voice to express
God's wishes. Audible only to those whom they visit, they speak a
language different from mortal tongues. For Joan, who knew nothing
of Scholasticism's baroque categorization of heavenly beings, the topic
presented the danger of her inadvertently revealing what traditions of
demonology would condemn as evidence of witchcraft. Counterfeits
of reality were held to be the work of the devil, not God, and Joan's
descriptions of her angels evolved under the pressure of relentless
questioning from voices accompanied by a great light to solid beings
whom Joan not only saw and heard but touched and kissed.

Was their hair long, did it hang down, was it the only thing
between their heads and their crowns? Was it Saint Michael who told
her to wear male clothing? Did Saint Margaret speak English? Did
she have arms and legs or a "different kind of member"? In what form
exactly had Saint Michael appeared? Was he carrying a set of scales?
(The archangel's role on Judgment Day was to weigh souls.)

Joan was clever enough to avoid answering questions she understood as traps but too proud to hide her exasperation.

"Was Saint Michael naked?"

"Do you think God has not wherewithal to clothe him?" she
countered.

"Did he have any hair?"

"Why should it be cut off?"

Cauchon, who "had invited a number of prominent people to
watch him prosecute what he believed would be a clear case against
an illiterate nineteen-year-old peasant girl who was either a fraud or
possessed by evil spirits, or both," had anticipated a glorious public
triumph. By the conclusion of the sixth session, which focused on
her alleged promotion of the cult of personality that had developed
around her, it was clear he was to be disappointed, at the least. If
Cauchon's cronies weren't amused by Joan's impertinence, and his
unwilling accomplices too cowed to smile, the audience of bigwigs
the bishop had collected to bear witness to his crowning glory—and
no seat went untaken, there wasn't standing room—felt no such loyalty. Joan had an audience, and she couldn't resist playing to it. Jean

Le Sauvage, a Dominican who spoke of the case "with great repugnance," said he had "never seen a girl of that age wreak such havoc with her examiners."

"Did your own party firmly believe you to be sent from God?"

"I do not know whether they do, and I refer you to their own opinion. But if they do not, nevertheless I am sent from God."

"Do they believe rightly in deeming you to be sent from God?"

"If they believe I am sent from God they are not deceived."

"Are you king of the Jews?" Pontius Pilate asked.

"You have said so," Jesus said.

As the Sanhedrin's predawn convocation hadn't been official, if the crucifixion was to be accomplished according to the letter of the law, the accused had to be arraigned before the Roman prefect. "Do you not hear how many things they testify against you?" Pilate asked Jesus.

"But he gave him no answer, not even to a single charge, so that the governor wondered greatly."

"Have nothing to do with that righteous man," Pilate's wife warned him, with as much success as Nicolas de Houppeville had had with Cauchon.

From March 4 to March 9, Joan had a respite. Cauchon, on the other hand, was very busy. He called his henchmen to his home every day to review the minutes of the trial and submitted them to an esteemed expert in clerical law, Jean Lohier, for review, expecting praise rather than the opprobrium he received. Lohier pointed out that the hearings had been held within a castle's locked hall, not in ecclesiastical chambers. No one had apprised the accused of the so-called evidence against her. Jailed in a military prison, she was under predation by enemy guards. She had no counsel to help her, an untutored nineteen-year-old, respond to the questioning of up to sixty judges at once, and anyone who attempted to visit and advise her was "harshly turned back and threatened." In the opinion of Jean Lohier, the trial was invalidated by any one of these irregularities.

Livid, Cauchon commanded Lohier to attend the remainder of the hearings. But the visiting expert wanted "no more to do with" a process he understood to be motivated "more from hate than anything else," and Lohier left town for Rome, never to return. If he informed the pope of what was unfolding in Rouen, no document suggests any action was taken or even considered. After deliberating with a handful of University of Paris colleagues, Cauchon made the decision to "go on with our trial as we have begun," with one exception. Now the examinations would take place in Joan's cell because, the bishop explained, the assessors' "various occupations" made it impossible for more than a few of them to attend at once. The unstated was so obvious it hardly needed stating. Cauchon wanted to terminate the involvement of assessors he suspected might be sympathetic to Joan's plight and remove the trial from the public eye.

From Saturday, March 10, until Saturday, March 17, Joan was interrogated in her cell nine times. Among the disadvantages for her was that as she no longer hobbled back and forth between the keep and the castle's great hall, she could no longer look forward to the respite of a few minutes outdoors, spring unfolding into the air, or of occupying a room other than her cell. The only sky Joan saw was through the grilled square of her one window. Too, she was at the mercy of enemies who had suddenly drawn that much closer and invasive, coming and going as they pleased and crowding into the room in which she slept and ate and knelt by her bed with her hands clasped. On each occasion, Cauchon's lieutenant, Jean de la Fontaine, Nicolas Midi, Gérard Feuillet, at least one notary, and one or more of the toadying minor assessors accompanied the bishop. For the final session Thomas de Courcelles and Jean Beaupère joined them. The topics addressed in the private sessions included the design of her standard, her leap from the tower at Beaurevoir, her foreknowledge of her martyrdom, her blasphemy in receiving the sacrament of the Eucharist while wearing men's clothes, and her alleged theft of the bishop of Senlis's horse.

"It was bought for two hundred saluts. Whether he received them or not, I do not know, but there was an arrangement and he was paid. I wrote him that he could have the horse back if he wished. I didn't want it, for it was no good for carrying a load." But even an otherwise useless hackney was good enough to trot the discourse back to either Joan's "sumptuous and ostentatious clothes" or her angels. As Lohier had warned Manchon, the judges were determined "to catch her out if they can with her own words—that is to say, in her assertions concerning her visions when she says 'I am sure about them.' Were she to say 'it seems to me' instead of 'I am sure,' in my opinion no one could find her guilty."

But Joan was sure and, as she said repeatedly, more afraid of displeasing her voices than of displeasing a mortal bishop. No amount of explaining the critical difference between the Church Militant and the Church Triumphant could save someone who said, "It seems to me that God and the Church are one, and no difficulty should be made about this. Why do you make difficulties about this?"

A document dated March 14, 1431, and signed by Dunois, acknowledges his receipt from Charles of three thousand *livres tournois* to finance a military campaign in Normandy. It can't prove but only intimate that, as France had made no attempt to officially ransom Joan, Dunois had at last convinced Charles to attempt her rescue. The following month, La Hire received six hundred *livres tournois* for his "agreeable service," as Charles put it, in accomplishing unnamed "causes that move us." If an attempt to rescue Joan was made, it eluded the notice of any chronicler. Joan's would-be saviors didn't have to send spies into Rouen to discover the mortal, if not divine, impossibility of penetrating the guard surrounding Joan. From a distance it was obvious that the English had absolute control over a supremely fortified city. To attempt Joan's rescue would have been certain suicide.

On March 18, a Sunday, and on Thursday, March 22, Cauchon "convoked a group of the assessors at his house to discuss future procedure." It was given to Jean d'Estivet, as promoter, to draw up the charges, many redundant, some absurd. Cauchon and a few assessors visited Joan in her cell on Saturday, and she was read the transcript of all their questions and the answers she made to them—an opportunity to show off powers some of her judges attributed to either divine or diabolical inspiration rather than mortal genius. Her memory for detail was infallible, and not just in the short term. According to the assessor Pierre Daron, who testified for the nullification, "they were interrogating her on a point on which she had already been interrogated a week before, she answered, 'I have been asked that before, on such a day,' or 'I was interrogated about that a week ago and I answered like this' . . . Then they read the answers for that particular day and found that Joan was speaking the truth."

In answer to her request to attend Mass the following day, March 25, Palm Sunday, Cauchon told her she could, provided she wore women's clothing, which she refused to do.

It was the first Holy Week Joan ever spent in a cell, and by its conclusion she wouldn't have been to Mass even once, because she'd refused to trade her male clothing for the Eucharist on Easter as well. But bars couldn't dampen the exaltation of Rouen's church bells announcing the Messiah's resurrection, and thus life everlasting for the faithful. Five hundred, it's estimated, all pealed at once, enough that were Joan to have set a hand against the wall or pressed her palms to the floor, she would have felt the shiver.

On Monday, a group of assessors met to review the articles of accusation; on Tuesday, Joan was brought before the forty or so judges assembled in the room just off the castle's great hall, where she was, for the first time, "offered counsel with the explanation that since she was not learned in letters and theology she might choose one of those present to advise her how to answer." Joan, who had little reason to trust in such an offer, said she had "no intention of separating herself from God's counsel," and so the reading of the articles commenced. Each article began with an accusation, the evidence upon which it was based, and the date the evidence was given. One by one, Joan listened and responded, usually by referring to her previous testimony or sometimes dilating her original denial. On certain topics, Joan asked for a few days or even a week to respond; she wanted to consult her voices.

Jean Le Maître's assistant, Isambart de la Pierre, who had been present for all the private interrogations, was so "troubled by the course of inquiry" that he contrived to find a place near to Joan so he could signal and even nudge her. His efforts were useless and costly. Joan didn't heed his advice, and as soon as Warwick had the opportunity, he attacked Isambart "most spitefully and indignantly, with biting abuse and scornful invective."

"Why do you keep touching that wicked woman? Why did you go on making signs to her? 'Sdeath villain, if I catch you again trying to get her off or helping her with warnings, I will have you thrown in the Seine."

Joan was given until Saturday, March 31, to address those points on which she had temporized. Would she "submit to the judgment of the Church which is on earth in her every act and saying, whether good or evil, and especially in the causes, crimes and errors of which she was accused, and in everything concerning her trial?"

"In all these I submit to the Church Militant provided it does not command me to do the impossible . . . I will not deny them for anything in the world," she said of her "visions and revelations." If the Church commanded her to do anything contrary to what she understood as God's bidding, she would "by no means undertake it."

After this last interview, Manchon explained, it was "decided by the counselors, especially by the gentlemen from Paris, that, according to custom, all these articles and answers must be reduced to a few short articles, covering the principal points, so that the matter could be presented briefly and so that the deliberations might be better and more swiftly concluded." From April 3 to the fifth, the seventy were edited down to twelve before Cauchon did "command and beseech" each assessor to weigh the abridged evidence before him to determine if Joan's beliefs and actions were "contrary to orthodox faith or suspect with regard to Holy Writ, opposed to the decrees of the Holy Roman Church and the canonical sanctions, scandalous, rash, noxious to the public weal, injurious, enveloped in crimes, contrary to good customs and in every respect offensive." Each assessor's conclusion was to be delivered to Cauchon in writing and bearing his personal seal. No one could recuse himself.

The greater part of the charges addressed Joan's voices, her saints—that she "sees and hears them, embraces and kisses them, touches and feels them . . . and has seen parts of their bodies whereof she has chosen not to speak." Under the direction of these demons she mistook for angels, Joan had assumed male clothing and slept among men without any female companion or chaperone. The glaring illogic of denouncing a proven virgin of sexual promiscuity didn't prevent its inclusion among other trumped-up charges. The charges that did not address Joan's direct experience of her angels concerned the powers with which they endowed her, the presumptions they inspired, the liberties they convinced her to take—including jumping from the tower at Beaurevoir and refusing to submit to the Church Militant while claiming certain inclusion among the Church Triumphant— and her insistence on wearing male clothing, the last more offensive than all the rest because it represented her defiance, advertised it.

The word "submit" appears ninety-four times in the trial record. It was impossible to look at Joan without being forced, each time, to consider her insurrection. And this disobedient creature had the audacity to say that "St. Catherine told her she would have aid, and she does not know whether this will be her deliverance from prison, or if, whilst she is being tried, some tumult might come through which she can be delivered. And she thinks it will be one or the other. And beyond this the voices told her she will be delivered by a great victory."

"Take everything peacefully," Joan's voices told her. "Have no care for thy martyrdom; in the end thou shalt come to the Kingdom of Paradise."

"Her martyrdom she called the pain and adversity which she suffers in prison," the record stated, "and she knows not how it will end."

CHAPTER
XI

A Heart
That
Would Not Burn

On the evening of April 15, Bishop Cauchon made the unusual gesture of sending Joan a piece of carp for dinner, a little respite from whatever prison fare she might expect that evening. It was Friday, on which it was not permitted to eat any meat or fowl, only fish, and while the peasantry could afford no better than preserved and unpalatably salty fish, aristocrats ate fresh carp or sometimes salmon. Whether or not the gift reflected a genuinely charitable impulse, its result was punitive. A few hours after retiring for the night, Joan woke with a fever and began vomiting. Hours passed until the guard changed and her condition was reported to John Gray and then Warwick, who responded with concern enough to dispatch not one but two physicians, Guillaume de la Chambre and Jean Tiphaine, whose directions were to make sure Joan recovered.

Escorted to her cell by Jean d'Estivet, the physicians found Joan shackled, as always, to the block at the end of her bed. No one had attended to her. According to the guards in her cell, "she had vomited a great deal" and felt ill enough to ask the doctors to summon a priest to hear her confession and administer last rites, which was not the hysterical response it might be judged today. Joan lived in an era of few and primitive remedies, when the onset of acute gastroenteritis wasn't the treatable ailment it became once medicine offered artificial means of rehydration. The stress, physical abuse, and compromised hygiene of captivity meant prisoners routinely fell ill and died, and fever accompanied by a severe or prolonged bout of vomiting might characterize not only food-borne illnesses but also incipient typhus, cholera, even plague. Guillaume testified that he had felt "her on the right side and found her feverish. So we decided to bleed her. When we reported this to the Earl of Warwick, he said to us, 'Take care with your bleeding. For she is a cunning woman and might kill herself.'

The king valued her highly and had paid dearly for her and he did not want her to die except by the hands of justice. He wanted to have her burned . . . Nevertheless she was bled, and this immediately improved her condition."

The other attending physician, Tiphaine, testified that he'd "asked her what was wrong and where she felt pain. She answered that a carp had been sent to her by the Bishop of Beauvais, of which she had eaten, and that she thought that to have been the cause of her illness. Then Jean d'Estivet upbraided her, saying that this was false."

In fact, he called Joan a whore and liar and accused her of using herbal emetics, ignoring the fact that she had no means of obtaining them nor advantage to be gained by their effects. " 'It is you, you wanton,' Jean d'Estivet said, 'who have taken aloes and other things that have made you ill.'

"This she denied," Tiphaine said, "and there was a liberal exchange of abuse between Joan and d'Estivet," upon which Joan's condition immediately deteriorated, as corroborated by Guillaume de la Chambre, who recalled separately, "Once she was cured, a certain Master Jean d'Estivet came on the scene and exchanged some abusive language with Joan . . . which so greatly annoyed Joan that she had a relapse and became feverish again."

It's tempting to accuse Cauchon of deliberately poisoning his victim. DeMille doesn't resist; he guides the bishop's hand to withdraw a tiny vial of poison from the decorative carving of his throne-like chair and pour its contents into a goblet of wine he offers not to Joan but to Charles, a toast to his coronation. In the film, as in history, the king himself is the ultimate target of the bishop's attempts to invalidate the Armagnac claim to the throne. Joan bends to give the bishop's hand a kiss of respect and recoils from his flesh, as if it, not the wine, is tainted. A luminous sword only she can see points its glowing tip at the poisoned cup, and Joan seizes it before Charles can put it to his lips.

A food-borne pathogen whose vector was fish handled without refrigeration or contaminated by an unclean serving vessel is a more likely cause of Joan's illness than any intent to poison the one key player in Cauchon's grand spectacle, but her exaggerated response to Jean d'Estivet's attack raises the question of a third possibility. If his presence and his verbal abuse upset her to the point of relapse, even raising her body temperature, the course of her illness might have been psychosomatic. The fervor of vocation that granted Joan her extraordinary tolerance for pain and the ability to transcend injury and exhaustion that felled the strongest among mortal warriors suggests a sympathy between spirit and flesh that might have left her body as vulnerable to emotional agitation and revulsion as it was to the force of her will. Joan knew Cauchon sought her death, and that was enough to provoke a violent rejection of a meal he'd offered and she literally could not stomach. No matter the organic cause of Joan's illness, she attributed it to the gift of a murderous enemy.

Like the stag that won the Battle of Patay, a poisoned fish enters the story of Joan's life bearing a meaning that a tainted bit of mutton or pheasant cannot bring to the narrative—yet another detail that tethers Joan to Jesus. Before the reign of Clovis, whose conversion transformed what had been a capital crime into a requirement of the state, early Christians relied on secret signs to point the way to clandestine meetings for worship, typically held underground, in catacombs.* Among these, the most commonly used was the fish, *ichthys* in Greek, an animal that, like a dove or a stag, represents a messiah who promised to make his disciples Peter and Andrew "fishers of men," and has the advantage of providing an acronym for *Iēsous Christos, Theou Yios, Sōtēr*—"Jesus Christ, God's Son, Savior." People still use the symbol to identify themselves as Christians. Joan's illness and the fish she blamed it on are documented; it isn't possible to interpret them as imaginative additions, no more than it is to prevent the fish from striking an unconscious note of significance: a wicked man purporting to be Christ's representative on earth fed Joan a fish in what was a perversion of Jesus's multiplying fish to sustain five thousand of his followers.

---

* First recorded use in the fifteenth century, from *catacumbae*, derived from *cata tumbas*, Latin for "among the tombs." Tradition holds that the Apostles (among them Saint Peter, over whose remains Saint Peter's Basilica was constructed) were buried underground in a network of tunnels later used for holding the Mass.

Two days later, on April 18, Cauchon, accompanied by the assessors Guillaume Le Boucher, Jacques de Touraine, Maurice du Quesnay,
Nicolas Midi, Guillaume Adelie, and Gérard Feuillet, visited Joan in
her cell, where they found her very weak and fretting over the possibility of dying unconfessed and unabsolved. The bishop told her the
reason he'd come to her sickbed was his concern for her immortal soul,
for which he was "disposed to seek salvation." He "reminded her that
for many different days in the presence of many learned persons she
had been examined on grave and difficult questions concerning the
faith, to which she had given varied and divergent answers . . . found
to contain words and confessions that from the point of view of the
faith were dangerous." Joan was, the bishop reminded her, "unlettered
and ignorant," himself generous in his offer "to provide her with wise
and learned men, upright and kindly, who could duly instruct her." If
she insisted on "trusting to her own mind and inexperienced head"
rather than selecting an adviser from the six judges he had brought
with him, he was afraid her case would be lost and the Church "compelled to abandon her."

"It seems to me," Joan said to Cauchon, ignoring an offer she suspected was a trick, "seeing how ill I am, that I am in great danger
of death. If it be that God desires to do His pleasure on me, I ask to
receive confession and my Savior [the Eucharist] also, and a burial in
holy ground."

"If you wish to receive the sacraments, Joan, you must do as good
Catholics are in duty bound. You must submit to the holy Church. If
you do not," Cauchon said, looking down on the stubborn figure in
the bed, "the only sacrament you will receive is that of penance. That
we are always ready to administer."

"I cannot now tell you anything more," Joan said.

"The more you fear for your life because of your illness," Cauchon
told her, "the more you ought to amend that life. You will not enjoy
the rights of the Church if you do not submit to the Church."

"If my body dies in prison, I trust you will have it buried in holy
ground. If you do not, I put my trust in Our Lord."

Before Cauchon took his leave, once again, the record states, Joan was "summoned, exhorted and required to take the good counsel of the clergy and notable doctors and trust in it for the salvation of her soul."

Forced into the position of Cauchon's lieutenant, Guillaume de la Fontaine was not Joan's enemy. A close friend of Nicolas de Houppe-ville, who had risked his own freedom by passing a letter to the jailed prelate, Guillaume was so disturbed by the tenor of the bishop's "charitable exhortation" to Joan that on May 1, in anticipation of the following day's public admonition, he made his way to her cell with Martin Ladvenu, who served as Joan's confessor in the last month of her life, and Isambart de la Pierre, whom Warwick had threatened to have drowned for trying to aid Joan in responding to the asses-sors' questions. It was Isambart de la Pierre's impression that it had never been explained to Joan that the Church Militant included the recently convened ecumenical Council of Basel and the newly elected Pope Eugene IV. It was not limited to the judges who had assembled in Rouen to try her. Aware how dire was her situation, the three cler-ics advised Joan to appeal directly to the pope, with the unfortunate result that the next day, when Joan asked for what Cauchon knew she hadn't before understood was her right, the bishop went immediately to her guards to find out who might have planted such an idea in her head. Manchon testified that when he found out, Cauchon "stormed most angrily . . . and threatened to do them a violent mischief." Le Maître made excuses for Isambart and Martin and "begged for their pardon, saying that if any mischief were done to them he would not take part in the trial." Guillaume didn't feel sufficiently protected by such limited collateral and left town for fear of his life, and the Earl of Warwick forbade Joan any visitors who had not been first approved by Cauchon. As there was no one who would dare carry an appeal from Joan to Pope Eugene, the request was effectively, and unlawfully, denied.

Even had an appeal reached the pope, it might have accomplished little. The schism had come to an end in 1417 with the election of Martin V by the previous ecumenical council, of Constance, which chose a candidate acceptable to all three warring papacies—one in Pisa having in 1409 joined those in Rome and Avignon. Martin V was, as he would have necessarily been, a politician with a gift for compromise. After Martin's death, on February 20, 1431, his successor, Eugene IV, would spend his term in conflict with the reform movement that grew out of the Council of Constance, its aim to limit the supreme power of the papacy by making the pope accountable to an assembly of prelates: an indefinite ecumenical council. Eugene could not have been ignorant of Joan's predicament, but whatever desire he might have had to adjudicate either for or against her, his term was consumed by defending what would once have been his uncontested rights against the new council, of Basel. The inquisitorial arm of the Church wielded ever more influence in the wake of Martin V's making war on the Hussites, and a witch trial whose foregone verdict was a critical matter of international politics is unlikely to have tempted his involvement. Too, even before her capture, Joan had already tumbled inadvertently into the controversy that remained twenty-five years after the schism was officially but not popularly ended. Factions remained, as did confusion. Twenty years earlier, Pierre Cauchon had been made chaplain of Saint-Étienne of Toulouse in recognition of his campaigning for the Avignon pope, Benedict XIII, to renounce the papacy.

"Asked if she had not had letters from the count d'Armagnac," the trial record states, "asking which of the three sovereign pontiffs he should obey," she answered that she'd been in too great a hurry to respond properly in the moment and asked the count to wait for a reply.

"The count's messenger arrived when I was mounting my horse to set off for Paris."

"Did you not profess to know, by the counsel of the King of Kings, what the count should hold in this matter?"

"I know nothing about that. The count asked whom God wanted him to obey. I didn't know how to instruct him."

"Whom do you believe to be the true Pope?"

"Are there two of them?"

"Do you entertain any doubts concerning whom the count should obey?"

"I believe we should obey our Holy Father in Rome."

"Why then did you write that you would give an answer at some other time, since you say you believe in the Pope at Rome?"

"I was referring to another matter. I told the count's messenger other things, which were not written." No less impatient than usual to get where she was going, Joan had dismissed the question without properly considering it. "If the messenger had not gone off at once he would have been thrown into the water," she said, "but not through me."

⊕

On May 2, Joan was taken from her cell to the room adjoining the castle's great hall to receive an amplified version of the admonition Cauchon had delivered in her cell, when she was recovering from her illness. Before the sixty-three assessors who had assembled for the occasion, Cauchon announced that "an old and learned master of theology, one particularly understanding in these matters," Jean de Châtillon, archdeacon of Évreux, would undertake "the present task of demonstrating to this woman certain points on which she is in error" and "persuade her to abandon her faults and errors and show her the way of truth." He invited any judge who "thinks he can say or do any good thing to facilitate her return or helpfully instruct her for the salvation of her body and soul . . . to speak to us or to the assembly." No one came forward with a suggestion.

Jean began by reviewing the articles of faith—in essence, the credo Joan said her mother had taught her. "If she wished to reform," the archdeacon said, "as a good devout Christian must, the clergy were always ready to act towards her in all mercy and charity to effect her salvation. If, however, out of arrogant and haughty pride she desired to persist in her own views, and imagine she understood matters of faith better than doctors and learned men, she would expose herself to grave danger." Her crimes were again tallied: "She would not submit to the Church Militant or any living man, but intended to refer herself to God alone in respect of her acts and sayings." She "persisted in wearing man's dress" and was "in error when out of a strange insistence upon her disgraceful dress she preferred not to receive the sacrament of the Eucharist" on Palm Sunday and Easter "rather than put off her male costume." She did "attribute the responsibility for her sins to God and His saints," justifying her bloodlust as ordained. She had "searched curiously into things passing our understanding, to put faith in what was new without consulting the opinion of the Church and its prelates." In predicting the future and detecting hidden objects, she had "usurped the office of God." Unsurprisingly, Joan's foreknowledge of the sword hidden behind the altar at Sainte-Catherine-de-Fierbois had been amplified by enthusiastic storytellers, accruing tales of her divining the whereabouts of "a married priest and a lost cup." At Beaurevoir, she had either attempted suicide or presumed on the grace of God to break her fall; either was blasphemy.

"You are in great peril of body and soul," the archdeacon warned, "your soul in danger of eternal fire and [your] body of temporal fire by the sentence of your judges."

"You will not do as you say against me," Joan told him, "without evil overtaking you, in body and soul."

The convocation was then adjourned, as Joan "made no further reply."

A week after Joan's disappointingly unfazed response to her public admonition, not to mention her irrepressible insolence, Cauchon called a meeting to determine "if it was expedient to put Jeanne to the torture." Of those thirteen whose responses were recorded, nine thought it not expedient, one "deferred to the popular opinion," and three supplied high-minded rationales to support its efficacy. Master Aubert Morel valued torture as a means "to discover the truth of her lies." Loiseleur "thought it good for the health of her soul," and Thomas de Courcelles praised it as "wise." In the end, the pragmatic voice of the treasurer Raoul Roussel prevailed: "Torture was not expedient, lest a trial so well conducted should be exposed to calumny."

Nonetheless, there was no harm in threatening her, and on May 9 Joan was taken down to the dungeon of the castle keep, where "instruments of torture were displayed before her." The Church inherited its understanding of torture from the Greeks, who considered it invaluable for managing their slaves, as they believed information obtained through torture to be more reliable than whatever a prisoner might give up willingly, without the leverage of pain. Truth lay hidden in the body, which could be compelled to relinquish it. The Inquisition favored the rack for the extraction of secrets withheld, and its operators stood by, prepared to pull Joan's bones out of joint. The artistry was in knowing just when to advance one of the ratchets, knowing by feel just how far, how much, to maximize its effects. Most people stood pain better than the noises, surprisingly loud, joints made as they came apart. Pincers were reserved for stubborn cases, their specialized grips designed to pull out fingernails and toenails, and the application of hot coals to exposed flesh was equally persuasive. But the sight of the rack had no more effect on Joan than had the previous week's threats of excommunication.

"I should afterwards declare that whatever I said you had compelled me to say it by force," she observed of the prospect of being winched into pieces. One of the torturers, Maugier Leparmentier, testified that when Joan was interrogated in the dungeon, "she replied with so much wisdom that everyone present was astonished. In the end, my colleague and I retired without touching her." If Cauchon wasn't among those astonished by Joan's self-possession, he was increasingly frustrated by her demonstrating a sangfroid that made her appear invulnerable.

On Holy Cross Day, May 3, she boasted that the angel of annunciation had appeared to her the day before, after she'd been publicly admonished. "I know by my voices it was Saint Gabriel who came to comfort me," she told Cauchon, "and I asked counsel of my voices . . . [who] told me that if I desired Our Lord to aid me I must wait upon Him in all my doings.

"I asked if I would be burned, and my voices answered that I must wait upon God, and He would aid me."

Michelet, who observed that Joan didn't fully recover from her illness until her public admonishment, wondered if her symptoms might not have been a physical manifestation of the inner turmoil provoked by a profound internal shift, when "Michael, the angel of battles, who was no longer sustaining her, yielded his place to Gabriel, the angel of grace and divine charity." Gabriel appeared to Joan as he had to

Mary, with an annunciation of glory through martyrdom. Like Joan, Mary was a mortal who partook of the divine, not God, but his closest mortal relative. Thomas Aquinas might have declared Jesus to be the sole perfect mediator between man and his creator, but the precepts of a thirteenth-century theologian had little weight against Christians' ever stronger conception of what salvation really looked like: a mother with the mercy and compassion of mothers and the usual weight over her son's opinions. Mary acquired the title mediatrix in the Church's infancy, and the cult of the Virgin exploded from the fifth to the fifteenth century. As the Church grew, the need for a figure of redemption that seemed within closer reach than Jesus was ever more apparent. Mother of God, Queen of Heaven, Mother of the Church, Our Lady: "Addressed as the one who could bring cleansing and healing to the sinner," Jaroslav Pelikan wrote, she was also "the one who would give succor against the temptations of the devil," offering the possibility for the faithful to regain what Eve lost—redemption that could only be purchased with sacrifice. Like Mary, Joan was an intermediary: those who thronged to touch her believed she was a physical bridge to the divine.

"The God of that age was the Virgin, far more than Jesus," Michelet wrote, and went on to make an unambiguous equation between Mary and Joan. "The Virgin was needed, a Virgin descending upon earth in the guise of a maid from the common folk, young, fair, gentle, and bold." Composed in AD 145, *The Infancy Gospel of James* identifies Mary as a sacrifice given willingly to God by her mother, Anne, who receives an annunciation very like the one Gabriel delivers to Mary. "An angel of the Lord appeared, saying unto Anna: 'Anna, the Lord hath hearkened unto thy prayer, and thou shalt conceive and bear, and thy seed shall be spoken of in the whole world.' And Anne said: 'As the Lord my God liveth, if I bring forth either male or female, I will bring it for a gift unto the Lord my God, and it shall be ministering unto him all the days of its life.'" And when the time came, Mary's father, Joachim, said, "Let us bring her up to the temple of the Lord that we may pay the promise which we promised."

Mary wouldn't die by flames; she wouldn't die at all; instead, she would be assumed directly into heaven. But a mother might prefer martyrdom to the excruciation of bearing witness to her son's crucifixion.

On Sunday, May 13, Warwick threw a grand formal dinner, attended by 110 guests, including his daughter, married to Talbot, still held hostage by the Armagnacs, and others who played a role in Joan's story. It was an unusually sumptuous feast, the purchases for which filled two pages of the earl's household account book, rather than the usual single page required for a party of that size. For a nightcap to the festivities, Warwick escorted a party of select guests to Joan's cell; the keep was a short walk from his home. "I have a dirty virgin witch girl tucked away on a litter of straw in the depths of a prison here in Rouen," Anouilh's Warwick says.

Although he thought it "inopportune" to pay such a call, Cauchon was among Joan's unwelcome visitors, as was her old captor, Jean of Luxembourg. "I have come here to offer you ransom," Jean said, "on condition that you promise never again to take up arms against us." In his cups, he found the taunt funny enough that he repeated it several times.

"In God's name," Joan said. "You are mocking me. I know well you have neither the wish nor the power to do so . . . I know very well that the English will have me killed, believing that after my death they will win the kingdom of France. But even if there were a hundred thousand Goddams* more than are here at present, they will not gain the kingdom."

Haimond de Macy, the knight who had tried, unsuccessfully, to fondle Joan's breasts, testified that the Earl of Stafford, also present, "was incensed by this speech and half drew his dagger to strike her, but the Earl of Warwick prevented him."

---

* French slang for "English" as they so often repeated the expletive "Goddamn" heard by the French as *Goddam*.

Last days vanish quickly, even in a cell. On May 14, the university faculty of theology convened to draft their response to the twelve articles of condemnation, which Jean Beaupère, Nicolas Midi, and a third cleric, Jacques de Touraine, had brought to Paris for them to review. By the morning of May 19, the envoys had returned with the expected endorsement, and the bishop summoned all the assessors to the chapel for a reading of the results of the faculty's deliberations: a unanimous consensus. The "iniquitous and scandalous demoralization of the people" that Joan inspired must come to an end. With respect to her voices, considering "the quality of the person and the place, and the other circumstances, . . . either these are imagined, corrupting and pernicious lies, or . . . these apparitions and revelations are superstitious, from malign and diabolical spirits such as Belial, Satan and Behemoth," the three demons chosen to represent Joan's three angels. Belial appears in both the Old Testament and Second Temple Judaic texts the Church classifies as apocryphal. The Dead Sea Scrolls describe him as the leader of the Sons of Darkness. Satan, the adversary, is the proud angel who fell from heaven, who tempted Jesus and ushered Joan off the roof of Beaurevoir. Behemoth, a rapacious primeval monster, stalks through the book of Job, summoned by God to demonstrate his power over evil as well as good, a land-bound Leviathan.

The Paris faculty judged Joan one who "believes lightly and affirms rashly . . . her belief is evil and she strays from the faith." Her miracles and precognition were accomplished through sorcery. She was "impious toward her parents." By dressing as a man, she committed blasphemy, "setting aside divine law." She was a "traitress, deceitful, cruel, and thirsty for the shedding of human blood, seditious and an inciter of tyranny." That she asserted she would go to Paradise was "a presumptuous and rash assertion, a pernicious lie." Her clothing, and the disgrace of having worn it countless times while receiving the Eucharist, revealed her as someone who defied "sacred doctrine, and the laws of the Church." She was an apostate who held "a reprehensible view on the unity and the authority of the Church"—a schismatic.

On May 23, at the instruction of the Paris faculty, Joan was "charitably exhorted" once more. "Jeanne was led to a room near her prison in the castle of Rouen and into the presence of her judges assembled in tribunal," among them Jean de Châtillon, Beaupère, Midi, Professor Guillaume Érard of the Sorbonne, and Pierre Maurice, canon of Rouen, a young theologian who "displayed a great deal of fervor in attempting to enlighten Joan," "expounded Joan's faults to her . . . and caused her to be warned to abandon these shortcomings and errors, to correct and reform herself, to submit to the correction and decision of our Holy Mother the Church."

"Jeanne, dearest friend," Maurice said,

> it is now time, near the end of your trial, to think well over all that has been said . . . although you have been shown the perils to which you expose your body and soul if you do not reform . . . nevertheless up till now you have not wished to listen. Do not permit yourself to be separated from Our Lord Jesus Christ who created you to be a partaker in His glory. Do not choose the way of eternal damnation with the enemies of God who daily endeavor to disturb men, counterfeiting often the likeness of Christ, His angels and His saints.
>
> If you persevere in this error, your soul will be condemned to eternal punishment and perpetual torture, and I do not doubt that your body will come to perdition. Let not human pride and empty shame . . . hold you back because you fear that if you do as I advise you will lose the great honors which you have known . . . you will lose all if you do not as I say.

Joan would say nothing that she hadn't before, during the trial. "If I were condemned and saw the fire and the faggots alight and the executioner ready to kindle the fire, and even if I myself were in it, I would say nothing else. I would maintain until death what I said in the trial."

The next day, Thursday, May 24, was Pentecost, commemorating the descent of the Holy Spirit on the disciples, their baptism by fire after Jesus had been crucified and resurrected, a great crowd of 120 astonished when "suddenly from heaven there came a sound like the rush of a violent wind, and it filled the entire house where they were sitting. Divided tongues, as of fire, appeared among them, and a tongue rested on each of them. All of them were filled with the Holy Spirit and began to speak in other languages, as the Spirit gave them ability." For the occasion of Pentecost, Cauchon "organized a spectacle designed to impress the prisoner" with the looming threat of fire.

Two scaffolds had been erected in the cemetery of the abbey of Saint-Ouen, a stone's throw from the Cathedral of Rouen. One was for judges, notables, notaries, prelates, and bureaucrats, the other for Joan, visited early that morning by the cathedral's canon, Jean Beaupère, who explained that she was to be taken to a public scaffold where a sermon would be delivered to her. Somewhere en route from her cell to the cemetery, Loiseleur drew her into a "certain small doorway." "Trust me," he said, "and you will be saved. Accept your [woman's] dress, and do everything they tell you, or you are in danger of death. If you do as I say . . . you will be turned over to the Church."

Under heavy guard, Joan was escorted to her scaffold by Massieu. It was the first time the public had been invited to look at Joan, now raised above their gaping mouths and staring eyes. She faced the hoary old professor, Érart, who preached a venomous sermon that veered into melodrama whenever he addressed Joan directly. "Oh, royal house of France, you have never known monsters till now!" he raved. "But now you are dishonored for giving your faith to this woman, this witch, heretic, and child of superstition."

"Do not speak of my king," Joan said. "He is a good Christian."

"I am speaking to you, Joan, and I tell you your king is a heretic and a schismatic."

"By my faith, lord, . . . he is the noblest Christian and loves the faith and the Church better than any. He is not as you say."

"Make her shut up," Érard said to Massieu.

Once Érard concluded the spewing of invective and name-calling that passed for a homily, Jean Massieu read Joan the "schedule of abjuration"—a document, he later testified, that was no more than eight lines long, which made it a different document from the one included with the official trial record, a long abjuration composed by Nicolas de Venderès, a licentiate in law and English partisan, that enumerated the specific errors of faith Joan was alleged to have committed and which she was now renouncing. Of the one he read and Joan signed, Massieu remembered only that it stipulated she was never again to dress as a man, cut her hair short, or bear arms. A version of that eight-line schedule discovered with the Orléans manuscript of the trial's French minutes is considered by some historians to be a copy of the original that Joan signed.

"I, Joan, called the Pucelle, a miserable sinner . . . confess that I have grievously sinned in falsely pretending to have revelations from God and His angels, St. Catherine and St. Margaret, etc."

So radical an abridgment of a document of such importance was unorthodox enough to be suspect. It may explain the curious form of the abjuration Joan was asked to sign: a "slip of parchment designed to be attached to a legal document" that appeared to have been prepared in haste. Massieu was certain "Joan did not understand the schedule or the danger she was in." Pressed to sign it, she asked that the clerics review it first.

"Let it be seen by the Church in whose hands I ought to be placed," she said. "If they advise me that I should sign it and do as I'm told, I will do it gladly."

"Do it now," Érard said. "Or else you will end your life today in the fire."

A tumbrel waited to wheel Joan off to the stake, already set with piles of fagots and tinder and raised high on a platform assembled for the occasion. By some accounts it was made of stone; others called it "plastered"—a means, presumably, of fireproofing an otherwise flammable wood scaffold. Cauchon made sure Joan had been taken to the cemetery by way of the marketplace so that she might see what awaited her should she fail to abjure. "In principle, the pains of fire were only applicable to a relapsed heretic," one of the clerics who had been present at the abjuration testified, speculating that Cauchon had "set his snare solely for the purpose of subsequently making a relapsed heretic of Joan." Warwick had made the expectations of the English clear: it wasn't enough that Joan be executed; they wanted her burned as a witch.

"I will sign it rather than be burned," Joan answered Érard. At hearing her submit, the crowd grew very restless. Some threw stones as they screamed, "Death to the witch," and the English soldiers had to restrain the mob by means of force. "Never were the Jews filled with such hatred against Jesus as the English against the Maid," Michelet wrote, for she had "wounded them at their most sensitive point, in the naïve and profound esteem they have of themselves."

"Now," the Evangelist Matthew recorded, "the chief priests and the elders persuaded the crowds to ask for Barabbas and to have Jesus killed. The governor again said to them, 'Which of the two do you want me to release for you?'"

"Barabbas," they said, choosing a "notorious criminal."

"Then what should I do with Jesus who is called the Messiah?"

All of them said, "Let him be crucified!"

"Why, what evil has he done?" the governor asked. But they shouted all the more.

"Let him be crucified!"

Cauchon turned to the bishop of Winchester to ask what was to be done now in response to Joan's submission.

"You will have to receive her as a penitent," Beaufort said.

If this exchange was staged—as it probably was, the embezzling cardinal having already established his deceitful nature—"the principal Englishmen," kept unaware of any such tampering, "were most indignant with the Bishop of Beauvais, the doctors, and the other assessors in the case," a cleric who had been present testified, "because she was not found guilty, sentenced, and handed over for execution."

"Do not worry, my lord," the bishop was heard to say to Warwick. "We shall catch her all right."

Much has been made of two unexplained and perhaps connected aspects of the abjuration. First, Joan, who knew how to sign her name, "mockingly drew a kind of circle" on the schedule in place of a signature. Second, when pressed to improve on the circle, she added an X and was observed to laugh or smile when she thus "signed" the document that repudiated her voices. Earlier, under interrogation about military correspondence, Joan said she'd added an X to intentionally misleading letters meant to fall into enemy hands so that her own men would know the information they contained was false. Now, on the most important document of her life, Joan made no more mark than an X, leading to suggestions that she was not only taunting the judges who were to end her life but refusing to honor a document she distrusted by signing her name on it.

Loiseleur praised Joan before she was led away from the cemetery. "Please God, you've done a good day's work and saved your soul."

"Now will you churchmen take me to one of your own prisons so that I shall not be in the hands of the English any longer?" she asked.

"Take her where you brought her from," Cauchon said. As she was led back to the keep, English soldiers shouted the usual insults at her.

Once locked in her cell, "she was given woman's dress which she put on immediately she had taken off the male costume," the trial record states. "She desired and allowed her hair, which had hitherto been cut short round the ears, to be shaved off and removed."

Accounts vary as to what transpired in the three days between the abjuration and Cauchon's discovery that Joan had "relapsed" into the same wickedness that proved her a heretic: she exchanged her dress for her twenty-times-two laced hosen. Certainly, he was aware that in a military prison, it would be, as Régine Pernoud judged it, "ludicrously easy to compel Joan in one way or another to resume those clothes," thus committing a capital offense, as stipulated by the abjuration she signed. Her confessor Martin Ladvenu testified for the nullification that he had "heard from Joan's own lips that a great English lord entered her prison and tried to rape her. That was the reason, she said, why she had resumed male clothes." Isambart de la Pierre, the only priest aside from Ladvenu who remained loyal to Joan and acted in good conscience toward her until the last minutes of her life, saw her "weeping, with her face running with tears, and so outraged and disfigured that [he] felt pity and compassion for her."

Joan told Massieu, he testified, that two days after her abjuration her guards "pulled off the women's clothing that covered her and emptied the sack in which were her male clothes." As she had no other, when she could no longer wait to use the latrine, she was forced to put them on. The guards reported her relapse, and the bishop came running.

"You promised and swore," Cauchon said, "not to take man's dress again."

"The promises made to me have not been kept. I was told I could go to Mass and that my chains would be taken off. If I were put in a gracious prison [guarded by women], I would be good and obey the Church."

"And the voices of St. Catherine and St. Margaret," Cauchon said, "have you heard them since last Thursday?"

"Yes. God sent word through St. Catherine and St. Margaret of the great pity of this treason . . . by which I saved my life. They told me I damned myself to save my life. For I am sent from God. And my voice told me I did a great evil in declaring that what I had done was wrong. It was only for fear of the fire that I said what I did. They told me I had saved my body to spite my soul." She had done that, and worse: she'd emptied the past of meaning, called her vocation a sham, and denied the only companions who had remained ever faithful to her. Three days was enough to convince Joan she didn't want the life she'd saved.

"I would rather do penance once and for all, I would rather die than endure any longer the suffering of this prison."

Cauchon was heard laughing as he walked back from Joan's cell to his apartments. A "crowd of English notables and soldiers" were waiting in the courtyard. "Farewell! Be of good cheer!" Cauchon called out to Warwick. "It is done. We have got her."

"The soldiers of the governor took Jesus into the praetorium, and they gathered the whole battalion around him. And they stripped him and put a scarlet robe upon him, and plaiting a crown of thorns, they put it on his head and put a reed in his right hand. And kneeling before him they mocked him, saying, 'Hail, King of the Jews!' And they spat upon him, and took the reed and struck him on the head. And when they had mocked him, they stripped him of the robe, and put his own clothes on him, and led him away to crucify him."

The Passion of Joan of Arc, a film by Carl Theodor Dreyer, presents an unambiguous equation between Joan and Jesus; during the trial Joan is made to wear a crown of plaited straw (Fig. 31). DeMille's *Joan the Woman*'s opening credits are followed by what amounts to a visual incantation: Interrupted at her spinning by a great light, the Maid looks up and raises her arms toward heaven. Just as the light gathers into a halo, her expression shifts from one of ecstasy to one of horror, her arms fall slowly, not all the way to her sides; instead, they stop, outstretched. Light crucifies her, then, nailing her not to a cross but to a great fleur-de-lis. Martyr and patriot, she casts her eyes heavenward before her head sinks to her breast. Her halo still burns, even though her life has departed (Fig. 34).

On Wednesday, May 30, Martin Ladvenu was dispatched with a Dominican friar, Jean Toutmouillé, to inform Joan, he testified, "by what death she was to die that day, by order and decree of her judges, and when she had heard the hard and cruel death that was so near to her, she began to cry out most sadly and pull and tear at her hair," her composure at last dismantled.

"Alas," she keened, "am I to be so cruelly and horribly treated that my pure and unblemished body, which has never been corrupted, must today be consumed and burned to ashes!" Joan's body was unblemished only in the moral sense. Her flesh bore scars another nineteen-year-old girl's would not, from a great many small abrasions and cuts as well as injuries significant enough to report, the crossbolt she took to the breast and the injuries to her thigh and the foot that came down on the *chausse-trappe*, all recent enough to appear livid against what was by now her very pale skin.

Though she admitted her fear of the flames, the vehemence of her response to the idea of losing her corporeal self was inspired by the catechism of a Church that promised resurrection of both soul and body. But not if fire left nothing for God to repair and resurrect—this is why the Catholic Church forbids cremation. Joan's reverence for flesh she'd defended against male predation so fiercely and for so long is betrayed by the single rupture in her otherwise perfect asceticism: Joan never tried to resist dressing her body as the sacred object she understood it to be. Uncorrupted, untouched by any man. A vessel pure enough to hold God's grace.

"Oh," Toutmouillé said she keened. "I had rather be seven times beheaded than be burned like this. Alas, if only I had been in the prisons of the Church to which I have submitted, if I had been guarded by churchmen and not by my enemies and foes, I should not have come to this miserable end.

"I call upon God, the great Judge, to see the great wrongs and griefs that are done me," Joan said to Ladvenu and Toutmouillé, who testified that "she complained exceedingly of the oppressions and violences that had been done to her in prison by her jailers and by others who had been let in to harm her.

"After these lamentations, the aforementioned Bishop entered, and she said to him immediately, 'Bishop, my death is your doing.'"

"Be patient, Joan," Cauchon told her. "You are to die because you did not keep your promise to us, and because you returned to your former sin."

"If you had only put me in the Church court's prisons and entrusted me to decent and proper ecclesiastical warders, this would never have happened. Therefore I appeal against you to God."

✠

"One of the criminals who were hanged railed at him, saying, 'Are you not the Christ? Save yourself and us!' But the other rebuked him, saying, 'Do you not fear God, since you are under the same sentence of condemnation? And we indeed justly; since we are receiving the due reward of our deeds; but this man has done nothing wrong.' And he said, 'Jesus, remember me when you come into your kingdom.' And he said to him, 'Truly I say to you, today you will be with me in Paradise.'"

"Where shall I be tonight?" Joan asked Pierre Maurice, who visited her in her cell before she was taken to the pyre waiting in the marketplace.

"Do you not trust in God?" Maurice said.

"I do," Joan told him. "And with God's aid I shall be in Paradise."

Church law denied the sacraments to a relapsed heretic, but Cauchon allowed Ladvenu to hear Joan's confession and administer the Eucharist to her as well. In fact, when the friar Guillaume Duval came to her cell bearing nothing but bread, Ladvenu sent him to fetch wine, as well, and his stole, salver, and candles. "I administered our Lord's Body to her," her confessor testified, "which she received with such humility, devotion, and copious tears as I could not describe."

Luc Besson's *The Messenger* allows Joan no more than an apparition to answer her plea.

"You want to confess?" God asks from under a black hood more commonly associated with the Grim Reaper. "I'm listening."

"I've committed sins, my Lord, so many sins." Joan clasps her hands, looks into her lap. "I saw . . . so many signs."

"Many signs," God agrees.

"Ones I wanted to see. I fought out of revenge and despair. I was all the things people believe they're allowed to be when fighting for a . . . a . . . cause."

"For a cause," God echoes.

"I was proud and stubborn."

"Selfish," God adds, "cruel."

"Yes," Joan says.

"You think you are ready now?"

"Yes." Joan's eleventh-hour examination of her conscience leaves her with the dubious comfort of a god who doesn't promise redemption.

⊕

Church law proscribed Cauchon, as an ecclesiastic, from attending a secular execution, just as it officially denied the sacraments to Joan, but the bishop stepped outside a number of conventions on what he expected to be the day of his glory. He allowed Joan the illegal privilege of the Eucharist, but he hadn't been satisfied by how distraught Joan had been in her cell. She'd had the audacity to condemn him before God. He was too fixed on the idea of her begging and weeping and denying her voices in public to deny himself the chance to see what he expected to unfold—groveling for mercy in a dress, crude as it was, her head, too, stripped of the brazen crown of disrespect she'd made of her hair.

Abandoned to the secular arm and, once received, given no hearing and no conviction, Joan was placed immediately in the care of the executioner. Anywhere between eighty and eight hundred (accounts vary) soldiers carrying swords and sticks and little axes accompanied the tumbrel that took Joan from her cell to the marketplace, a moving moat of bodies wide enough to prevent any rescue attempt. "So many indeed," Manchon said of the soldiers, "that there was no one bold enough to speak to her except Friar Ladvenu and Jean Massieu," the usher. Although, Nicolas Taquel testified, her old, false confessor, Loiseleur, suffered an improbable last-minute crisis of conscience, and, "weeping, tried to climb into the cart to ask her pardon, . . . the English shoved him away and might have killed him but for the intervention of the earl of Warwick, who warned him to leave Rouen at once."

The soldiers parted the crowd to allow Joan's delivery to her place in the drama about to be enacted, and the tumbrel rolled slowly through a chaotic mob, the sinister carnival atmosphere electric with anticipation. As most of the citizens of Rouen supported Joan's great enemy, the Duke of Burgundy, as many as ten thousand people had gathered to see the burning hand of God devour a great wickedness. "The crowd was enormous, and seething with excitement; it was evident that, if things did not go exactly as they wished, trouble might be expected from the English." Four stages had been raised: one for the ecclesiastical judges and notable personages, another for the secular judges and bailiff, a third on which Nicolas Midi would preach a final sermon to Joan, and, finally, the highest and most visible of all, on which the stake had been set. The army was kept busy restraining the ugly press of people who trampled one another to get as close as possible to the pyre. "And it was not only the common soldiery, the English *mob*, that evinced that thirst for blood," Michelet wrote. "Substantial people, men of high station, the lords, were as savage as the rabble."

Joan was dressed in a rough tunic, either gray or black, "and on the mitre which she had upon her head was written the following words," Clément de Fauquembergue recorded: "Heretic, relapse, apostate, idolater." A placard set before the fagots bore a legend: "Joan who had herself named the Pucelle, liar, pernicious person, abuser of people, soothsayer, superstitious woman, blasphemer of God, presumptuous, unbeliever in the faith of Jesus Christ, boaster, idolater, cruel, dissolute, invoker of devils, apostate, schismatic and heretic."

"You are fallen again—O, sorrow!—into these errors and crimes as the dog returns to his vomit,"* Cauchon pronounced after Nicolas Midi's "long, redundant" sermon was concluded. "You are a relapsed heretic," he charged, "and by this sentence which we deliver in writing and pronounce from this tribunal, we denounce you as a rotten member, which, so that you shall not infect the other members of Christ, must be cast out of the unity of the Church, cut off from her body, and given over to the secular power: we cast you off, separate and abandon you."

The Church, and the Church's female body. Joan a rotten member to be cut off, lest she pollute that female body. Whoever noticed didn't dare say it: the Church's definition of feminine virtue was based not, as it exhorted endlessly, on her sexual incorruptibility but on her willingness to submit.

Burned, not beheaded, for only fire provides a bridge between this world and the next. The word chosen by the Torah for burnt offering

---

* "Like a dog that returns to its vomit is a fool who reverts to his folly." Proverbs 26:11.

is *olah* (עֹלָה)—"that which goes up in smoke." Joan's head could not roll; her body couldn't be broken and left to decay but must be carried up toward the heavens, reduced to "a smell pleasing to the Lord."

"Oh, Rouen, I am much afraid that you may suffer for my death," Joan was heard to say as she was led to the pyre. Like Jesus, she asked God's forgiveness for her persecutors, and "she most humbly begged all manner of people, of whatever condition or rank, to . . . kindly pray for her, at the same time pardoning any harm they had done her," Massieu testified. "When she was handed over by the Church I remained with her and she asked most fervently to be given a cross. And when an Englishman who was present heard this he made her a little one out of wood from the end of a stick, and handed it to her and she received it and kissed it most devotedly." She put the cross inside her clothes, against her breast, and asked Massieu to bring the crucifix from the church and hold it where she could see it.

"If it will save from the nought of Hell Souls of the damned that are maddened there, I give up my soul to the nought of Hell," Péguy's Joan says, lingering to bid her life—her vocation—good-bye. "Have Lord my soul for the nought of Hell. Take my soul into nothing."

"What, priest, are you going to keep us until dinnertime?" an English captain heckled Massieu from the opposing platform. The executioner, Geoffroy Thérage, complained that the height of the platform on which the stake had been set hadn't allowed him to cast a rope around Joan's neck and strangle her, a mercy routinely extended to those being executed before they had to smell themselves cook, for if the wind blew just right, or wrong, neither heat shock nor smoke inhalation would save them from that. It was a "slow, protracted burn-ing," Michelet wrote, that Cauchon wanted, hoping it would accom-plish what the rack had denied him and "expose at last some flaw . . . wrench from her some cries that might be given out as a recantation," or "at the very least some confused, barely articulate words that could be so twisted."

"Ego te absolvo in nomine Patris, et Filii, et Spiritus Sancti," Luc Besson's Grim Reaper says to Joan. She cannot see the crucifix Massieu holds before her face—already her eyes are aflame. The hem of her robe catches fire, and in a second the crude dress has burned away, a flag of fire twirling skyward. A chorus of voices unite—a hymn of increasing ecstasy as flames lick between her toes, rush over her head, a halo of impossible beauty, her features gilded, beautiful, as is Fleming's Ingrid Bergman, in her bride-white robe, the chains that bind her to the stake girdling her waist and crossing her breast, rendering it into a Grecian gown. Fire is the only suitor for so solitary and frigid a bride, Leonard Cohen sings in "Joan of Arc," and furious fire spun "the dust" of Joan of Arc heavenward, and "high above the wedding guests / He hung the ashes of her wedding dress."

"And when the sixth hour had come, there was darkness over the whole land until the ninth hour," "while the sun's light failed." "And at the ninth hour Jesus cried with a loud voice, 'E'lo-i, E'lo-i, la'ma sabach-tha'ni?'" which means, "My God, my God, why hast thou forsaken me?"

"And Jesus uttered a loud cry, and breathed his last. And the curtain of the temple was torn in two, from top to bottom."

"And the earth shook, and the rocks were split; the tombs also were opened, and many bodies of the saints who had fallen asleep were raised, and coming out of the tombs after his resurrection they went into the holy city and appeared to many."

"Jesu," Joan called as she died, "Jesu!" Her essence was transformed by light too hot to touch—heir to Moses's burning bush, to the blinding flash that made Saul into Paul.

The Bourgeois of Paris, a genuine eyewitness—the population of Rouen swelled with voyeurs from all classes—reported that after Joan was dead and her clothes burned away, "the fire was raked back, and her naked body," lifted above the eyes of the marketplace, "was shown to all the people, with all the secrets that could or should belong to a woman to remove any doubt from the people." When "they had seen enough and looked as long as they liked at the dead body bound to the stake, the executioner started a great fire again round her poor carcass . . . and flesh and bone were reduced to ashes."

As he watches the fire consume her in Gastyne's *La merveilleuse vie de Jeanne d'Arc*, the executioner turns away, his face contorted with fear. "We have burned a saint!" he screams, and the petrified onlookers turn their backs to run in panic.

"Abba!" Jesus called, begging for delivery. "Father!"

"Jesu!" Joan cried when the flames engulfed her, her voice the last to sound in Schiller's play. "Look! Do you see the rainbow in the sky? Heaven is opening its golden gates . . . Clouds lift me up—my heavy armor's changing—I am on wings—I rise—up—up—earth falls away so fast."

Signs abounded. Many who watched Joan die above the heads of the mob spoke of seeing "Jesus" "written in the flames of the fire in which she was burned." When an English soldier who had been particularly vocal about his hatred for Joan heard her call on Jesus as she burned, he succumbed to "rapture" so intense it left him insensible. Once revived "with the aid of strong drink," he spoke of seeing "a white dove flying from the direction of France at the moment she was giving up the ghost." Birds exulted at her birth, beating their wings and proclaiming the savior's arrival. Silent now, they swept Joan heavenward, at last granted her wish "to be sent back to God, from whence I came."

Bresson's camera swings from Joan's head, caught in a cloud of white smoke, to a skylight, translucent but not transparent. Overhead, the silhouettes of doves move restlessly, waiting for her ascent through that ceiling between earth and the light beyond it. Dreyer's flock wheels over Joan's head, and her eyes follow them until they close, her gaze wet with light. A woman runs past, a white lamb in her arms.

"We made a lark into a giant bird," Anouilh's Warwick laments, a bird "who will travel the skies of the world long after our names are forgotten, or confused, or cursed down."

The executioner, Thérage, who had been instructed to incinerate Joan's clothes, shoes, plate, spoon—whatever belongings a prisoner might own—along with every scrap of her flesh and throw all the ash into the Seine, approached Ladvenu and Isambart de la Pierre and "said and affirmed that notwithstanding the oil, sulphur, and charcoal that he had applied to Joan's entrails and heart, he had not found it possible to burn them or reduce them to ashes. He was astonished at this as at a patent miracle."

By noon Thérage was on his knees before a priest, weeping for his lost soul, begging for absolution in which he couldn't believe: so horrific was his crime.*

"I never wept as much for anything that befell me," Guillaume Manchon testified, "and could not finally stop weeping for a whole month afterward."

* According to records in France's national library, Thérage recovered sufficiently to continue in his line of work and received, on March 25, 1432, "111 livres et 13 sous pour 104 exécutions."

CHAPTER
XII

Life
Everlasting

Poisoned by disappointment over Joan's having not in the end denied her voices, on June 7, 1431, a week after she was burned, Cauchon summoned a handful of assessors to a closed meeting at the archbishopric's palace in Rouen. Among them were the three clerics who had kept Joan company on the last morning of her life and who would have heard any last-minute disavowal of her voices, had she made such a thing: Pierre Maurice, Martin Ladvenu, and Jean Toutmouillé. All three proved sufficiently ductile to suborn; they joined several others in the creation of "ex officio information upon certain words spoken by the late Jeanne before many trustworthy persons, whilst she was still in prison and before she was brought to judgment." The fraudulent affidavit was devised to be attached like a postscript to the official Latin trial record Thomas de Courcelles would assemble over the next six months. Present at the closed meeting, Thomas, who elided his name here as he did wherever he found it in the French trial minutes, swore that Joan admitted her voices "were evil spirits who had promised her deliverance and that she had been deceived." In the end, he said, she had agreed that their having failed to save her was proof of their malevolence. Nicolas de Venderès, who wrote the exhaustive abjuration included in the official record—not the brief one read to Joan—agreed she had renounced her angels as *mauvais esprits*, as did Nicolas Loiseleur. Apparently, his crisis of conscience was of insufficient strength or duration to inspire his disobeying Cauchon. Not only did Loiseleur claim that on the morning of Joan's execution he had "heard her say that it was she, Jeanne, who had announced to her king the crown mentioned in the trial, that she was the angel, and there had been no other angel but herself"; he also testified that when led to the stake, Joan had not asked God to forgive any of her persecutors but "was heard to ask with great contrition of heart pardon of the English and Burgundians for having caused them to be slain, put to flight and, as she confessed, sorely afflicted." The flourish suggests Cauchon ordered Loiseleur to openly atone for groveling before Joan on the day she was executed.

More apologia than affidavit, the "ex officio information," in reversing all Joan held to be true, amounted to a blanket pardon for her persecutors even as it provided them with evidence that Joan finally confessed that the infamous heavenly sign presented to Charles at Chinon was no crown but a "pure fiction." Left unsigned by all three notaries, the document was produced as the necessary preamble to a second unorthodox postscript to the trial record. A letter dated June 28, 1431, was carried from Bishop Pierre Cauchon to "the emperor, kings, dukes and other princes of all Christendom." Writing both for and as the nine-year-old King of England, who hadn't the faculties to manufacture the statement at hand, Cauchon qua Henry "thought it wise to make known that the certain woman whom the vulgar called The Maid" was dead, condemning Joan, "who with an astonishing presumption, and contrary to natural decency, had adopted man's dress, assumed military arms, dared to take part in the massacre of men in bloody encounters and appeared in divers battles," until, by an act of God, she had been delivered into the young king's hands. "As befits a Christian king reverencing the ecclesiastical authority with filial affection," Henry had relinquished "the said woman to the judgment of Our Holy Mother Church." But, as no effort was great enough to save a woman of such grave wickedness, after Joan had been handed over to the secular arm,

> the fire of her pride which then seemed stifled, renewed by the breath of devils, suddenly burst out in poisonous flames; this wretched woman returned to her errors, to her false infamies which she lately had vomited away. Finally, as the ecclesiastical sanctions decree, to avoid the infection of the other members of Christ, she was given up to the judgment of the secular power which decided that her body was to be burned. Seeing then the nearness of her latter end, this wretched woman openly acknowledged and fully confessed that the spirits which she claimed had visibly appeared to her were only evil and lying spirits, that her

deliverance from prison had been falsely promised by the spirits, who she confessed had mocked and deceived her.

Cauchon closed his self-congratulatory pronouncement by underscoring the necessity that the people "be taught not to put their faith lightly in superstitions and erroneous frivolities, especially at a time such as we have just experienced." Joan hadn't been the answer to desperate war-torn prayers. She had been not God's envoy but the devil's, "shedding human blood, causing popular seditions and tumults, inciting the people to perjury and pernicious rebellions, false and superstitious beliefs, by disturbing all true peace and renewing mortal Wars, permitting herself to be worshiped and revered by many as a holy woman."

His victory was a paper one, but Cauchon prevailed in having it broadcast from pulpit to pulpit throughout Europe. Once they'd gone up in smoke with their owner, Joan's clothes took on even greater significance than they had in the trial. On August 9, Jean Graverent— the *Journal d'un bourgeois de Paris* identified him only as "a friar of the Order of Saint Dominic"—preached a great public sermon that trended toward outright fiction and hysteria, claiming Joan had admitted "she had persisted in [wearing] the clothing of a man when she was about fourteen years old, and that from that time on her mother and father would gladly have brought about her death if they could have done so without staining their consciences. So she had therefore left them, accompanied by the devil, and since then had killed Christian people, full of fire and blood." Having "recanted, and been assigned penance . . . of which she did not do a single day, but was waited on in prison like a lady," she was paid a visit by Satan's emissaries, disguised as saints, who "said to her, 'Miserable creature who changed your dress for fear of death! Do not be afraid. We will protect you effectively from them all.' So she then immediately undressed and put on all the old clothes she wore when riding, which she had pushed into the straw of her bed. She trusted this devil so much that she said she was sorry that she'd ever agreed to give up her clothes."

By the end of November 1431, six months after Joan's execution, the official trial document had been completed, copied, bound, and distributed. Three original copies survive, each authenticated by Cauchon's seal. Extant receipts and documents authorizing payments made to "Pierre, bishop of Lisieux, formerly bishop of Beauvais . . . for the trial for heresy of the deceased Joan, formerly called the Maid," have allowed scholars to calculate the total cost of Joan's trial and execution at 10,865 *livres tournois*. All but 770 wrung from Normandy's taxpayers were disbursed from the English king's treasury in six sums, five received by the bishop during the year 1431 and the last delayed by England's wartime financial predicament until 1437.

A first-class lawyer of the time would have earned as much as three hundred livres a year; the village curé for a town like Domrémy received but five. Had Jacques d'Arc leased the house in which his family lived, he would have paid his landlord about two or three livres a year. Had he convinced Joan to marry, the wedding feast and dowry together would have cost little more. And had there been anything left of his daughter to bury, Jacques d'Arc would have set himself back a good ten livres for even an inexpensive funeral, with minimal bell ringing, clergy, and refreshments.

On December 16, Pierre Cauchon, thus swaddled in considerable riches as well as entitlements, attended Henry VI's coronation in Paris. As reported by Enguerrand de Monstrelet, the bishop of Winchester joined him, along with the Duke of Bedford, the Earls of Warwick, Suffolk, and Salisbury, and Louis of Luxembourg. At the formal banquet that followed the anointing, the bishop sat close to the newly anointed king. Beautiful or not, already the trial and execution of Joan of Arc had provided Cauchon with the altitude he'd anticipated; within a few years his diplomatic status would soar as high as mortally possible. In 1435, he attended the Council of Basel and then the Congress of Arras. He was general envoy for Henry VI; he was the English queen's chancellor as well. During 1439 and 1440, his career took him back and forth across the channel, chasing the peace he never lived to see, as on December 18, 1442, he died at his home in Rouen, suddenly, while being shaved.

Little more than a decade would pass before his heirs had occasion to write to "the judges of the nullification trial, through the intermediary of its procurator, Jean de Gouvis, to disclaim any responsibility" for their great-uncle Pierre's infamous crimes. "Hard-pressed to remain in the good graces of the new [French] government . . . they rejected him [Cauchon] absolutely."

A larger sliver of poetic justice could be tweezed from the creeping years-long torture of Nicolas Midi's dying by degrees, a literally untouchable pariah. The biblical scourge of leprosy descended on the venerable theologian three years after he delivered the "solemn sermon" on the morning Joan died, the one he conceived for her "salutary admonition and the edification of the people."

"Most diligent care must be taken," Midi called out to his barbarous audience, eager to get past the preaching and on to the stake, "to prevent the foul contagion of this pernicious leprosy from spreading to other parts of the mystic body of Christ." And he cut off the limb he misjudged and ordered it be burned.

As Midi had been the one who boiled Joan's interrogation down to the twelve articles that summarized her "doctrine," his fate was almost immediately interpreted as a divine punishment. Not only was his death gruesome; it was slow enough that the once revered doctor of the Church was forced to witness the enjoyment his torture inspired in those he'd once counted his friends. It was, perhaps, unfortunate to have chosen the affliction that ended up killing him as a metaphor for Joan's heresy.

⊕

From the time of Joan's capture until her execution, the war had fizzled and stalled. The French continued to teeter on the brink of bankruptcy, and the English, having discovered the challenge of marshaling forces in thrall to even a captured and chained witch of such formidable power, funneled their dwindling resources into Joan's trial. But by executing the girl who insisted peace was to be found only at the tip of a lance, they'd also removed the greatest obstacle to Charles's attempts at reconciliation with Philip, Duke of Burgundy, and England's continued presence in France depended on its alliance with Burgundy. Despite the efforts of the esteemed general envoy of the English, Pierre Cauchon, at the Congress of Arras, in

1435, that alliance was undone. Charles agreed to make reparation for the death of John the Fearless, and Burgundy, though it remained a free state, recognized Charles as the King of France, significantly undermining Henry VI's claim to his throne. Paris, the jewel of all Europe, was once again the French capital.

Emboldened by the shift in his fortunes, by 1441 Charles had recovered the aggressive flair that characterized the teenage dauphin who had yet to be emasculated by his mother's betrayal. The king of France, thirty-eight years old, once again climbed on a charger, took the lead of his army, and discovered how vitiated were the forces on which his nation's independence relied. A truce from 1444 to 1449 allowed him to redirect what revenues he could muster from making war into reorganizing his ragged ranks of mercenaries, feudal levies, and volunteers into the "first professional, permanent, national standing army that Europe had seen since Rome." Now there were *compagnies d'ordonnances*, their senior officers appointed by the king, who disbursed funds directly to those officers to pay his men-at-arms. Locally recruited corps of anywhere between one hundred and four hundred knights, most of whom were cavalry and whose archers now carried longbows, replaced demoralized bands of ill-equipped, underpaid, and hungry soldiers. Thanks to the brothers Jean and Gaspard Bureau, whose innovations in the use of gunpowder made French artillery the most advanced in all Europe, French "cannons quickly pulverized one English-held fortress town after another." In 1449, the once impenetrable walls of Rouen, with their sixty towers, fell, and by 1453 the Hundred Years War was over. Had Joan lived to see what she had prophesied, she would have been forty-one years old.

The Maid's enemies died off, and her friends multiplied. Fantastic rumors spread. If Saint Michael hadn't set Joan free, then mortal knights had ridden to her rescue. Too many and too shining for the enemy to hold at bay, they swept through the old market like crusaders storming Jerusalem. They trampled the English, and they freed the Maid who freed Orléans and brought the French king his crown.

Not only were there sightings of Joan's apparition; there were flesh-and-blood impostors. One among the flurry of alleged Maids even attracted international attention. A woman named Claude des Armoises, whose repertoire of parlor tricks included prestidigitation (she was said to be able to make broken glass and torn napkins whole again), emerged in 1436, two of Joan's brothers her unlikely accomplices. Petit-Jean, or as he preferred to be called, Jean du Lys, passed through Orléans on August 5, en route to see Charles, for whom he claimed to carry a message from his sister. Two weeks later he was back in town, grumbling that although the king had promised him a hundred livres—probably in consideration of Jean's having bankrupted himself to pay his own ransom from the English—the king's officers had given him only twenty, to which the ever-grateful people of Orléans added another twelve. It was one thing, however, to claim to be his illustrious dead sister's messenger as a means of jimmying himself past La Trémoille's cadre to speak with the king about financial restitution, another to embrace a fraud in front of an audience. The *Chronique du doyen de Saint-Thibault-de-Metz* recorded that on May 20, 1436, a woman claiming to be the Maid and using the alias Claude des Armoises came to Metz in person, and there met with the local nobility as well as with her brothers Pierre and Jean. They had, they said, "believed she had been burned; but when they saw her they recognized her and she also recognized them." The last mention of this "Joan" was as the guest of honor at a banquet in Orléans on July 18, 1439. The *Journal d'un bourgeois de Paris* reported that Claude des Armoises was ultimately unmasked and "confessed her imposture before the University of Paris."

By the time the nullification trial was under way, any hope of monetary gain to be wrung from proximity to the Maid had evaporated, and Jean acquitted himself to the degree that he testified as to his sister's innocence. Popular accounts of what is generally called the "retrial" of Joan of Arc suggest it was undertaken at the behest of Joan's grieving and outraged mother, but it was, of course, Charles and his advisers who initiated the process, determined to neutralize whatever taint of illegitimacy might remain from Joan's role in his anointing, a taint that hadn't faded so much as changed in the twenty years since she'd died. Joan was on her way to becoming a national icon, a heroine more widely beloved with every year that passed. On

February 15, 1450, Charles appointed Cardinal Guillaume Bouillé, a University of Paris professor who was known to be ashamed of the institution's contemptible role in Joan's persecution and death, to initiate an inquiry into the trial of condemnation.

"A long time ago," the king wrote, with the air of embarking on a fairy tale, "Joan the Maid was taken and captured by our ancient enemy," and they "had her tried . . . and during this trial they made and committed many errors and abuses," and they "put her to death very cruelly, iniquitously, and against reason." To redress this shameful injustice, Charles did "command, instruct, and expressly charge" Bouillé to collect the evidence needed to begin the process of Joan's vindication. The cardinal, deputized by royal decree, was to be provided access to whatever documents he wanted: to refuse him was to disobey the king. Bouillé was not the only cleric eager to redress what was as much an embarrassment to the Church as to the crown. By 1452 the grand inquisitor of France, Jean Bréhal, had joined the investigation into what they would discover had been more of a travesty than a properly conducted trial. Most of the documents generated by the inquiry have been lost, but it is known that from May 2 to May 8, 1452, twenty-two witnesses were interviewed, among them Guillaume Manchon, Jean Massieu, Isambart de la Pierre, and Martin Ladvenu. The papal legate, Cardinal d'Estouteville, sent a messenger to Charles on May 22. The inquisitor of the faith and Bouillé would arrive shortly with a dossier for the king to examine, he reported. "They will reveal to you most clearly all that has been done in the trial of Joan the Pucelle. And because I know this matter greatly touches your honor and estate, I have acted with all my power." Sufficient to mandate an official inquiry, the statements collected in Rouen were later included in the nullification trial record.

On June 11, 1455, Pope Calixtus III wrote to the bishops of Paris and Coutances and the archbishop of Reims, charging them to begin the work required to "wipe out this mark of infamy suffered wrongfully." Three years had passed, not long by Rome's clock, papal politics as byzantine then as now. The nullification proceedings opened in Paris on November 7, 1455, with a petition from Isabelle Romée, who read from a prepared statement asking the Church to redress what she presented as not only the destruction of her daughter's life but also "an insulting, outrageous and scornful action towards the rulers and the people . . .

"After having taken away all means of defending her innocence," she continued, they "condemned her in a baneful and iniquitous way, flouting all the rules of procedure, charging her falsely and untruthfully of many crimes." At last, they "had her burned most cruelly in a fire, to the damnation of their souls, provoking tears from all and heaping opprobrium, infamy and an irreparable wrong on this Isabelle and her [family]."

Within a month, investigators were dispatched to Domrémy to collect testimony from those who had known Joan when she was a child. Others went to Vaucouleurs and Toul. In February and March 1456, forty-one witnesses were deposed in Orléans, the Bastard Dunois, among them. Simon Charles, the Duke of Alençon, Jean Pasquerel, Louis de Coutes, Thomas de Courcelles, and the two physicians who attended Joan when she was ill in prison, Jean Tiphaine and Guillaume de la Chambre, all gave their testimony in Paris in April. Guillaume Manchon, Jean Massieu, and Seguin Seguin testified in May in Rouen, and Joan's squire, Jean d'Aulon, was deposed in Lyon on May 2. And, at last, on July 7, 1456, the three prelates chosen by the pope to render judgment on the trial of condemnation convened in Rouen's archiepiscopal palace, where twenty-five years earlier Joan had been dragged, fettered, before Pierre Cauchon.

"We say and pronounce that we judge this trial record and sentences that contain deceit, slander, contradiction and manifest error of law and of fact," and "the execution of all that then ensued, were and are null, invalid, without effect or value. And nevertheless, as is necessary and required by reason, we quash, suppress, and annul them, removing all of their strength." Whatever "mark or stain of infamy" might cling to the family of Joan of Arc was thereby officially neutralized.

The "execution of the sentence" was to be accomplished, the document stipulated, through "its solemn publication in two places in this city, straight away in one, that is to say the square of Saint-Ouen"—the cemetery where Joan had been forced to abjure, replacing the name she knew how to write with an X—"with a general procession to start and a public sermon." The second half of the spectacle would take place the following day, when the sentence of nullification would be read aloud, again, "in the Old Market, that is to say where Joan died in a cruel and horrible fire." In addition, there was to be "the erection there of a worthy cross in her perpetual memory," a cross that stands there still, just outside Rouen's church of Sainte-Jeanne-d'Arc.

Joan's passage through the city of Rouen was thus commemorated. From the archiepiscopal palace that provided the condemnation trial's courtroom, to the cemetery at Saint-Ouen, to the marketplace where she was burned alive, pilgrims retrace her steps, as they do the stations of the cross in Jerusalem, marking where Christ was condemned and beaten and where he fell, three times, under the weight of the cross on which he died.

The first official biography of Joan of Arc was undertaken in 1500, by order of King Louis XII. By then she'd ridden through countless histories, but only as a cameo; the story of the Virgin from Lorraine was inserted into chronicles of the cities through which she'd passed. This book was her own, and as the goldsmith Johannes Gutenberg had overtaken the quills of countless scriveners across Europe with an avalanche of movable type, the story of her life was printed in great quantities and translated.

Across the channel, it was 1593, and she still hadn't left off mocking the English. "Glory is like a circle in the water," Shakespeare overheard her say to the dauphin, "Which never ceaseth to enlarge itself / Till by broad spreading it disperse to nought. / With Henry's death the English circle ends."

"Was Mahomet inspired with a dove?" Charles wonders at the power of his sorceress. "Thou with an eagle art inspired then."

At home in France, now 1636, a founding member of the Académie Française, Jean Chapelain, began what he imagined would become France's *Aeneid* and unfortunately spent the next twenty years advertising it as such. When at last Chapelain completed *La Pucelle; ou, La France délivrée: Poème héroïque*, the epic filled twelve volumes and the work that had consumed him for so long collapsed under the weight of his ambition, universally lampooned as the labor of a tiresome pedant, and not only in his own day. Ridicule persisted.

"Gentlemen," Voltaire addressed the Académie Française in 1760, complaining, with arch indignation, of "this shameful abuse of attributing to us, works which are not of our composition, and of falsifying and mutilating those that are, and thus vending [profiting by] our name." As a member of the academy, he demanded redress for what had begun as a dinner party lark thirty years earlier, when his host, Armand, Duke of Richelieu, challenged him to write an epic poem about Joan of Arc. The story was so fantastical, Voltaire said, that he would undertake it only as satire, which he did, tossing off a dozen cantos of a mock chanson de geste that included a swipe at Chapelain and took its place among the most popular accounts of Joan's life. Voltaire, squinting in the glare of the Enlightenment, imagined his pen mightier than the Maid's sword, and he, too, grasped the hem of her gold cloak and pulled her down to where Dunois, "spite of his caution, would oftimes leer on Joan with wanton eye."

Although Voltaire insisted he'd been jeering at the mythologized Maid and not at Joan herself, *The Maid of Orléans* enraged enough readers that it was banned and burned throughout Europe for all the eighteenth and nineteenth centuries, guaranteeing a wide readership. Had Joan the misfortune to encounter herself as a burlesque heroine of lusty appetites, not so much virgin warrior as the highest cherry to be picked, arousing the desire "to ravish that which has been kept so long," she might have found it difficult to resist throwing a dart of retribution from on high. The bawdy sexual references that became an embarrassment to Voltaire were plagiarized, mimicked, and malarial. No sooner had he recovered from one bout than another commenced. The scene of Dunois ravishing the Maid in the wake of their great victory at Orléans was a particular favorite for drawing-room dramatizations.

The City of Ladies "will last for all eternity," Lady Reason promised Christine de Pizan. "It will never fall or be taken . . . it will never be lost or defeated." Reason set Christine to work digging the city's foundation in the "Field of Letters . . . on flat, fertile ground . . . where every good thing grows in abundance." She describes the landscape in *The Book of the City of Ladies*. She tells how Reason brought the bricks and mortar to build "such high walls that the city inside will be safe from assault."

Lady Rectitude carried a "yardstick of truth which separates right from wrong and distinguishes between good and evil." It would serve Christine de Pizan, Rectitude explained, "to plan the city which you have been commissioned to build" and measure its "towers, houses, and palaces which will all be covered in bright gold."

Relieved of carrying a set of scales, Lady Justice held in her right hand the "vessel of pure gold"—a grail—God had given to her "to share out to each person exactly what he or she deserves." And when the city was complete, Justice set a crown on the Virgin Mary's head and named her Queen of all its inhabitants.

It was to be, Rectitude said, a "city full of worthy ladies," and Justice closed its strong gates and placed the keys in Christine's hands. What choice did ladies have, Reason asked, but to separate themselves from those who "have attacked all women in order to persuade men to regard the entire sex as an abomination"?

But Joan had promised the King of Heaven to take up a sword and "do the fairest deed ever done for Christendom," and how was she to accomplish such a quest cloistered behind "such high walls"? She couldn't stay in the City of Ladies. She had to make her way through the perils that lay beyond its gates.

From Domrémy to Vaucouleurs, Chinon, and Poitiers, and on to Orléans and Reims, the Maid rode in a circle of light too strong for death to dim. Who didn't recognize the Virgin from the marshes of Lorraine? She was the girl to whom God's angels spoke, walking out of the air to burn her ears with words too hot for ordinary mortals.

"Be good," they told her, "be chaste and pure," and they dressed her in bright shining armor and lifted her onto a white horse. They hung the King of Heaven's banner over her head, and they gave her its staff to hold.

Joan of Arc was tried seven times by the Church for which she gave, and lost, her life. Summoned in 1428 by the young man to whom her father had promised her hand in marriage, she appeared, sixteen years old, before her local bishop and was released from honoring a contract to which she had never agreed.

Upon her arrival at Chinon, on March 4, 1429, she was examined by the hastily assembled tribunal that sent her on to Poitiers, where she waited from March 11 to March 22 for the clerics gathered there to assess her claim of a divine mission. It was during a break from this third trial that she assuaged her impatience by composing her letter to the English.

"Know well that the King of Heaven will send a greater force to The Maid and her good men-at-arms than you in all your assaults can overcome," she dictated to a scribe. "By blows shall the favor of the God of Heaven be seen."

In May 1431 she was tried twice: condemned as a heretic and sentenced to life in prison on the twenty-fourth; on the thirtieth she was condemned as a lapsed heretic and burned at the stake.

The sixth trial overturned the verdict of the fifth, and on July 7, 1456, the nullification of the sentence was read aloud in the marketplace where her stake had been set and her life ended.

The cause for her beatification was first championed in 1869 by the bishop of Orléans, Félix Dupanloup, who began by summoning all the other bishops through whose dioceses Joan had passed. No matter what she had come to represent in the centuries since her death, the Maid of Orléans was a saint, he was sure of it, and his passion was persuasive; his colleagues joined with him in petitioning the pope. But, as a twentieth-century prelate explained, "a cause of canonization is never a matter of urgency," and from 1873 to 1877 Rome was preoccupied with a petition for the beatification of Christopher Columbus, ultimately denied "on grounds that the proofs for Columbus's marriage to the mother of his son Ferdinand, Beatrice Enríquez de Arana, were insufficient," casting suspicion of sexual impropriety on the great conquistador.

The seventh jury Joan faced, again in absentia, accused her of crimes she might have predicted, so familiar had they become. The first of three devil's advocates said she'd "boasted of her virginity . . . but she was not always careful of modesty or free of imprudence . . . nor did she keep herself from the anger that is customary of military persons." She refused to share her visions and revelations with the Church, he said, and "did not face death like a martyr, but suffered it with great anguish and fear."

"What was heroic about her faith?" the second demanded. She'd jumped off the tower at Beaurevoir. She'd wept when she was wounded "and carried on in a way unbefitting" to a heroine. She admitted freely that she was afraid of going to prison, unlike "the saints of history, who positively desired to suffer out of love for God."

Witnesses were lacking, said the third. He took exception to her defenders' producing sometimes-contradictory testimony from documents five centuries old, and he cited the opinion of an unidentified distinguished father who found it "surprising to read that only Gabriel was sent to the Most Holy Virgin to announce the incarnation of the divine Redeemer, whereas two archangels, Gabriel and Michael, appeared to Joan, and in such a way that she really saw, heard, and even touched and adored them. Who knows whether she did not suffer some hallucination and cultivated it as consonant with her own genius."

The charges didn't stick. Joan of Arc was beatified on April 18, 1909, and canonized on May 16, 1920.

Who is it, Scripture asks, "who makes his angels winds, and his servants flames of fire?"

"The voice was gentle," Joan told the examiner. "The voice was soft and low."

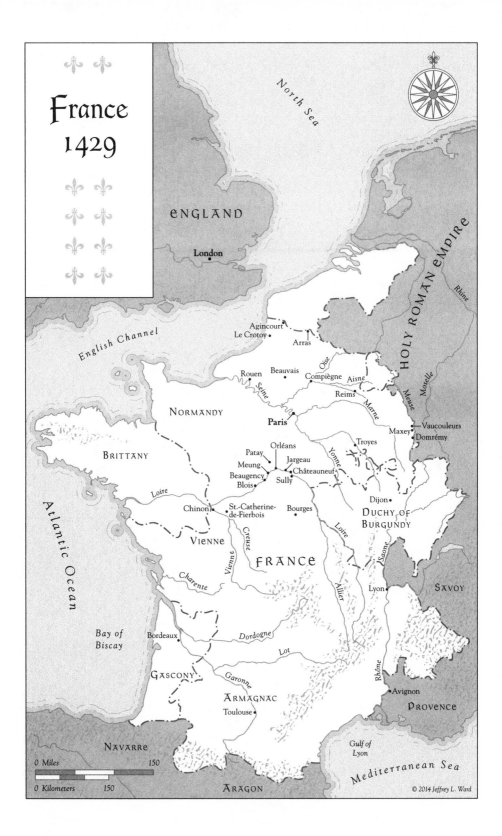

France
1429

North Sea

ENGLAND

London

HOLY ROMAN EMPIRE

Rhine

English Channel

Agincourt
Le Crotoy
Arras

Oise

Rouen
Beauvais
Compiègne
Aisne

Seine
Reims

Marne

Meuse

Moselle

NORMANDY

Paris

Maxey
Vaucouleurs
Domrémy

Troyes

BRITTANY

Patay
Orléans
Meung
Jargeau
Beaugency
Châteauneuf
Blois
Sully

Yonne

Loire

Chinon
St.-Catherine-
de-Fierbois
Bourges

Dijon

DUCHY OF
BURGUNDY

Atlantic Ocean

VIENNE

Creuse

Vienne

FRANCE

Loire

Saône

Charente

Allier

Lyon

SAVOY

Bay of
Biscay

Bordeaux

Dordogne

Lot

Rhône

Avignon

GASCONY

Garonne

PROVENCE

ARMAGNAC

Toulouse

Gulf of
Lyon

NAVARRE

0 Miles   150

0 Kilometers   150

ARAGON

Mediterranean Sea

© 2014 Jeffrey L. Ward

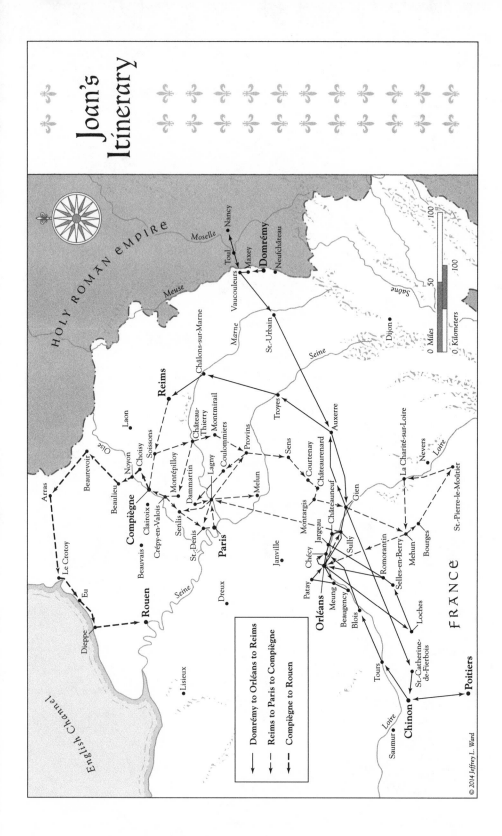

Chronology

1412

January: Joan of Arc is born.

1424

Summer: Joan first receives "a voice from God to help and guide her."

1425

Burgundians raid Domrémy, whose inhabitants, including Joan's family, flee to Neufchâteau.

1428

May 13: Joan travels with Durand Laxart to Vaucouleurs, on her first attempt to enlist support for her mission from Robert de Baudricourt.

July: Burgundian forces again raid Domrémy. Joan's family takes refuge in Neufchâteau, where they remain for two weeks, at an inn owned by La Rousse.

October 12: The English lay siege to Orléans.

Joan is summoned to Toul, where the bishop of the local diocese dismisses a suit brought against her by a local youth.

1429

January: Joan accompanies Durand Laxart to his home in Burey, near Vaucouleurs, on the pretext of helping his wife during childbirth. Again she meets with Baudricourt.

February: Joan assumes male dress; she meets with Duke Charles of Lorraine.

February 12: Baudricourt has Vaucouleurs's parish priest "exorcise" Joan before granting her an escort to Chinon.

February 22: Joan leaves Vaucouleurs for Chinon, three hundred miles west through enemy-occupied territory. She is accompanied by Jean de Metz, Bertrand de Poulengy, Richard the Archer, and their servants.

March 2–3: At Sainte-Catherine-de-Fierbois, Joan awaits permission to approach the dauphin, in Chinon, twenty-five miles to the west.

March 4: Joan arrives in Chinon with her escort.

March 6: Joan meets, and convinces, the dauphin Charles, who has her housed in the Tour de Coudray.

March 7: The Duke of Alençon, upon seeing Joan's riding skills, gives her a warhorse of her own.

March 10: Joan is interrogated by what few local theologians can be gathered promptly in Chinon. They advise the dauphin to have Joan more thoroughly tried at Poitiers.

March 11–22: A tribunal of eighteen renowned theologians examines Joan in Poitiers and find "no harm in her."

March 27: Joan is officially presented to the wider court at Chinon.

April 6: Accompanied by her new squire, Jean d'Aulon, and her two pages, Louis de Coutes and the army's new bursar, Jean de Metz, Joan arrives in Tours to be outfitted for battle; a standard is made to the specification of her angels; she is introduced to Jean Pasquerel, who becomes her confessor.

ca. April 10: At Joan's request the sword of Charles Martel is retrieved from the shrine at Sainte-Catherine-de-Fierbois.

April 21: Joan departs from Tour to Blois, where she joins the convoy of provisions for Orléans and meets Jean Dunois, Bastard of Orléans.

April 24: Joan sends her "Letter to the English" from Blois.

April 29: The citizens of Orléans welcome the Maid into their city.

May 4: Joan leads her army to victory at the battle for the bastille of Saint-Loup.

May 6: Joan's army takes the bastille of the Augustins.

May 7: Joan is wounded by a crossbolt, returns to battle, and takes the Tourelles.

May 8: The siege of Orléans is lifted.

May 13: Joan goes to Loches (or possibly Tours) to petition Charles for more forces and provisions to attack Jargeau.

May 22: In Selles-en-Berry (now Selles-sur-Cher), Joan meets Guy and André de Laval.

ca. May 27–29: Joan visits the Duke of Alençon at his home in Saint-Laurent, where she meets his mother, Mary of Brittany, and his wife, Jeanne.

May 29–June 6: In Selles-en-Berry, Joan mobilizes for Jargeau.

June 11–12: Joan's army takes Jargeau in heavy fighting.

June 15: The French recapture the ridge at Meung-sur-Loire.

June 16–17: The French take Beaugency.

June 18: At Patay, a stag surprises and scatters the English army; France prevails.

June 19: Joan and her captains return to Orléans, where they await the dauphin's permission to approach the court at Gien.

June 25: Joan and her forces arrive at Gien, from which Joan dispatches a circular announcing the triumph of her Loire campaign.

June 27: Joan, her army, the dauphin, and the French court set out for Reims.

June 29–July 16: The Loire towns of Cravant, Bonny, Lavau, Saint-Fargeau, Coulanges-la-Vineuse, Auxerre, Saint-Florentin, Brinon, and Saint-Phal welcome Charles as the King of France.

July 17: In Reims, Charles is anointed the King of France.

July 21–23: Charles touches for scrofula at Corbeny.

July 29: Joan mobilizes her troops at Château-Thierry.

July 31: Charles declares the citizens of Domrémy and Greux exempt from taxation.

August 7: The Duke of Bedford and the Duke of Burgundy declare Charles's anointing invalid.

August 14: Joan and her troops skirmish with the English forces at Montépilloy.

August 28: Charles signs a four-month truce, of which Joan is unaware, with the Duke of Burgundy.

September 8: Joan's thigh is pierced by a crossbow in a failed attack.

September 9: In gratitude for having not lost her life or freedom, Joan makes the offering of a suit of armor on the altar at Saint-Denis.

October: Joan recuperates from the wound in her thigh in Bourges, where she challenges Catherine de La Rochelle to produce her "White Lady."

November 4–8: Joan besieges Saint-Pierre-le-Moûtier.

November 24–December 24: Joan attempts and fails to besiege La Charité.

December 25: Joan retreats to Jargeau, where she receives letters from Charles conferring nobility on her and her family.

1430

January 19: Joan attends a banquet in her honor at Orléans.

February–March: Joan is detained at Sully-sur-Loire.

March 29: Joan takes Lagny.

April: According to witnesses, Joan raises an infant from the dead.

May 23: Joan is captured at Compiègne by a liege of Jean of Luxembourg-Ligny with her brother Pierre and squire, Jean d'Aulon.

May 24–July 10: Joan is held captive at Beaulieu-les-Fontaines, from which she nearly succeeds in freeing herself and her fellow prisoners.

July 11–early November: Joan is held captive at Beaurevoir.

October: In an attempt to escape, Joan leaps from the top of the tower at Beaurevoir.

November 9–11: Joan is held in Arras.

November 21–December 20: Joan is held in Le Crotoy.

December 23: Joan arrives in Rouen.

1431

January 9: The first day of the trial of condemnation. Preliminary investigations into Joan's character begin in Domrémy and Vaucouleurs.

January 13: The assessors consider what evidence they have against Joan thus far.

February 13: Bishop Cauchon appoints his officers of the court.

February 21: Joan is presented to her judges at the first public session of the trial of condemnation.

February 21–March 1: The judges examine Joan in public.

March 4–9: Bishop Cauchon holds a closed meeting; it is decided that Joan's public appearances have been so disruptive as to necessitate a private venue.

March 10: The trial sessions are moved to Joan's cell, into which only the bishop's cadre can fit.

April 15: Joan falls seriously ill after eating fish sent to her by Cauchon.

April 18: Cauchon delivers a "charitable exhortation" in her cell.

May 1: Martin Ladvenu, Jean de la Fontaine, and Isambart de la Pierre secretly advise Joan to make an appeal to the pope.

May 2: Joan is publicly admonished for failing to submit to the Church Militant, persisting in wearing male clothing, and practicing witchcraft.

May 9: Disappointed by having failed to crack Joan's composure, Cauchon has her threatened with torture, to no effect.

May 13: The Earl of Warwick escorts a handful of dinner party guests, including Cauchon, to Joan's cell, where her old captor Jean of Luxembourg-Ligny taunts her.

May 14–19: Joan's inquisitors draw up twelve articles of condemnation against her.

May 23: The judges assemble to hear the canon of Rouen, Pierre Maurice, formally charge Joan for heresy and witchcraft.

May 24: Joan appears before a crowd gathered in the cemetery of Saint-Ouen, where she is publicly accused and where she allegedly abjures. Taken back to prison, she puts on the dress of a woman.

May 28: Joan resumes dressing as a man and is subsequently accused of being a relapsed heretic.

May 29: The judges deliberate.

May 30: Joan is burned alive in the old marketplace in Rouen.

1450
February 15: Charles appoints Cardinal Guillaume Bouillé to initiate an investigation into Joan's trial of condemnation.

1456
January 28: Inquest begins at Domrémy.

February 12–March 16: Inquest continues at Orléans.

July 7: Joan's 1431 condemnation is nullified on the basis of the trial's procedural flaws.

1909

April 18: Joan of Arc is beatified.

1920

May 16: Joan of Arc is canonized.

Acknowledgments

Gerry Howard, my inspired editor, suggested Joan of Arc as a subject, and I know I'll look back on the time devoted to this book as some of the headiest and happiest of my writing life. I bear him boundless gratitude. Jeremy Medina, Bette Alexander, Ingrid Sterner, and Benjamin Hamilton helped shepherd this book into the world, and John Fontana gave it a sublime jacket. My agent, Amanda Urban, has made everything possible from the very beginning.

Lia Ottaviano and Samantha Kristia Smith provided me expert research assistance, and Sarah Harrison shouldered the endnotes. Chris and Catherine Snidow were expert guides in France, and Thomas Dubiaha made sure I made it home.

My husband, Colin, and our children, Sarah, Walker, and Julia, are always their generous selves. Everyone knows how many dinners were takeout and that it's been years since I sorted the socks.

Notes

Chapter I: In the Beginning Was the Word

In the beginning was: John 1:1. All biblical citations are taken from the Revised Standard Version.

3   "Have you not heard": Pernoud, *Retrial of Joan of Arc*, 99.

4   Throughout the text, I have relied on W. P. Barrett's translation of the trial of condemnation. Unless otherwise cited, all quotes attributed to Joan or her judges are taken from that translation. As it was the custom during the Middle Ages to record testimony in the third rather than first person, I have on occasion returned the inquisitor's examination of Joan to its original dialogue form.

5   "seeing may not see": Luke 8:10.

5   "new and everlasting covenant": The Church of Jesus Christ of Latter-day Saints' conflation of Isaiah 55:3, Jeremiah 32:40, and Hebrews 8:13 and 12:24.

5   "the most noble life": Twain, *Personal Recollections*, xvi.

7   "In preference to all the brave men": Craig Taylor, *Joan of Arc*, 105.

7   Her *Ditié de Jehanne*: "The Song of Joan" is generally known as "The Song of Joan of Arc," but as the suffix "d'Arc" is an anachronism added centuries after her death, I have left it off.

7   a "young maiden, to whom God gives": Craig Taylor, *Joan of Arc*, 102.

8   summoned as a trio: Fraioli, *Joan of Arc*, 61.

8   the fifth century BC: Heraclitus, 12th frag.

8   "Behold, battles resound": Fraioli, *Joan of Arc*, 62.

8   "For unto us a child is born": Isaiah 9:6.

8   prophets Isaiah, Daniel, and Hosea: Isaiah and Hosea in the eighth century BC, and Daniel in the second.

9   "triumphant and victorious is he": Zechariah 9:9.

9   "All this has taken place": Matthew 26:26.

9   "set at liberty those who are oppressed": Isaiah 58:6.

9   "great sufferings": Pernoud, *Retrial of Joan of Arc*, 115.

10   "bad form to praise": Huizinga, *Waning of the Middle Ages*, 22.

10   "to see only its suffering": Ibid., 28.

12   Isaiah, Ezekiel, and Zechariah: Isaiah 40:11 and 44:28; Ezekiel 34:12, 23, 24; Zechariah 11:16.

12   lumped Joan in among the herd: Duby, *France in the Middle Ages*, 288.

14   "even cooking instructions": Tuchman, *Distant Mirror*, 32.

15   "went down into the abyss": Cervantes, *Don Quixote*, 601.

16   hairdressers: Hubert Demory, *Monsieur Antoine: Grand maître de la haute coiffure française* (Paris: L'Harmattan, 2006).

Chapter II: By Angels' Speech and Tongue

20   The strategy was intended: Gies, *Joan of Arc*, 19.

21   Born in 1375: According to some accounts, he was born in 1380.

22   "true and good Catholics": Pernoud, *Retrial of Joan of Arc*, 73.

22   "Honest farmers": Ibid., 71.

22   "the only house in the village": Richey, *Joan of Arc*, 26.

23   "It was during the night": Sackville-West, *Saint Joan of Arc*, 31.

23   "Wonderful to relate": Ibid., 31.

24   The Evangelist Matthew chose Bethlehem: Micah 5:2.

24   "You, oh Bethlehem": Matthew 2:1.

25   "We have found him": John 1:45.

26   "bears herself vigorously": Gies, *Joan of Arc*, 48.

26   "never had any carnal desire": Pernoud, *Retrial of Joan of Arc*, 160.

26   "Although she was a young girl": Ibid., 174.

26   "found that she was *stricta*": Wheeler and Wood, *Fresh Verdicts*, 299.

27   "Black and swart before": William Shakespeare, *Henry VI, Part One*, act 1, scene 2.

28   "was very small and looked": Craig Taylor, *Joan of Arc*, 229.

28   "A white dove will fly up": Schiller, *Joan of Arc*, 136.

28   "in the skies of France": Anouilh, *Lark*, adapt. Hellman, 35.

28   "making sparrows, then slapping": Charlesworth, *Historical Jesus*, 65.

28   "saw the Spirit of God descending": Matthew 3:17.

30   "accompanied the mayors": Larissa Juliet Taylor, *Virgin Warrior*, 6.

30   "the daughter of a shepherd": Craig Taylor, *Joan of Arc*, 112.

30   "young girl who had only": Ibid., 90.

31   "mendacious propositions": Pernoud, *Retrial of Joan of Arc*, 61.

31   "Ladies who cast spells": Ibid., 72.

32   "leaves and branches come down": Ibid., 84.

33   posthumously acquitted of the crime: Warner, *Joan of Arc*, 41.

33   "a whole century" : Huizinga, *Waning of the Middle Ages*, 9.

33   "Their only liege": Michelet, *Joan of Arc*, 7.

34   "near continuous incursions": Larissa Juliet Taylor, *Virgin Warrior*, 12.

35   "used to go down on her knees": Pernoud, *Retrial of Joan of Arc*, 87.

35   "it was her habit": Ibid., 143.

35   "seized with a marvelous": Ibid., 142.

35   as Satan is called: Revelation 12:20.

35   "the primordial feat of arms": Huizinga, *Waning of the Middle Ages*, 56.

36   "The first maker of the gods": James, *Varieties of Religious Experience*, 74.

36   "orison of union": Teresa of Avila, *Life of Saint Teresa of Jesus*, 158.

37   "ineffable light and splendor": Saint Bridget of Sweden, *Birgitta of Sweden*, 203.

37   "air opened as bright": Kempe, *Margery Kempe*, 42.

37   "dead from the middle downwards": Julian of Norwich, *Revelations of Divine Love*, 19.

37   "the red blood trickl[ed] down": Ibid., 21.

38   "The Roman soldier who stuck": Péguy, *Mystery of the Charity of Joan of Arc*, 34.

38   "malicious semblance": Julian of Norwich, *Revelations*, 153.

38   "Satan, in an abominable shape": Teresa of Avila, *The Life of Saint Teresa of Jesus*, 168.

38   "comes to snare a soul": Anouilh, *Lark*, trans. Fry, 7.

40   "her reluctance to discuss": Sackville-West, *Saint Joan of Arc*, 298.

41   "A light came over the sun": Anouilh, *Lark*, adapt. Hellman, 7.

41   "Born in the shadow": Michelet, *Joan of Arc*, 9.

43   "Virgins would be rewarded": Duby et al., *History of Women in the West*, 29.

43   "an explosion of female categories": Ibid., 74.

43   Sexually immature girls: Ibid.

43   "Art thou not formed": Rogers, *Troublesome Helpmate*, 67.

43   "foul substance was blamed": Duby et al., *History of Women in the West*, 65.

43   Aristotle taught that the gaze: Ibid.

43   "a temple built over a sewer": Grant, *Journal of the American Academy of Religion*, 483. Grant corrects the widely held misperception, attributing the words to Marcion.

43   "whitewashed tombs": Matthew 24:13–36.

44   "In her, the life of the spirit": Michelet, *Joan of Arc*, 9.

44   "I was only born the day": Anouilh, *Lark*, adapt. Hellman, 54.

44   "She gave alms gladly": Pernoud, *Retrial of Joan of Arc*, 84–85.

45   "She was deeply devoted": Ibid., 79.

45   "I and the others": Ibid., 87.

45   "I say my prayers, yes, Joan": Péguy, *Mystery of the Charity of Joan of Arc*, 17–18.

45   "She liked going to church": Pernoud, *Retrial of Joan of Arc*, 81.

45   "when her parents thought": Ibid., 72.

46   "You were crying out": Anouilh, *Lark*, adapt. Hellman, 11–12.

Chapter III: A Small, Nay, the Least, Thing

51   "escalating tensions between the warring factions": Larissa Juliet Taylor, *Virgin Warrior*, 30.

51   "She was not so much warned": Craig Taylor, *Joan of Arc*, 109.

51   "A terrible contract binds me": Schiller, *Joan of Arc*, 173.

52   "The terms in which earthly women": Gies, *Knight in History*, 54.

53   "completely human in her origin": Pelikan, *Mary Through the Centuries*, 107.

53   "Daily was she visited": Anonymous, *The Gospel of the Nativity of Mary*, chap. 7.

53   "appeared in front of me": Schiller, *Joan of Arc*, 157–58.

55   "If anyone comes to me": Luke 14:26; 33.

55   "He'd been a good son": Péguy, *Mystery of the Charity of Joan of Arc*, 46.

55   "well-behaved, pious, and patient": Pernoud, *Retrial of Joan of Arc*, 86.

55   "Was it not said that France": Ibid., 86.

56   "give her a good slapping": Ibid.

56   "I saw her there": Ibid., 102.

56   "The King of Heaven": Sackville-West, *Saint Joan of Arc*, 74.

57   "kick [her] in the place": Anouilh, *Lark*, adapt. Hellman, 15.

57   "The village girls": Anouilh, *Lark*, trans. Fry, 20.

57   "they only laughed": Craig Taylor, *Joan of Arc*, 250.

57   "Don't get involved": Brecht, *Saint Joan of the Stockyards*, 13.

57   "In a dark time of cruel confusion": Ibid., 7.

58   "We are soldiers of God": Ibid., 9.

58   Joan "did not like": Pernoud, *Retrial of Joan of Arc*, 85.

59   "Do you know": Péguy, *Mystery of the Charity of Joan of Arc*, 36–38.

61   "loved her very dearly": Ibid., 81.

61   "When she went away": Ibid., 82.

61   "All I know": Ibid., 84.

61   "No eggs! No eggs!!": Shaw, *Saint Joan*, 1.

61   "There is no milk": Ibid., 3.

62   "I heard it said": Pernoud, *Retrial of Joan of Arc*, 87.

62   "What are you doing here": Ibid., 96.

62   "Before mid-Lent": Ibid.

62   "for that she was born": Ibid., 100.

62   "sought him and would have kept him": Luke 4:43.

62   "I had great trust": Pernoud, *Retrial of Joan of Arc*, 98.

62   "I believed in what she said": Ibid., 99.

63   "reading and writing in French": Tuchman, *Distant Mirror*, 53.

64   "We have not nurtured and cherished": Goldstone, *The Maid and the Queen*, 70.

65   "I saw Robert de Baudricourt": Pernoud, *Retrial of Joan of Arc*, 98–99.

65   "all good Christians": Gies, *Joan of Arc*, 185.

65   "I asked her": Pernoud, *Retrial of Joan of Arc*, 96–97.

66   "some people of Vaucouleurs": Ibid., 97.

66   "infinity of hats": Tuchman, *Distant Mirror*, 20–21.

67   "attributes sublime virtues": Huizinga, *Waning of the Middle Ages*, 49.

67   "God, the theory went": Duby, *History of Private Life*, 569.

67   "It was characteristic of the time": Michelet, *Joan of Arc*, 91.

67   "Mark what I say": Shaw, *Saint Joan*, 95.

68   "If a woman could": Craig Taylor, *Joan of Arc*, 127.

69   "warlike thoughts": Schiller, *Joan of Arc*, 136.

69   "the primordial feat of arms": Huizinga, *Waning of the Middle Ages*, 56.

70   A sacred vessel: Loomis, *Grail*, 152.

70 Galahad wore flaming red armor: Campbell, *Power of Myth*, 249.
70 Saint Joseph of Arimathea: Matthew 27:57–60; Mark 15:43–46; Luke 23:50–54; John 19:38–41.
70 "about four parts in five": Tuchman, *Distant Mirror*, 62.
71 "the worst conceivable crime": Gies, *Knight in History*, 125.
71 "massacre and torture": Ibid., 43.
71 "Dismembered bodies lay": Ibid.
72 "he was sinning": Pernoud, *Retrial of Joan of Arc*, 123.
72 "She was very bold": Craig Taylor, *Joan of Arc*, 255.
73 "It's no good": Anouilh, *Lark*, trans. Fry, 16.
73 "If God didn't mean": Ibid., 9.
73 "I would much prefer to stay": Pernoud, *Retrial of Joan of Arc*, 96.
74 "I am a soldier": Shaw, *Saint Joan*, 45.

Chapter IV: The King's Treasure
77 "I was sent for this purpose": Luke 4:43.
77 *Joan of Arc Leaving Vaucouleurs*: 1887, Musée des Beaux-Arts, Orléans.
78 "the mother of her country": Acocella, *Twenty-Eight Artists*, 510.
78 "A mother bears children": Ibid.
79 "a contemporary debate between": Craig Taylor, *Joan of Arc*, 157.
79 "traveled in Joan's region": Larissa Juliet Taylor, *Virgin Warrior*, 19.
80 "to arm her because she knew": Warner, *Joan of Arc*, 90.
80 "In God's name, Robert de Baudricourt": Twain, *Personal Recollections*, 53.
81 "French knights [who] continued": Richey, *Joan of Arc*, 16.
81 "No member of the noble class": Ibid., 15.
81 "the noble-born English knights": Ibid., 20.
81 "individualistic glory-seekers": Ibid.
82 "no roads and no bridges": Michelet, *Joan of Arc*, 17.
82 "some soldiers who had gone": Pernoud, *Retrial of Joan of Arc*, 112.
83 "heard it said": Ibid., 122.
83 "Joan's intimates say": Ibid., 119–20.
83 "I afterward heard the men": Ibid., 124.
84 "We escorted her": Ibid., 98.
84 "Le Berger was spared": Sackville-West, *Saint Joan of Arc*, 256 n.
85 "a virtual temporal state": Tuchman, *Distant Mirror*, 26.
86 "fetters, shackles, balls": Warner, *Joan of Arc*, 163.
86 "was going into the royal lodgings": Pernoud, *Retrial of Joan of Arc*, 182.
87 "most faithfully records": Preminger, *Saint Joan*, 107.
87 "because of that letter": Ibid., 108.
87 "There is nothing in that court": Anderson, *Joan of Lorraine*, 26.
88 "pressed in the King's name": Pernoud, *Retrial of Joan of Arc*, 108.
88 "And while the generals discussed": Schiller, *Joan of Arc*, 153–54.
88 "moral, serious, and ethical": Fraioli, *Joan of Arc*, 12–13.
88 "a respected but entirely independent": Ibid., 17.
89 "make himself ridiculous in the eyes": Ibid., 18–19.
90 "French people of all ages": Gastyne, *La merveilleuse vie de Jeanne d'Arc*.

90	"crowds of people": Anderson, *Joan of Lorraine*, 23.
90	"through the territory of the King's enemies": Pernoud, *Retrial of Joan of Arc*, 108.
90	"There is something strange": Anouilh, *Lark*, adapt. Hellman, 25.
91	"When the King learned": Pernoud, *Retrial of Joan of Arc*, 108.
91	"appeared before His Royal Majesty": Ibid., 116.
92	"a black doublet": Gies, *Joan of Arc*, 48.
92	"If he can make three": Anderson, *Joan of Lorraine*, 27.
92	"The Maid talked with our lord": Pernoud, *Retrial of Joan of Arc*, 162.
92	"After hearing her": Ibid., 108.
94	"humble silent request in prayer": Pernoud and Clin, *Joan of Arc*, 24.
94	"When Joan came to find the King": Pernoud, *Retrial of Joan of Arc*, 153.
95	"After dinner the King went": Ibid.
95	"I saw her completely covered": Craig Taylor, *Joan of Arc*, 93.
95	"When the King had seen and heard": Pernoud, *Retrial of Joan of Arc*, 116.
95	"When Joan came to the King": Ibid., 182.
95	"keep personal watch over Joan": Ibid., 161.
96	"The Queen said and told": Ibid., 163.
96	"I lived in that tower with Joan": Ibid., 175.
97	Their tax-exempt status: Gies, *Knight in History*, 196.
97	"the King's prosecutors dragged": Tuchman, *Distant Mirror*, 42.
98	Herod's incestuous marriage: Herod had abandoned his own wife to poach his brother's. Mark 6:17–18.
98	all four of the Gospels: Matthew 26:24–25; Mark 14:18–21; Luke 22:21–23; John 18:4.
98	"For many bore false witness against him": Mark 14:56–59.
98	Once crowned, Charles: Craig Taylor, *Joan of Arc*, 15.
99	"she appeared to have studied": Ibid., 110.
99	*Sola cum multis*: Fraioli, *Joan of Arc*, 49.
99	"Besides myself": Pernoud, *Retrial of Joan of Arc*, 112.
100	"a gathering of the finest": Fraioli, *Joan of Arc*, 48.
100	"Ask Who, What, Why": Craig Taylor, *Joan of Arc*, 14.
100	"By following Holy Writ": Ibid., 73.
100	"soul must be probed": Fraioli, *Joan of Arc*, 45.
100	"Afterward, when she was taking her meal": Pernoud, *Retrial of Joan of Arc*, 154.
101	"oldest remaining considerable fragment": *New Oxford Annotated Bible*, 298.
101	"Up; for this [is] the day": Judges 4:14.
101	"a subtly planned anti-Semitic pogrom": *New Oxford Annotated Bible*, 603.
101	equated piety with patriotism: *New Oxford Annotated Apocrypha*, 76.
101	"The Lord has struck": Judith 13:15.
102	"Many will come in my name": Mark 13:6.
102	"inclined toward a certain indecency": Craig Taylor, *Joan of Arc*, 117.
102	"had been given to her": 1 Corinthians 11:15.
102	"A woman shall not wear": Deuteronomy 22:5.

102 "There is neither Jew": Galatians 3:28.

102 "Adam was not deceived": 1 Timothy 2:14.

102 "no woman to touch": Ibid., 2:12.

102 "I asked her again": Pernoud, *Retrial of Joan of Arc*, 113.

103 "You said the voice told you": Ibid.

103 "In God's name!": Ibid.

103 "Heaven never helps the men": Sophocles, *Tragedies and Fragments*, 2:165.

103 "What language do your voices speak?": Pernoud, *Retrial of Joan of Arc*, 113.

104 "God cannot wish us": Ibid.

104 "I have not come to Poitiers": Ibid.

104 "An evil and adulterous": Matthew 12:39.

104 "I do not know A from B": Pernoud, *Retrial of Joan of Arc*, 118, 124.

104 "no evil is to be found": Craig Taylor, *Joan of Arc*, 73.

104 "much pious belief": Ibid., 80.

104 "In the end they agreed": Anouilh, *Lark*, trans. Fry, 56.

105 "splendid apartment": Sackville-West, *Saint Joan of Arc*, 122.

106 "he withdrew behind the others": Pernoud, *Retrial of Joan of Arc*, 108.

107 "Because you have the cruelest face": Brecht, *Saint Joan of the Stockyards*, 19.

107 "the same bows": Craig Taylor, *Joan of Arc*, 250.

109 "fully adequate to express": Huizinga, *Waning of the Middle Ages*, 191.

Chapter V: Who Is This Then, That Wind and Seas Obey?

111 "Who Is This Then": Mark 4:41.

113 "peasant army": "Royal Financial Records Concerning Payments for Twenty-Seven Contingents in the Portion of Joan of Arc's Army Which Arrived at Orléans on 4 May 1429," Joan of Arc: Primary Sources Series (Historical Academy for Joan of Arc Studies, 2006), online.

113 "To the Master Armorer": Larissa Juliet Taylor, *Virgin Warrior*, 52.

113 "She was armed as quickly": Pernoud and Clin, *Joan of Arc*, 224.

113 To furnish context: Taylor, *Virgin Warrior*, 52.

113 "the 'steel' used": www.oakeshott.org/metal.html.

114 "handed down from grandfathers": Gies, *Knight in History*, 145.

114 Contrary to the irresistible: Literally farcical, as its first known appearance was in *When Knights Were Bold*, by Harriett Jay (who used the male pseudonym Charles Marlowe), a British comedy first performed in 1907.

114 Experiments with genuine: http://www.metmuseum.org/toah/hd/aams/hd_aams.htm#details.

115 The open-faced *bascinet*: http://www.metmuseum.org/toah/hd/aams/hd_aams.htm#details_b.

115 "often went about": Pernoud and Clin, *Joan of Arc*, 224.

115 "I never saw the man": Joan told the examiner she "was at Tours or Chinon" when she sent for the sword—she didn't remember which. That an "armorer of Tours" fetched the sword suggests she was in that city.

116 "sharp, two-edged sword": Revelation 1:16.

116 "Do not think that I came": Matthew 10:34.

117 "as a prize of war": DeVries, *Joan of Arc*, 51–52.

117   "chase a girl who was with the soldiers": Pernoud, *Retrial of Joan of Arc*, 160.

117   a battle sword typical: http://www.metmuseum.org/toah/hd/aams/hd
        _aams.htm#weight_b.

117   "All of them. In a mess of tears": Anderson, *Joan of Lorraine*, 34.

117   Jesus, too, was described: John 2:14–15.

118   "Do you not know": 1 Corinthians 6:19.

118   "You think you have a right": Brecht, *Saint Joan of the Stockyards*, 55.

118   "the virgin sword": Michelet, *Joan of Arc*, 52.

118   "Hauves Poulnoir": Larissa Juliet Taylor, *Virgin Warrior*, 52.

119   A dove descended: Duby, *France in the Middle Ages*, 15.

119   likely inspired by the yellow iris: Pierre-Augustin Boissier de Sauvages, *Dictionnaire languedocien-françois* (1765), 253.

121   "astonished at his teaching": Matthew 7:28–29.

121   "Go to the shrine at Puy": Fleming, *Joan of Arc*.

122   "I served her as chaplain": Pernoud, *Retrial of Joan of Arc*, 184.

122   "With all your sins": Anouilh, *Lark*, adapt. Hellman, 43.

123   "King of England": Joan's "Letter to the English" is included in the record of the Trial of Condemnation. This translation is by W. P. Barrett.

125   These were the men: Fraioli, *Joan of Arc*, 73.

125   "a preemptive strike against": Ibid., 76.

125   "Now you shall see what": Exodus 6:1.

126   "Go and tell Talbot": Michelet, *Joan of Arc*, 28.

126   "not girl's work": Anderson, *Joan of Lorraine*, 14.

126   "Oh, if I could speak": Ibid., 16.

127   "wolves and . . . hyenas": Twain, *Personal Recollections*, 100.

128   "the whole of France": Huizinga, *Waning of the Middle Ages*, 146.

128   "told La Hire, whose habit": Pernoud, *Retrial of Joan of Arc*, 114.

128   "he might swear by his bâton": Twain, *Personal Recollections*, 102.

128   "had a horror of the game": Pernoud, *Retrial of Joan of Arc*, 125.

128   It was a horror: Mark 15:24; Matthew 27:35.

128   "when we were in her company": Pernoud, *Retrial of Joan of Arc*, 144.

128   "Joan bade me assemble": Ibid., 184.

129   "a heroic defense": Tuchman, *Distant Mirror*, 75.

129   "Le feu! Le feu!": Villemarqué, *Barzaz-Breiz*, 321.

130   "Whoever listened to the voice": Twain, *Personal Recollections*, 103.

130   "When Joan departed from Blois": Pernoud, *Retrial of Joan of Arc*, 184–85.

130   "awoke bruised and weary": Sackville-West, *Saint Joan of Arc*, 151.

131   "the lord de Villars, seneschal": Pernoud, *Retrial of Joan of Arc*, 134.

131   "rough band of looters and libertines": According to Jean-José Frappa, the screenwriter of Gastyne's *La merveilleuse vie de Jeanne d'Arc*.

131   "immediately collected a great number": Pernoud, *Retrial of Joan of Arc*, 134.

132   "instead of going straight": Ibid., 136.

132   "I answered that I and others": Ibid.

132   "in actual fact it had": Gies, *Joan of Arc*, 68–69.

132   "as a test for Joan": Gondoin, *Joan of Arc and the Passage to Victory*, 40.

132   "many wagons and carts": DeVries, *Joan of Arc*, 70–71.

132 "shallow, rapid, but navigable": Gies, *Joan of Arc*, 62.

132 "In God's name": Pernoud, *Retrial of Joan of Arc*, 136.

Chapter VI: Surrender to the Maid

140 estimated twenty thousand: Larissa Juliet Taylor, *Virgin Warrior*, 56.

140 "sallied out in great strength": DeVries, *Joan of Arc*, 74.

140 "begged her to agree": Pernoud, *Retrial of Joan of Arc*, 137.

140 "succeeded in rendering them": "Royal Financial Records Concerning Payments for Twenty-Seven Contingents in the Portion of Joan of Arc's Army Which Arrived at Orléans on 4 May 1429."

140 "Her entrance was greatly desired": Pernoud, *Retrial of Joan of Arc*, 145.

141 "men, women, and small children": DeVries, *Joan of Arc*, 75.

141 "There was a very extraordinary rush": Pernoud, *Retrial of Joan of Arc*, 145.

141 "such was the press around her": Sackville-West, *Saint Joan of Arc*, 166.

142 "been sent for the consolation": Pernoud, *Retrial of Joan of Arc*, 125.

142 "Who is going to give": Péguy, *Mystery of the Charity of Joan of Arc*, 22.

142 "Who was it that touched me?": Luke 8:45–46.

142 "Jesus, your people are hungry": Péguy, *Mystery of the Charity of Joan of Arc*, 32.

142 "If their baseness": Brecht, *Saint Joan of the Stockyards*, 29–30.

143 "Foxes have holes": Matthew 8:20.

143 "still in so great a state": Sackville-West, *Saint Joan of Arc*, 176.

143 "she would kill": DeVries, *Joan of Arc*, 77.

143 "went to see the Bastard": Pernoud, *Retrial of Joan of Arc*, 176.

144 "a certain bulwark": DeVries, *Joan of Arc*, 77.

144 "called the Bastard of Granville": Pernoud, *Retrial of Joan of Arc*, 176.

144 "absence of echeloned units": Gies, *Joan of Arc*, 85.

144 "Since you pay more heed": Sackville-West, *Saint Joan of Arc*, 172.

145 "written in her mother tongue": Pernoud, *Retrial of Joan of Arc*, 138.

145 "From that moment the English": Ibid., 146.

145 "torture and burn her": DeVries, *Joan of Arc*, 77.

145 "left Orléans for Blois": Ibid.

145 "the town militia": Gies, *Joan of Arc*, 68.

146 "presented money and gifts": DeVries, *Joan of Arc*, 78.

146 "as soon as she learned": Pernoud, *Retrial of Joan of Arc*, 166.

147 "observed the rules that children": Sackville-West, *Saint Joan of Arc*, 166–67.

147 "on a couch that was": Pernoud, *Retrial of Joan of Arc*, 166.

147 "Oh wicked boy!": Ibid., 176.

148 "When I had harnessed": Ibid.

148 "she never saw French blood": Ibid., 167.

148 "she found many wounded": Ibid., 186.

148 "By 1429 purchases of gunpowder": Gies, *Joan of Arc*, 86.

149 "protectors and defenders": Anonymous, *Lancelot of the Lake*, 52.

149 "The Franks there strike": Anonymous, *Song of Roland*, 115.

149 "assault with very few": Pernoud, *Retrial of Joan of Arc*, 167.

150   "They're dead": Anderson, *Joan of Lorraine*, 40–41.

150   "The voice of Heaven": Schiller, *Joan of Arc*, 175.

150   "You men of England": Craig Taylor, *Joan of Arc*, 84.

150   "She took an arrow": Pernoud, *Retrial of Joan of Arc*, 167.

151   "when the Maid and her people": Ibid., 187.

151   "cross to a certain island": Ibid., 168.

152   "the most imposing fortifications": DeVries, *Joan of Arc*, 62.

152   "to use the power": Richey, *Joan of Arc*, 15.

152   "being 'the most courteous'": Gies, *Knight in History*, 165.

152   "managed to subordinate French notions": Richey, *Joan of Arc*, 17.

153   "Any attack or charge": Pernoud, *Retrial of Joan of Arc*, 109.

153   "and many other knights": DeVries, *Joan of Arc*, 84.

153   "La Hire and the Maid": Pernoud, *Retrial of Joan of Arc*, 168.

153   "sallied out of the Tourelles": DeVries, *Joan of Arc*, 84.

153   "strong and harsh": Ibid.

153   "majority of the enemy": Pernoud, *Retrial of Joan of Arc*, 168.

154   "Get up early tomorrow": Ibid., 188.

154   "Seeing that the city": Ibid.

154   "You have been to your council": Ibid.

154   "Behold you scoffers, and wonder": Acts of the Apostles 13:41; the Evangelist Luke is considered the author of Acts.

154   Habakkuk's apocalyptic message: Habakkuk 1:5.

155   "The just shall live": Ibid., 2:4.

155   "bloodiest military engagement": DeVries, *Joan of Arc*, 87.

155   "spectacular assault during": Ibid.

156   "rode up hastily": Sackville-West, *Saint Joan of Arc*, 191–92.

156   "penetrated her flesh": Pernoud, *Retrial of Joan of Arc*, 138.

156   "When some soldiers saw her thus": Ibid., 189.

157   "that when they saw": Ibid., 178.

157   "Glasdale, Glasdale, give in": Ibid., 189.

157   "Afterwards [Glasdale] was fished up": Gies, *Joan of Arc*, 81.

157   "Then the Maid came up to me": Pernoud, *Retrial of Joan of Arc*, 139.

158   "took up her standard": Craig Taylor, *Joan of Arc*, 281.

158   "shook the standard so vigorously": Pernoud, *Retrial of Joan of Arc*, 171.

158   "The she-warrior": Craig Taylor, *Joan of Arc*, 110.

158   "a maid all alone": DeVries, *Joan of Arc*, 95.

159   "There fell by the hand": Craig Taylor, *Joan of Arc*, 239.

159   "heard from the soldiers": Pernoud, *Retrial of Joan of Arc*, 155.

159   "the myth of English invincibility": Richey, *Joan of Arc*, 64.

159   "eight sous for having beached": Sackville-West, *Saint Joan of Arc*, 196.

159   "giving wondrous praise": DeVries, *Joan of Arc*, 91.

160   "He was transfigured before them": Matthew 17:2.

160   "glistening . . . as no fuller": Mark 9:3.

160   "And when they lifted": Matthew 17:8.

160   "withered away to its roots": Mark 11:20.

160   "the appearance of his countenance": Luke 9:29.

160 "suddenly a light": Acts of the Apostles 9:3–5.

160 "Moses did not know": Exodus 34:29–30.

160 "lo, a bright cloud": Matthew 17:5.

161 "O unique virgin": Craig Taylor, *Joan of Arc*, 111–12.

161 "Master Pierre de Versailles": Ibid., 303–4.

161 "And all the crowd": Luke 6:19.

161 "bringing paternosters": Pernoud, *Retrial of Joan of Arc*, 125.

Chapter VII: A Leaping Stag

165 "had her supper, eating": Pernoud, *Retrial of Joan of Arc*, 139.

165 "Take and eat": Matthew 26:26.

165 "very abstemious": Craig Taylor, *Joan of Arc*, 296.

165 "In the Middle Ages": Huizinga, *Waning of the Middle Ages*, 30.

166 "as a trainer holds back": Sackville-West, *Saint Joan of Arc*, 199.

166 "Look back and see": Ibid., 200.

166 "Oh God! What do I see!": Schiller, *Joan of Arc*, 172.

166 "departed discomfited and in confusion": Pernoud, *Retrial of Joan of Arc*, 172.

167 The *Chronique de la Pucelle* reported: DeVries, *Joan of Arc*, 99.

168 "Do not take such long and copious": Pernoud, *Retrial of Joan of Arc*, 141.

168 "say here in the presence": Craig Taylor, *Joan of Arc*, 283.

168 "some verisimilitude": Sackville-West, *Saint Joan of Arc*, 165.

169 "through their great prowess": Craig Taylor, *Joan of Arc*, 86.

169 "commanded the nobles of all": DeVries, *Joan of Arc*, 99.

170 "a very small thing": Craig Taylor, *Joan of Arc*, 93.

170 taken at the Battle of Verneuil: Pernoud, *Retrial of Joan of Arc*, 157.

171 "not to fear the numbers": Craig Taylor, *Joan of Arc*, 306.

171 "set off to the attack": Ibid., 157.

171 "surrender this place": DeVries, *Joan of Arc*, 104.

172 "Oh gentle duke": Ibid., 105.

172 "defended themselves most virtuously": Ibid.

172 "Our Lord has doomed the English": Pernoud, *Retrial of Joan of Arc*, 158.

172 "During the attack": Ibid., 157.

173 "large garrison of their own": DeVries, *Joan of Arc*, 108.

173 "lords, knights, squires, captains": Ibid.

174 "news came that the English": Pernoud, *Retrial of Joan of Arc*, 159.

174 "Ah, my good constable": Craig Taylor, *Joan of Arc*, 308.

174 "Joan, it has been said": Ibid., 111.

175 "a man's heart inside a woman's body": Goldstone, *The Maid and the Queen*, 248.

175 "6,000 soldiers of which": DeVries, *Joan of Arc*, 112.

175 "Many of the King's men": Pernoud, *Retrial of Joan of Arc*, 159.

175 "poorly timed . . . incredibly ineffective": DeVries, *Joan of Arc*, 114.

176 "In God's name!": Pernoud, *Retrial of Joan of Arc*, 159.

176 "in the leading and drawing up": Ibid., 121.

176 "In the conduct of war": Ibid., 160.

177   six thousand men: Ibid., 117.

177   "one of the most lopsided": Richey, *Joan of Arc*, 22.

177   "vanguard, supplies, artillery": DeVries, *Joan of Arc*, 118.

177   "five hundred elite mounted archers": Ibid.

178   "uttered a great cry": Pernoud and Clin, *Joan of Arc*, 61.

178   In one Christian legend: Martin, *Book of Symbols*, 285.

178   a manifestation of purity and nobility: Psalms 42:1, 18:33.

178   "Flying Stag . . . arising": Craig Taylor, *Joan of Arc*, 96–97.

179   diminish the stag's role: DeVries, *Joan of Arc*, 218.

179   "the unplanned, that turns the tide": Ibid., 120.

179   The English soldiers' attention: Richey, *Joan of Arc*, 71.

179   "four thousand men in dead": Pernoud, *Retrial of Joan of Arc*, 141.

179   "master of the horse": Larissa Juliet Taylor, *Virgin Warrior*, 200.

179   "Whatever the relationship": Gies, *Knight in History*, 43.

180   "had been crowned and consecrated": Craig Taylor, *Joan of Arc*, 283.

180   The letter was a circular: DeVries, *Joan of Arc*, 125.

180   "copied and transmitted": Craig Taylor, *Joan of Arc*, 94.

180   "chased the English out": Ibid.

181   "a small piece of paper": Larissa Juliet Taylor, *Virgin Warrior*, 80.

181   "welcomed the soldier and the Maid": DeVries, *Joan of Arc*, 128–29.

182   "told continually by their Anglo-Burgundian leaders": Ibid., 131.

182   a popular preacher could summon: Michelet, *Joan of Arc*, 4 n.

182   "since it was he who was entrusted": Pernoud, *Retrial of Joan of Arc*, 101.

182   "Joan the Maid commands and informs": Craig Taylor, *Joan of Arc*, 94.

183   "In God's name": Pernoud, *Retrial of Joan of Arc*, 143.

183   "set up all of the French gunpowder": DeVries, *Joan of Arc*, 132.

183   "the dauphin dealt mercifully": Ibid.

184   "Look over there!": Schiller, *Joan of Arc*, 199.

184   Regnault's flock hadn't seen him: Sackville-West, *Saint Joan of Arc*, 221.

185   "lance, which wounded Our Lord": Anonymous, *Song of Roland*, 76.

185   "secreted away by monks": DeVries, *Joan of Arc*, 133.

185   "Magic Porridge Pot": Grimm and Grimm, *Grimm's Fairy Tales*, 475.

185   "all night long the city resounded": Sackville-West, *Saint Joan of Arc*, 221.

185   "ornamented by hundreds of precious stones": Huizinga, *Waning of the Middle Ages*, 229.

186   "I anoint you for the realm": Larissa Juliet Taylor, *Virgin Warrior*, 94.

186   "the royal entourage judged": Pernoud and Clin, *Joan of Arc*, 67.

186   "Everyone cried 'Noel!'": Sackville-West, *Saint Joan of Arc*, 224.

186   "When the Maid saw": DeVries, *Joan of Arc*, 134.

186   "questions of precedence and etiquette": Huizinga, *Waning of the Middle Ages*, 33.

187   "from the infinite Creator": Lovejoy, *Great Chain of Being*, 190.

188   "This girl is ambitious and unscrupulous": Anderson, *Joan of Lorraine*, 39.

189   "as a means of hiding": Wheeler and Wood, *Fresh Verdicts*, 43.

189   the ten plagues God visited on Egypt: Exodus 7:14–12:29.

189   "whenever and wherever tournaments": Horrox, *Black Death*, 130.

189 "You stand alone": Shaw, *Saint Joan*, 82.

190 "the Maid," Dunois testified: Pernoud, *Retrial of Joan of Arc*, 143–44.

190 "I sometimes heard Joan say": Ibid., 160.

190 "produced an extraordinary perception": Pernoud and Clin, *Joan of Arc*, 70.

191 "You Charles, King of France": Craig Taylor, *Joan of Arc*, 100–101.

191 "the proof Joan offered": Ibid., 98.

191 "The famous holy oil": Shaw, *Saint Joan*, 72.

192 "Great and mighty prince": Craig Taylor, *Joan of Arc*, 95–96.

193 "I wrote to you and sent": Ibid., 97.

193 "among the most violent": Michelet, *Joan of Arc*, 64.

Chapter VIII: Black Horseman

197 While Charles lay prone: Craig Taylor, *Joan of Arc*, 119.

197 "in a frenzied and gory assault": Richey, *Joan of Arc*, 59.

198 "sympathetic magic": Frazer, *Golden Bough*, 26–27.

198 "for purpose of removing": Ibid., 489.

199 "If my Voices do not answer": Anderson, *Joan of Lorraine*, 64.

199 "Oh, dear Dunois": Shaw, *Saint Joan*, 69.

199 "You will miss the fighting": Ibid., 73.

199 "the medieval Western European conception": Richey, *Joan of Arc*, 40.

200 "massive gate houses . . . with angular towers": DeVries, *Joan of Arc*, 148.

200 "What voices do you need": Shaw, *Saint Joan*, 76.

200 as many as six or seven thousand: As with most medieval head counts, this one varies from source to source—by thousands.

200 "the duke of Bedford would come": DeVries, *Joan of Arc*, 142.

200 "expressing optimism that the King": Craig Taylor, *Joan of Arc*, 118.

200 "eight months of drifting about": Twain, *Personal Recollections*, 213.

201 "The expedition seemed": Michelet, *Joan of Arc*, 44.

201 "Joan the Pucelle sends you her news": Craig Taylor, *Joan of Arc*, 118–19.

202 "without cause entitle yourself King": Ibid., 119–21.

203 "ordered in a good formation": DeVries, *Joan of Arc*, 142.

203 "so that a prince of the blood royal": Pernoud and Clin, *Joan of Arc*, 74.

203 "rode about the battlefield": Ibid.

203 "as close as the shot": Ibid.

204 it took his entire entourage: Richey, *Joan of Arc*, 79.

204 "his assailants' daggers": Ibid., 74.

204 Charles agreed to surrender four cities: DeVries, *Joan of Arc*, 145.

204 "was deeply grieved that he wished": Pernoud and Clin, *Joan of Arc*, 76.

204 "We have feasted in Campiegne [sic]": Anderson, *Joan of Lorraine*, 64.

205 "stayed away from the new king": DeVries, *Joan of Arc*, 136.

205 "equip your men": Pernoud and Clin, *Joan of Arc*, 76.

205 "the defenses of Paris were strengthened": DeVries, *Joan of Arc*, 136.

206 "as much to intimidate any enemy": Ibid., 149.

206 "They began by bombarding the walls": Ibid., 150.

206 "The attack was hard and long": Ibid.

206 "so full of great error": Gies, *Joan of Arc*, 126.

206   "a very savage attack": DeVries, *Joan of Arc*, 151.

206   " 'See here, you whore, you slut' ": Craig Taylor, *Joan of Arc*, 230.

207   "remained the whole day": Ibid., 256–57.

207   "fired into their backs": DeVries, *Joan of Arc*, 152.

207   "defected from the city": Ibid.

207   "over the vehement objections": Ibid., 153.

207   "was broken the will": Gies, *Joan of Arc*, 127.

208   "And this was why the Jews": John, 5:16–18.

208   "he said to them, 'The Sabbath' ": Mark 2:27–28.

209   "While Joan had been victorious": DeVries, *Joan of Arc*, 156.

209   "where he could balk and hinder": Twain, *Personal Recollections*, 212.

210   "member of a vagabond": Pernoud and Clin, *Joan of Arc*, 200.

210   "On the first night, Jeanne": Sackville-West, *Saint Joan of Arc*, 244–45.

210   "The business of this Catherine": Pernoud and Clin, *Joan of Arc*, 80.

210   "Catherine later reciprocated by testifying": Ibid., 200.

210   "Her army, of which she was": DeVries, *Joan of Arc*, 157.

210   the area was controlled: Ibid., 157–58.

211   fourteen thousand: Charles VI had restyled the old *écu d'or*, or shield of gold—named for its escutcheon design—as the *écu à la couronne*, or crown, valued at ten times the *écu d'argent*, or shield of silver. In 1577, the last of the Valois monarchs, Henry III, officially abolished the livre in favor of the ecu. Philip Grierson, *Coins of Medieval Europe* (London: Seaby, 1991), 144.

211   "the French were forcibly compelled": Pernoud, *Retrial of Joan of Arc*, 172–73.

211   "gunpowder, saltpeter, sulphur, arrows": Craig Taylor, *Joan of Arc*, 131.

211   the French could make no effective attack: DeVries, *Joan of Arc*, 164.

212   "even without any relief": Pernoud and Clin, *Joan of Arc*, 81.

212   "thanks for the multiple": Ibid.

212   "acted like a minister of state": Ibid., 82.

212   "The candidate [for knighthood] first was bathed": Gies, *Knight in History*, 85.

213   "the activity of royalist 'partisans' ": Pernoud and Clin, *Joan of Arc*, 82.

213   "Joan the Pucelle has received": Craig Taylor, *Joan of Arc*, 131.

214   "She will restore harmony": Ibid., 105.

214   "For some time now": Ibid., 132.

215   "the protest of the individual": Shaw, *Saint Joan*, 65–66.

215   of like mind and scruples: Pernoud and Clin, *Joan of Arc*, 71.

215   "Slums breed immorality": Brecht, *Saint Joan of the Stockyards*, 38.

215   "I know their money": Ibid., 56.

215   "clerks, artisans, and merchants": Pernoud and Clin, *Joan of Arc*, 82.

216   "resolute to undergo every risk": Ibid., 83.

216   "to betray the city": Craig Taylor, *Joan of Arc*, 133.

216   "She went to the town": DeVries, *Joan of Arc*, 168.

217   "Each and every captain": Larissa Juliet Taylor, *Virgin Warrior*, 111.

217   plot recently uncovered in Paris: Pernoud and Clin, *Joan of Arc*, 85.

218   "the incident was trumpeted": Gies, *Joan of Arc*, 138.

218   "But if I do them [perform miracles]": John 10:38.

219   "that whatever you ask from God": Ibid., 11:22.

219   " 'I have said this on account' ": Ibid., 11:42–44.

219   "the chief priests and the Pharisees": Ibid., 11:47–48.

219   "from that day on": Ibid., 11:53.

219   "Never," Péguy's Joan says: Péguy, Mystery of the Charity of Joan of Arc, 56.

219   "a newborn baby": Pernoud and Clin, Joan of Arc, 85.

219   "a curious incident": Gies, Joan of Arc, 138.

219   "Have you cured people": Bresson, Trial of Joan of Arc.

219   its script based on the French trial minutes: Ibid.

220   "Are you so tired already": Schiller, Joan of Arc, 193.

220   "amassed a large army": DeVries, Joan of Arc, 169.

220   "fought large skirmishes": Ibid., 171.

221   "the pleasure of seeing": Sackville-West, Saint Joan of Arc, 256.

221   "refused to allow Jeanne and her followers": Ibid.

221   "300–400 more soldiers": DeVries, Joan of Arc, 172.

221   On May 22, spies reported: Sackville-West, Saint Joan of Arc, 259.

222   "Does thou not see": DeMille, Joan the Woman.

222   "I have not long!": Ibid.

Chapter IX: The Golden Cloak

225   "a secret hour": Pernoud and Clin, Joan of Arc, 86.

225   "and entered the town": Sackville-West, Saint Joan of Arc, 259.

225   "without confusion nor disturbance": DeVries, Joan of Arc, 172.

225   "a small and unsuspecting garrison": Sackville-West, Saint Joan of Arc, 260.

225   "young, violent and formidable": Ibid., 259.

226   "let God deliver him now": Matthew 27:43.

226   "mounted on her horse": DeVries, Joan of Arc, 174.

226   "large and forceful skirmish": Ibid., 173.

226   "archers and men with crossbows": Sackville-West, Saint Joan of Arc, 260.

227   "charged forward strongly": DeVries, Joan of Arc, 174.

227   "The English who were there": France, Joan of Arc, 152.

227   She spoke to her men: DeVries, Joan of Arc, 174.

227   "was really beyond redemption": Sackville-West, Saint Joan of Arc, 261.

227   "a rough and very sour man": DeVries, Joan of Arc, 176.

228   "bribery to achieve the surrender": Ibid., 177.

228   "fell on his face and prayed": Matthew 26:39.

228   "Why didn't you take special": Redacted from testimony of Pierre Daron, Pernoud, The Retrial of Joan of Arc, 209.

229   "Of that day and hour": Matthew 24:36.

229   "the rush of a violent wind": Acts of the Apostles 2:2.

229   "My Lord," she whispers: Besson, Messenger.

229   "We will draw down the curtain": Twain, Personal Recollections, 217.

229   "Holy and terrible one": Schiller, Joan of Arc, 227.

230   "when you see that your prayers": Péguy, Mystery of the Charity of Joan of Arc, 75–76.

230   "the one putting his hand": DeVries, *Joan of Arc*, 175.

230   "she did not wish to pay attention": Pernoud and Clin, *Joan of Arc*, 91.

230   He hadn't the courage to admit: Sackville-West, *Saint Joan of Arc*, 256.

230   "Have I not been punished": Shaw, *Saint Joan*, 103.

231   "tremendous and immediate excitement": Sackville-West, *Saint Joan of Arc*, 262.

231   "more joyous than if": Larissa Juliet Taylor, *Virgin Warrior*, 118.

231   England's royal account books: Sackville-West, *Saint Joan of Arc*, 264.

231   "the Burgundian and English partisans": Pernoud and Clin, *Joan of Arc*, 88.

231   "The woman called the Maid": Ibid., 90.

232   "as soon as it can be done safely": Ibid., 91.

233   "savored all the fruit": Ibid., 98.

233   "the noblest Christian of all Christians": Pernoud, *Retrial of Joan of Arc*, 237.

233   "not actually in the diocese": Michelet, *Joan of Arc*, 65.

233   For her second meeting: Pernoud and Clin, *Joan of Arc*, 92.

234   "the choice of a more suitable": Ibid.

234   "conceived a great devotion": Sackville-West, *Saint Joan of Arc*, 266.

234   "greatly distressed by her obstinate": Ibid., 266–67.

235   "black hair, cut round": Gies, *Joan of Arc*, 48.

235   "cast herself at [her nephew's] feet": Michelet, *Joan of Arc*, 67.

235   "to heavy legal penalties": France, *Joan of Arc*, 190.

235   "the younger son of a younger son": Sackville-West, *Saint Joan of Arc*, 264.

235   "had a lien on French prisoners": Ibid.

236   "placed him in charge": Pernoud and Clin, *Joan of Arc*, 209.

236   "for 153 days, 'Pierre Cauchon took leave'": Ibid., 97.

236   "of which 10,000 was set aside": By some accounts, it was 6,000.

236   "the great expenses": Pernoud and Clin, *Joan of Arc*, 192.

237   "a kind of frenzy": Sackville-West, *Saint Joan of Arc*, 267.

237   "the argument continued daily": Ibid., 268.

237   "offers his right-hand glove": Anonymous, *Song of Roland*, 72.

237   "she ceased to listen": France, *Life of Joan of Arc*, 181.

238   She landed in the castle's dry moat: Gies, *Joan of Arc*, 149.

238   "Her body was at Beaurevoir": Michelet, *Joan of Arc*, 69.

239   "The devil took him": Matthew 4:5–6. "For he commands his angels with regard to you, to guard you wherever you go. With their hands they shall support you, lest you strike your foot against a stone." Psalm 91:11–12.

239   Jesus answered him: Matthew 4:7, quoting Deuteronomy 6:16.

240   "wait here alone, in the darkness": Anderson, *Joan of Lorraine*, 64.

240   "As he returns through": Craig Taylor, *Joan of Arc*, 106.

240   "paraded throughout many of the lands": DeVries, *Joan of Arc*, 181–82.

241   they called her a dirty cunt: From the Middle English *cunte*, via Middle Low German *kunte*; first recorded use in the fourteenth century.

243   "She received the ladies": Sackville-West, *Saint Joan of Arc*, 276.

243   who also heard her confession: Ibid., 277.

Chapter X: The Tower Keep

247   "I have heard from Étienne Castille": Pernoud, *Retrial of Joan of Arc*, 211.

247   "I saw it being weighed": Ibid.

248   "Joan was brought to this city": Ibid.

248   "lined with buildings": Gies, *Joan of Arc*, 152.

248   "very dark": Pernoud, *Retrial of Joan of Arc*, 210.

249   "a great bed in it": Ibid.

249   "unable to stir from her place": Ibid.

250   "greatly displeased some": Ibid., 215–16.

250   "tried several times playfully": Ibid., 194.

250   "complained to the Bishop": Ibid., 213.

250   "She's lived with soldiers": Bresson, *Trial of Joan of Arc*.

251   "injury from riding horseback": Gies, *Joan of Arc*, 154.

251   "if she were robbed of it": Michelet, *Joan of Arc*, 107.

251   "two layers of hosen": Allen Williamson, "Primary Sources," 1–2.

252   Once her virginity had been confirmed: Gies, *Joan of Arc*, 154.

252   "a gentleman in the service": Ibid.

252   "A case must quickly be": Pernoud, *Retrial of Joan of Arc*, 202.

252   "they reckoned that while": Ibid.

253   "moved by fear": Ibid., 208.

253   "took no part in": Gies, *Joan of Arc*, 156.

253   "There was no one": Pernoud, *Retrial of Joan of Arc*, 206.

253   "The English instituted the prosecution": Ibid., 205.

253   "We only gave our opinions": Ibid., 207.

253   "came of their own": Gies, *Joan of Arc*, 156.

253   "spoke exultingly with great joy": Pernoud, *Retrial of Joan of Arc*, 274.

254   "a wanton and a whore": Ibid., 215.

254   "loose woman and a filthy": Ibid., 62.

254   "Somebody important from Lorraine": Ibid., 92.

255   the single precondition required: Gies, *Joan of Arc*, 158.

255   "zealous university man": Pernoud and Clin, *Joan of Arc*, 211.

256   "vast holocaust": Gies, *Joan of Arc*, 159.

256   "subjected to the Inquisition's tactic": Ibid.

256   "very highly regarded": Pernoud and Clin, *Joan of Arc*, 214.

256   "pretended to be a man": Pernoud, *Retrial of Joan of Arc*, 50.

257   "to defy the court": Gies, *Joan of Arc*, 159.

258   "two white wings reaching": Anouilh, *Lark*, trans. Fry, 3.

258   "Now you have heard": *New Oxford Annotated Bible*, 1209.

258   "He deserves death": Matthew 26:66–68.

258   "sought false testimony": Ibid., 26:59.

258   "You will see the Son of man": Ibid., 27:64.

258   "There came one": Daniel 7:13–14.

259   "just when one of them": Pernoud, *Retrial of Joan of Arc*, 217.

259   "surprised to see how well": Ibid.

259   "they often asked Joan questions": Gies, *Joan of Arc*, 163.

260   "alone, sitting on a high chair": Pernoud, *Retrial of Joan of Arc*, 225.

261   "leading Joan from her": Ibid., 216.

262   "the malice inherent": Pernoud and Clin, *Joan of Arc*, 208.

264   Instead, she used a scrap: Craig Taylor, *Joan of Arc*, 148.

266   "La Barbe-Bleue": Perrault, *Complete Fairy Tales*, 104.

267   "surpassing all others": Tuchman, *Distant Mirror*, 22.

267   "only a hard shell": Ibid., 479.

267   They stand in roads: Numbers 22:23.

267   they sit under oak trees: Judges 6:11.

267   wrestle: Genesis 32:24.

267   climb up and down ladders: Ibid., 28:12.

267   and brandish swords: Numbers 22:31.

267   the mouths of donkeys: Ibid., 23:28.

267   go up in flames: Judges 13:20.

268   Counterfeits of reality: Warner, *Joan of Arc*, 128.

268   "had invited a number": Gies, *Joan of Arc*, 174–75.

269   "with great repugnance": Pernoud, *Retrial of Joan of Arc*, 221–22.

269   "Do you not hear": Matthew 27:13–14.

269   "Have nothing to do": Ibid., 27:19.

270   "harshly turned back": Pernoud, *Retrial of Joan of Arc*, 225.

270   "no more to do with": Gies, *Joan of Arc*, 176.

271   "to catch her out": Pernoud, *Retrial of Joan of Arc*, 273.

271   "causes that move us": Larissa Juliet Taylor, *Virgin Warrior*, 172.

271   "convoked a group of the assessors": Gies, *Joan of Arc*, 190.

272   "they were interrogating her": Pernoud, *Retrial of Joan of Arc*, 222–23.

272   Five hundred: Michelet, *Joan of Arc*, 94.

272   "offered counsel with the explanation": Gies, *Joan of Arc*, 191.

273   so "troubled by the course": Ibid.

273   "Why do you keep touching": Pernoud, *Retrial of Joan of Arc*, 227.

273   "decided by the counselors": Ibid., 57.

Chapter XI: A Heart That Would Not Burn

277   "she had vomited": Pernoud, *Retrial of Joan of Arc*, 214.

277   "her on the right side": Ibid., 215.

278   "asked her what was wrong": Ibid., 214.

278   " 'It is you, you wanton' ": Ibid.

279   "fishers of men": Matthew 4:19.

281   "stormed most angrily": Pernoud, *Retrial of Joan of Arc*, 228–29.

282   Twenty years earlier: Ibid., 209.

284   "instruments of torture": Ibid., 213.

285   Truth lay hidden in the body: DuBois, *Torture and Truth*, 5.

285   "she replied with so much wisdom": Pernoud, *Retrial of Joan of Arc*, 224.

285   "Michael, the angel of battles": Michelet, *Joan of Arc*, 89.

286   "the one who would give succor": Pelikan, *Mary Through the Centuries*, 133.

286   "The God of that age": Michelet, *Joan of Arc*, 25.

286   "An angel of the Lord": *Infancy Gospel of James* 4:1–2.

286   "Let us bring her up to the temple": Ibid., 7:1.

287 rather than the usual single: Pernoud and Clin, *Joan of Arc*, 128.

287 "I have a dirty virgin": Anouilh, *Lark*, adapt. Hellman, 6.

287 "I have come here to offer": Pernoud, *Retrial of Joan of Arc*, 194.

287 "In God's name": Ibid., 195.

287 "was incensed by this speech": Ibid.

288 "the quality of the person": Craig Taylor, *Joan of Arc*, 213.

288 Belial appears in both the Old Testament: 1 Samuel 2:12; Proverbs 6:12.

288 stalks through the book of Job: Job 40:15–24.

288 "believes lightly and affirms rashly": Craig Taylor, *Joan of Arc*, 214.

289 "displayed a great deal of fervor": Pernoud and Clin, *Joan of Arc*, 216.

289 "suddenly from heaven": Acts of the Apostles 2:1–4.

290 "organized a spectacle": Pernoud, *Retrial of Joan of Arc*, 129.

290 "Trust me": Gies, *Joan of Arc*, 211–12.

290 "Oh, royal house of France": Pernoud, *Retrial of Joan of Arc*, 236.

291 "slip of parchment designed": Pernoud and Clin, *Joan of Arc*, 130.

291 "Joan did not understand": Pernoud, *Retrial of Joan of Arc*, 237.

291 "In principle, the pains of fire": Ibid., 239.

292 "Never were the Jews filled": Michelet, *Joan of Arc*, 106.

292 "the chief priests and the elders": Matthew 27:20–23.

292 "were most indignant": Pernoud, *Retrial of Joan of Arc*, 240.

292 "Do not worry, my lord": Ibid.

293 "mockingly drew a kind of circle": Gies, *Joan of Arc*, 214.

293 "Please God, you've done": Pernoud, *Retrial of Joan of Arc*, 241.

293 "ludicrously easy to compel": Ibid., 241.

293 "heard from Joan's own lips": Ibid., 242.

294 "pulled off the women's clothing": Ibid., 241.

294 "crowd of English notables": Gies, *Joan of Arc*, 218.

295 "The soldiers of the governor": Matthew 27:27–31.

295 *Joan the Woman*'s opening credits: DeMille, *Joan the Woman*.

295 "by what death she was": Pernoud, *Retrial of Joan of Arc*, 245.

296 "I had rather be seven times": Ibid., 245.

296 "she complained exceedingly": Ibid.

297 " 'Truly I say to you' ": Luke 23:39–43.

297 "Where shall I be tonight?": adapted from Pernoud, *Retrial of Joan of Arc*, 250.

297 "I administered our Lord's Body": Ibid., 248.

298 accounts vary: According to Michelet, eight hundred; to Gies, eighty to one hundred. Michelet, *Joan of Arc*, 115; Gies, *Joan of Arc*, 222.

298 "So many indeed": Pernoud, *Retrial of Joan of Arc*, 254.

298 "weeping, tried to climb": Gies, *Joan of Arc*, 222.

298 "The crowd was enormous": Sackville-West, *Saint Joan*, 325.

299 "And it was not only": Michelet, *Joan of Arc*, 104.

299 "and on the mitre": Craig Taylor, *Joan of Arc*, 228.

300 "a smell pleasing": See, for example, Genesis 8:21.

300 "Oh, Rouen, I am much afraid": Pernoud, *Retrial of Joan of Arc*, 250.

300 "she most humbly begged": Ibid., 247.

300   "If it will save": Péguy, *Mystery of the Charity of Joan of Arc*, 42.

300   "What, priest, are you going": Pernoud, *Retrial of Joan of Arc*, 248.

300   "slow, protracted burning": Michelet, *Joan of Arc*, 116.

300   "Ego te absolvo": Besson, *Messenger*.

301   solitary and frigid: Leonard Cohen, "Joan of Arc," *Songs of Love and Hate*, Universal Music Publishing Group, Sony/ATV Music Publishing LLC, 1970.

301   "And when the sixth hour": Mark 15:33.

301   "while the sun's light failed": Luke 23:45.

301   "And at the ninth hour": Mark 15:34.

301   "And Jesus uttered": Ibid., 15:37–38.

301   "And the earth shook": Matthew 27:51–53.

301   "the fire was raked back": Craig Taylor, *Joan of Arc*, 233–34.

302   "Look! Do you see": Schiller, *Joan of Arc*, 238.

302   "We made a lark": Anouilh, *Lark*, adapt. Hellman, 56.

303   "said and affirmed": Pernoud, *Retrial of Joan of Arc*, 283.

303   "I never wept as much": Ibid., 254.

Chapter XII: Life Everlasting

309   "a friar of the Order of Saint Dominic": Craig Taylor, *Joan of Arc*, 234.

310   "Pierre, bishop of Lisieux": Pernoud and Clin, *Joan of Arc*, 236–37.

310   As reported by Enguerrand de Monstrelet: Ibid., 209–10.

310   "the judges of the nullification trial": Ibid., 210.

312   "first professional, permanent, national standing army": Richey, *Joan of Arc*, 85.

312   "cannons quickly pulverized": Ibid.

313   "believed she had been burned": Pernoud and Clin, *Joan of Arc*, 234.

313   "confessed her imposture": Ibid.

314   "A long time ago": Craig Taylor, *Joan of Arc*, 260.

314   "They will reveal to you": Ibid., 261.

314   "wipe out this mark": Ibid., 264.

315   "After having taken away": Ibid., 265.

315   "execution of the sentence": Ibid., 349.

316   "Was Mahomet inspired": Shakespeare, *Henry VI, Part One*, act 1, scene 2.

316   imagined would become France's *Aeneid*: Pernoud, *Retrial of Joan of Arc*, 238.

317   "this shameful abuse": Voltaire, *Maid of Orleans*, 143.

317   *The Maid of Orléans* enraged enough readers: Heimann, *Joan of Arc in French Art and Culture*, 13.

317   "to ravish that which": Voltaire, *Maid of Orleans*, 84.

317   "will last for all eternity": Christine de Pizan, *City of Ladies*, 12.

317   "Field of Letters": Ibid., 16.

318   "such high walls": Ibid., 13.

318   "yardstick of truth": Ibid.

318   "towers, houses, and palaces": Ibid., 15.

318   "vessel of pure gold": Ibid., 14.

318 "city full of worthy": Ibid., 15.
318 "have attacked all women": Ibid., 17.
318 "such high walls": Ibid., 13.
319 "a cause of canonization": Woodward, *Making Saints*, 23.
319 "on grounds that the proofs": Wheeler and Wood, *Fresh Verdicts*, 208.
320 "boasted of her virginity": Ibid., 210.
320 "did not face death": Ibid.
320 "What was heroic": Ibid., 217.
320 "the saints of history": Ibid.
320 "surprising to read": Ibid.
320 "who makes his angels": Hebrews 1:7.

Bibliography

Abbott, Elizabeth. *A History of Celibacy*. New York: Scribner, 2000.

Acocella, Joan. *Twenty-Eight Artists and Two Saints*. New York: Pantheon, 2007.

Allmand, Christopher, ed. *War, Government, and Power in Late Medieval France*. Liverpool, U.K.: Liverpool University Press, 2000.

Anderson, Maxwell. *Joan of Lorraine*. New York: Dramatists Play Service, 1974.

Anonymous. *Lancelot of the Lake*. Translated by Corin Corley. Oxford: Oxford University Press, 1989.

Anonymous. *The Gospel of the Nativity of Mary*. The Library of Alexandria, 2000.

Anonymous. *The Song of Roland*. Translated by W. S. Merwin. New York: Modern Library Classics, 2001.

Anouilh, Jean. *The Lark*. Adapted by Lillian Hellman. New York: Dramatists Play Service, 1985.

———. *The Lark*. Translated by Christopher Fry. Oxford: Oxford University Press, 1956.

Astell, Ann W., and Bonnie Wheeler, eds. *Joan of Arc and Spirituality*. New York: Palgrave Macmillan, 2003.

Barstow, Anne Llewellyn. *Joan of Arc: Heretic, Mystic, Shaman*. Lewiston, N.Y.: Edwin Mellon, 1986.

Besson, Luc, dir. *The Messenger: The Story of Joan of Arc*. Gaumont, 1999.

Brecht, Bertolt. *Saint Joan of the Stockyards*. Edited by John Willett and Ralph Manheim. Translated by Ralph Manheim. London: Methuen Drama, 1991.

Bresson, Robert, dir. *The Trial of Joan of Arc*. Agnes Delahaie, 1962.

Bridget of Sweden. *Birgitta of Sweden: Life and Selected Writings*. Edited by Marguerite T. Harris. Mahwah, N.J.: Paulist Press, 1989.

Bynum, Caroline Walker. *Holy Feast and Holy Fast: The Religious Significance of Food to Medieval Women*. Berkeley: University of California Press, 1988.

Campbell, Joseph. *The Power of Myth*. New York: Anchor Books, 1991.

Cassagnes-Brouquet, Sophie. *La vie des femmes au moyen âge*. Rennes: Ouest-France, 2009.

Cervantes, Miguel de. *Don Quixote*. Translated by Edith Grossman. New York: HarperCollins, 2003.

Charlesworth, James H. *The Historical Jesus: An Essential Guide*. Nashville: Abingdon Press, 2008.

Christine de Pizan. *The Book of the City of Ladies*. New York: Penguin Books, 1999.

D'Aquili, Eugene G., and Andrew B. Newberg. *The Mystical Mind: Probing the Biology of Religious Experience*. Minneapolis: Fortress, 1999.

DeMille, Cecil B., dir. *Joan the Woman*. Cardinal Film, Paramount Pictures, 1916.

DeVries, Kelly. *Joan of Arc: A Military Leader*. Stroud, U.K.: Sutton, 1999.

DuBois, Page. *Torture and Truth*. New York: Routledge, 1991.

Duby, Georges. *France in the Middle Ages, 987–1460*. Translated by Juliet Vale. Malden, Mass.: Blackwell, 2009.

Duby, Georges, Michelle Perrot, and Christiane Klapisch-Zuber, eds. *History of Women in the West*. Vol. 2, *Silences of the Middle Ages*. Translated by Arthur Goldhammer. Cambridge, Mass.: Harvard University Press, 1992.

Duby, Georges, ed. *A History of Private Life: Revelations of the Medieval World*. Cambridge, Mass.: The Belknap Press of Harvard University Press, 1988.

Enders, Jody. *The Medieval Theater of Cruelty: Rhetoric, Memory, Violence*. Ithaca, N.Y.: Cornell University Press, 1999.

Fraioli, Deborah A. *Joan of Arc: The Early Debate*. Woodbridge, U.K.: Boydell, 2000.

———. *Joan of Arc and the Hundred Years War*. Westport, Conn.: Greenwood Press, 2005.

France, Anatole. *The Life of Joan of Arc*. Vol. 2. Translated by Winifred Stephens. Oxford: Benediction Classics, 2011.

Frazer, James George. *The Golden Bough: A Study in Magic and Religion*. Edited by Robert Fraser. Oxford: Oxford University Press, 2009.

Gastyne, Marco de, dir. *La merveilleuse vie de Jeanne d'Arc*. Pathé-Natan, 1929.

Gies, Frances. *Joan of Arc: The Legend and the Reality*. New York: Harper & Row, 1981.

———. *The Knight in History*. New York: Harper & Row, 1984.

Girault, Pierre-Gilles, and Angela Caldwell. *Joan of Arc*. Paris: Jean-Paul Gisserot, 2004.

Goldstone, Nancy. *The Maid and the Queen: The Secret History of Joan of Arc*. New York: Viking, 2012.

Gondoin, Stéphane W., and Ludovic Letrun. *Joan of Arc and the Passage to Victory, 1428–29: The Siege of Orléans and the Loire Campaign*. Translated by Jennifer Meyniel. Paris: Histoire & Collections, 2010.

Gordon, Mary. *Joan of Arc*. New York: Viking, 2000.

Grant, Robert M. Review, *The Body and Society: Men, Women and Sexual Renunciation in Early Christianity* by Peter Brown, in *Journal of the American Academy of Religion*. Vol. 58, no. 3.

Greene, E. A. *Saints and Their Symbols: A Companion in the Churches and Picture Galleries of Europe*. London: Isaac Pitman, 1924.

Grimm, Jacob, and Wilhelm Grimm. *Grimm's Fairy Tales*. New York: Pantheon, 1994.

Happold, F. C. *Mysticism: A Study and an Anthology*. New York: Penguin, 1986.

Heimann, Nora M. *Joan of Arc in French Art and Culture (1700–1855)*. Burlington, Vt.: Ashgate, 2005.

Hobbins, Daniel, trans. *The Trial of Joan of Arc*. Cambridge, Mass.: Harvard University Press, 2005.

Horrox, Rosemary, ed. and trans. *The Black Death*. Manchester, U.K.: Manchester University Press, 1994.

Hotchkiss, Valerie R. *Clothes Make the Man: Female Cross Dressing in Medieval Europe*. New York: Garland, 1996.

Huizinga, Johan. *The Waning of the Middle Ages*. Lexington, Ky.: Benediction Classics, 2010.

Inglis, Erik. *Jean Fouquet and the Invention of France*. New Haven, Conn.: Yale University Press, 2011.

James, William. *The Varieties of Religious Experience*. New York: First Library of America, 2010.

Jewell, Helen M. *Women in Late Medieval and Reformation Europe, 1200–1550*. Basingstoke, U.K.: Palgrave Macmillan, 2007.

Johnston, Ruth A. *All Things Medieval: An Encyclopedia of the Medieval World*. Santa Barbara, Calif.: Greenwood, 2011.

Julian of Norwich. *Revelations of Divine Love*. Guildford, U.K.: White Crow Books, 2011.

Kelly, John. *The Great Mortality*. New York: Harper Perennial, 2005.

Kempe, Margery. *The Book of Margery Kempe*. Translated by B. A. Windeatt. New York: Penguin, 2004.

Lang, Andrew. *The Maid of France, Being the Story of the Life and Death of Jeanne d'Arc*. New York: Cosimo, 2007.

Le Roy Ladurie, Emmanuel. *Montaillou: The Promised Land of Error*. Translated by Barbara Bray. New York: George Braziller, 2008.

Levack, Brian P. *The Witch Hunt in Early Modern Europe*. 3rd ed. Harlow, U.K.: Pearson Education, 2006.

Lightbody, Charles Wayland. *The Judgements of Joan: Joan of Arc: A Study in Cultural History*. London: George Allen and Unwin, 1961.

Loomis, Roger Sherman. *The Grail: From Celtic Myth to Christian Symbol*. Princeton, N.J.: Princeton University Press, 1991.

Lovejoy, Arthur O. *The Great Chain of Being: A Study of the History of an Idea.* Cambridge, Mass.: Harvard University Press, 1936.

Magill, R. Jay, Jr. *Sincerity.* New York: Norton, 2012.

Martin, Kathleen, ed. *The Book of Symbols: Reflections on Archetypal Images.* Cologne: Taschen, 2010.

McBrien, Richard P. *Catholicism.* Minneapolis: Oak Grove, 1981.

Michelet, Jules. *Joan of Arc.* Translated by Albert Guérard. Ann Arbor: University of Michigan Press, 2006.

Murphy, G., and S. J. Ronald. *The Owl, the Raven, and the Dove: The Religious Meaning of the Grimms' Magic Fairy Tales.* Oxford: Oxford University Press, 2000.

The New Oxford Annotated Bible with the Apocrypha. Edited by Herbert G. May and Bruce M. Metzger. Oxford: Oxford University Press, 1977.

Otto, Rudolf. *The Idea of the Holy: An Inquiry into the Non-rational Factor in the Idea of the Divine and Its Relation to the Rational.* Translated by John W. Harvey. New York: Oxford University Press, 1958.

Pagels, Elaine H. *Adam, Eve, and the Serpent.* New York: Random House, 1988.

―――. *Revelations: Visions, Prophecy, and Politics in the Book of Revelation.* New York: Penguin, 2012.

Péguy, Charles. *The Mystery of the Charity of Joan of Arc.* Translated by Jeffrey Wainwright. Adapted by Jean-Paul Lucet. Manchester, U.K.: Carcanet, 1986.

Pelikan, Jaroslav. *Jesus Through the Centuries: His Place in the History of Culture.* New Haven, Conn.: Yale University Press, 1985.

―――. *Mary Through the Centuries: Her Place in the History of Culture.* New Haven, Conn.: Yale University Press, 1996.

Pernoud, Régine. *The Retrial of Joan of Arc: The Evidence for Her Vindication.* Translated by J. M. Cohen. San Francisco: Ignatius, 2007.

―――. *Those Terrible Middle Ages: Debunking the Myths.* Translated by Anne Englund Nash. San Francisco: Ignatius, 2000.

Pernoud, Régine, and Marie-Véronique Clin. *Joan of Arc: Her Story.* Edited by Bonnie Wheeler. Translated by Jeremy duQuesnay Adams. New York: St. Martin's, 1998.

Perrault, Charles. *The Complete Fairy Tales.* New York: Oxford University Press, 2009.

Perroy, Édouard. *The Hundred Years War.* New York: Capricorn, 1965.

Peters, Edward. *Inquisition.* Berkeley: University of California Press, 1989.

Prestwich, Michael. *Knight: The Medieval Warrior's Unofficial Manual.* London: Thames & Hudson, 2010.

Procès de condamnation et de réhabilitation de Jeanne d'Arc, dite La Pucelle. Paris: Libraires de la Société de l'Histoire de France, 1844.

Rankin, Daniel S., and Claire Quintal, trans. *The First Biography of Joan of Arc, with the Chronicle Record of a Contemporary Account.* Pittsburgh: University of Pittsburgh Press, 1964.

Richey, Stephen W. *Joan of Arc: The Warrior Saint.* Westport, Conn.: Praeger, 2003.

Rogers, Katharine M. *The Troublesome Helpmate: A History of Misogyny in Literature.* Seattle: University of Washington Press, 1966.

Ronnenberg, Ami, and Kathleen Martin, eds. *The Book of Symbols.* Cologne: Taschen, 2010.

Sacks, Oliver. *Hallucinations.* New York: Knopf, 2012.

Sackville-West, Vita. *Saint Joan of Arc.* New York: Grove, 1936.

Salih, Sarah, ed. *A Companion to Middle English Hagiography.* Cambridge, U.K.: D. S. Brewer, 2006.

Schiller, Johann Christoph Friedrich von. *Joan of Arc.* In *Mary Stuart/Joan of Arc.* Translated by Robert David MacDonald. London: Oberon, 1995.

Schneider, Kirk J. *Horror and the Holy: Wisdom-Teachings of the Monster Tale.* Chicago: Open Court, 1993.

Schweitzer, Albert. *The Quest of the Historical Jesus.* New York: Macmillan, 1961.

Shaw, George Bernard. *Saint Joan.* Lexington, Ky.: GBS, 2011.

Sophocles. *Tragedies and Fragments, with Notes Rhymed, Choral Odes, and Lyrical Dialogues.* Translated by E. H. Plumptre. Charleston, S.C.: BiblioBazaar, 2009.

Spoto, Donald. *Joan: The Mysterious Life of the Heretic Who Became a Saint.* New York: HarperOne, 2007.

Stone, Merlin. *When God Was a Woman.* San Diego: Harvest, 1976.

Sullivan, Karen. *The Interrogation of Joan of Arc.* Minneapolis: University of Minnesota Press, 1999.

Taylor, Craig. *Joan of Arc: La Pucelle.* Manchester, U.K.: Manchester University Press, 2006.

Taylor, Larissa Juliet. *The Virgin Warrior: The Life and Death of Joan of Arc.* New Haven, Conn.: Yale University Press, 2010.

Teresa of Avila. *Life of Saint Teresa of Jesus.* Middlesex, U.K.: The Echo Library, 2011.

The Très Riches Heures of Jean, Duke of Berry. New York: George Braziller, 1969.

The Trial of Jeanne d'Arc. Translated by W. P. Barrett. New Orleans: Cornerstone, 2008.

Tuchman, Barbara Wertheim. *A Distant Mirror: The Calamitous 14th Century.* New York: Ballantine, 1978.

Twain, Mark. *Personal Recollections of Joan of Arc.* New York: Dover, 2002.

Villemarqué, Théodore Hersart de la. *Barzaz-Breiz: Chants populaires de la Bretagne.* Vol. 1. Paris: A. Frank, 1846.

Voltaire. *The Maid of Orleans (La Pucelle d'Orléans)*. New York: DuMont, 1901.

Ward, Benedicta, ed. *The Life of Teresa of Jesus: The Autobiography of Teresa of Avila*. New York: Doubleday, 1991.

Warner, Marina. *Alone of All Her Sex: The Myth and Cult of the Virgin Mary*. Oxford: Oxford University Press, 2013.

———. *Joan of Arc: The Image of Female Heroism*. Berkeley: University of California Press, 2000.

Wheeler, Bonnie, and Charles T. Wood. *Fresh Verdicts on Joan of Arc*. New York: Garland, 1996.

Williamson, Allen. "Primary Sources and Context Concerning Joan of Arc's Male Clothing," Historical Academy for Joan of Arc Studies, 2006.

Wilson-Smith, Timothy. *Joan of Arc: Maid, Myth, and History*. Stroud, U.K.: History Press, 2006.

Woodward, Kenneth L. *Making Saints: How the Catholic Church Determines Who Becomes a Saint, Who Doesn't, and Why*. New York: Simon & Schuster, 1996.

Young, Robert. *Analytical Concordance to the Bible on an Entirely New Plan*. Grand Rapids, Mich.: William B. Eerdmans, 1964.

Illustration Credits

Fig. 3. Courtesy Thomas Dubiaha

Fig. 4. Courtesy Thomas Dubiaha

Fig. 5. © Cardinal Film Corporation

Fig. 6. Courtesy the Metropolitan Museum of Art

Fig. 8. Musée des Beaux-Arts, Orléans, France / Giraudon / The Bridgeman Art Library

Fig. 9. *Jeanne la Pucelle I: Les Batailles* © Bac Films

Fig. 10. Louvre, Paris, France / Giraudon / The Bridgeman Art Library

Fig. 11. © RKO Radio Pictures

Fig. 12. Courtesy the Metropolitan Museum of Art

Fig. 14. Henri-Alexandre Wallon, *Jeanne d'Arc* (2 vols., 1860; 2nd ed., 1875)

Fig. 16. Bibliothèque nationale de France

Fig. 17. Wolverhampton Art Gallery, West Midlands, UK / The Bridgeman Art Library

Fig. 18. Society of Antiquaries of London, UK / The Bridgeman Art Library

Fig. 19. Musée des Beaux-Arts, Dijon, France / Giraudon / The Bridgeman Art Gallery

Fig. 20. Musée des Beaux-Arts, Orléans, France / Giraudon / The Bridgeman Art Library

Fig. 21. Louvre, Paris, France / Giraudon / The Bridgeman Art Library

Fig. 22. *Joan of Arc at the Coronation of Charles VII at Reims, 1429*, painted by Jules Eugène Lenepveu, © Stephane Compoint

Fig. 24. United Artists / Photofest, © United Artists

Fig. 26. Bibliothèque nationale de France

Fig. 27. © RKO Radio Pictures

Fig. 28. © Columbia Pictures

Fig. 29. Courtesy Thomas Dubiaha

Fig. 31. Photofest

Fig. 33. *Procès de Jeanne d'Arc*, Pathé Contemporary Films / Photofest, © Pathé Contemporary Films

Fig. 34. © Cardinal Film Corporation

Fig. 36. Library of Congress Prints and Photographs Division, Washington, D.C.

Fig. 37. *Joan of Arc* (December, 1950) by Classics Illustrated, © Gilberton Company, Inc.

Index

Kathryn Harrison has written the novels *Thicker Than Water, Exposure, Poison, The Binding Chair, The Seal Wife, Envy,* and *Enchantments.* Her autobiographical work includes *The Kiss, Seeking Rapture, The Road to Santiago,* and *The Mother Knot.* She has also written a biography, *Saint Thérèse of Lisieux,* and a book of true crime, *While They Slept: An Inquiry into the Murder of a Family.* She lives in Brooklyn with her husband, the novelist Colin Harrison, and their three children.